THE *Essential* COOK

THE
Essential
COOK

Everything You REALLY Need
to Know about Foods and Cooking

Charles Delmar

Hill House Publishing Company
Chapel Hill, North Carolina

TM The paper used in this book meets the minimum requirements of American National Standard for Information Sciences—Permanence of Paper for Printed Library Materials, ANSI Z39.48-1984.

Hill House Publishing Company

Printed in the United States of America
10 9 8 7 6 5 4 3 2

Library of Congress Catalog Card Number: 88-82339

ISBN 0-929694-00-7

In this work, when it shall be found that much
is omitted, let it not be forgotten that much likewise
is performed.

> *Dr. Samuel Johnson, 1775,*
> *upon completion of his dictionary*

---

*This handsome book was created by a team of talented
and dedicated professionals from California:*

Editor: John Bergez, San Francisco
Producer: David Hoyt, Pacific Grove
Designer: Katherine Minerva, Monterey
Illustrators: Ronald G. Grauer, Pacific Grove
           Carole Minou, Pacific Grove
           Rolland Dingman, Brookdale
Compositor: Graphic Typesetting Service, Los Angeles
Layout Artist: Michèle Judge, Pacific Grove
Proofreaders: Ellen Brownstein, Pacific Grove
           Jean Thurman, Pacific Grove
Manufacturing Manager: Harry Timmins, Carmel

Contents in Brief

Contents

Chapter Four

Hot Sauces   127

Chapter Five

Cold Sauces or Dressings   163

What This Book Is (and Is Not) and How to Use It

CHAPTER ZERO

The Craft of Cooking
How to Use This Book
Acknowledgments
Other Good Source Books

*T*his is not just a cookbook. It is a book about cooking. What's the difference? Cookbooks are collections of recipes. This book has none. Not in the conventional sense, that is. Recipes give detailed instructions for making a particular dish using exact amounts to repeat the way someone has made the dish before. In this book we consider *basic concepts and fundamental techniques of cooking*—the essential elements from which recipes are made.

Most cooks learn these essential concepts and techniques the hard way: backwards, through trial and error (lots of trials and too many errors). As they gain experience and acquire information from recipes and other cooks, though, they gradually learn what they should have known from the start—the essentials that make for successful cooking. Then they can work around recipes and begin to cook more creatively. Eventually, they might be able to cook without having to use recipes at all.

Instead of trying to teach cooking by starting with recipes and letting you learn the essential concepts and techniques through experience, this book presents these essentials first, explicitly for what they are. In this way you can learn what you need to know to do things right to begin with. If you're already an experienced cook, you should still find plenty of useful information in this book, and perhaps a different slant on some of the things you already know.

Another difference between this book and cookbooks is that cookbooks seldom account for such fundamental instructions as how to bake a potato, steam broccoli, make a casserole (any casserole), broil a beef steak, and other plain and simple ways of cooking basic foods. Yet those are what most cooks do most of the time to cook most of the foods they serve. Such essentials are not accounted for by recipes. They are accounted for by the chapters and topics in this book.

A good deal of what is covered here can be learned by reading the seemingly endless number of newspaper and magazine articles about cooking, from the hints and tips that appear in many recipes, or from other cooks. But snippets of information from these sources are but bits and pieces of the whole. They are also a chore to find and keep track of and, all too often, they are not correct. It was to bring together in one place most of the correct information any cook really needs to know that this book was written.

The Craft of Cooking

So that you might better appreciate why the information in this book really is essential, and why it is presented the way it is, consider the following definition of cooking.

The process or craft of cooking includes the following steps and stages.

1. **Planning** what to cook as well as when to cook it
2. **Selecting** foods and ingredients
3. **Storing** foods and ingredients to preserve their flavor, texture, and appearance
4. **Preparing** foods for a particular recipe or cooking method
5. **Combining** foods for special effects
6. **Seasoning** the foods
7. **Cooking** foods using one or more of the basic cooking methods
8. **Serving**
9. **Dining**
10. **Cleaning up**

But good cooking is more than just a craft. It is also an art. Like other arts, it is mastered only with experience and practice. I hope that this book will enable you to develop the craft and help you on your way to developing your cooking into an art—an art that reflects your own creativity and imagination.

How to Use This Book

Although the parts of this book build on one another, some cooks will want to put the book to use right away and start cooking. These cooks may want to go immediately to Part Three for detailed descriptions of various foods and how to select, store, prepare, cook, season, and serve them. This part of the book is a reference to use as you plan or prepare meals using specific foods.

Most cooks also look for ready-made instructions that will lead to instant success. The step-by-step "How to" sections that appear throughout the book are for them. Those instructions are detailed enough so that even an inexperienced cook should be able to follow them with success. However, references to more detailed information are provided in them in case you need it. To locate the "How to" you need, scan the table of contents, or use the index in the back of the book.

The more experienced cooks become, the more they will appreciate the general information provided in the text. It is from reading the text that you will learn what you need to know in order to become a good cook. Just what does a good cook need to know?

Good cooks need to know about basic cooking methods and techniques. Part One covers those methods and techniques in more detail than you are likely to find in any other source. The following parts of the book build upon the foundation presented in Part One.

Good cooks need to know about working tools, planning, shopping, sanitation and safety, diet, and the other "facts of life" covered in Part Two.

Good cooks need to know about foods and basic ingredients: how to select them, how to store them, how to prepare them, how to cook them according to one or more basic techniques, what seasonings go well with them, and how to serve them. These are the topics covered in Part Three.

Finally, good cooks must know about the language of cookery, especially if they cook using recipes. Because knowing what words mean is so important to good cooking, a great deal of this book can be thought of as an explanation of basic terms. The extensive glossary and index can serve as your guide to the language used in this and other books.

Acknowledgments

Knowledge about cooking has been handed down through the ages and written about in literally thousands of books. Still, most of us learn as much or more about cooking from

talking with other cooks as we learn from books. I certainly have, and I want to give credit here to the many friends and reviewers who have helped me. It is through their encouragement and helpful criticism that this book came to be. It is to them that it is dedicated.

Thank you, one and all: John Bergez, Bob Brown, Joan Cassilly, Michael Coverstone, Lee Culpepper, Judith Delmar, Beth Dodge, Nancy Lafferty Evans, Mark Gershenson, Benjamin Keaton, Sue Lamb, Michael Lohr, Miriam Nathanson, Jim Parker, Ned Rice, Lori Rutter, Adeline Shell, Ruby Sheridan, Walter Snyder, Ranny Umberger, Steven Vogel, Dean White, Leonard White, Terry Wortley, and last but not least my mother, Maggie Lee Delmar, who never taught me any of this. I also owe special thanks to my "bosses" Tom Orsi, Michael Needham, Peter Cokinos, Donald Browning, Ray Coleman, and Harold Parnes. Each of them in his way helped make this book possible.

Other Good Source Books

A great deal of the information presented here has been gleaned over the years from other books. It is impossible now to give credit exactly where it is due, but I can at least list many of the books in my collection and commend them to you. So that no preference is implied, they are listed alphabetically by title.

The ABC's of Cooking, by Charlotte Adams, published in 1983 by Doubleday, Garden City, New York.

The American Family Cookbook, edited by Melanie De Profit, published in 1974 by the Culinary Arts Institute, Chicago.

The American Heart Association Cookbook, third edition, published in 1980 by Ballantine Books, New York.

Barbeque Cookbook, edited by Carol D. Brent, published in 1972 by Tested Recipe Publishers, Chicago.

Better Homes and Gardens Complete Step-by-Step Cookbook, edited by Gerald Knox, published in 1978 by Meredith Corporation, Des Moines, Iowa.

Betty Crocker's Kitchen Secrets, published in 1983 by Random House, New York.

The Complete Family Cookbook, edited by Ann Bramson, published in 1977 by Octopus Books, London.

Cooking for the Professional Chef, by Kenneth C. Wolfe, published in 1982 by Delmar Publishers, Albany, New York.

Cooking without Recipes, by Helen Worth, published in 1965 by Gramercy Publishing, New York.

The Cook's Book, by Howard Hillman, published in 1981 by Avon Books, New York.

The Cook's Companion, by Frieda Arkin, published in 1968 by Doubleday, Garden City, New York.

The Cook's Companion, by Doris McFerran Townsend, published in 1978 by Rutledge Books, New York.

The Escoffier Cook Book, by A. Escoffier, published in 1969 by Crown Publishers, New York.

Festival of Meat Cookery, by Wilson Sinclair, published in 1971 by Western Publishing, New York.

Foods, seventh edition, by Gladys E. Vail and others, published in 1978 by Houghton Mifflin, Boston.

Foods of the World series, by the editors of Time-Life Books, published by Time-Life Books, Alexandria, Virginia.

The French Chef Cookbook, by Julia Child, published in 1968 by Alfred A. Knopf, New York.

From Julia Child's Kitchen, by Julia Child, published in 1975 by Alfred A. Knopf, New York.

The Good Cook series, by the editors of Time-Life Books, published by Time-Life Books, Alexandria, Virginia.

The Good Housekeeping Illustrated Cookbook, by Zoe Coulson, published in 1980 by Hearst Books, New York.

Handbook of Food Preparation, seventh edition, published in 1975 by the American Home Economics Association, New York.

House and Gardens Cook Book, published in 1968 by Bonanza Books, New York.

Issues in Nutrition for the 1980's, edited by Alice L. Tobias and Patricia J. Thompson, published in 1980 by Wadsworth Health Sciences Division, Monterey, California.

The Joy of Cooking, by Irma S. Rombauer and Marion Rombauer Becker, published in 1975 by Bobbs-Merrill, New York.

Kitchen Technique: A Complete Guide to Practical Cookery, by Wendy James and others, published in 1982 by Crescent Books, New York.

Mastering the Art of French Cooking, volume I, by Julia Child, published in 1961 by Alfred A. Knopf, New York.

Mastering the Art of French Cooking, volume II, by Julia Child, published in 1970 by Alfred A. Knopf, New York.

Meat and Fish Management, by Stephen A. Mutkoski and Marcia L. Schurer, published in 1981 by Breton Publishers, Boston.

The Professional Chef, fourth edition, by the Culinary Institute of America and the editors of Institutions Magazine, published in 1974 by Cahners Books, Boston.

The Professional Chef's Knife, prepared by the Learning Resources Center of the Culinary Institute of America, published in 1978 by CBI Publishing, Boston.

Professional Cooking, by Wayne Gisslen, published in 1983 by John Wiley & Sons, New York.

Reader's Digest Creative Cooking, published in 1977 by the Reader's Digest Association, Pleasantville, New York.

Reader's Digest Secrets of Better Cooking, published in 1977 by the Reader's Digest Association, Pleasantville, New York.

Souffle & Quiche: A 2 in 1 Cookbook, by Paul Mayer, published in 1972 by Nitty Gritty Productions, Concord, California.

Sunset Easy Basics for Good Cooking, by the editors of Sunset Books and Sunset Magazine, published by Lane Publishing, Menlo Park, California.

Sunset Ideas for Cooking Vegetables, by the editors of Sunset Books and Sunset Magazine, published in 1973 by Lane Publishing, Menlo Park, California.

Theory and Practice of Good Cooking, by James Beard, published in 1979 by Alfred A. Knopf, New York.

Uniform Retail Meat Identity Standards, published in 1973 by the Department of Merchandising of the National Live Stock & Meat Board, Chicago.

The Waiter & Waitress Training Manual, by Sondra J. Dahmer and Kurt W. Kahl, published in 1974 by Cahners Books, Boston.

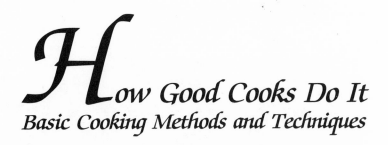

How Good Cooks Do It
Basic Cooking Methods and Techniques

PART ONE

If you want to know how to cook something, about all you have to do is find a recipe and follow it. Most cooks learn to cook by following recipes. Some, including some very good cooks, always follow recipes to the letter for everything they cook. Similarly, most cooking classes are little more than elaborate presentations that demonstrate a certain recipe or several recipes. Because recipes are so commonly used, it would seem that cooking is as simple as knowing how to follow a recipe. Or is it?

What do you do if you cannot find a recipe for something you want? What if the recipe you have doesn't account for some technique that is important but that you don't know? What if the recipe is for eight servings and you want six? What if you don't have certain ingredients that are called for?

Such "what if's" happen more often than not, and that is why knowing the basic principles and techniques of cooking is so essential. It is knowing how to account for them that makes good cooks good. These essential principles and techniques are covered in the five chapters of the first part of this book. The more you know about them, the better you will be able to handle those "what if" problems when they occur, and, consequently, the better cook you will be.

*A*bout Recipes

CHAPTER ONE

*I*n its most basic definition and role, a recipe is simply a record of what some cook has done before—a record that communicates the essential ingredients and how to's for preparing and cooking a dish so that it can be duplicated by others. A recipe is "good" if it communicates accurately to the reader. A recipe is "bad" if it does not. Individual tastes do vary, of course, and so the final product might taste "bad" even if the recipe is "good" and the cook has followed it well. No matter how good it might be, however, a recipe cannot relate everything that is important for all cooks to know and account for. Consequently, the cook usually must rely on his or her own knowledge and judgment to fill in the gaps if the final product is to turn out well. That is why knowing the basics is so important.

How Recipes Are Organized

Some cooks might be surprised to learn that there is really no common format for recipes. Most recipes list the ingredients before the instructions, which is a convenience for checking to see that you have everything, or for making a shopping list. The format for the instructions for combining ingredients, though, is less standard and can be confusing. Some recipes are not broken down into individual steps and stages. Some are cluttered with a lot of chitchat. Many recipes assume too much and leave out details that might be needed by inexperienced cooks. On the other hand, a recipe that includes every last necessary detail can be boring to more accomplished cooks.

Most recipes contain *recipes within recipes*. The main recipe might describe cooking a food or foods according to one or more of the basic techniques, such as baking and frying. But within that recipe there may be another that calls for making a sauce—a different task entirely. Recipes within recipes are especially common with braises and casseroles. Anytime a recipe calls for equal parts of flour and butter or other fat, for example, it is really telling you to "make a roux." If it goes on to instruct you to add milk or broth, it really means "make a white sauce."

(See "How to Make White Sauce," p. 144.)

If you consider recipes in this way, and if you know the basic principles of the different cooking tasks, then you will be able to spot those "recipes within recipes" and make modifications to suit your needs. Adapting recipes will be much simpler, cooking will be much easier, and the results will more than likely be better than they would be if you had stuck to following the recipe to the letter. The following "How to" sections discuss the fundamental steps in using and converting recipes.

How to Cook from a Recipe

For the beginning cook, recipes are vital. Even after reading this book, practicing the procedures described in it, and learning from experience, most cooks will still work from recipes, whether they follow them closely or not. That being the case, you should know how to use recipes intelligently. Here's how to do it.

1. **Read the entire recipe from top to bottom.** Be certain you have all the ingredients and implements that are called for.

2. **Plan your timing.** Many recipes give only the cooking time; preparation usually takes much longer. Allow adequate time to open packages, thaw foods, cut them, prepare sauces, and so forth.

(See "Planning Timing," p. 205.)

3. **Convert the number of servings if necessary.** The next "How to" discusses this step.

4. **Look for basic concepts and methods within the recipe.** Many recipes describe a "recipe within the recipe." The recipe may call for one of the sauces described in Chapters Four and Five, for example; or a recipe might fall into one of the categories of combination cookery described in Chapter Three.

5. **Number the steps** if that has not already been done.

6. **Underline important words and phrases** to cut out the chitchat.

7. **Look up any words you don't understand.** The Index and Glossary at the back of this book may help.

8. **Prepare.** Set out and organize the necessary tools and ingredients. It is often easiest to prepare and measure

ingredients and hold them in individual containers until needed.

9. **Do it.** Begin at the beginning and proceed step by step to the end. If you have planned properly and organized your recipe, your time, your tools, your ingredients, and your thoughts, then everything should come out just fine.

10. **Save it.** If the recipe works and you like it, save it so you can refer to it easily in the future.

∎

How to Convert a Recipe

1. **Define the "multiplier."** Let's call that *M*. To get it, divide the number of portions desired (called *D*) by the number of portions called for in the original recipe (called *O*). We can express this step by the following simple formula:

$$M = \frac{D}{O}$$

2. **Multiply the amount of each ingredient listed in the original recipe by *M*.** You will then have the correct amounts of each of the ingredients needed for the converted recipe.

Example A. Suppose the original recipe is for six portions but you want twelve. In this case, $D = 12$ and $O = 6$. Since 12 divided by 6 equals 2, the multiplier (*M*) is 2. To get the proper amounts for the converted recipe, multiply all the amounts in the original recipe by 2.

An Illustration of Recipes within a Recipe

Notice that most of the ingredients in the recipe on the facing page are blended together to make a sauce. Specifically, this is a velouté white sauce, about which we will learn more in Chapter Four. Steps 3 to 7 provide detailed information for making this sauce, including ways to cook the flour thickener ("roux") so that it does not form lumps or have a starchy taste.

If you recognize these instructions for what they are—a recipe for making a white sauce—and if you know as much as you should about how to make white sauces, then you won't need to concern yourself with most of the little details included in this recipe. Furthermore, if you recognize this recipe as being for a basic casserole dish, and if you know and understand the basic considerations for making casseroles that are described in Chapter Three, then you can substitute ingredients or modify this recipe in a number of ways. The entire set of instructions can be interpreted basically as this:

Chicken Divan

A casserole in which sautéed chicken pieces and broccoli are combined with a white sauce flavored with cheese and enriched with cream.

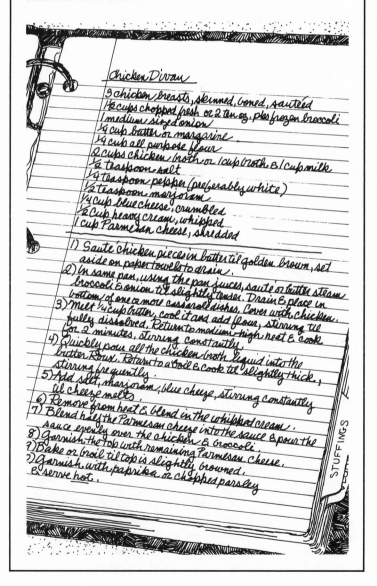

Chicken Divan

3 chicken breasts, skinned, boned, sautéed
1½ cups chopped fresh or 2 ten oz. pkg frozen broccoli
1 medium sized onion
¼ cup butter or margarine
¼ cup all purpose flour
2 cups chicken broth or 1 cup broth & 1 cup milk
½ teaspoon salt
¼ teaspoon pepper (preferably white)
½ teaspoon marjoram
¼ cup blue cheese, crumbled
½ cup heavy cream, whipped
1 cup Parmesan cheese, shredded

1) Saute chicken pieces in butter til golden brown, set aside on paper towels to drain.
2) In same pan, using the pan juices, saute in butter steam broccoli & onion til slightly tender. Drain & place in bottom of one or more casserole dishes. Cover with chicken.
3) Melt ¼ cup butter, cool it and add flour, stirring til fully dissolved. Return to medium-high heat & cook for 2 minutes, stirring constantly.
4) Quickly pour all the chicken broth liquid into the butter Roux. Return to a boil & cook til slightly thick., stirring frequently.
5) Add salt, marjoram, blue cheeze, stirring constantly til cheeze melts.
6) Remove from heat & blend in the whipped cream.
7) Blend half the Parmesan cheeze into the sauce & pour the sauce evenly over the chicken & broccoli.
8) Garnish the top with remaining Parmesan cheese.
9) Bake or broil til top is slightly browned.
9) Garnish with paprika or chopped parsley & serve hot.

STUFFINGS

Example B. Suppose the recipe calls for six portions but you want two. In this case $D = 2$ and $O = 6$. Since 2 divided by 6 equals 1/3, the multiplier (M) is 1/3. Multiply all of the amounts in the original recipe by 1/3.

Note: Herbs and spices do not convert exactly by this formula. With herbs and spices, it's best to start with small amounts and then add more to taste. In recipes for frying, specified amounts of cooking oil or fat should be varied in relation to the frying method (sauté, pan-fry, and so on) and the size of the pan (see pp. 56–60).

(See "Seasonings," p. 305.)

■

Recipes and Cooks

Many cooks seem to take recipes too literally, as though they were absolute and had to be followed to the most minute detail. Good cooks, though, are able to *read and work around* recipes. They use recipes as a beginning, not an end. They know that it is the idea behind the dish that is important, not the details; that it is the relationships among ingredients that count, not the exact measures. (One qualification: exact measures *are* important for breads, pastries, and other foods in which flour is a primary ingredient.) Good cooks know that substitutions can be made and that there is always room for creativity and innovation—*if you know what you're doing.*

Cooks who do know what they are doing can use recipes loosely and creatively. It's usually these creative cooks who have the reputation for being *really* good. Furthermore, they seem to enjoy cooking more than cooks who stick rigidly to the recipes of others. However, to be creative requires knowledge and experience. A good bit of the knowledge is conveyed in this book. Experience is something you will have to acquire.

Recipes and the Language of Cookery

The language of cookery is complicated because it draws from so many different countries. Even within the same country, various "schools" of cookery might use the same term to mean things that are quite different. For example, to some cooks the word *sauté* means to fry quickly in a small amount of fat, but to others it means to fry the food partially and then complete the cooking in a liquid. That second definition is what many cooks (including myself) mean by the term *braise*. If you add liquid when none is needed or desired, the results will be quite different—perhaps unfortunate. Add in incorrect language translations, together with misunderstandings and misinterpretations of the language that have been passed down through the years, and you end up with a cooking language that is not very standardized. The result is that words used in recipes can be confusing. Believe that. Be aware of it as you read other books and talk to other cooks. When you're not sure you understand something, try checking the glossary of the book you are using. In addition, the Index and Glossary at the back of this book should be quite helpful.

Recipes and Your Health

Many recipes have been passed along through the ages—ages when it was thought that for something to be good it had to contain large amounts of fat, sugar, and salt. In modern times, more and more recipes have come to be based on prepackaged processed foods, such as bread stuffing mix or dried soup. These foods often contain large amounts of fat, sugar, and salt or other high-sodium ingredients, as well as chemical preservatives. Either way, recipes that call for such ingredients should be labeled "Danger! Could be hazardous to your health." That is not to say those recipes are not good, or that you should never use them. For health reasons, however, you might want to substitute ingredients that are better for you, or at least reduce the amounts of harmful ingredients. For example, use fresh homemade soup or white sauce instead of the prepackaged products specified in recipes, and reduce the specified amounts of sugar, fats, and high-sodium ingredients. The results can still be good, and your physical health as well as your figure will be a lot better for it. (See Chapter Six, "Eating Smart.")

Recipe Collections

Every cook has his or her favorite recipes collected from many sources. Managing them requires some system of organization, and different cooks have different systems, ranging from the basic "cut it out and paste it on a file card" method to complete rewrites using a special format.

Although it requires a good bit of work, perhaps the best way to keep recipes is to print or type them on individual sheets of paper. That will leave plenty of room to make changes and add notes as you want. Rewriting each recipe will also cause you to give some thought to its organization and the basic concepts involved. You might be able to simplify the original recipe, modify it, or make the instructions more clear.

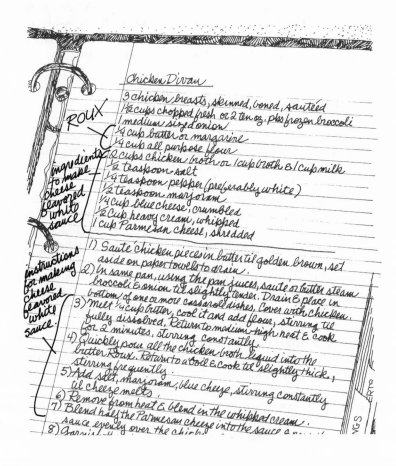

For the sake of clarity, use a standard format for all of your recipes. The sample recipe for Chicken Divan is as good a model as any, and better than most. Look again at that recipe for a moment, and consider how it is presented.

Notice that the ingredients are all listed at the top, in the order in which they will be used. That is a fairly standard procedure. However, the way these ingredients are listed differs from most recipes in that substitutions are listed also: margarine instead of butter, one cup of milk instead of a second cup of chicken broth. Having recipes with these features is a real convenience, especially if you plan to pass copies of your recipes along to others.

The steps of this recipe are grouped logically, and they are all numbered—a good practice that will simplify the instructions. If you wanted to make the steps even more clear, you might group the basic concepts involved and label them as such. That would produce instructions such as those in the box below.

When you have several recipes, you will find it best to group them together, usually by food type or concept (chicken dishes, desserts, casseroles, and so forth). For convenience, you might want to use a three-ring binder, dividing the groups with labeled separator cards you can obtain in any office supply shop. Take care of your recipes, and they will take care of you when you need them.

Chicken Divan: A Chicken/Broccoli Casserole

1. **Chicken:** Skin, bone, and sauté until golden brown. Set aside.

2. **Broccoli:** Chop and parboil or sauté until slightly tender. Drain and place evenly over the bottom of one or more prepared casserole dishes. Cover with chicken pieces.

3. **Roux:** Cool the butter and add flour, stirring it in until fully dissolved. Return to medium-high heat and cook for 2 minutes, stirring constantly.

4. **Cheese sauce:** Quickly pour all the liquid into the roux, bring to a boil, and cook until slightly thick, stirring frequently. Add salt, marjoram, and crumbled blue cheese, stirring constantly until the cheese has melted. Blend half the Parmesan cheese into the sauce. Pour the sauce over the chicken and broccoli.

5. **Garnish** the top of the casserole with the remaining Parmesan cheese.

6. **Bake or broil** until the top is slightly browned.

7. **Optional:** Garnish with paprika or chopped parsley.

8. **Serve** hot, accompanied with rice, bread, and a fresh garden salad.

Three (and Maybe Four) Ways to Cook

CHAPTER TWO

*A*s you might already know, and as the accompanying chart clearly shows, there are many different methods of cooking. If we think of the main thing that distinguishes these methods—the medium used for cooking—and if we then group them accordingly, then all of them can be placed into one of three distinct groups: cooking in liquids, cooking in dry heat, and cooking in fat. That is what I mean here by "three ways" to cook. In addition, there is also microwave cooking, which isn't really a fourth way to cook at all, but simply a way to cook by one of the three basic ways more quickly.

Each of the three ways to cook is distinguished from the others by four things: (1) what heats and flavors the food, the cooking *medium;* (2) what the medium does to the *texture* of the food; (3) what the food is cooked in, the *vessel;* (4) how the cooking is done, or the different techniques or *methods* that can be used with the given medium.

These four elements for each of the three ways to cook are the most fundamental and important concepts in all cookery. They are what most recipes assume a cook already knows, and indeed what a cook must know in order to cook well. In this chapter, we consider each of these elements in detail for each of the different ways to cook.

Cooking in Liquids

Any and all foods are commonly cooked in liquids. As a cooking medium, liquids make foods more tender and add

| Three Ways to Cook | | |
Cook in Liquids	Cook in Dry Heat	Cook in Fat
Boil	Bake	Sauté
Parboil ("blanch")	Oven-broil	Grill-fry
Simmer	Pan-broil	Pan-fry
Poach	Oven-roast	Deep-fat-fry
Steam	Grill-roast	Stir-fry
Stew	Spit-roast	Wok-fry
Braise	Barbecue	Oven-fry

flavor to them. If this kind of cooking is done correctly, the foods will be flavorful, nutritious, and tender but firm in texture. However, if the food is cooked too long, it can be robbed of its texture, nutrients, and flavor.

Salt is the chief robber of foods cooked in liquids. It leaches flavors and nutrients from them into the liquid. If the liquid is then poured off, the flavor and nutrients go with it. Really, salt should be included in any cooking liquid only when the liquid will be served with the food.

Since liquids in which foods are cooked contain nutrients and flavors, it is wasteful to throw them out. Instead, save them to use for reheating the food, or for making soups or sauces.

What Heats and Flavors the Food: Liquids

Water is the most common liquid used for cooking, but any number of other liquids can be used in addition to or instead of water to make foods more flavorful and more interesting. Fruit juices, broths, milk, beer, and wine are just some of the liquids that can be used for cooking. Each liquid has its own flavor and cooking characteristics that you must account for. Let's take a look at the main considerations involved in cooking with various kinds of liquids.

□ *Water*

Water is used to simmer and poach eggs, vegetables, and fish, as well as to make soups, braises, and stews. The only consideration for using water as a cooking medium is that it adds virtually nothing to either the taste or the nutritional value of any food. All too often, in fact, a good bit of the flavor and nutrients from a food are poured off along with the water in which it was cooked. To prevent that, add a few drops of vegetable oil to cooking water. The oil will cling to the food, holding flavors and nutrients with it even if the water is poured off. By the way, you can add oil to other liquids as well as water to help preserve flavors and nutrients.

□ *Broth, Stock, or Bouillon*

These liquids are used for making soups, stews, and braises; they may also be used to simmer vegetables, meat, or fish, as well as to make rice and pasta. If there ever were any differences in the meanings of the terms *broth, stock,* and (See "Broth," pp. 106–108.) *bouillon,* they have long since been lost through misuse. Each is correctly defined as "the liquid in which a food has been cooked." In other words, any liquid in which one or more foods have been cooked becomes a broth, stock, or bouillon. For the sake of consistency, such liquids will be referred to throughout this book as "broth."

Basic broth is made from meat, poultry, or fish cooked in lightly salted water. Onions, celery, carrots, and usually herbs and spices are often cooked along with the base food to give the broth more flavor.

About the only considerations for using broth as a

medium for cooking foods are its flavor and the amount of salt and seasonings it contains. Beef broth goes well with meats, poultry, and some vegetables. Vegetable broth and poultry broth go well with meats as well as with poultry and vegetables. Fish broth, however, usually is used only with fish.

Canned or powdered broths (those labeled "bouillon," especially) contain enough salt, MSG (monosodium glutamate), or other sodium products that usually no more needs to be added to the liquid when it is used for cooking other foods. A popular powdered bouillon product, for example, has salt, sugar, and MSG listed as the first three ingredients, and "beef extract" (whatever that might be) listed last following seven other chemical products! To control what you get and don't get in your broth, make your own. It will be cheaper, probably tastier, and certainly better for you.

(See "How to Make Broth," p. 111.)

☐ *Soups, Vegetable Juices, and Fruit Juices*
These liquids are used to add flavor to casseroles, braises, and stews, as well as to vegetables and other foods that are simmered or poached. More than broth, the flavors of soups and juices must be accounted for when they are used as a cooking medium. You don't want the flavor of the liquid to clash with or overpower the flavor of the food. Juices or soups with a strong flavor should be diluted with water, milk, wine, broth, or combinations of these to mellow their flavor.

Because the flavors of these liquids are so rich, they may be made into a sauce to accompany the food. If the liquid

(See "Thickeners," p. 130.)
is thin, add cornstarch, arrowroot, or a roux to thicken it. If it is thick, thin it with water, broth, wine, or milk.

☐ Milk, Cream, and Other Milk Products

(See "Milk Products," p. 302.)
Milk and milk products may be used alone to cook foods, especially vegetables and fish, but more often they are mixed with other liquids to reduce the chances of scorching or curdling. Because milk and milk products do curdle easily when heated, they must be cooked at low temperatures and should be stirred frequently. If milk does begin to curdle, you may be able to rescue it by removing it from the heat, stirring the liquid rapidly, and adding cold water or milk to cool it. If it still tastes scorched, there is no saving it. Throw the mess out and start over.

☐ Beer and Wine

Certainly the most expensive liquids you can use for cooking, beer and wine contribute unique flavors that can make them well worth the cost. Beer is used most often for braising meats and for steaming or boiling shellfish. Wine is used for simmering, poaching, stewing, or braising just about any food. Beer can be used alone or diluted with water or broth to make its flavor more subtle. Wine, on the other hand, is seldom used alone. It is usually mixed with water or broth to mellow its flavor. That is especially true for red wines, whose strong flavors might easily overpower the delicate flavors of most foods.

Both the color and the flavor of wine must be accounted for to match it to a food. A hearty red wine might be good with beef or lamb, but it would discolor and overpower delicate fish or shellfish. As a guide, use bold-flavored wines with bold-flavored foods and delicate-flavored wines with delicate foods. White wines can be used with virtually any foods, but red wines are best reserved for red meats.

For most cooking purposes, any table wine is perfectly acceptable. Don't waste your money using expensive wines, because the subtle flavors that make them worth the price will be cooked away. Vermouth makes a good all-purpose cooking wine. There are also special cooking wines with salt in them that are fine for cooking, but not for drinking. Be careful to account for their salt content before adding more salt to the dish, or foods might end up tasting too salty. (See "Wines," p. 286.)

☐ *Hot Sauces*

When you want to create something special out of any basic foods, or when you want to reheat leftovers and make them taste different, just heat them in one of the hot sauces described in Chapter Four. The taste of the sauce will be added to that of the food, and the two can be served together. Not only are hot sauces good for reheating leftovers; they are also used as one of the elements in casseroles and other specialty dishes described in Chapter Three.

☐ *Butter and Margarine*

When we think of cooking with butter or margarine, most often we think of frying. However, either of these fats can be added to any cooking liquid to enrich its flavor. When they are used alone in a covered cooking vessel, the food steams in the fat and becomes infused with its flavor. This technique is called *butter steaming*, and it is especially good for cooking delicate foods such as vegetables and fish. Don't use butter steaming if the food requires lengthy cooking, however, because it will make the food taste greasy. (See "Special Forms of Butter and Margarine," p. 291.)

□ *Combinations*

Different liquids can be combined to make many interesting flavors. Tomato juice and sour cream, apple juice and chicken broth, wine and chicken soup, beer and beef stock, are but a few examples. And of course, butter, margarine, or one of the milk products can be added to any liquid to enrich its flavor. Experimenting with different combinations and blends should be an exciting and rewarding experience for the good cook.

What Happens to the Food: Textures

Foods cooked in liquids will be moist and tender. That's fine for most foods, but remember that the texture will be weakened and the food can become too soft or even mushy if it is cooked or held in the liquid for too long. That is especially true for delicate foods such as fish, fruits, and many vegetables. To prevent such foods from overcooking, always remove them from heat (or their cooking liquid) while they are still firm and slightly undercooked. They will continue cooking in their own heat, so they can easily overcook if you're not careful.

What to Cook in: Vessels

Cooking with liquids is ordinarily done in a covered container on top of a range burner. It can also be done in the oven or over an open fire in any covering that will hold moisture in and around the food. For instance, so-called baked potatoes cooked in aluminum foil will be soft and moist, not dry and mealy, the way real baked potatoes should be. That's because the wrapped potatoes are really steamed, not baked. In other words, it is the presence of moisture, not where the food is cooked, that determines the resulting texture. Anything that holds in moisture so food cooks in steam or liquid can be used as a vessel for cooking in liquids.

□ *Pots and Pans*

For boiling water or for quick heating of foods such as vegetables in a liquid, a pot made of any metal can be satisfactory. The only consideration is that it be large enough to contain the food with an inch or two of space at the top to allow room for the liquid to foam. A pot that is too large for the amount of food wastes energy.

Pots made of aluminum with an inner lining of non-stick material are about the least expensive and most practical all-purpose vessels for cooking in liquids. Pots made of stainless steel are fine if they are small, but stainless steel heats slowly and distributes heat unevenly, so it is not a good material for very large pots. Pots made of copper or treated aluminum heat most evenly, but they are very expensive. Bare aluminum or copper will interact chemically with some foods, affecting their flavors. Pots made of iron are good for long, slow cooking, but iron is heavy, heats slowly, retains the flavor of foods, and interacts with some foods. Enameled iron is preferred over plain iron because there is no chance for chemical reactions or flavor retention. However, enameled iron can be expensive, and the enamel can chip off to expose the plain iron with all of its shortcomings.

(See "Cooking Vessels," pp. 250–253.)

Here are some other considerations for cooking pots:

· The deeper the pot, the more slowly the food will cook.
· The heavier the pot or the better it conducts heat, the less energy it will require to cook the food.
· The thicker the liquid, the more important it is to have a pot that will conduct heat evenly, the lower the cooking temperature should be, and the more frequently the food should be stirred.

French steamer.   This is a special rack on stilts that is used to hold a food above the cooking liquid. It is porous to allow steam to reach the food and usually is collapsible so that its size can be changed to fit into different pots. If

Crock Pot

Double Boiler

Pressure Cooker

you do not have a regular steamer, you can substitute any porous container, such as a colander, tea strainer, or wire basket. The important considerations are that the steamer must prevent the food from touching the liquid and allow steam to pass freely so that the food can cook evenly. For most steaming, especially if a lot of food is being steamed at one time, the food should be stirred or shaken occasionally so that the steam can cook it evenly.

"Waterless" cookware.   This is the name given to special pots and pans made so that their lids form a vacuum seal when heated. They are not really waterless, however. A very small amount of liquid is needed to form the seal for the lid as well as to steam the food.

Pressure cooker.   This is a special heavyweight pot in which foods are cooked under pressure. This method permits the cooking temperature to be very hot, so that foods cook in only seconds or minutes.

Crock pot.   An appliance called a *crock pot* is especially useful for cooking soups and stews very slowly at low temperatures. The ceramic pot conducts heat evenly over its entire surface, so the food cooks evenly without having to be stirred. This is a real convenience, especially when you want food to cook while you're away from home. The long, slow cooking allows the flavors of the stew or soup to blend, making the taste particularly good.

Double boiler.   A double boiler allows foods to be cooked or kept warm at low temperatures because the upper pot is held above the heated liquid. This is especially important for cooking very delicate foods that might burn or curdle if allowed to get too hot. Egg dishes, sauces, chocolate, and cream dishes are some common examples of foods that are usually cooked in a double boiler.

Wrap cookery.   This is a way to cook foods in liquid using dry heat. Wrap cookery is just a fancy name for what can be a fancy process, such as steaming fish in lettuce leaves soaked in sherry. It can also be something as simple as cooking moist foods in a covered casserole dish or wrapped in aluminum foil. The important consideration is that the food be moist and sealed in such a way that it is protected from the dry heat and can steam in the moisture contained in the wrap.

(See "How to Wrap-steam Fish," pp. 386–388.)

Aluminum foil is an economical, convenient, and effective material for wrap cookery. It can be folded two ways. The *drugstore wrap* is good to use with meats and other solid foods. (1) Tear a rectangular sheet large enough to contain the food plus one or two inches. Place the food in the center and bring the two longest sides of the foil up and over it. (2) Place the two sides together and fold them down in a series of locked folds. Fold the ends in a series of locked folds.

(See illustration on p. 32.)

The *pyramid wrap* is useful for cooking vegetables and food pieces. Tear a square of aluminum foil and place the food in its center. Bring the four corners of the foil up to form a pyramid shape. Fold the edges over one another in a series of locked folds.

(See illustration on p. 33.)

How to Do It: Methods

Any of the methods listed here may be done by placing the cooking vessel on a range burner or in an oven. A range burner is usually more economical and convenient.

The fundamental difference between each of these methods is the temperature of the liquid. Since boiling is the highest temperature to which a liquid can be heated and still remain liquid, all of the other methods are defined in relation to it.

Should you heat the liquid slowly or quickly? That depends on how thick the liquid is and on what is in it. The thicker the liquid, or the more solid food it contains, the more slowly its temperature should be raised to allow more time for the food to cook evenly. Plain water can be

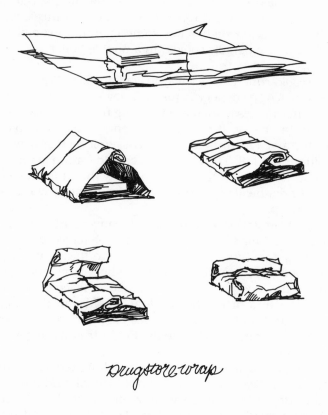

Drugstore wrap

brought to a full boil rapidly over high heat without hurting it. A thick soup or stew, on the other hand, should be brought up to cooking temperature slowly, with frequent stirring as it heats.

Should you add the food before or after the liquid is heated? If the food is simply to be heated or cooked, and the liquid is not to be served with it, then add the food after the liquid is hot. That way, more flavor and nutrients will be retained in the food. On the other hand, if the liquid will be eaten with the food, as in the case of a stew, then add the solid food at the beginning to maximize the exchange of flavors between the food and the liquid.

□ Boiling

Boiling is the stage at which a heated liquid bubbles profusely on its surface. Since the agitation of boiling is neither needed nor desired for cooking most foods, boiling liquids are seldom used for cooking. Virtually the only foods

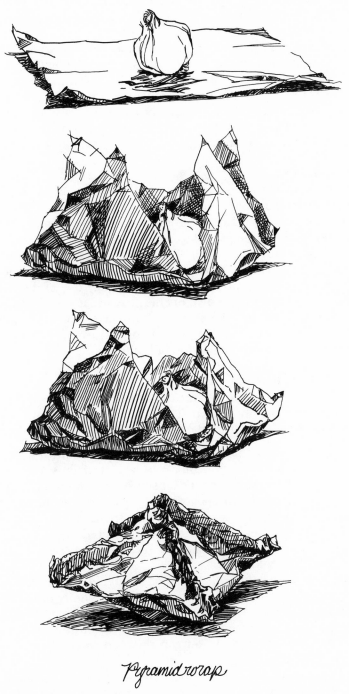

Pyramid wrap

that should be boiled are crabs and lobsters. For other foods, the liquid should be brought to a boil, then reduced so as to simmer, stew, or poach.

Boiling occurs at the highest temperature to which the liquid can be heated before it turns to gas. For water, that is 212 degrees Fahrenheit (F.) at sea level. Boiling temperature varies according to the thickness of the liquid, the distance above sea level, and other things such as the amount of salt or sugar contained in the liquid. In other words, there is no one temperature at which boiling occurs.

(See "Cooking Considerations for Cooking in Liquids," p. 36.)

□ *Simmering*

Simmering is the method used most often for cooking foods in liquids, especially vegetables and eggs. To *simmer* means to cook in a liquid with bubbles just barely breaking on the surface. As some cooks describe it, "You let the liquid smile, not laugh out loud." The liquid is first brought to a boil and then the temperature is reduced. The difference between boiling and simmering is literally one of degree. Boiling allows a great deal of energy to escape in the bubbles that break on the surface. Simmering, on the other hand, retains almost the same temperature, but without the energy loss and agitation of boiling.

□ *Parboiling or Blanching*

To *parboil* or to *blanch* means to boil or simmer a food until it is partially cooked. There are three different ways of doing it, each with a particular purpose.

1. *To cook vegetables partially so they remain somewhat firm, or to set the color and seal nutrients in foods that will be cooked further by some other method:* First immerse the food into a pot of rapidly boiling water. Immerse the food slowly, so as not to disrupt the boil. Reduce the heat and simmer the food in an uncovered pot. Pour off the hot water and soak the food in cold water ("refresh" it) to stop the cooking.

2. *To make the skins of foods such as tomatoes or peaches easier to peel, or to remove the shells or husks from almonds or other nuts:* Plunge them into boiling water or pour boiling water over them until the skin or husk is tender enough to peel. Refresh the food in cold water to stop the cooking.

3. *To remove strong flavors or odors from foods such as salted ham or variety meats:* Place the food into a pot of cold water. Slowly bring the water to a boil. Reduce the

heat to a simmer. Leave the pot uncovered while the food cooks to allow gases to escape.

□ *Poaching*

Poaching is used mostly for cooking fish, eggs, fruits, and other foods that are too delicate to cook by boiling or simmering. To cook smaller pieces, heat the liquid before adding the food to it. If the food is large—a large whole fish, for example—place it in cool liquid first and then heat the liquid slowly. That allows time for the inside of the food to cook before the outside cooks too much.

Poaching differs from boiling and simmering in three ways. First, the liquid should just barely cover the food. Most often, poaching is done in a wide, shallow pot or pan with a large surface area, so that the food rests on the bottom. Second, the liquid should be kept just hot enough that the bubbles barely break on the surface—a "slow" simmer. Third, the cooking vessel must be partially uncovered to allow steam to escape so that the liquid never gets hot enough to simmer or boil.

□ *Stewing and Braising*

Stewing and braising are so similar that it is difficult to distinguish between them. Foods that are braised are always fried briefly before being cooked in liquids. With stews, the frying is optional. Then there is the matter of how much liquid is used. In stew, all the solid food is covered completely by the cooking liquid. A braise would have only half or less of the food immersed in the liquid so that the top part cooks in the steam, not in the liquid itself.

(See "Braises and Stews," p. 95.)

Either stewing or braising is used to cook foods slowly in a liquid at a low temperature for a long period of time. Both methods are especially good for cooking tougher meats and older, tougher poultry, but vegetables and even fish or shellfish may be stewed also. The longer the food cooks, the more tender it will be. Not only does the long, slow cooking tenderize the solid food, but it also draws out flavors so that they blend in with the cooking liquid. The flavored liquid is usually served as a sauce along with the food. The liquid may be reduced as it cooks to make it thicker, or a thickening agent may be added.

□ *Steaming*

Steaming, like poaching, is usually used for cooking delicate foods such as vegetables, fish, or shellfish. It offers the particular advantage of allowing the food to hold its color, nutrients, and flavors rather than losing them in a cooking liquid. The medium is not the liquid itself, but the steam it gives off. It is important, therefore, that the food not touch the liquid. If the container is cooked in dry heat, as when a potato wrapped in aluminum foil is cooked in the oven, then the food must be wrapped tightly enough to seal it off from the dry heat so that the moisture in it does not evaporate.

Many cooks and books will tell you that steam is hotter than a boiling liquid and that steamed foods cook faster. They are wrong. Steam does not impart as much heat as a boiling liquid; consequently, foods that are steamed require slightly *more* time to cook than those that are boiled or simmered.

Wrap steaming.   A long neglected method of steaming, but one growing in popularity, is *wrap steaming.* This method is often used to cook fish, but it can also be used to cook poultry, meats, and vegetables. All that is required is a wrap that seals in moisture. Covered casserole dishes are the easiest to use; alternatively, the food can be wrapped in aluminum foil or cooking parchment. Butter, margarine, cooking oil, or some other liquid is used to moisten the food as well as to contribute its flavor. Seasonings, onions, sweet bell peppers, and other vegetables also add flavor. To give the food more color and a firmer surface texture, first sauté it lightly and then wrap-steam it to cook it to completion. The description of how to wrap steam fish on pages 386–389 can be used as a model for wrap steaming any food. (Also see p. 31 for descriptions of ways to wrap foods in aluminum foil.)

Cooking Considerations for Cooking in Liquids

1. Any container or wrap that holds in steam around a food as it cooks will make the food soft and moist. In other words, if you want a food to cook in dry heat, don't wrap it, cover it, or use devices such as roasting bags—otherwise, the food will cook in steam, not dry heat.

2. Salt in any cooking liquid will extract flavor and nutrients from foods. That's fine for stews and braises, because the liquid is eaten. With other cooking, however, it is best to leave salt out of the liquid, or at least reduce the amount by half. For the best flavor, use a dash of sugar and other seasonings in the cooking liquid and add salt to foods after they have been cooked.

3. A few drops of cooking oil, butter, or margarine in a cooking liquid will cling to the food, holding in some of the flavors and nutrients along with it when the cooking liquid is poured off.

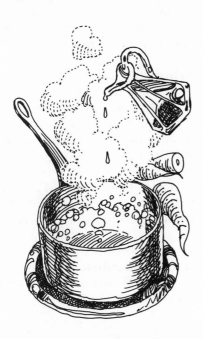

4. To cook foods more evenly in a liquid, stir them frequently. The thicker the liquid or the greater the amount of solid food being cooked in it, the more frequently it should be stirred.

5. Solid foods, thick liquids, and liquids containing milk or milk products are likely to stick on the bottom of the pot and scorch. To minimize scorching, use a pot or pan with a special non-stick inner coating. Alternatively, do the following: (a) Prepare the bottom inside of the pot with a thin coating of vegetable shortening. (b) Stir frequently. (c) Place a heat-retarding device such as an asbestos pad between the burner and the pot.

6. The higher the temperature of a liquid before it is heated, the less time and energy will be required to bring it to a boil.

7. A covered vessel heats liquids faster and requires less energy to maintain a constant temperature than an uncovered one. As the saying goes, "A watched pot never boils."

8. As the elevation goes up, the temperature at which a liquid boils goes down. In other words, the higher the elevation, the more time will be required to cook foods (see table).

Boiling temperatures of water at different elevations

	Fahrenheit	Celsius
Sea level	212 degrees	100 degrees
+2,000 feet	208	98
+5,000 feet	203	95
+10,000 feet	194	90

9. Foods will retain more nutrients and flavors if they are introduced quickly into a liquid that is already boiling. (Allow the liquid to return to a boil before reducing the heat.) However, if the object is to draw the flavors and nutrients into the liquid (as in stews and braises), put the food in cold liquid and then bring the liquid to a boil.

10. It is best to serve foods that have been cooked in a liquid as soon after cooking as possible. However, they may be held in the liquid at a temperature of between 100 and 120 degrees F. without cooking them further. Don't hold them that way for more than thirty minutes, however, or some bacterial growth might occur.

11. Liquids that have been used for cooking foods ("broths") contain flavors and nutrients. Save leftover broths and use them for making soups and sauces, or for reheating foods.

Cooking in Dry Heat

Among the many foods and specialty dishes cooked using dry heat are roasts, casseroles, pies, cakes, and pastries. There are several distinct methods for cooking in dry heat: baking, broiling, pan-broiling, roasting, and grilling. Each method has its own special effect on the texture of the food. The distinctions between them are sometimes subtle, but they are important.

The terminology used to distinguish these methods can be confusing, because different terms are often used in varied and even inconsistent ways. For example, the word *roast* can mean a large piece of meat or poultry as well as a cooking process. Many cooks and books will tell you that the difference between roasting and baking is that you "roast" meats and "bake" vegetables, but then they will usually go on to tell you how to bake ham and roast corn. You can bake in an oven but not over an open fire. You can roast or broil either over an open fire or in an oven. And so it goes.

Knowing basic definitions and distinctions between terms is the first step toward avoiding confusion and controlling what you do. If what follows seems to be as much a lesson in language as a lesson in cooking, that's why.

What Cooks the Food: Dry Heat

Whatever the method, food cooked in dry heat is cooked by two or even three kinds of heat: (1) the *radiant* heat from the heat source; (2) the heated air that reaches the food by *convection*; and (3) the heat that is *conducted* to the food from the cooking vessel, if one is used. If the food is held in a vessel so that it is cooked by both heated air and the heat from the cooking vessel, it is *baked.* Baking is done in a closed oven to hold in the heated air so that the food cooks evenly. If no vessel is used, and heated air can reach the entire surface of the food, then it is *roasted.* Roasting can be done either in an oven or in the open air. If a food is roasted in the open air, the cooking process is sometimes called *grilling* and the food is said to be *grilled.* If the heat source is hot enough, usually so hot that it glows, and the food is exposed directly to it, then the food is *broiled.* Broiling can be done either in an oven or in the open air.

How Dry Heat Cooks

Radiation: All heat sources radiate heat in the form of infrared rays. An open fire or gas flame, glowing coals, or the heat coil inside an electric appliance are sources of radiant heat used for cooking. The hotter the heat source, or the closer a food is to it, the greater the radiation and the faster the food cooks. If the heat source is so hot that it glows, the food is *broiled.*

Convection: When an object is not exposed directly to the heat source, or if it is far away from it, then it may be heated primarily by the air that touches it. This kind of heat is called *convected* heat, and the cooking process is called *convection cooking.* Convected heat cooks best when it is contained in a closed oven. The more evenly the air around a food is heated, and the more evenly the oven holds it, the more evenly the food will cook. That is why some ovens, called *convection ovens,* have fans built into them. The fans circulate the heated air so that it cooks more evenly.

Conduction: An object—heated either by radiation or by convection—will then conduct that heat. Cooking vessels conduct heat to their contents. Foods being cooked conduct heat from their outer surface inward. Either way, the amount of conducted heat decreases as the distance over which it is conducted increases. That is why the center of a food—a large roast, for example—takes longer to cook than the outside areas, and why the food cooks less on the inside than on its surface. If a food is cooked in a vessel, it is cooked by heat that has been conducted to it by the vessel. Different materials conduct heat better than others. Metals conduct heat much better than glass or ceramics, so if you want to cook the outer surface faster than the inside—cake baking is a good example—you should use a metal pan. If you want the food to cook more evenly throughout, use a vessel made of glass or a ceramic material that is a less efficient heat conductor.

What Happens to the Food: Textures

Because the cooking medium is dry, foods cooked in dry heat will be dried as they cook. Dry heat—broiling, especially—also causes sugar and starches to caramelize, giving foods a beautiful sheen, crunchy crust, and added flavor. However, since caramelization is the final step before burning, care must be taken to prevent foods from becoming so dry that they burn. (Charred or burned foods are now believed to be carcinogenic, meaning they can cause cancer.) Here are some precautions to help prevent foods from burning in dry heat.

1. *Adjust the temperature of the heat.* The lower the temperature, the slower the outer parts of the food will cook. That allows more time for heat to be conducted to the inner parts. Use lower heat for larger, thicker foods and for foods to be cooked well done. Use higher heat for thinner foods and for meats to be cooked rare.

2. *Adjust the distance from the heat.* If you want the surface well cooked but the inside less so, put the food closer to the heat. If you want the food to cook more evenly throughout, move the food away from the heat.

3. *Cover the surface of the food.* Meats, poultry, fish, and vegetables are most often coated with cooking oil or fat to protect them from direct heat and to keep them moist. Casseroles, cakes, or roasts can be covered lightly with aluminum foil, but do leave room for the steam to escape if you want the surface texture to be dry.

4. *Use a "Mary's bath"* (also called "Bain Marie"). This is simply a pan of water used to hold the vessel in which a food is being cooked. As the food cooks, the water prevents the bottom from browning too quickly. The water also produces a steam which, if contained in an oven, will cause the surface texture of the food to be moist. If you don't want the surface to be too moist, open the oven door a crack to allow the steam to escape.

(See the illustration on p. 93.)

What to Cook in: Vessels

For *baking*, using the proper vessel will make the crucial difference between success and failure. The sides must be low enough to allow the heated air to reach the top surface of the food so that it can cook evenly. Cookies should be baked on a flat sheet with almost no sides. A casserole should be cooked in a glass or ceramic dish large enough to contain it, with the surface of the casserole no more than three-quarters of an inch from the top edge. Cakes and breads require metal pans with sides high enough to contain them after they have risen.

(See "Oven-cooking Vessels," pp. 251–252.)

Should the cooking vessel be metal or glass? Glass, porcelain, or ceramic dishes heat more slowly and retain heat longer than all but the heaviest metal containers. They are best suited for cooking pies and casseroles so their innermost parts have time to cook before the outer surface browns. Glass has the added advantage of being clear, allowing you to see the bottom and sides of the food and thus prevent burning.

Heavy metal pans are good for cooking casseroles and some breads. Cakes and pastries, on the other hand, are quite delicate. They require cooking pans that respond more rapidly to temperature changes in order for the outer surface to be browned while the center remains soft and moist. Aluminum is the best metal for pans used for baking cakes, breads, and pastries. If the aluminum is too light, though, it will bend and warp easily, causing uneven cooking.

For most baking, unless the instructions specify otherwise, the pan or dish should be *prepared.* That is, the inner bottom and sides should be coated with fat so that foods will not stick to them and burn. The best fat for this purpose is vegetable shortening. It has little flavor, it won't burn, and it won't be absorbed by the food. Butter or margarine will burn at high temperatures. Oils will run down the sides, collect on the bottom, and be absorbed by the food. To further prepare pans for baking cakes, pastries, and cookies, sprinkle a little flour over the coated surface, distribute it evenly, and shake out any excess. The flour will keep the dough from becoming gummy and allow it to spread out more evenly.

Roasting or grilling requires that the entire surface of the food be exposed to air in order for it to acquire a uniform color and crunchy texture. What happens to the food's texture is what distinguishes the roasting process. To roast properly, foods must not be contained in a vessel but should be cooked on a rack or a spit coated with vegetable shortening or other fat to prevent the food from sticking. If a pan is used to catch the drippings, its sides must be below the bottom of the food so that air can reach the food. There should never be enough liquid in the pan to cause the bottom of the food to steam or simmer.

How to Do It: Methods

☐ Baking

Baking is done in an oven using convected heat. If the food is in a vessel, then the vessel also cooks the food by conduction. Any food you can name can be baked. That includes casserole dishes, breads, cakes, pies, and pastries, as well as the basic foods such as vegetables, fish, shellfish, meats, and poultry. Most foods that are baked should be cooked evenly, which means that they should not be too close to the heat source or to the top or bottom of the oven. Here are some other considerations for successful baking.

Cooking Considerations for Baking

1. Both the top and bottom of an oven are hotter than its center. To cook foods evenly, position them near the center of the oven. If you want the top of the food to brown more than its bottom, place it closer to the top of the oven.

2. The temperature at the rear of an oven is usually slightly higher than at the front, where small leaks around the door can allow heated air to escape. To cook foods most evenly, turn the cooking vessel occasionally as the food cooks.

3. Air must reach all surfaces in order to cook them evenly. If more than one food is baked at a time, separate the foods so that one doesn't cut the heated air off from the others.

4. To cook the surface of foods more than their insides, preheat the oven before putting the foods in.

5. Heat should be constant. When the oven door is opened, heat is lost, disrupting the cooking process. For best results, open the door only when necessary and then close it as quickly as possible.

6. A clean oven distributes heat more evenly than a dirty one.

7. An aluminum drip pan or strips of heavy aluminum foil can be used to line the bottom of an oven to make cleaning it easier. However, reflected heat can affect cooking temperatures. If you do line your oven, check the temperatures in various locations with an oven thermometer to determine whether some parts of the oven are hotter than others.

8. The thermostat in any oven can go wrong. It is a good practice, therefore, to use an oven thermometer to check the thermostat for accuracy at least once a year.

9. Many recipes specify a definite baking temperature. Others use only general terms such as "slow" or "hot" oven. The temperatures corresponding to these terms are listed in the accompanying table.

Temperatures corresponding to common baking instructions

Oven Description	Degrees Fahrenheit
Very slow	250–300
Slow	300–325
Slow moderate	325–350
Moderate	350–375
Quick moderate	375–400
Moderate hot	400–425
Hot	425–450
Very hot	450–500
Extremely hot	500–525
Broil	Surface of food is exposed to radiant (glowing) heat source

☐ *Broiling*

Meats, poultry, fish, shellfish, some vegetables (such as eggplant), and even some casserole dishes may be broiled. Broiling uses mostly radiant heat to cook foods so that the surface exposed directly to the heat source browns quickly, before the innermost parts have time to cook much at all.

Foods can be broiled over an open fire or in an oven. The heat source should be glowing hot, and the food's surface must be exposed directly to it. Broiling foods correctly requires that they be placed a proper distance from the heat. If a food is broiled in an oven, all of the cooking considerations for baking apply. Here are some others.

Cooking Considerations for Broiling

1. The heat source should be extremely hot (over 500 degrees F.) before the food is exposed to it.

2. The thickness of the food and its distance from the heat must be accounted for to ensure that it cooks thoroughly throughout without being overcooked on the surface or undercooked inside. The thicker the food, the farther it should be from the heat source.

3. Meats and other thick foods are usually turned after the surface first exposed to the heat has browned. Casseroles, fish, shellfish, vegetables, and other thin foods usually are not turned.

4. **The side that is turned to the heat last will cook in one-third the time required to cook the first side.**

5. When broiling in an oven, if a drier surface texture is desired, leave the door open a crack. That allows moisture to escape and also lowers the cooking temperature.

6. Broiling can burn foods quickly. Watch foods carefully as they cook.

☐ *Pan-broiling*

Pan-broiling is a special form of broiling reserved for fatty meats such as bacon, hamburger, and fatty beef steaks. Instead of being exposed directly to radiant heat, the meat is cooked on a very hot pan or metal griddle. As the meat cooks, the fat runs out and prevents the meat from sticking. Excess fat should be poured off so that the food doesn't fry.

Professional chefs use a technique called *striking* to give pan-broiled meats a special flavor and texture. Coat the hot griddle or pan with a thin layer of salt just before placing the meat on it. The salt absorbs some of the melted fat and also flavors the meat.

☐ *Roasting*

The term *roast* can be used as a verb for the cooking process or as a noun to refer to large cuts of meat or poultry. Roasting can be done either in an oven or over an open fire. Meats, poultry, fish, shellfish, and some vegetables such as corn and sweet bell peppers are foods that are sometimes roasted.

When roasted properly, foods will have a uniformly crisp and dry surface texture. To have the best texture, the food must be fully exposed to the hot, dry air so that it can cook evenly all over. The food must rest on a rack, not in a pan, or its bottom will simmer or steam. If roasting is done in an oven, then all of the cooking considerations for baking apply. Here are some others.

Cooking Considerations for Roasting

1. If the food's surface is to cook evenly, hot air must reach it evenly. When roasting food in the open air, turn it often so that it can cook evenly.

2. Small food pieces may become very dry when roasted. They are usually better broiled, pan-broiled, or fried.

3. To prevent a food from charring before it cooks throughout, coat the surface with cooking oil before roasting. For thick roasts, if more fat is needed it may be applied by barding or larding. *Barding* means to drape fat over the food or bind it in place with kitchen twine. *Larding* requires a special needle that is used to pierce through the meat and insert a thin strip of fat, called a *lardon*. Lardons should be placed every one to two inches. (See "How to Bard or Lard Meats," p. 420.)

4. Any salt on the surface of a food will draw moisture from it, thereby lessening the browning.

5. Fats and pan juices that accumulate in a cooking pan are good for basting the food to prevent it from becoming too dry. If additional juices are needed, use cooking oil. If water or other liquids are used for basting, they will cause the surface to dry.

6. If too much liquid accumulates in the pan, the bottom of the food might steam and become soggy. To prevent steaming, use a bulb baster or long-handled spoon to draw off excess juices.

7. To prevent the top of the food from becoming too brown, lay a tent of aluminum foil loosely over the top so that it is covered but hot air can still circulate to reach most of the food's surface.

8. Pan drippings can be used to make gravy or sauce to accompany the roasted food. Pour off excess fat and combine it with flour or cornstarch to make a roux. Add liquid to the pan to deglaze the drippings, and add the roux to it to make the sauce. (See "How to Make Gravy," p. 138.)

☐ *Grilling, Griddling, and Barbecuing*

Grilling, griddling, and barbecuing are commonly used methods for cooking meats, poultry, fish, and shellfish. These three terms are often used interchangeably, as if they all meant the same thing. They do not. Let's look at the differences between these methods, using their proper names to distinguish them.

Grilling means to cook in the open air using either a metal grill or a griddle. A *grill* is an open grate that allows air to circulate around the food so that it roasts. Grilling, then, is just the open-air version of roasting. A *griddle* is a solid sheet of metal, and griddling is just a form of pan-broiling. Foods cooked on a griddle will not have the same flavor or dry surface texture as those cooked on a grill.

Barbecuing means to cook a food in a special sauce. Usually the sauce is hot and spicy, and most often the food is marinated in it as well as basted with it as it cooks. Barbecuing can be done by baking, roasting, grilling, or griddling. Most often, it is done by grilling. (See "Marinades," p. 102.)

Cooking in Fats: Frying

Frying means to cook in hot fat in an uncovered vessel. Usually frying is done on a range burner, but it can also be done in special appliances or even in an oven. There are many ways of doing it, as well as many considerations for doing it well.

Because frying is done with fats, it has come to be controversial for dietary reasons. Fats add calories to foods. In fact, fats contain twice the number of calories that comparable measures of proteins or carbohydrates do. Furthermore, some kinds of fats contain cholesterol. In other words, cooking fats are not good for your figure or for your health. (To learn more about fats and your health, see Chapter Six.)

On the other hand, fats used for frying give foods special texture and added flavor. So many foods taste good when fried that life and some of the foods that make it pleasurable would be diminished if we never used frying at all. The solution, then, is to eat fried foods in moderation and to use fats that contain little or no cholesterol. Other than accounting for the dietary considerations, there are many things to know about fats and about the various cooking techniques using them that will make the foods you fry tastier and more attractive.

What Heats and Flavors the Food: Fats

Most cooks and books use the word *fats* to apply to both solid fats and cooking oils. Beyond the fact that cooking oils are liquid at room temperature, there are some important differences between the two kinds of fats. For one thing, solid fats are always saturated, and most of them contain cholesterol. Liquid oils are not saturated, and most of them contain little or no cholesterol. Solid fats and cooking oils also differ in price, taste, temperature at which they burn, and ability to remain stable with repeated use. Even though recipes may specify a particular type of fat— and sometimes even a particular brand—you can substitute one kind for another for frying so long as its cooking characteristics are the same.

☐ *Rendered Animal Fat ("Grease")*

When animal flesh is heated, fats are released in liquid form. This process is called *rendering,* and the rendered fats can be collected and used for cooking other foods. Bacon grease is saved by many cooks for frying. Excess fat trimmed from meat can be melted and used to baste the meat as it cooks. Many recipes instruct you to brown bacon or some other meat and then use the rendered fat to brown onions and other vegetables. (Of course, you can usually substitute a cooking oil, which will be much better for your health.) Lard is rendered pork fat sold in cans for baking and frying. Rendered animal fats may also be present in shortening or other mixed fats sold commercially.

For frying foods, animal fats can be used at high cooking temperatures, but they do not hold up well for extended or repeated use. They have a distinctive flavor that may be desirable for some dishes, such as meats and gravies to accompany meats, but too strong for some sauces, casseroles, fish, shellfish, or other dishes that have subtle flavors.

(See "Fats," pp. 194–195.)

Animal fats are highly saturated, and they contain a great deal of cholesterol. Cholesterol can build up in your blood and literally "clog the tubes," causing heart problems. In short, animal fats aren't good for you. Anything that can be done using animal fats can usually be done just as well, if not better, using vegetable oils or shortening. Either is better for your diet and your health.

□ *Butter*

For sautéing as well as for adding flavor to other fats used for frying at low temperatures, butter is the favorite of most good cooks. Because it smokes and burns at medium to high temperatures, butter cannot be used at the high temperatures required for pan-frying or deep-fat-frying. Even for sautéing at low temperatures, butter should be mixed with at least an equal amount of vegetable oil to reduce its chances of burning. Better still, cook the food almost fully in oil and then add butter during the last minute or so of cooking—just enough to flavor the food but with no danger of burning. Butter does not hold up well for long or repeated use, so it is best to dispose of it after it has been used once. Finally, butter is high in cholesterol. If you want to reduce cholesterol in your diet, use a low-cholesterol margarine or butter-flavored shortening instead.

(See "Butter and Margarine," pp. 290–292.)

□ *Clarified or Drawn Butter*

Clarified butter is butter that has been heated at a low temperature until the solid milk particles separate from the liquid butterfat. The liquid is then poured ("drawn") off. Clarified butter tastes different from regular butter, and it will cook at higher temperatures without smoking. Otherwise, all that was said about butter holds true for clarified butter as well.

(See "How to Clarify Butter," p. 291.)

□ *Margarine*

Margarine usually is made from vegetable oils. Most brands contain no saturated fats, and many contain polyunsaturated fats. That means margarine is better for your health than butter, for which it can always be substituted. Since margarine costs about half as much as butter, it is also better for your pocketbook. Like butter, margarine smokes and burns at medium to high cooking temperatures, so it cannot be used for pan-frying or deep-fat-frying. It does not hold up well with long or repeated use and should be disposed of after one use.

□ *Mixed Vegetable Oils and Shortening*

Mixed vegetable oils, as the name implies, are mixtures of oils from different vegetables. Shortening consists of liquid oils that have been mixed with hydrogen ("hydrogenated") to make them solid. Shortening may also contain animal fats. Unlike pure liquid vegetable oils, which usually are low in cholesterol, mixed oils and shortening may contain coconut or palm oils, both of which are highly saturated and contain cholesterol. Don't assume that just because the label says "vegetable oils," the product is not bad for you. Read the list of ingredients to know what you are really getting.

For frying, mixed oils and shortenings have the same characteristics as other liquid oils or solid animal fats. When a recipe calls for lard or other animal fat, shortening can be substituted and is much better for you.

□ *Pure Vegetable Oils*

Pure vegetable oils—corn oil, safflower oil, peanut oil, olive oil, and so on—are probably the most desirable of all frying media. For convenience, they can be poured, measured, used, and cleaned up easily. With the exception of coconut oil and palm oil, they all contain no cholesterol, and some contain polyunsaturated fats. Each has a distinctive flavor, and most will cook at high temperatures without smoking or burning. Furthermore, they will all hold up well for long and repeated use if they are used properly.

Any vegetable oils may be used for frying any foods. Some, though, seem to go better with some foods than with others. Just which goes best with what foods is something for you to work out to suit your own taste. Here are some suggestions:

· Fish: Peanut oil
· Chicken: Corn, peanut, soybean, or cottonseed oils
· Veal: Olive oil
· Vegetables: Safflower, corn, peanut, soybean, or olive oils

How to Care for Fats

1. **Water in fats damages them and lessens their cooking ability.** Water also makes hot fat spatter, making a mess and possibly causing burns. To minimize water in fats, heat them slowly to allow any water in them to evaporate. Keep the moisture in foods being fried at a minimum.

2. **Never let a fat get so hot that it smokes.** Hot fats can burst into flames, and a smoking fat is very near the flash point.

3. **Keep fat clean.** Remove food particles before they have a chance to burn and impart a bad flavor to other foods. After each use, strain the fat through cheesecloth held in a colander or a tea strainer.

4. **Never mix fats with different foods.** If a fat is used once to fry fish, for example, then reserve it for cooking only fish. You can remove some of the food flavors from a fat by frying a few slices of potato in it.

5. **Do not add cool fat to hot fat.** New fat can be added to replace good fat that has evaporated or been absorbed in foods, but the hot fat should first be cooled for a couple of minutes so that it does not scorch the new fat.

6. **Salt or sugar in fat causes it to require higher cooking temperatures.** Foods containing salt or sugar will require longer cooking and will therefore absorb more fat. It is best to leave salt or sugar out of foods until after they have been fried.

7. **Throw out used fats, except for cooking oils.** To save money, reuse cooking oils. Pour the used oil through cheesecloth or a coffee filter to filter out any food particles and refrigerate the oil for later use.

8. **When a fat is worn out, throw it out.** Do not reuse a fat that smells bad, has a bad flavor, or foams excessively when foods are added to it. A worn-out fat will require higher cooking temperatures and will not hold heat well, so foods fried in it will taste greasy.

9. **Dispose of solid fats in the garbage.** Fats should never be poured down the drain of a sink. They will build up and eventually cause plumbing problems. Pour warm fat into a can or other heat-proof container with a lid so that it can be covered and disposed of. Use paper towels to soak up any fat remaining in cooking vessels.

■

What Happens to the Food: Textures

In frying, fats are heated to very high temperatures, so that the outer surface of the food cooks much faster than the inner parts. To compensate, a coating is usually used to protect the food and allow time for it to cook throughout. Even when a coating is to be used, however, larger food pieces may require partial cooking by some other method before being coated and fried. Large pieces of chicken, for example, are usually parboiled for three to five minutes before they are fried.

Not only does a coating give a food longer to cook, it also forms a crisp, tasty crust that adds texture, flavor, nutrients, and calories. There are many different coatings and countless recipes and variations of any one. The following descriptions are of the four basic types: dry coating, dipped batter, wet batter, and breading. Any one of them can be changed by varying the ingredients, but what is said about each one will hold true even if the ingredients are modified.

□ *Dry Coating*

Dry coatings are the simplest and probably the most commonly used coatings of all. A food is simply coated with flour or other dry ingredient that will form a crust when fried.

The ingredients

Base: Plain white all-purpose flour is used most often, but self-rising flour or pancake mix can be used just as well. You can also use dark flour, cornmeal, cracker crumbs, or breading, but be aware that they will brown more quickly than white flour. Many cooks mix all-purpose or self-rising flour with cornmeal or breading to give different flavors and textures.

Seasonings are usually mixed into the coating, but they can also be applied directly to the surface of the food before it is coated.

Dredge it...

How to make it

1. The food should be slightly moist so that the seasonings and the dry coating will stick to it. If the food is dry, coat it lightly with vegetable oil.
2. Mix seasonings evenly into the dry coating, or sprinkle them lightly over the entire surface of the food.
3. Apply the dry coating thoroughly and evenly, using one of the following methods:

   a. *Dredge it.* Place the food in a pan and shake ("dredge") the dry coating onto it. Turn the food and repeat the coating process until it is coated evenly all over.

   b. *Bag it.* Place the dry coating and a few pieces of the food in a paper or plastic bag and shake the bag gently. Do not do this with delicate foods such as fish, or they might fall apart.

Bag it...

c. *Beat it.* For tougher meats that are to be braised, such as veal scallops, Swiss steaks, or stew beef, pound in the flour until the meat won't hold any more. Use a meat mallet or the back of a long knife blade. To minimize the mess, shield the food by putting it between two pieces of waxed paper or plastic wrap.

4. Shake off excess dry coating and place the food on a plate or wire rack. Keep all pieces apart so that they don't rub the coating off one another.

5. Fry the food right away, or hold it in the refrigerator for up to two days. The crust will be crisper if the food is allowed to set for 30 minutes before frying.

Beat it!

□ *Dipped Batter*

This batter adds a wet "dip"—or "wash," as it is also called—to the dry coating. The dip binds the dry coating together and holds it to the food. The resulting crust is firmer and less crumbly than a crust made with a dry coating alone. Fish, chicken, and most vegetables are exceptionally good fried in a dipped batter.

The ingredients

Base: Any of the dry coatings described above may be used. Plain all-purpose flour, breading, and a mix of flour and breading are the most popular.

Liquid: The liquid dip or wash may be milk, cream, yogurt, beer (even flat beer), broth, or combinations of these.

Egg: Beaten eggs—whole eggs, or yolks or whites alone—may be used as a dip. Also, you can enrich any of the liquids just listed by adding eggs to them. For a very light crust, use only the egg whites, beating them until they peak before using in the dip. Egg dip cooks very quickly, causing the crust to brown very fast. For that reason, use egg dip for cooking only small pieces or delicate foods such as fish or vegetables that require little cooking time.

Seasonings may be mixed into either the dry coating or the dip, or they can be applied directly to the surface of the food.

How to make it

1. Prepare the dip in a bowl. Blend it well, but don't beat it so much that it foams. Air bubbles in the dip will keep it from coating the food evenly.

2. Prepare a dry coating as described above. The dry coating can be applied before or after the food is dipped, or both before and after.

3. Season the dry coating, the dip, or the surface of the food.

4. *Optional:* Coat the food with the dry coating by dredging or bagging it.

5. Drop the food gently into the dip. Use a dry hand to handle the food when it is dry, the other hand to handle the food when it is wet. That will tend to minimize lumps of coating falling off into the fat. (Lumps can burn and give the frying fat, and consequently the food, a bad flavor.)

6. Remove the dipped food to a plate or wire rack to drain. Keep the pieces separated so that they can all drain freely and evenly.

7. *Optional:* When the food has drained, coat it once again with breading or other dry coating. Shake off any excess and place the food on a plate or wire rack. Keep all pieces apart so that they don't rub the batter off one another.

□ *Wet Batter or Fritter Batter*

Wet or fritter batter is basically a mixture of a dry coating with a dip. If it is very thick, it can bind small food pieces together to make fritters. If it is thinner, it makes a batter that forms a firm and solid crust over foods. Moist foods, especially okra, onion rings, and oysters, seem to cook especially well in a wet batter. The crust firms up quickly to seal in moisture and the food steams in its own juices, thereby conserving its delicate flavors.

The only drawback to using a wet batter is that it requires some advance time—at least one hour, and preferably three or more—to allow the batter to set. The longer the batter sets, the smoother and more solid the crust will be. If it is used right after it is mixed, the texture will be quite different and not as good. Don't worry about having to plan too carefully, though. Wet batter keeps well for as long as three days.

The ingredients

Unlike other batters in which the dry and wet ingredients are kept apart, it is the mixture of the two that makes this batter work. How much is needed? One cup of batter is enough to coat about four to eight servings of most foods.

How thick should it be? The thicker the batter, the thicker the crust. For fritters, a thick mixture is needed. More delicate foods such as shrimp or vegetables are usually better with a more delicate crust made from a thin batter. A mix of equal parts of flour and liquid is a good all-purpose mixture for most foods. Start with this mix and then vary it to suit your taste.

Base: Use all-purpose flour, self-rising flour, or pancake mix.

Liquid: Milk and beer are the most popular liquids, although water, broth, or any other liquid can be used just as well. Beer seems to give a crust with a darker color than either water or milk.

Egg: For each cup of batter, mix in one whole egg or one to two yolks or whites. For a lighter crust, separate the eggs and hold the whites to be beaten and incorporated as a leavener just before the food is dipped.

Seasonings should be incorporated into the mixture.

Optional leavener: Baking soda (which is already in self-rising flour and pancake mix), carbonated beverages (including fresh beer), or well-beaten egg whites that are included in the batter will make the crust puffy and light. If you use beaten egg whites, they should be added to the batter just before the food is dipped. Any leavening agent will gradually lose its power the longer it sits.

How to make it

1. Mix equal parts of the base and liquid. One cup of batter will coat four to eight servings.

2. For each cup of batter, blend in one whole egg, or two yolks or two whites (see step 6 below), and seasonings.

3. Blend the batter until it is smooth.

4. Adjust the thickness: thin for most foods, thick for fritters. Add flour to thicken, liquid to thin. For a really thick batter, allow it to sit for an hour or longer, and then pour off the excess liquid.

5. Allow the batter to sit either at room temperature for one to two hours, or in the refrigerator for at least three hours. It will keep well if refrigerated for up to three days.

6. *Optional:* Just before dipping the food, add well-beaten egg whites or other leavener.

7. Dip the food into the batter, coating it thoroughly and evenly all over.

8. Drain off excess batter and place the food on a plate

or wire rack to hold it before frying. The longer the coated food sits, the more batter will drain off. The less batter, the less crust.

9. *Optional:* Just before frying, dip the battered food in breading. Press the breading in so that it sticks.

□ *Breading*

Breading is used to give special added texture and flavor to fish, veal, pork, and vegetables—delicate foods that can cook in the short amount of time needed to brown the breading.

The ingredients

(See "How to Make Bread Crumbs," p. 288.)

Finely ground bread crumbs, cornmeal, cracker meal, fish meal, matzoh meal, or combinations of these are the most popular "breadings." Finely ground rolled oats, cornflakes, or other breakfast cereal can also be used. To make the breading lighter, mix it with as much as an equal amount of white all-purpose flour, self-rising flour, or pancake mix. For special flavor, you can mix in finely ground nuts or hard cheese (as much as one part in four).

How to make it

Breading may be applied as a dry coating or as a dip. The dip method gives better results. Whichever method you use, press or pat the crumbs into the food just before it is fried to make the breading stick. It is best to fry breaded foods within a very short time after they have been dipped (thirty minutes maximum). If breaded foods are held very long, the breading sweats and may become soggy.

Method 1. Follow the steps for applying a dry coating (pp. 50–51), substituting breading for all or part of the flour.

Method 2. Follow the steps for applying a dipped batter, using breading in the final step. For best results, use a thick dip. (See pp. 51–52.)

Method 3. Use a fritter batter or a dip. Dip the food into the batter, drain it thoroughly, coat it with breading, and fry it as quickly as possible. (See pp. 52–53.)

What to Cook in: Vessels

(See "Range-top Vessels," p. 250.)

Any pan used for frying should rest flat on the surface of the burner. Some pans are so light that the weight of their handle can cause them to tilt. The result is that most of the fat runs to one side, and foods cook unevenly.

Pans that are very light can warp because of the high temperatures used for frying. This is especially true if they are subjected to rapid temperature changes caused by putting a hot pan onto a cold surface. A warped frying pan will allow the fat to settle around the outer edge. Again, foods will cook unevenly.

Each of the methods used for frying has a particular type of cooking vessel that suits it best.

To grill-fry, use a solid pan (called a "griddle") made of heavy cast aluminum or iron, The bottom should be flat, and the sides should be just high enough to contain the small amount of fat used.

griddle

Sautéing requires a pan that can respond rapidly to temperature changes, so that foods do not overcook. Pans made of either copper lined with tin or treated aluminum are the best, but they are expensive. Aluminum pans coated with a non-stick inner lining are a splendid but inexpensive substitute. Pans made of heavyweight stainless steel or iron are not good for sautéing because they hold heat for a long time, which means that foods might overcook if you're not careful.

The **pan-fry** method calls for cooking at high temperatures, with the fat temperature kept as constant as possible. Pans made of heavy stainless steel, heavy aluminum with an inner lining of stainless steel, or commercial-weight treated aluminum are the best. Even though they are expensive, they are worth the cost. Lightweight pans made of any material are likely to warp. Enameled iron is an excellent material, but pans made of it are heavy and expensive. Pans made of plain iron are functional and cheap, but they are very heavy. They can also hold the flavors of foods cooked in them and convey those flavors to other foods.

skillet

To deep-fat-fry, use a vessel deep enough to allow the food to be immersed completely in the fat, with the fat filling the vessel no more than halfway to allow room for foam. There are special appliances made for deep-fat-frying that have built-in thermostats so that the temperature of the fat can be controlled, but you can also use any large, heavy pot. Pots made of heavyweight treated or clad aluminum are the best, because they distribute heat evenly and hold it.

deep fryer

For stir-frying, a wok is the best thing to use, but any good heavy pan will do.

wok

How to Do It: Methods

Virtually every recipe in which frying is used will have instructions reading "Melt two tablespoons of butter . . ." or "In 1/4 cup cooking oil . . ." or something similar specifying exact amounts. But it is *not* the amount of fat that counts; it is *the amount of fat in relation to the size of the cooking vessel.* That's because it is the *depth* of the fat in the pan *in relation to the food being fried* that determines the outcome, not the size of the pan or the sheer amount of fat.

The depth of the fat in relation to the food being cooked is what distinguishes one frying method from another. If you know these methods by name, as well as the amount of fat and other considerations involved in using them, you can vary recipes intelligently and produce good results. Simply "sauté," "pan-fry," or use one of the other methods to fry the food the way you want. The "Cook's Guides" in Part Three of this book use these terms to indicate the ways in which particular foods can be fried.

□ Grill-frying

Grill-frying is similar to pan-broiling because it is done on a solid sheet of metal that may be called a "grill." It is more correct, however, to call it a *griddle* to distinguish it from the grated grill used for roasting. Whereas in pan-broiling the food provides its own fat, in grill-frying the griddle is coated with a thin layer of fat to keep foods from sticking to it. Eggs, lean meats, thin vegetables, and seafood pieces are all good grill-fried.

□ *Sautéing*

Sauté is a French word that comes from the verb meaning "to hop" or "to jump." Either meaning conveys the idea of the sauté method, which is to cook foods quickly, just enough to remove their raw characteristics. Delicate foods such as fish, vegetables, and thin slices of veal are sautéed—often without coating or batter—to give them the flavor of the frying fat. Use only a small amount of fat and cook over low to moderate heat, stirring or shaking the food constantly to coat all the food's surface with the fat and cook it evenly. You can serve a good bit of the fat with the food to give it more flavor.

How much fat do you use? Just enough to prevent the food from sticking, and not so much that it covers the food to any degree. That's a depth of about one-sixteenth to one-eighth of an inch.

What kind of fat? Most good cooks insist that plain or flavored butter, clarified butter, margarine, or olive oil are the only fats to use because of their rich flavors. Any of these can burn easily, however, so it's best to mix them with an equal part of vegetable oil. An even better technique is to cook the food at least halfway in vegetable oil and then add butter, margarine, or olive oil for flavor.

Many cooks and books tell you that the word *sauté* means to brown a food lightly in fat and then add a small amount of liquid to cook it to completion. This technique may also be called *braising*, which is discussed in Chapter Three. Whatever you call it, if you add liquid to cook delicate foods that have been browned lightly in fat, add only enough liquid to cool the fat and prevent the food from burning. Too much liquid will make the food soggy. If the liquid evaporates before the food cooks fully, add a little more.

□ *Pan-frying*

Perhaps the most popular method for frying is pan-frying. When you fry chicken, fish, French fried potatoes, and most vegetables, you will usually use the pan-fry method. For pan-frying, use a metal pan with sides high enough to contain a fairly large amount of fat as well as the food. How much fat? Enough to cover about one-half the thickness of the food so that the food will be cooked throughout with only one turning.

What kind of fat? Pan-frying involves high temperatures, which rules out butter, clarified butter, margarine, and olive oil, because they will smoke and burn. That leaves any and all of the other fats and cooking oils. Which ones you choose depends on your own taste and health considerations.

□ *Deep-fat Frying*

Just as the name says, in deep-fat frying the fat is deep. How deep? Deep enough for the food to be completely immersed and even to float in the fat so that it will cook throughout all at the same time. Croquettes, fritters, doughnuts, and small pieces of fish and vegetables all cook well in deep fat. Because there is so much fat, it retains heat well, so foods cook faster and therefore absorb less fat. It is a good practice, though, to stir or shake the food occasionally so that it cooks evenly.

Because fats will boil up when cold foods are introduced into them, the cooking vessel should never be more than half full of fat. The fat should be very hot (325 to 400 degrees F.), but never so hot that it smokes.

What kind of fat? Again, butter, clarified butter, margarine, and olive oil cannot be used because they will burn at high temperatures. Vegetable oil is preferred to solid fat not only for health reasons, but for convenience of measuring, pouring, and cleaning. With the large amounts of fats used, it is most economical to clean and store them to reuse later on.

□ *Stir-frying or Wok-frying*

Stir-frying is a form of frying used mainly for cooking small pieces of food in the Oriental style. Vegetables and small pieces of fish, poultry, and meat are all very good stir-fried. Cooks often use a special pan called a *wok* that has a small bottom and high sloping sides. The higher up the sides the food is cooked, the lower the heat, so the cook has some control over the cooking temperatures. If you don't have a wok handy, use a solid griddle or any pan that would be appropriate for pan-frying.

In stir-frying, a thin layer of fat (traditionally, peanut oil) is used to coat the cooking surface evenly. The wok or pan is then heated over medium to high heat until the fat

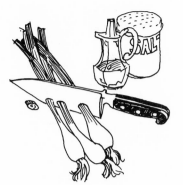

sizzles. Salt may be sprinkled lightly over the entire cooking surface before the food is cooked, a technique similar to the "striking" process used with pan-broiling.

Foods are usually cut into very small pieces, all about the same size, so that they can cook evenly in the same length of time. It is customary to cut the foods crosswise at a forty-five degree angle; that way, a greater portion of their surface is flavored with the fat. Cook the food pieces by stirring them rapidly around the cooking surface to coat them with fat so that they cook evenly.

Another common practice in wok cookery is to cook the food lightly in the fat and then finish it in a liquid as in the braising process described in the next chapter. The liquid usually contains a thickener to make a "wash" (see p. 131). The liquid may be water, broth, or fruit juices, used alone or mixed together. The thickener is usually cornstarch or arrowroot, either of which produces sauces that are clear and glossy.

□ *Oven Frying or "Ovenizing"*

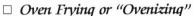

Oven frying is a less well-known method that is becoming more popular, especially for cooking fish, vegetables, and small pieces of poultry. It is done by placing a food that has been coated with a dry coating or batter into a shallow metal pan with about one-sixteenth of an inch of hot fat in it. The food is rolled in the hot fat to coat it evenly and then baked in a preheated oven at 400 to 500 degrees F. Poultry and meats may be turned after their tops have browned so that their undersides can brown also. The second side will require less than half the time to brown as the first. Fish or thin vegetables need not be turned.

Is this baking or is it frying? It's really both. Even though they are baked in the oven, foods will have a crunchy crust because of the coating and the fat. Done properly, this will produce a texture that is uniformly crisp. Be careful, though: too much fat and the food will steam, making it soggy or greasy.

□ *Pressure Frying*

The new technique of pressure frying has recently grown in popularity because "the Colonel" and other fast-food chains have been using it to cook chicken and other foods. Now a special cooker is available for doing it in the home. Foods are first partially fried in deep fat in a special heavy pot. A pressure lid is then securely fastened on so that the food cooks under pressure in a very short time. The fried food will have a moist texture, but it won't be greasy the way it ordinarily would be if it had cooked in its own steam.

Cooking Considerations for Frying

1. *Danger!* Fats and cooking oils can catch fire. When they begin to smoke, they are just below the flash point where they burst into flame. In case of fire, cover the pan or fire with a pot lid or sprinkle salt or baking soda on the burning surface. *Don't* try to put out a burning fat with water. That will only spread it. Never try to carry a pan that is on fire. You will most likely drop it and spread the burning fat over a much larger area, including yourself.

2. Only foods that are tender should be fried. They may be naturally tender, like chicken, fish, and most vegetables, or you can tenderize them by parboiling them or beating them with a mallet or the back side of a long knife blade.

3. Foods that are large or that require longer cooking times should be parboiled before frying to ensure that they cook throughout.

4. The side of the food that is browned first will be the most attractive for serving.

5. The side that is browned last will cook in one-third to one-half the time required to brown the first side.

6. Fats should be heated slowly to allow moisture in them to evaporate before foods are introduced.

7. The lower the temperature of the fat, the longer it will take to cook the food. If the temperature is too low, the food will taste greasy.

8. To check whether the fat is hot enough when pan-frying or deep-fat-frying, put a one-inch cube of stale bread into the fat. If the fat is ready, the bread should cook to a crusty brown within sixty seconds.

9. Introducing large amounts of food into the fat will lower the temperature, thereby lengthening the cooking time and causing the foods to absorb more fat. Crowding foods in the fat will do the same. So, add foods slowly, and don't crowd them.

10. To prevent spattering and to keep from lowering the temperature of the fat too much, lower foods gradually into hot fat. For safety, hold the foods with tongs or a long-handled spoon.

11. Foods at room temperature or warmer will cook more rapidly and absorb less fat than foods that are chilled or frozen.

12. The longer a food is in the fat, the more fat it will absorb.

13. The larger the surface area of the food, the more fat it will absorb.

14. Foods with high sugar content will absorb more fat than foods with little or no sugar.

15. Soft, doughy, or watery foods will absorb more fat than more solid foods.

16. Frozen foods require about twenty-five percent longer cooking times than foods that are fully thawed.

17. Except in pressure frying, don't cover the cooking vessel. If you do, the foods will cook in their own steam. As a result, they will become limp and will probably taste greasy.

18. Never salt a fried food over the fat. Salt in fats will shorten their life. Salt also lessens the crispness of fried foods unless it is added after the food has been fried.

19. Bread flour or other high-gluten flours will absorb less fat than soft wheat flour such as cake or pastry flour.

20. To avoid messy and dangerous spills, always turn the handles of frying pans away from you and away from range burners.

21. When deep-fat-frying, use a fry thermometer to determine the tempera- ture of the fat. For most purposes 365 degrees F. is about right. Remember that just by thinking of the number of days in a year.

22. Cold fats added to hot fats might scorch and affect the flavors of foods fried in them. To avoid scorching, never add cold fats to any fats that are over 250 degrees F.

23. Solid fats should never be poured down a sink drain. They will build up in the pipes and cause plumbing problems.

Microwave Cooking: A Fourth Way to Cook?

All of the three ways to cook covered so far in this chapter have been used by cooks since the beginning of civiliza- tion. Now there is a new cooking device that some regard as revolutionary: the microwave oven. Is it truly revolu- tionary? That is, does it give us a fourth way to cook, or is it simply a device that allows each of the three basic ways to be done faster?

The greatest difference between microwave cooking and conventional methods is the length of time required. Depending on the amount, most foods will cook fully in a microwave device in only one-fourth to one-half the time required by conventional methods. Otherwise, what microwave cooking does is fairly conventional, and doing it well requires the same knowledge of the three basic ways to cook as ordinary cooking does.

Other than the time required to cook foods, two things that truly have been revolutionized by microwave cooking are the thawing of frozen foods and the reheating of pre- viously cooked foods. Frozen foods can be thawed in a frac- tion of the time required by other methods, and the texture of the food is less likely to be diminished in the process. Foods that have just been cooked can be rewarmed for serving in seconds. They won't be dried out, and they will hold their heat longer than foods reheated by conventional

methods. Cold foods that have been cooked previously will retain their original flavors when reheated by microwaves with less chance of having a peculiar "leftover" taste.

One other advantage of microwave cooking cries out for attention: cleaning up is much easier. Foods can be cooked right in the containers in which they will be served. In fact, foods can be frozen, cooked, *and* served in the same container. That saves a lot of dirty dishes. And because there are seldom any spills, splashes, or spatters, microwave cooking virtually eliminates constant cleaning of countertops, range burners, and ovens.

What Heats the Food: Microwaves

Microwaves are a form of high-frequency radio waves. They are similar to those used by radio transmitters but much shorter, approximately four to six inches long. The radio waves cause the molecules in foods to vibrate fast enough to produce friction, which in turn produces the heat that cooks the food.

Because microwaves penetrate into the food—about three-fourths to one and one-half inches—some cooks and books have suggested that foods cook from the inside out. That notion is not exactly accurate, but it does give some insight into why foods cook much faster in microwaves without browning their surfaces. What really happens is that the microwaves agitate molecules within the food, thereby producing heat that is then conducted by the food in both directions, toward the center as well as toward the outer surface.

The rapid motion of the food's molecules accounts for another characteristic of microwave cooking. The food continues to cook for many seconds, and even minutes, after the energy is turned off. That is why instructions call for letting foods set a period before serving. That is also why timing can be more difficult unless you are following a tried and proven recipe.

What Happens to the Food: Textures

Probably the worst thing to have happened to the world of microwave cookery was the decision to label the device an "oven." That's because the very things done best in an oven—baking and roasting—are the things microwaves do *least* well. Baked goods such as breads and pastries quite often have a gummy texture when microwaved and might not be browned. In some cases, foods—breads, especially—can overcook and become dry and hard. Meats, poultry, and fish may lack the darkened, crisp surface texture associated with broiling or roasting. Their appearance, flavor, and taste are diminished as a result.

A number of foods don't brown in a microwave device the same way they do in a conventional oven. Bacon, meat roasts, and turkeys may brown nicely, but beef steaks, fish, shellfish, and most casseroles won't. Browning those foods can be accomplished in several ways, but each has its drawbacks. (1) If the food is cooked long enough, heat conducted from inside the food will brown the surface to some degree. Unfortunately, by the time that occurs the inside is usually overcooked. (2) A "browning liquid" can be applied to the surfaces of meats, poultry, or fish before they are cooked. Worcestershire or soy sauce, other meat sauces, or special browning sauces are all suggested for this purpose. However, each imparts its own flavor to the food, and most are loaded with sodium, sugar, or both. (3) Some microwave ovens have a heating element built into them to cook the food by conventional radiation and convection heat in addition to the microwaves. Those are the ovens that cost most. By the time the food has cooked in them enough to brown, however, the process has taken about as much time as it would in a conventional oven. Also, meats and poultry will spatter, making as big a mess in a microwave as they would in a conventional oven. (4) Finally, there are "browning trays" that heat up enough to cook the surface of the food, much as pan-broiling does. Browning trays seem satisfactory for many purposes, but not all cooks are pleased with their results. All in all, your baking and roasting will probably be more satisfactory if you do them in a conventional oven and use the microwave device for other things.

So if a microwave cooker isn't very good for things you would ordinarily do in an oven, what is it good for? If you think of it as a range instead of as an oven and use it accordingly, it will serve you very well. Foods high in moisture content (such as vegetables, fruits, fish, and shellfish), fatty foods (such as bacon), or foods that are cooked in liquids (including casseroles and stews) all taste exceptionally good cooked by microwaves.

Another way to think of your microwave cooker is as an aid for preparing foods, much like a good knife, mixer, or food processor. Thawing foods quickly, melting butter, cooking foods partially (instead of parboiling them), and reheating foods (except breads) are all feats that can be done so quickly in a microwave "range" that you will wonder how you ever got along without one.

What to Cook in: Vessels

The only vessels that ordinarily cannot be used in microwave devices are those made of metal, especially metal pots and pans. Microwaves reflect off metal containers like balls bouncing off a wall, so they cannot reach the food inside. Also, microwaves reflected from metal surfaces can arc off the magnetron tube that produces the microwaves, causing it to burn out. Manufacturers of microwave devices usually specify precautions for using containers made of metal and other materials, so check the manual.

Aluminum foil can be used in small amounts to protect parts of foods from overcooking (chicken wings or bones in roasts, for example). Use small pieces of foil and cover only the part to be protected.

Heat-resistant glass, heavy plastic, porcelain, pottery, and even paper or styrofoam containers can all be used for microwave cooking. Lightweight plastic such as food storage bags or delicate glass should *not* be used. Delicate glass might shatter, and lightweight plastic might melt from the heat conducted to it by heated foods. Mugs or other earthenware with handles or other parts that are glued on should not be used because the glue might be loosened by the heat. Dinnerware or any vessels with a metal rim or decoration should not be used because the metal might cause an electronic arc with the magnetron tube.

Because microwaves pass through the vessel, they do not heat it. That's why some vessels can be handled comfortably after their contents have been heated. Remember, though, that the vessel *will* be heated by heat conducted to it from the food inside. For safety, always handle cooking vessels with a hotpad or cooking mitt whether or not you think they will be hot.

How to Do It

Timing is the key to failure as well as success with microwave cooking. And timing, you will find, is a difficult thing to plan unless you are using a proven recipe with known results in a particular microwave cooker. The power of the device as well as the power settings used vary from manufacturer to manufacturer and from model to model. The amount of food being cooked at one time is another variable that causes cooking times to be different. The more food, the longer the cooking time. For these and other reasons, it is impossible to provide any specific "how to" information for using all microwave devices. If you have a microwave cooker, use the instruction booklet and any other materials provided by its manufacturer to guide you.

What Kind to Buy

If you don't already own a microwave device and are planning to shop for one, you will find that the variety and number of available features can be downright bewildering. You can pay a great deal to get many features you might not need and that most cooks can well do without. Here are some points to consider about various features.

Since most microwave units are made to sit on a countertop, **size considerations** must account for two things: the cooking space inside and how much counter space will be lost. Any unit with an interior space under one cubic foot is fine for cooking one thing at a time but just can't handle two or more dishes or even one very large food such as a turkey. The largest units can cook even a large turkey and perhaps three or even four dishes at once, but they take up a great deal of counter space. The question is, will you be cooking enough things often enough to justify the loss of counter space that comes with a large unit? If the answer is no, then perhaps you should choose a smaller one. An oven capacity of about one to one and one-quarter cubic feet is suitable for most needs.

Most units available today provide at least three **temperature settings:** low, medium or "defrost," and high. You will need all three. Temperature settings other than those are nice to have, but aren't likely to be used often enough to be worth their cost.

Cooking **timers** can be set by a conventional clock switch or by push buttons. Push-button timers are more precise and require less maintenance, but they do cost more.

Some units provide **automatic features.** The more you get, the more you pay. **Temperature probes** are used for roasting meats as well as for cooking casseroles and other foods to some preset temperature. **Automatic defrost** allows foods to be defrosted by their weight. You simply specify the food and its weight, and the timing will be accounted for automatically. **Auto sensor** cooking allows certain foods to be cooked according to a preprogrammed time that is activated when a puff of steam from the heating food touches a sensing device. All you have to do is punch a button that has been preprogrammed for a specific food. Some units provide for only a limited number of foods; others allow the cook to program times for dozens of foods and even for specific recipes.

Most foods require turning or moving as they cook in a microwave device, in order to cook them evenly. Some manufacturers claim that their built-in fans provide even cooking; others build in a carousel turntable to turn foods as they cook. You can add a spring-powered turntable to any microwave cooker if it's needed.

As I noted earlier, foods cooked using microwaves alone sometimes lack the color and texture of foods baked or roasted in a conventional oven. To compensate for this, some microwave models provide a **broiling unit.** These models are usually the top of the line, the most expensive ones with most if not all of the other features I've described. Are they worth it? If you don't have a conventional oven, then maybe they are. If you do have a conventional oven, however, then you can get along very well using your oven for baking and roasting foods, and a less fancy and much less expensive microwave device for doing other things.

Cooking Considerations for Microwave Cookery

1. The energy in a microwave cooker is not distributed evenly. For foods to cook evenly, they must be rearranged as they cook. The more often they are rearranged, the more evenly they will cook. Stir liquids, and periodically change the position of solids or rotate their cooking vessel. A carousel turntable is a real convenience.

2. Cooking times vary according to how much food is being cooked at the same time. The larger the food, or the more foods being microwaved, the longer the time required for them to cook.

3. Foods that have an irregular shape, such as whole fish and chicken breasts or drumsticks, take longer to cook in their thicker parts. To help them cook evenly, place the thickest parts to the outside of the dish, where they will receive more energy.

4. Small foods cook faster than large ones. To speed cooking, cut pieces smaller

than two inches. For even cooking, make all pieces the same size.

5. The shallower the food in its vessel, the faster it will cook.

6. Porous, airy foods take less time to cook than heavy, compact foods.

7. Coverings on foods will cause them to steam, thereby making them moist. To prevent steaming, use plastic wrap and turn back one side or poke holes in it to allow steam to escape.

8. Foods sealed in skins, shells, or containers will expand when microwaved and can explode. To cook potatoes, apples, hot dogs, and the like in their skins, first poke holes in them. Always remove eggs from their shells and break the yolks. Never try to cook foods in cans, bottles, or other sealed containers.

9. Paper towels placed under breads, crackers, or breaded foods absorb moisture and keep the food's surface more dry and crisp.

10. Don't attempt to fry foods in fats or cooking oils in a microwave cooker. The fats might overheat and catch fire.

Combination Cookery
What to Do with Leftovers

CHAPTER THREE

*T*he term *combination cookery* can be used to categorize the many cooking methods other than the basic "three ways to cook" covered in Chapter Two. If one food is cooked by two or more basic cooking methods, or if two or more foods are combined and cooked by one or more cooking methods, then they fall into this category. Soups, braises, and casseroles are some examples. Such combination dishes make up the great majority of specialty dishes with which recipes are concerned. They are also dishes that are commonly made using leftovers of foods that have been cooked originally by one of the three ways described in Chapter Two.

The difference between the information contained in this chapter and the instructions given in recipes is simple: this information is quite general and very, very basic. These are the themes for which recipes are the variations. Instead of telling you how to make one braise, one casserole, or one soup, I'll deal with how to go about making all braises, casseroles, soups, and other combination dishes. If you master the contents of this chapter, including the detailed instructions that are given, you will be able to work with recipes more intelligently and flexibly. In fact, if you learn what is covered here, you just might not have to use recipes at all.

I won't attempt to cover all the possible forms of combination cookery here, just the ones used to make main meal dishes. No breads or desserts, in other words. Still, that is quite a lot. Braises and casseroles, for example, are only two combination methods, but between them they account for the vast majority of all main meal dishes that might be classified as combination dishes.

Also included here are several "fancy" dishes such as quiches and soufflés. Those are the kinds of specialty items with which many good cooks like to show off. If you have never tried to cook them, you might think they must be difficult. They really aren't. In fact, they're fun to do, and they are excellent ways to serve even the simplest leftovers to make very special and tasty main dishes.

Casserole Cookery: Basic Casseroles, Gratinées, and Pot Pies

Basic casseroles are called by many names, and the number of different recipes for them is legion. They range from leftover vegetables cooked in cream soup through pot pies cooked in pastry crust, with chicken, vegetables, or fish cooked in white sauce in between. Names and ingredients may differ, but the basic method and cooking considerations for any casserole will always be about the same.

Know Your Cooking Terms

Casserole: (1) One or more foods combined with a sauce and baked in a casserole dish. (2) The dish in which a casserole is cooked.

Gratinée or au gratin: A basic casserole that has a topping to give it added texture, color, and flavor.

Pot pie: A basic casserole with an added topping—or a shell and a topping—made of pastry dough that browns to form a pie-like crust.

The Ingredients

Recipes, cookbooks, and too many cooks focus entirely on specific ingredients and their amounts for one particular dish or another. Casseroles are a good example. Bean casseroles, chicken casseroles, and cheese soufflés certainly have different ingredients, but the elemental parts of which they are composed are really very much the same. Those common elements are a base food, optional filler, sauce, seasonings, and perhaps a topping or garnish.

□ *Base*

The base food is the most important ingredient and therefore should be the most prominent. Meats, fish, poultry, and most vegetables can all serve as the base ingredient for making casseroles. Whatever the food, its size and abundance relative to the other ingredients should leave little doubt that it is the main one. If a filler is used along with it, the base food should account for at least half of all the ingredients. If the base food is tough, it might require precooking, at least partially, before it is combined with the other ingredients.

☐ *Optional Filler*

"Fillers" are usually combined with the base (up to an equal amount) to add flavor and texture and to make more servings. Among the common fillers are vegetables (especially onions, celery, peas, sweet bell peppers, carrots, and mushrooms), pasta, rice, hominy, and bread crumbs. Whatever you use, always remember that the filler should not be so strongly flavored or abundant that it overwhelms the taste and texture of the base. In most cases the filler must be partially precooked before being combined with the other ingredients. That is especially true for pasta or rice, which absorb the liquid in which they are cooked. Vegetables, however, ordinarily should not be precooked fully, since most of them will cook in the time required to cook the casserole.

☐ *Sauce*

A sauce is used to unify and bind the solid ingredients as well as to contribute its own flavor to a casserole. Any thick seasoned liquid can serve as a sauce. Sometimes the main item or filler—tomatoes, for example—generates enough liquid to make a sauce. Prepared white sauce, tomato sauce, brown sauce, sour cream, yogurt, mayonnaise, thickened broth, or combinations of these are liquids used for sauce. Canned soups—onion, cream of celery, cream of mushroom, cream of chicken, tomato—are also popular.

The two most important considerations for any sauce are its taste and its thickness. The taste should be compatible with the food but not be so imposing that it overpowers it. The sauce should not be so thin that it is runny, but it should not be so thick that the casserole cooks to be solid and dry. (Remember that many sauces will thicken as they cool.) Thick soups, mayonnaise, sour cream, or yogurt can be thinned with milk, broth, cream, wine, or plain water. Thin liquids may be thickened with eggs, roux, sour cream, yogurt, grated cheese, or cornstarch. (See "Thickeners," p. 130.)

☐ *Seasonings*

Since you'll normally prepare the base, filler, and sauce separately (especially when using leftovers), you need to account for salt, pepper, and any other seasonings you've used in the original preparation of the foods before adding more. When you do add seasonings, either mix them into the sauce or sprinkle them evenly over the layers of the casserole to distribute them evenly.

□ *Topping*

A topping for any casserole is optional. Some casseroles— especially those made with a cheese sauce, heavy cream, or mayonnaise—may brown on top so that an additional topping won't be needed. When you do add a topping, use one that will be attractive and compatible with the flavors of the casserole. Some of the most popular toppings are grated or thinly sliced cheese, browned onion rings or other chopped vegetables, breading, or combinations of these.   (See the box on pp. 74–75.)

□ *Garnish*

Like the topping, a garnish is optional. Garnishes are distinguished from toppings by degree. Whereas a topping covers all or most of the top of the casserole, a garnish is more a bit here or a strip there that dresses up the surface. A garnish may well be uncooked, whereas a topping is invariably cooked to brown it.

Foods used as garnishes include parsley or other fresh herbs, pimiento, tomato, sweet bell pepper, other fresh vegetables, fruits, nuts, and other raw foods. The only requirements are that they be compatible with the flavor of the casserole and that they be arranged attractively— even decoratively—on top.

What to Cook in

If a casserole is a combination of foods baked in a casserole dish, then just what is a casserole dish? Any ovenproof dish can be used. The only real requirement is that the sides must be high enough to contain the food, but not so high that they prevent hot air from reaching its surface so it doesn't brown evenly.

Dishes made of ceramic materials are most preferred because they are less likely to burn the bottom and sides of foods. For easier serving, use dishes that are attractive enough to be served at the table. For real convenience, make individual servings using custard cups, ramekins, au gratin dishes, or even large muffin tins. To prevent

Favorite Toppings and Garnishes for Casseroles

Raw vegetables: Cut into strips or small pieces, raw vegetables are often used to top or garnish casseroles. Place the pieces attractively over the top and bake or broil them just before serving to soften and brown them a bit.

Cheese: Cut into strips, cheese can be arranged into interesting designs. It can also be applied in thin sheets or grated and sprinkled evenly over the top. Add the cheese in the final minutes of cooking so that it cooks only long enough to melt and brown but not burn. If you are using a broiler, place the top of the casserole four to five inches from the top of the oven.

Breading and batter-fried vegetables: These should be added only in the final minutes of cooking, just before the casserole is served. If they are added too early, they may become soggy or burn before the casserole is fully cooked.

Fruits: Use fruits more as a garnish than as a topping. Use them fresh and uncooked, and use them sparingly. Slices of lemon or avocado go well with seafoods. Pineapple, poached apple slices, or orange sections go well with ham, pork, chicken, and many vegetable casseroles.

continued

Pastry dough: For a crusty topping, use a pastry dough. You can make it from scratch or from a biscuit mix, or you can even use frozen biscuits or pie shells. If the dough covers the entire surface of the casserole, poke holes in it to allow steam to escape. To make casseroles particularly attractive, arrange the dough in interesting patterns. You can bake the dough separately and lay it on the casserole before it is served, or bake it on top of the casserole in the last ten to fifteen minutes it cooks. To prevent the dough from becoming soft and mushy ("doughy"), be sure the casserole is bubbling hot when you place the dough on it. For a golden color, brush the top with a little milk, egg white, Dijon mustard, or a combination of these after the dough has cooked enough to become firm. (See "How to Make Pastry Crust for Casseroles, Quiches, and Pies," p. 79.)

Nuts: Like fruits, nuts are used more as a garnish than as a topping. Halved, sliced, or crushed, most nuts go well with most casseroles. Take care, though, to try to match the flavor of the nuts with the flavor of the casserole. A robust-flavored nut such as black walnut might be too strong for a delicate fish dish. Almonds or pine nuts, on the other hand, have delicate flavors that complement the flavors of delicate dishes very nicely.

foods from sticking, prepare the bottom and sides of casserole dishes by coating them with a thin layer of shortening.

Hollowed-out vegetables—tomatoes, squash, sweet bell peppers, onions, and eggplant, especially—make wonderful "dishes" for casseroles that can be eaten dish and all. Stuffed vegetables, in other words, are really casseroles if you just think of them that way.

When a vegetable is used as a dish, take care to bake it only long enough to make it tender. You may need to precook the other ingredients so that they need no more time for final cooking than that required to cook their vegetable shell. On the other hand, if the stuffing will take little cooking time, the vegetable shell might need to be parboiled before it is stuffed so that it will become tender in the time it takes to cook the stuffing.

How to Make It

If the casserole is cooked in a covered vessel, it will cook in the liquid and the steam it produces. When it is cooked uncovered, however, the cooking considerations for baking come to be more important. For example, the heated air will dry out the food from its top down—an important consideration for getting the texture you want, especially if a topping is used. You must take care, therefore, to have the casserole dish far enough from the heat source that its bottom or top doesn't burn before it is cooked throughout.

(See "Cooking Considerations for Baking," p. 42.)

The secret to having a really good casserole is to have each of its ingredients fully cooked at the same time, with no one cooked too much or too little. To do that may require precooking the base food or the filler at least to the point where it will cook fully in the time needed for the casserole to cook. Cooking times for casseroles vary from thirty to sixty minutes depending on the size of the dish, the degree to which the ingredients were precooked, and whether or not the casserole has a pastry crust.

The flavor of most casseroles is improved if they are cooked partially, allowed to cool and sit refrigerated for a period—even a day or two—and then reheated for serving. That allows their flavors to blend.

If you plan to freeze a casserole, line the dish with aluminum foil and cook the casserole for about half the full cooking time. Cool the casserole and then fold the foil over its top to seal it. Freeze it in its cooking dish. When it is

fully frozen, remove the wrapped food from the dish. Keep
the casserole frozen in its wrap, and use the dish for cooking other things.

How to Make Casseroles, Gratinées, and Pot Pies

Model for four servings
  White sauce: 1 cup liquid, 2 Tbsp. butter or margarine,
2 Tbsp. flour
  Food base: 1 to 1 1/2 cups
  Filler: 1/2 to 3/4 cups
  Seasonings: Salt, pepper, and other seasonings that go
well with the base food
  Optional topping or garnish: 1/8 to 1/4 cup
  Vessels: 1 mixing bowl, 1 to 4 baking dishes

0. **Before you begin:** Read all the steps below. Review the
    description of casseroles above as well as the principles
    of baking (pp. 41–42) if necessary.
1. **Plan** 1/2 to 1 cup per serving. Most casseroles require
    15 to 30 minutes to prepare and 30 to 60 minutes to
    cook. They usually taste better if they are cooked half-
    way, cooled, and then reheated to completion.
2. **Prepare the sauce:** Allow 1/4 to 1/3 cup per serving.
    Use a white sauce (p. 144), brown sauce (p. 148), tomato
    sauce (p. 151), thinned condensed soup, sour cream,
    yogurt, mayonnaise, or combinations of these. Butter
    or margarine may be included for added flavor. Keep
    in mind that any raw egg or cheese in the sauce will
    thicken it as it cooks.
3. **Season the sauce to taste,** accounting for any sea-
    sonings that have already been used in the sauce, base,
    or filler. Mix seasonings into the sauce to distribute
    them evenly throughout the casserole.
4. **Prepare the base:** Allow 1/4 to 1/3 cup per serving.
    Delicate watery vegetables or fruits may be used raw,
    but do account for their moisture by using less liquid
    in the sauce. Sauté or parboil tougher vegetables until
    they are slightly tender. Cook meats or poultry almost
    fully. Tender vegetables, fish, shellfish, and fruits need
    not be precooked.
5. **Optional filler:** If a filler such as vegetables, rice, or
    pasta is desired, use up to one-half the amount used

for the base. Rice and pasta should be fully cooked. Vegetables should be cut into small pieces. Tougher vegetables should be parboiled or sautéed until they are slightly tender.

6. **Preheat the oven:** Most casseroles are cooked at 325 to 375 degrees F. The larger the dish, the lower the temperature should be. This will allow the casserole to cook evenly throughout without burning its top.

7. **Prepare the vessel:** Use a dish or dishes that can be filled to within 3/4 to 1/2 inch of the top. Coat the bottom and sides with a thin layer of shortening. For a pot pie, line the bottom and sides with pastry dough (see p. 79).

8. **Combine the ingredients:** Distribute the solid ingredients evenly across the bottom of the dish. Mix them up or place them in alternating layers. Leave a space of 3/4 inch from the top of the dish to allow room for expansion. Pour in the sauce to cover the dry ingredients.

9. **Optional topping:** Distribute the topping evenly and attractively over the top. For a delicate topping or a garnish, cook the casserole almost fully, and then add the topping or garnish to cook in the last 15 minutes.

10. **Cook the casserole:**

    a. Place the dish into the preheated oven. The larger the dish, the closer to the oven's center it should be. For a browner top, place the dish closer to the top of the oven.

    b. Set a timer for the approximate cooking time (30 to 60 minutes). The larger the dish, the longer the cooking time. Casseroles with ingredients that are drier will require less cooking than those with ingredients that are moist or liquid.

    c. Halfway through the approximate cooking time, turn the dish 180 degrees. The end that had been facing the rear of the oven will now be facing the front.

    d. Cook until the top and/or bottom browns to your liking.

11. **Serve hot** right away, or cover to hold in heat and moisture.

■

How to Make Pastry Crust for Casseroles, Quiches, and Pies

Models for various sizes of pastry crust

	Sifted Pastry Flour	*Salt*	*Shortening*	*Cold Water*
One crust, 8–9 inches	3/4 cup	1/2 tsp.	1/4 cup	2 Tbsp.
Two crusts, 8 inches	1 1/2 cups	1 tsp.	1/2 cup	4 Tbsp.
Two crusts, 9 inches	1 3/4 cups	1 tsp.	2/3 cup	5 Tbsp.

Note: All-purpose flour may be used, but the texture will be less flaky and more mealy. If all-purpose flour is used, do not add salt.

1. Place all ingredients, except water, in a mixing bowl.
2. With an electric mixer, blend at low speed for 30 seconds, or until the mixture has the consistency of lumpy cornmeal.
3. Add the cold water and mix at low speed for about 15 seconds, until the dough clings together.
4. Coat your hands lightly with flour and roll the dough into a ball.

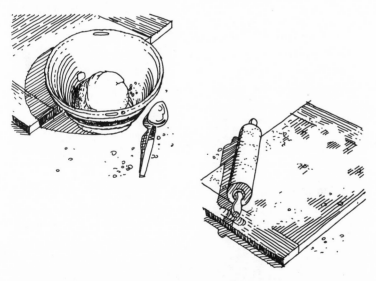

5. Coat a pastry board or cloth and a rolling pin lightly with flour.
6. Fold the dough onto the prepared board or cloth, and roll it into a circle about 1/8 inch thick. Roll from the center to the edge lifting the pin a bit as you approach

the edge. To keep the thickness even, do this in four directions. If the edges split, pinch the dough together with your fingers.

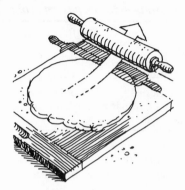

7. *For a pie shell:*

   a. Place the cooking vessel upside down in the center of the dough and cut a circle around it as much wider as the vessel is deep. (You want the dough to be large enough to fill the vessel plus some overhang.)

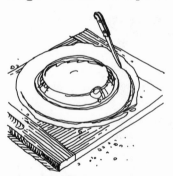

   b. Fold the dough lightly over the rolling pin. Lift the rolling pin over the vessel and unfold the dough loosely into the vessel without stretching the dough.

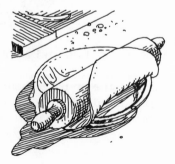

c. Use a knife to trim the dough from the outer rim of the vessel. Fold the dough over the lip and use your fingers or a fork to flute the edge all around.

d. Seal the shell:
  · Preheat an oven to 450 degrees F.
  · Prick the bottom and sides of the pastry with a fork.
  · Baste the bottom and sides (but not the lip) of the pastry with unbeaten egg white or Dijon mustard.
  · Bake 5 to 10 minutes, until the bottom is firm and golden.
  · When the bottom crust is golden brown, pour the filling in.

8. *For a top crust:*
  a. Roll out a crust 1/8 inch thick and large enough to extend 1/2 inch beyond the edge of the vessel.
  b. Brush one side with unbeaten egg white to seal it so it is not softened by steam from the filling as it cooks.
  c. Carefully lift the top pastry and place it basted side down over the filling.

d. Fold the edge under the outer rim of the lower crust, and use your fingers or a fork to flute it all around.

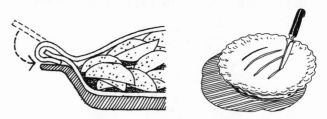

e. Cut vents into the top to allow steam to escape.

9. Bake at 350 to 400 degrees until the crust browns to your liking.

■

Fancy Casseroles: Quiches, Timbales, and Puddings

Served hot or cold, as an hors d'oeuvre, main course, or side dish, for breakfast, brunch, lunch, dinner, or snack, a quiche, timbale, or pudding is gracious and special. These dishes are also delightful ways to serve small amounts of leftovers. Unfortunately, most people think of them as being beyond the capabilities of all but the most skilled cooks. If you think of them as being just fancy casseroles, though, then perhaps they will be less intimidating and more inviting to cook.

The Ingredients

Like the more basic casseroles I've described, these "fancy" casseroles are made of a base, filler, sauce, seasonings, and perhaps a topping or garnish. Just about everything said about casseroles so far applies to quiches, timbales, and puddings as well. The one thing that distinguishes them and makes them special is their sauce. All are made using a basic custard sauce. Because custard sauce is so rich in fats and cholesterol from the egg yolks, these dishes should be enjoyed infrequently.

□ Base
Meats, fish, poultry, and most vegetables are all commonly used as the base ingredient for these dishes. The same

Know Your Cooking Terms

Timbale (pronounced *tim-bel* or *tim-BAHL*): A casserole made using a batter of *chopped* solid food blended with a custard sauce. Usually served hot with a topping of white sauce or Hollandaise sauce.

Pudding: A casserole made exactly like a timbale except that the food is pureed. A pudding may be served hot or cold, with or without a serving sauce.

Quiche (pronounced *keesh*): A casserole made with pureed food, like a pudding, or with chopped food, like a timbale. What distinguishes a quiche is that it is cooked in a pastry shell. A quiche does not need a serving sauce, and it may be served hot or cold.

considerations for the food base of any casserole apply here as well. In particular, the base food should be abundant enough that it is not overwhelmed by any filler. At least half the ingredients should be the base food. Cut it into small pieces of about equal size for quiches and timbales, or puree it for puddings.

□ Filler

As with any casserole, the filler is optional. It should be compatible with the base food and no more than equal to it in amount. Some of the more popular fillers are grated hard cheese (especially for quiche) and chopped, sautéed onions, mushrooms, potatoes, or combinations of these.

□ Sauce

(See "Custard Sauce or Baked Custard," p. 159.)

The sauce is always a custard sauce. Extra egg yolks are usually added to make the custard sauce very rich. For the liquid, use whipping cream or half-and-half, either alone or mixed with equal parts of milk, broth, or fruit juice—whatever goes well with the base.

□ Seasonings

Be sure to account for any salt, pepper, or other seasonings you used for cooking the base, filler, or the sauce before adding more. Additional seasonings that are compatible with the ingredients should be mixed into the sauce.

□ Pastry Shell

The pastry shell is used only for making quiche. A frozen pie shell is simplest, or you can make your own from scratch or from a mix. Homemade or ready-made, the pie shell should be sealed so that it does not absorb the liquid from the batter and remains solid and crisp (see p. 79).

What to Cook in

Any of these dishes is usually cooked in a glass pie plate. Ramekins, custard cups, and even muffin tins may be used to make individual servings so long as they are at least an inch deep. Whatever the vessel, coat the inside with a thin layer of shortening to prevent the food from sticking. Quiches, of course, require a pie shell.

For a light crust on the bottoms of timbales or puddings, coat the inside of the baking dish with butter or margarine. Sprinkle in finely grated cheese or bread crumbs, and spread them evenly over the bottom and sides. Shake out the excess.

How to Make It

Because eggs are such an important ingredient, and because eggs cook so quickly, these dishes must be protected somehow from the dry heat so the custard has time to cook evenly throughout. In a quiche, the pastry shell protects the custard, so no other precautions are necessary. Timbales and puddings, on the other hand, often require a "Mary's bath." Place the cooking dish in a pan of hot water so that the height of the water outside the cooking vessel is about the same as the height of the sauce inside.

(See the illustration on p. 93.)

Cooking times will vary according to the size of the dish and the cooking temperatures. In most cases, the cooking temperature should be 350 degrees F. At that temperature, most dishes eight to ten inches in diameter will require thirty to forty-five minutes' cooking time; individual ramekins will cook in twenty to thirty minutes.

The egg sauce will continue to cook in its own heat after the dish is removed from the oven, so be careful that it does not overcook. Remove the dish when the custard is firm but the top is still glossy. A toothpick or knife blade inserted into the center should come out moist but with no liquid sticking to it.

How to Make Quiches, Timbales, and Puddings

Model for four servings

Food base: 2 to 3 cups

Custard sauce: 1 1/2 cups milk, half-and-half, cream, or combinations, plus 4 large eggs

Seasonings: Salt, pepper, nutmeg, and other seasonings that go well with the base food, "to taste"

Vessels: 2 mixing bowls plus either one 8–10-inch pie shell, or 1 to 4 baking dishes or ramekins at least 1 inch deep.

0. **Before you begin:** Read all the steps below. Review the descriptions of these dishes above as well as the principles of baking (pp. 38–42) if necessary.
1. **Plan** 1/2 to 3/4 cup of solid ingredients and 1/3 to

1/2 cup of sauce per serving. Allow 15 to 20 minutes preparation time and 30 to 60 minutes for cooking.

2. **Prepare the food:** Delicate, watery vegetables may be used raw, but account for their moisture by using less liquid in the sauce. Parboil or sauté vegetables that are firm. Cook meats and poultry almost fully.

   · *For a quiche:* Chop or puree the solid food.
   · *For a timbale:* Chop the foods into small pieces of about the same size.
   · *For a pudding:* Puree the solid ingredients.

3. **Prepare the vessel:** Coat the inside bottom and sides with a thin layer of shortening. Quiche, of course, requires a pastry shell. *Optional:* For a timbale or a pudding, decorate the inside of the dish with grated cheese, pimiento, tomato, parsley, etc., or with firm vegetable pieces that have been parboiled or sautéed to make them tender. Place the dish in the refrigerator to chill for 30 minutes before pouring in the batter.

(See "How to Make Pastry Crust for Casseroles, Quiches, and Pies," p. 79.)

4. **Make a custard sauce:** Allow 1/3 to 1/2 cup per serving, and follow the instructions given on page 160.

5. **Preheat the oven** to 350–375 degrees F. The larger the dish, the lower the temperature.

6. **Combine the ingredients:**

   · *For a quiche or timbale:* Distribute the solid ingredients evenly across the bottom of the dish or pie shell. Mix them up or place them in alternating layers. Pour the custard sauce over them evenly enough to cover. Leave a space of 1/4 inch from the top of the dish or pie shell to allow for expansion.
   · *For pudding:* Mix the custard into the pureed ingredients. The mixture should be fairly thick. Pour the mixture into the baking dish to within 1/4 inch of its top.

7. **Optional topping:** Use grated cheese, bread crumbs, pimiento, parsley, etc. If the sauce is very liquid, wait until it has baked enough to become firm before adding the topping.

(See the illustration on p. 93.)

8. **For timbales and puddings, use a "Mary's bath"** to prevent the bottom from burning. Place a pan of hot (not boiling) water on the bottom rack of the preheated oven. Put the baking dish or dishes into the Mary's bath. The water should come up to 1/2 to 2/3 of the height of the sides of the dish(es).

9. **Cook:**

   a. Place the dish into the preheated oven. Use the center rack for quiche, the bottom rack for timbales or puddings.

   b. Set the timer for the approximate cooking time: small individual dishes, 20 to 30 minutes; medium-sized dishes, 30 to 45 mintues; large dishes, 30 to 60 minutes.

   c. Halfway through the approximate cooking time, turn the dish 180 degrees so that the end that was facing the rear of the oven faces the front.

   d. Cook until the top and/or bottom browns to your liking. The center should be slightly underdone, because it will continue to cook in its own heat.

10. **Serve hot or cold** in individual slices. Timbales may be served in the baking dish but are much prettier if they are turned upside down and removed from the dish. To remove a timbale from its baking dish, first allow it to cool for five minutes. Next, cut around the edge with a sharp knife. Place a serving dish over the top and turn the baking dish upside down so the timbale falls onto the plate. If it does not come right out, bang it with the heel of your hand until it does.

11. **Optional sauce:** Serve a timbale accompanied by tomato sauce, white sauce, or one of the egg yolk and butter sauces. Hollandaise sauce is a favorite. (See Chapter Four, *Hot Sauces.*)

Really Fancy Casseroles: Soufflés

The fanciest casseroles of all are soufflés. You may have heard that soufflés are difficult to make and easy to botch up. They're not really all that difficult, however, and even if they happen to fall they can still be good to eat. The satisfaction of trying, to say nothing of the elation that comes with success when they come out well, makes soufflés well worth the effort.

The Ingredients

Like all the other casserole dishes described earlier in this chapter, soufflés are made of a base food, filler, seasonings, and a sauce, all mixed together and baked in a casserole dish. What distinguishes soufflés from all other dishes is egg whites and how they are used. For soufflés, egg whites are beaten until they hold in air. Much like tiny balloons, the egg whites expand when heated, causing the soufflé to rise.

□ *Base*

Virtually any food—meats, fish, poultry, fruits, vegetables, and even hard cheeses—can be used as the base food for a soufflé. Only two to three tablespoons of base are needed for each serving, so this is a good way to use small amounts of leftovers. The base should be cooked completely or close enough to it that it can be completed in the short time required for cooking the soufflé. It must be finely chopped, flaked, grated, or pureed so that the pieces will be small enough to be lifted by the air in the egg whites.

□ *Sauce*

(See "White Sauce," pp. 140–145.)

Any white sauce will do. Use one-half cup per serving. White sauce made with milk, or with milk mixed with fruit juice, goes well with any cheese or dessert soufflé. White sauce made with milk, broth, or the two mixed together goes well with meats, poultry, fish, or shellfish. The white sauce should be medium thick to allow for the further thickening that will come as the eggs cook. Heat and hold the thickened sauce in a double boiler just enough to cook the egg yolks only slightly and to melt cheese if it is used.

□ *Egg*

Allow one whole egg per serving plus an extra white for each two to three servings. Separate the eggs, using the yolks to enrich the sauce. Beat the whites to incorporate air into them. (See "How to Beat Egg Whites for Soufflés," p. 94.) Once the egg whites are beaten, be careful not to jar them, or you might break many of the tiny balloons. If the air in them escapes, the soufflé will not rise.

□ *Seasonings*

Use seasonings that go well with the base food, accounting for any that might have been used to cook the base or the sauce. Add seasonings to the batter after mixing the base and the sauce but before folding in the egg whites.

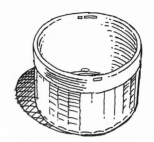

What to Cook in

Use a round dish with straight sides so that the rising soufflé is guided up, up, and away from the dish. It makes little difference whether the dish is glass, porcelain, ceramic, or metal, as long as the sides are straight, but a metal pan makes for faster cooking and a crisper crust. Of course, the dish must be ovenproof and should be attractive enough to be served at the table.

The size of the dish is important. A dish that is too large for the batter will conceal too much of the soufflé in its risen glory. If it is too small for the batter, the rising soufflé is likely to flop over the sides before it has cooked enough to become firm.

Prepare the inside of the dish by coating it with butter, margarine, or shortening. For a light crust, sprinkle in finely grated cheese or bread crumbs. Shake them around to coat the inside of the dish evenly, and shake out the excess. (For a dessert soufflé, use powdered sugar.) For best results, chill the prepared dish in the refrigerator for thirty minutes before pouring in the batter.

Fill the dish to within at least one inch of its top but no closer than three-fourths of an inch from it. Many recipes recommend building a collar, but they are likely to be more trouble than they are worth. If you observe the considerations given above, a collar should not be needed. Just in case, though, here's how to make one.

How to Make a Soufflé Collar

1. Cut a strip of heavyweight aluminum foil the height of the dish plus three inches, and long enough to encircle the dish completely.

2. Coat the shiny side of the foil with butter, margarine, or shortening to half its height.

3. Wrap the foil around the dish with the coated part above the dish facing in. Secure it with kitchen twine or straight pins. Smooth and shape the collar to be an extension of the sides of the dish.

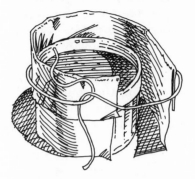

4. Remove the collar after the soufflé is fully cooked and just before serving.

■

How to Make It

Because a soufflé is so delicate, all of the "Cooking Considerations for Baking" given on pages 42–43 are especially important. You must always preheat the oven, and once you have placed the soufflé inside, you must not open the door until the cooking time is up. The cold air entering an opened door and hitting the soufflé might cause those tiny balloons to collapse, and the soufflé will fall.

Because a successful soufflé will rise to as much as twice its original volume, it is best to cook it on the bottom rack and to remove all the racks above it. To prevent the bottom from burning before the center is cooked, place the dish in a pan of warm water, a "Mary's bath."

You can hold a fully prepared soufflé for thirty minutes to an hour in the refrigerator before cooking it, but doing so is risky. If you do hold it, cover the top of the dish to protect the batter from drafts that might deflate the air bubbles. You can also freeze a fully prepared soufflé and store it for up to three months before cooking. Cook a frozen soufflé unthawed, adding fifteen minutes to its regular cooking time.

The cooking times for soufflés given in many recipes tend to be too long. As with any egg dish, a soufflé will continue to cook in its own heat even after it has been removed from the hot oven. A good soufflé should be moist and tacky in its center, and well puffed and firm across its top and sides. It should wobble just a little.

There is one cardinal rule for cooking a soufflé: it must be served immediately. As a guide for timing, have the diners in their places no less than ten minutes before the soufflé is to be served. That way they should be settled and ready for its presentation (presenting it is at least half the fun). Let the audience wait for the soufflé, for the soufflé certainly will not wait for them. Some cooks and books contend that soufflés can be held for as long as one hour in a closed oven at 250 degrees F. I recommend that you take no chances and serve them right away.

How to Make Soufflés

Model for four servings
   Food base: 3/4 to 1 cup
   White sauce: 2 cups liquid, 3 Tbsp. butter, 3 Tbsp. flour
   Seasonings: Salt, pepper, and other seasonings that go well with the base food, "to taste"
   Egg yolks: 4
   Egg whites: 6
   Vessels: 1 small bowl for egg yolks, 1 copper or stainless steel bowl for beating egg whites, 1 six-cup round baking dish with straight sides, 1 baking pan large enough to contain the baking dish, 1 sauce pot, 1 double boiler, 1 large mixing bowl

0. **Before you begin:** Read all the steps below. Review the description of soufflés given above as well as the principles of baking (pp. 38–42) if necessary.
1. **Plan** 2 to 3 tablespoons of base food, 1/2 cup white sauce, and 1 egg for each serving. Add an extra egg white for each two servings. Determine the cooking time (see step 13), adding 30 minutes to allow for preparation and for the cooking dish to chill. The base and sauce may be prepared well in advance, but the egg whites must be beaten and incorporated into the batter just before the soufflé is cooked.
2. **Separate cold eggs,** placing the whites into a bowl suitable for beating them (see the next "How to").
3. **Prepare the vessel** by coating the entire inner surface

with butter or margarine. Place it in the refrigerator to chill for 30 minutes or longer. *Optional:* Coat the inside of the prepared dish with finely grated cheese or bread crumbs; use powdered sugar for dessert soufflés.

4. **Prepare the base** by chopping the solid food into small pieces, or by pureeing them.

5. **Preheat the oven to 400 degrees F.** Remove all but the bottom rack to allow room for the soufflé to rise.

6. **Prepare a white sauce** of medium thickness (see p. 144). Allow 1/2 cup per serving. For each cup of white sauce use 6 Tbsp. roux (3 Tbsp. butter or margarine, 3 Tbsp. flour) and 1 cup milk, broth, or a mixture of the two.

   a. Heat the fat over low heat until it foams. Remove it from the heat and cool it for 1 to 2 minutes. Stir in the flour. Cook for 2 to 3 minutes, stirring constantly so the roux does not brown. Set the roux aside to cool.

   b. Heat the liquid slowly at a moderate temperature until it is warm but not hot. Allow it to cool for 1 minute before stirring in the roux.

   c. Mix the roux and liquid. Simmer the mixture, stirring constantly, for 2 to 5 minutes until it thickens.

   d. Season to taste.

   e. Allow the sauce to cool for about 5 minutes.

   f. Add 1 egg yolk per serving, beating the yolks into the sauce one at a time.

   g. Heat the sauce in a double boiler, stirring until it thickens.

   h. Adjust the seasoning and thickness. If the sauce is too thick, stir in liquid. If it is too thin, add a "wash" of cornstarch: for each cup of sauce, add 1 Tbsp. cornstarch dissolved in an equal amount of water, milk, or broth. Heat the sauce, stirring it constantly until it thickens.

7. **Stir the base food into the sauce** until it is incorporated fully. (Cheese, if it is used, should be melted thoroughly.) Pour the mixture into a bowl large enough to hold it plus the beaten egg whites.

8. **Beat the egg whites** (see the next "How to"). When they are solid enough to be cut with a knife but still glossy, not dry, gently fold the whites into the batter, leaving small amounts of white showing (see the next "How to").

9. **Pour the completed batter into the chilled baking dish** (or dishes). Fill the dish to within 3/4 to 1 inch from its top.

10. **Optional:**

    a. For an attractive topping, sprinkle finely grated cheese, bread crumbs, or other compatible topping lightly on the top.

    b. For a "top hat" effect, use the smooth handle of a clean knife and cut a circle all around the top about 1 to 1 1/2 inches from the outer edge.

11. **Prepare a "Mary's bath":** Fill a large pan about half full with hot water and carefully place the soufflé dish in its center.

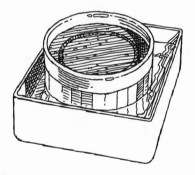

12. **Carefully place the soufflé and the Mary's bath in the oven,** on the center of the bottom shelf. Close the door gently and reduce the heat to 375 degrees F.

13. **Set a timer** according to the size of the dish: small dishes, 20 minutes; 6-cup dishes, 30 minutes; 8-cup dishes, 40 minutes. *Do not open the oven door until the cooking time is up!*

14. **When the cooking time is up and not before, gently**

open the door just enough to peek inside. If the soufflé has risen and wobbles only slightly when nudged, and if its top is a golden brown, it is ready and should be removed. If more cooking is needed, gently close the door and wait an additional 2 to 3 minutes before checking the soufflé again. *Note:* A soufflé can collapse from overcooking. If it is flat after the full cooking time has elapsed, it might be because it has overcooked, or failed to rise. Either way, if it wobbles only slightly and its top is golden brown, it is ready to be removed and served.

15. **When the soufflé is ready, carefully remove it from the oven and serve it immediately.** Handle it gently, or it might collapse. (Any soufflé will deflate a little bit, so don't worry about that.) A soufflé should be carried directly from the oven to the table and served from its cooking dish.

16. **To serve:** Use a large spoon and a fork placed back to back to slice down to the bottom of the soufflé, tearing and pulling it apart. Be careful not to press down too much, or you might just press the whole thing down. Use the spoon to gently lift out each portion for serving. Each portion should include a piece of the crust.

17. **Optional:** Accompany with white sauce.

■

How to Beat Egg Whites for Soufflés

1. Use grade AA or grade A eggs that are *several days old.* Separate them when they are cold. Any yolk present in the whites will diminish their volume when they are beaten. (See "How to Separate Eggs," p. 318.)

2. Bring the whites to room temperature before beating them.

3. Use a bowl made of copper or stainless steel that is just large enough to contain the whites after they are beaten. Egg whites should beat up to be about six times their original volume.

4. Start beating the whites as close to the time you will need them as you can. The longer they have to wait, the more they will deflate.

5. Beat the whites with a rotary beater or wire whisk

until they are a glossy mass of foam with small bubbles. Stop beating them before they peak.

6. To stabilize the beaten egg whites so they will hold air better, add 1/4 tsp. cream of tartar and/or a pinch of salt for every four whites.

7. Resume beating and continue until the whites have very small bubbles with a glossy smooth mass that forms firm peaks. The whites should be solid enough to be cut with a knife but still be glossy, not dry.

8. Pour about half the beaten whites onto the soufflé batter. Use a wire whisk to fold them in, making long, smooth strokes to cut them down through the center and pulling the mixture up the sides and over the top until most of the white is incorporated.

9. Use a rubber spatula to carefully fold in the remaining whites until a little white is seen throughout the batter. Don't blend too much, or some of the tiny balloons will deflate.

10. Treat the mixture with care. Every jolt and motion, even drafts of air, can deflate some of those tiny balloons.

Braises and Stews

You may never have heard of a dish called a "braise." In fact, you can pick up any number of cookbooks and never find the terms "braise" or "braising" used at all. What you will find, though, are thousands of recipes for "one dish meals" or for specialty dishes such as beef stew, Irish stew, hunter's stew, chicken fricassee, veal cacciatore, ragout of beef, Yankee pot roast, and so forth. All of these and hundreds of other dishes, including such common ones as chili and the meat sauce for spaghetti, are cooked by the same method: braising.

Braising combines the two basic methods of sautéing and stewing. The food is first sautéed in a little fat to brown its surface, soften its texture, and give it more flavor. Then liquid is added and the food is stewed until it is tender.

The Ingredients

No matter what you might call them, foods cooked by braising have a special flavor. Truly, the whole is more than the sum of its parts. The flavors of the ingredients all meld to produce a dish whose flavor and texture are quite different from those of the single ingredients. Depending on the foods used, the fat in which they are browned, the liquid in which they are stewed, and the seasonings, the combinations are virtually limitless, and the results are usually outstanding.

□ *Base*

Meats and poultry are used most often for the base, especially tougher, more flavorful cuts of meats and older, tougher birds such as stewing hens. Braising involves slow cooking and that makes these foods tender and brings out their rich flavors. Flour or other dry coating may be applied to the food before it is fried to add texture, color, and flavor, and to help thicken the liquid.

□ *Liquid*

Plain water lightly salted is the most fundamental and commonly used liquid. It becomes flavored by the foods as they cook to become a tasty broth to serve with the food. For a richer flavor, start with a ready-made broth instead of plain water. For variety, mix different broths with different foods: chicken broth with beef, beef broth with poultry. Wine can be added to any broth to give it more flavor. Fruit juices can be substituted for broth or mixed with it for even greater variety. Apple juice, for example, is excellent for braising pork. Orange juice goes well with poultry. Tomato juice goes well with anything. The number of possible combinations is vast, and part of the fun of braising is using various liquids in different amounts to "flavor to taste."

(See "Cooking in Liquids," p. 22.)

How much liquid? Foods coated with breading need only a small amount—enough to cool the fat and prevent the breading from burning after it has browned lightly. Chops, steaks, cutlets, pot roasts, and fricassees require only a quarter to a half inch of liquid; the top of the food cooks in steam instead of in the liquid itself. In a stew, the solid foods are covered completely by the liquid.

□ *Vegetables*

Onions, carrots, celery, sweet bell peppers, and potatoes are usually cooked and served along with the base food and its serving liquid. When braising delicate foods such as fish, small pieces of chicken, and any foods that will cook in thirty minutes or less, it's fine to cook the flavoring vegetables along with the food and serve them as they are. When cooking hens and meat roasts, however, cooking the flavoring vegetables for the time required to cook the meat will make them soft and neither as tasty nor as attractive as they should be. The solution is to cook some vegetables along with the base food for flavor, and then spruce up the dish with fresh vegetables near the end of the cooking time— just enough so that they will become tender. Use a *mirepoix* of chopped vegetables for flavoring (see the accompanying box for how to make it). Add the serving vegetables to the pot no more than thirty to forty-five minutes before the end of the cooking period. If you like, you can puree the mirepoix vegetables in the cooking liquid about an hour before the braise is done to create a thick, flavorful serving sauce.

☐ *Seasonings*

Most of the rich flavors of braises and stews come from the basic ingredients: base, liquid, and flavoring vegetables. A little salt in the cooking liquid may be all the seasoning needed. Careful, though: a little salt goes a long way, especially if you are using canned or powdered broth. If you add any other seasonings, use them sparingly. So that their flavors won't be cooked out, add them to the braise no more than thirty minutes before the cooking time is up.

☐ *Thickener*

The long, slow cooking will evaporate some liquid and break down some of the solid foods. Both of those will thicken the liquid to some degree. Any flour used to coat the base food before it is fried will also thicken the liquid. If the mirepoix vegetables are pureed in the liquid, that, too, will thicken the sauce. If after all of this the liquid still needs to be thickened, add a wash of cornstarch, a roux, or mannie butter. If the opposite occurs and the sauce seems too thick, add water, broth, or wine to thin it. Make final adjustments just before serving, remembering that the sauce will thicken as it cools.

(See "Thickeners," p. 130.)

What to Cook in

Brown the base food and vegetables in a pan suited to sautéing or pan-frying. If the pan is large enough, and if it has a lid, you can add the liquid after browning the base

Mirepoix: The Classic Flavoring

Use: 1 part celery, 1 part carrots, 2 parts onions. (*Optional:* Add up to 1 part each of garlic, mushrooms, and sweet bell peppers.)

Plan 1/4 cup mirepoix for each cup or two of liquid.

Chop vegetables very fine.

Sauté until the onions (and garlic, if used) are translucent but not brown.

Add the mirepoix to the cooking liquid.

Optional: To make a thicker, more flavorful serving sauce, an hour before the braise is done remove the base food and puree the mirepoix in its cooking liquid. Return all ingredients to the pot and complete the cooking.

and do all the cooking in one vessel. Otherwise, brown the foods in one pan and then put them in a larger pot that can be covered. The heavier the pot or the better it conducts heat, the more evenly it will cook the food.

□ How to Make It

The flavor of any braise or stew will be improved if the dish is cooked partially and then allowed to cool and rest for several hours or longer before serving (up to two days, if refrigerated). To make sure that it does not overcook when you reheat it, try the following method. Brown the base and flavoring vegetables in fat. Drain off the excess fat to reduce calories and cholesterol. Add liquid and stir any browned food particles into it. Stew the foods until the base food is not quite tender. Remove the pan from the heat and allow the food and liquid to cool. If you have cooked a mirepoix of chopped vegetables, puree them in the cooking liquid. Refrigerate the braise overnight or until you need it (up to forty-eight hours). One hour before serving, remove the braise from the refrigerator, skim any fat from the surface. Heat the braise slowly, stirring it frequently. Chop fresh serving vegetables and add them to the sauce.

Add seasonings and cook for thirty to forty-five minutes until the serving vegetables are tender. Adjust the thickness of the sauce and serve.

How to Make Braises and Stews

Model for four servings

Food base: 4 pieces of serving size, or 2 to 3 cups chopped pieces

Vegetables (optional): 2 to 4 cups

Liquid: Enough to cover 1/4 to all of the solid foods

Seasonings: Salt, pepper, and other seasonings that go well with the base food, "to taste"

Optional thickeners: Flour used to brown the food, pureed vegetables, cornstarch, roux, or mannie butter

Vessels: 1 sauté pan, 1 cooking pot with cover

0. **Before you begin:** Read all the steps below. Review the description of braises above as well as the principles of cooking with liquids (pp. 22–37) if necessary.

1. **Plan** 1 to 2 cups per serving. Allow 60 to 90 minutes for a base food that is tender, 2 to 4 hours for large pot roasts of tough meats and whole stewing hens. Most braised foods will taste better if they are cooked almost fully, allowed to cool for several hours or overnight, and then reheated for serving.

2. **Prepare the base food:**
   a. Allow 1 piece of serving size or 1/2 to 3/4 cup chopped pieces per serving.
   b. *Optional:* For added color and flavor, and to thicken the sauce, coat the food with seasoned flour.
   c. Sauté the food in cooking oil or fat until the surface is lightly browned.
   d. Drain off excess fat.

3. **Optional:** Prepare flavoring vegetables. The most popular mix is a classic mirepoix of 2 parts onions, 1 part celery, and 1 part carrots. Garlic, sweet bell peppers, mushrooms, and root vegetables such as turnips are popular also.
   a. Allow 1/2 to 1 cup of vegetables per serving. Cook about one fourth of the vegetables from the start for flavoring, reserving the remainder to cook in the last 30 to 45 minutes.
   b. Cut the vegetables to be used for flavoring into small

pieces, the remainder into a size suitable for serving.

    c. Sauté the flavoring vegetables in hot cooking oil or fat until they are soft but not browned.

    d. Drain off excess fat.

4. **Deglaze the vessel.** Add a small amount of liquid and stir any browned food particles into it.

5. **Put the foods in the cooking pot.**

6. **Add cooking liquid:** Use water, broth, wine, stewed tomatoes, tomato juice, fruit juices, or combinations of these. Stir in a very small amount of salt, sugar, or both. (Omit the salt if you are using powdered or canned broth.)

    · *For stew:* All of the food should be covered by liquid.

    · *For chops, cutlets, steaks, scallops, pot roasts, or fricassees:* Cover only from one-quarter to one-half of the food.

    · *Breaded foods:* Add only enough liquid to cool the fat and keep the food from burning. Add more if needed to replace liquid that evaporates.

7. **Stew the food:**

    a. On a range burner, slowly bring the liquid to a boil.

    b. When the liquid boils, lower the heat to a very slow simmer, or "stew."

    c. *Optional:* Remove the pot from the range burner to a preheated 250–300 degree F. oven.

    d. Stir and/or baste the food occasionally as it cooks.

    e. Remove any fat that appears on the surface.

    f. Cook until the base food is tender. Alternatively, cook partially and cool for several hours or overnight. Remove any fat that has accumulated on the surface. Reheat for serving.

8. **Optional:** Remove the base food to a warm serving dish and puree the flavoring vegetables to thicken and flavor the liquid. If a thicker sauce is desired, add roux, a wash, heavy cream, plain yogurt, or mannie butter.

(See "Thickeners," p. 130.)

9. **Add seasonings and serving vegetables** to cook during the last 30 to 45 minutes of cooking time.

10. **Adjust the thickness of the liquid.** To thin, add liquid; to thicken, add roux, a wash, or mannie butter.

11. **Adjust seasonings.**

12. **Serve** on a heated plate or in a hot serving bowl.

■

How to De-fat Liquids

Use a spoon, ladle, or bulb baster to lift most of the fat off the surface of the liquid. Then use one of the following methods to remove any fat that remains.

Method 1: To remove small amounts of fat on the surface of a liquid, fold several paper towels together and float them gently on the surface. When the towels are saturated with fat, lift them off and the fat will come with them. Repeat the procedure with fresh paper towels if needed. (Some stores now have a special "Magic Mop" that will remove fat in the same way as paper towels do.)

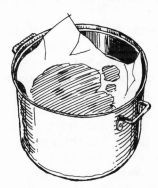

Method 2: There is now a special cup made for separating fats from liquids. The pouring spout is on the bottom. Since fats will always float to the top of a liquid, the pouring spout allows the liquid to be poured through the bottom, leaving the fat behind.

Method 3: If time permits, refrigerate the liquid until the fat firms up on the surface of the liquid. Use a slotted spoon or tea strainer to lift the fat off.

■

Marinades

Marinating is the process of soaking a food in a flavored liquid. Both the liquid and the final product are called "marinades." Barbecued meats or poultry, three-bean salad, and chicken or steak teriyaki are some popular marinated dishes.

Marinating liquids flavor foods. If the liquid contains acid, alcohol, salt, or sugar, it also protects the food from bacteria so that it holds up without spoiling for a longer period than it would otherwise. For example, poultry may be kept refrigerated in a marinade for up to five days, meats for seven days. Many vegetables may be held even longer, provided that the liquid does not contain so much acid or carbonation that it destroys their texture.

Any foods may be marinated, but the process is especially popular with tougher cuts of meats because it makes them more tender. The liquid causes the food to cook in its steam, thereby tenderizing it. If the liquid is acidic (vinegar and citrus juices) or if it is carbonated (cola drinks or beer), that too will tenderize the food.

Any marinating liquid may be used, then refrigerated or frozen and reused again as many as three or four times. If you have used it to marinate chicken, meats, or any fatty foods, keep the marinade refrigerated and boil it every two to three days and then once again just before use to destroy any harmful bacteria that might have grown in it.

The Ingredients

There is a seemingly endless number of commercial products as well as recipes for marinades that contain large amounts of catsup, sugar, honey, salt, soy sauce, MSG, and other ingredients that are not good for you. If you value your figure or your health, you will be wise to use such products or recipes infrequently. Instead of using commercial products or common recipes, you will be better off making your own marinades. Use the following description of ingredients as a guide.

□ Liquid

The most important consideration for selecting the liquid should be its taste and its compatibility with the food. Orange juice, for example, goes well with chicken but not with fish. Soy sauce and vinegar both have very strong flavors and must usually be diluted with broth, citrus juice, beer, wine, or some other liquid. Commercial or homemade sauces such as barbecue sauce or teriyaki sauce are popular for marinating meats, poultry, and fish. Vinaigrette dressings, mayonnaise, sour cream, yogurt, or combinations of these are good for marinating vegetables. Fruit juices, cream or melted ice cream, white wine, and liqueurs are wonderful for marinating fruits.

□ Oil

Although oil is sometimes omitted, most marinades do include at least some. If the food is cooked, the oil helps to keep it moist. Flavorless vegetable oils such as corn or safflower oil are most common, but more flavorful oils such as peanut oil, olive oil, or tahini oil may be used if a more assertive flavor is desired. In fact, you can use oil alone, flavored with herbs and spices, to marinate meats, fish, or poultry.

□ Seasonings

Since the liquid itself is the most important flavoring, how the sauce tastes is about how the food will taste. Add herbs and spices, sugar, root vegetables, and other ingredients for additional flavor. If you use garlic, onion, or other aromatic vegetables, sauté them briefly to mellow their flavors before adding them to the marinade.

How to Make It

Delicate foods such as fish and smaller pieces of any food may be thoroughly impregnated with the flavors of a marinade sauce in as little as fifteen to thirty minutes. Large pieces and tougher meats will require longer, perhaps as long as several days. The more acid or carbonation in the liquid, the faster it will flavor and tenderize the food. A heated liquid will flavor foods faster, but it will also cook them to some degree.

For some meats or poultry you may want to brown the surface in fat before marinating. This gives the finished product a firmer texture and usually a more attractive appearance. If the food is browned, however, it will require a longer period to soak for the marinade to penetrate the hardened surface. Asparagus, beans, and other vegetables that are to be marinated and served without cooking should be blanched in boiling water for a few seconds to set their color and make them tender.

Select the liquid and then flavor it the way you like. If you sauté root vegetables or brown the main food, allow them to cool before putting them in the marinade so that the liquid does not become hot enough to cook the food.

Soak the food in the marinade for thirty minutes or longer to infuse it with the flavors of the marinade. The food should be covered completely in the liquid if possible. If the food cannot be covered, turn it frequently so that it marinates evenly.

One of the most convenient and least messy ways to marinate any food is to put it in a sealable plastic bag. Less liquid will be required to cover the greatest amount of food, and all parts can be marinated evenly simply by turning the bag from time to time. For safety in case of leaks, keep the bag in a large bowl, pot, or pan.

Poultry and pork products should be kept refrigerated while soaking. Other meats, vegetables, and fruits can be marinated at room temperature, or they can be refrigerated.

Marinated fruits are usually not cooked. Vegetables can be served uncooked, or they can be simmered in the marinade until they are tender. Meats, poultry, and fish are usually baked, broiled, or roasted so that the outer surface dries while the inside remains moist. The most popular method for cooking these foods is to roast them on an open grill or barbecue.

To cook a food using dry heat so that it cooks throughout but without burning its outer surface, first simmer it in its marinade in a covered vessel for about one-fourth the time required for cooking it in a liquid. Complete the cooking using dry heat.

How to Make Marinades

Model for four servings
Sauce: 1 to 2 cups
Food base: Pieces of serving size to make 4 servings
Vessels: 1 covered bowl, pot, or pan large enough to hold the food and the sauce; a grill or roasting pan for cooking

0. **Before you begin:** Read all the steps below. Review the description of marinades above as well as the principles of dry heat cooking (pp. 38–45) if necessary.

1. **Plan** 1/4 to 1/2 cup sauce per serving. Allow enough "soaking" time for the food to become thoroughly impregnated with the flavors of the sauce. Usually, this can be done overnight in the refrigerator.

2. **Prepare the sauce:** Virtually any flavored liquid may be used. Vinaigrette dressings and commercially made sauces are the most popular for marinating meats and poultry. Vinaigrette and mayonnaise dressings are good with vegetables. Fruits can be marinated in fruit juices, white wine, cream, liqueurs, ice cream, sugar and water, or combinations of these.

3. **Prepare the food:** Cut it into pieces suited for serving. Meats or poultry may be browned in fat if desired. Vegetables may be parboiled for a few seconds to set their color and tenderize them.

4. **Soak the food in the marinade:** Put the food in a sealable plastic bag or in a bowl or pan large enough to hold it. Add enough sauce to cover from one-fourth to all of the food. Turn the pieces occasionally so that they marinate evenly in the sauce.

5. **Refrigerate the food**—meats and poultry, especially—if it is to marinate for longer than two hours.

6. **Optional:** Precook larger or tougher pieces of meat or poultry by simmering them in the marinade in a covered vessel for a short time.

7. **Cook meats, fish, and poultry using dry heat.** Roast, bake, or broil until the surface is browned but not burned. **Vegetables and fruits** may be served without cooking.

8. **Optional:** Serve extra marinade along with the food. If the food is hot, the serving sauce should be hot also.

9. **Danger!** Foods that contain fats—poultry, especially—can quickly grow dangerous bacteria. Keep the foods, the sauce, and any tools such as a basting brush at room temperature for no longer than one hour. If the sauce is to be saved for later use, boil it thoroughly before refrigeration and again before use. Wash hands and cooking utensils thoroughly after handling foods to prevent contamination.

(See "Bacterial Foodborne Illness," p. 242.)

■

Soups

Many people today enjoy soups from cans or made from powdered concentrates instead of homemade from scratch. Those ready-made soups can be very good, and they certainly are convenient, but they probably don't taste as good as homemade. You can have soups that taste better, cost less, and provide more nourishment by making your own.

The Ingredients

One of the biggest problems with canned soups or dried soup mixes is the amount of salt, monosodium glutamate (MSG), and other sodium products, sugar, and chemical preservatives they contain. Such ingredients are bad for your health (see Chapter Six, *Eating Smart*). If you make your own using your own ingredients, you won't have to worry about such things.

☐ Broth

As I noted earlier, the liquid in which a food has been cooked is called different things by different cooks and books. *Broth, stock,* and *bouillon* are the most common terms. For simplicity, the term *broth* is used throughout this book. Vegetable broth, meat broth, and poultry broth are all good for making any soup. Fish broth, though, has such a distinct flavor that it is usually reserved for fish soups alone.

It is very common and also desirable to mix broths to

(See "Broth, Stock, or Bouillon," p. 24.)

take advantage of their best qualities. Meat broth is thicker than poultry or vegetable broth and is often mixed with them to make them thicker. Conversely, the milder flavors of poultry or vegetable broth are often used to mellow the stronger flavor of meat broth.

(See "How to Make Broth," p. 111.)

Different Broths from Different Foods

Vegetable broth: Any vegetables may be used for making broth. The classic mixture, though, is simply a mirepoix of 1 part carrots, 1 part celery, and 2 parts onion, all cooked together in lightly salted water. Garlic is optional.

Meat broth: Traditionally, meat broth has been made from the meat and bones of beef, pork, or veal. (The flavor of lamb is too strong.) The bones are cut or broken into small pieces to expose more surface area and to extract more flavor from the marrow. The larger the pieces, the longer they will take to cook to extract their flavor. A mirepoix of carrots, celery, onion, and (optional) garlic is usually cooked along with the bones to give the broth more flavor.

Meats from different animals yield broths with different densities as well as different flavors. Veal is prized for making broths that are thick and gelatinous. Pigs' feet added to any broth will do the same. A typical recipe for meat broth will call for combinations of beef and veal or pigs' feet.

Meat broth can be made either "white" or "brown." White broth is usually made using veal alone, but beef can be used as well. Brown broth is made from bones that have been cooked in an oven at 450 degrees F. and turned occasionally until they are browned evenly all over.

Poultry broth: For economy, use pieces such as backs, necks, and wing tips that are less popular for serving. Cook the pieces for thirty to sixty minutes in just enough lightly salted water to cover them. A mirepoix of onions, carrots, celery, and (optional) garlic may be cooked along with the poultry to give the broth more flavor. (Tip: Pick the cooked meat from the bones and save it for making soups, salads, sandwiches, casseroles, and croquettes.)

Fish broth, "court bouillon," or "fumet": Use the trimmings (heads, fins, bones, and skins) as well as the meat of lean fish. (Broth made from oily fish such as herring or mackerel does not taste good.) The greater the variety of fish, and the fresher it is, the better the broth. Stew the meat and trimmings for about an hour and then discard them. A mirepoix of carrots, celery, onions, and (optional) garlic may be cooked along with the fish to give the broth added flavor.

What about using canned or powdered broth products? Canned broth tastes better than broth made from a powder, but it is much more expensive. Powdered products are strongly flavored and contain a good deal of salt, frequently augmented by MSG and other seasonings that will be beyond your control. One powdered beef bouillon product, for example, has twelve ingredients starting with salt, sugar, and MSG, with "beef extract" last and least of all.

To save money and to control flavors, I recommend that you make your own broth. For convenience, make it in large amounts and freeze it in plastic containers to use as needed. Frozen broth will remain flavorful for up to three months. (Tip: Freeze some in ice cube trays to use when only a little is needed.)

For very special flavor, substitute white wine for up to one fourth the amount of water used to make broth. Lemon juice also adds to the flavor, but use it sparingly—one to two teaspoons per quart of water.

□ *Solid Foods*
Any food or combination of foods may be used for making soup so long as the foods go well with the broth (and with each other, if more than one is used). The proportion of solid food to broth is usually very low. In other words, soups are usually quite thin. Unless the solid food is to be pureed, cook it only long enough to make it tender to retain its texture.

□ *Seasonings*
Seasonings in the basic broth should be limited to just a pinch or two of salt. After adding the solid foods to make the soup, put in herbs and spices that go along with them to suit your taste. Herbs and spices are best if they are cooked no longer than thirty minutes.

□ *Optional Thickener*
(See "Thickeners," p. 130.) For a thicker, richer soup, add cornstarch, pureed vegetables, cream, a liaison, or roux.

□ *Optional Garnish*
You can dress up the surface of a finished soup by adding a garnish. Chopped fresh vegetables, grated cheese, sau-

téed bread crumbs or croutons, a dollop of sour cream or yogurt, small pieces of toast, and other toppings add body and flavor to a soup as well as make it more attractive.

What to Cook in

Any pot will do for cooking broth or soup. The greater the amount of liquid, the better heat conductor the pot's material should be for even cooking with the least amount of energy. Lined copper is the best material. Treated or clad aluminum is also excellent, and either stainless steel or enameled iron is quite acceptable. Plain aluminum or plain iron might interact chemically with some foods.

(See "Range-top Vessels," p. 250.)

How to Make It

Other than just making broth and then adding things to it, about all there is to know about making soups is the different ways in which things can be combined and served. Here is a list of the main ones.

Clear soups or consommé consist of basic broth that has been clarified and flavored. For a really clear broth, use the optional step 8 in the procedure described below.

Compound soups are clear soups to which one or more solid foods are added, usually cut into bite-sized pieces. The amount of solid food will depend on how thick you want the soup to be. Don't use too much, or your soup might come to be more like a stew.

Thickened soups are clear or compound soups thickened by a small amount of roux, cornstarch, or pureed vegetables.

Puree soups are compound soups that have been run through a food mill, blender, or food processor to liquify the solid matter.

Cream soups are any soups into which cream, sour cream, half-and-half, or unflavored yogurt is blended to enrich the flavor and texture.

Bisques are shellfish broths that are thickened and then finished with cream.

Chowders are compound soups that usually contain fish or shellfish along with potatoes, milk, and perhaps cream or other thickener.

> ### *Old-fashioned Stock Pot Soup*
> Back in the "good old days" when people cooked on wood-burning stoves, a big stock pot was always kept just barely simmering on the back burner. Instead of throwing out cuttings and scraps that might be perfectly good to eat, people threw them into the stock pot, where they cooked along with water and other foods to make "stock." The stock was used as the base for an endless variety of soups. Since the stock pot had new things added to it daily, it changed constantly, and no two soups were ever the same.
>
> We lost the stock pot along with the wood-burning stove. (About all that is left is the expression "keep it on the back burner.") Now, though, we have the food freezer, which can serve the same purpose. Instead of putting scraps in the garbage or pouring liquids used for cooking down the drain, put them in a plastic container and store them in the freezer. Keep them all together, or separately in labeled containers. When you have enough, cook them with broth, add seasonings, and puree them. Like real stock pot soups, no two of your creations will ever be the same. And all of them will be nutritious, probably delicious, and free.

How to Make Soups

Model for four servings
  Broth: 4 to 8 cups
  Solid food(s): 1 to 2 cups
  Optional: Cream or milk to thicken and flavor
  Optional: Topping or garnish
  Vessels: 1 large pot with lid
  Seasonings: Salt, pepper, herbs, and spices "to taste"

0. **Before you begin:** Read all the steps below. Review the description of soups above as well as the principles of cooking in liquids (pp. 22–37) if necessary.
1. **Plan** 1 to 2 cups per serving. Allow 1 hour or longer to prepare and cook. Soups are usually best if they are made in advance and allowed to set for a day in the refrigerator before serving.
2. **Prepare the broth.** For making broth, see the next "How to." If you use a prepared broth, heat it and proceed to step 3.
3. **Add solid foods.** Cut the foods into bite-sized pieces. For best flavor, sauté vegetables lightly before adding

them to the broth. Add long-cooking foods first, short-cooking foods near the end.

4. **Simmer over low heat** until the solid food is tender.
5. **Add seasonings to taste.**
6. **Optional:** To thicken the soup, use pureed vegetables, (See "Thickeners" p. 130.) roux, or cornstarch. *For a pureed soup,* run it through a food mill or food blender. *For a cream soup,* add milk, half-and-half, or cream.
7. **Serve hot or cold.**
8. **Optional:** Garnish with fresh herbs, thinly sliced fresh vegetables, grated cheese, croutons, or bread crumbs.

■

How to Make Broth

Tip: Make broth in large amounts and freeze it for later use.

1. **Place bones, meat, and/or vegetables in a cooking pot.** Use a pot that is large enough to hold the food and the liquid with one inch of space at the top to allow for foam.
2. **Cover the food with cold water,** leaving at least an inch to spare. Add a pinch or two of salt or 1 teaspoon lemon juice for each quart of water. For special flavor, substitute white wine for up to one fourth the water.
3. **Optional:** For added flavor, add a mirepoix of chopped vegetables, 1/2 cup per quart of liquid. The classic mix is two parts onions, one part carrots, and one part celery plus (optional) crushed garlic. Mushrooms are also a popular ingredient. Chop all the vegetables very fine. If you want the flavor but not the vegetables in your soup, tie them in cheesecloth so they can be retrieved.
4. **Slowly bring the liquid to a boil.** The slower the better for producing a clear broth.
5. **Stir the foods occasionally** as the liquid heats so that they don't stick on the bottom and burn. Skim off any scum that accumulates on the surface. (Scum is coagulated protein that will cloud the broth if it is broken up and mixed into the liquid.)
6. **When the liquid barely boils, reduce the heat** so that the surface trembles just slightly. Cover the pot only

partially to keep the temperature below the boiling point. Boiling or stirring from this point on will cloud the broth.

7. **Cook for 30 to 60 minutes.** That will be long enough to extract the flavors from the food.

8. **Optional:** For a really clear broth, do the following.

    a. Rest the bottom of the cooking pot half on and half off a range burner and simmer the liquid gently, uncovered. The impurities will rise to the surface and be trapped by a skin that will develop gradually around them. When the skin has formed, use a spoon or tea strainer to remove it along with the trapped impurities. Repeat this as many times as needed to clarify the liquid to your liking.

    b. In addition, you might drop a well-beaten egg white or two into the broth as it simmers. When the white hardens, it will entrap small food particles. Strain out the egg. (Some recipes recommend including the egg shell. Egg shells, though, are unsanitary and should not be used.)

9. **Optional:** Clarify the broth. Line a colander with wet cheesecloth and pour the broth through it into a pot.

Save food pieces to add to the soup later or to use in some other dish. If you like, puree the cooked vegetables to thicken the soup.

10. **De-fat the liquid.** (See "How to De-fat Liquids," p. 101.)

■

Salads

Salads make healthful and tasty dishes that supply many nutrients most of us need, but without too many calories. Fresh green salads are a welcome accompaniment to most main meals. "Feature" salads in which some basic food is the primary ingredient—tuna, chicken, or shrimp, for example—make fine light meals in themselves, or they can be used for making sandwiches.

The Ingredients

Salads range from something as simple as a few pieces of lettuce coated with a little seasoned oil and vinegar to elaborate feature salads dressed with homemade mayonnaise. No matter how simple or elaborate they might be, most salads will include the following ingredients.

□ Base
Leaves from lettuce and other greens provide the base for most salads. Use one type of leaf alone, or mix several together for variety of taste, color, and texture. Lettuce is by far the most popular salad base, but the leaves of spinach and other greens can be used also. (See the sections on lettuce and greens in Chapter Eighteen.)

□ Feature Food
Optionally, chicken, tuna, shrimp, potatoes, macaroni, and other foods can be featured as the main ingredient (an excellent way to use leftovers). Whatever food you use, it should be cooked fully and thoroughly cooled before being mixed with the other ingredients.

□ Vegetables
Onions, celery, tomatoes, and sweet bell peppers are the most popular vegetables that are combined with greens to give added colors, flavors, and textures to salads. Cucum-

bers, avocados, mushrooms, and radishes are popular also. Nuts (especially light-flavored nuts such as pine nuts and almonds) and fruits such as apples and raisins are delicious additions to many salads, especially those served with mayonnaise.

□ *Dressing*
Vinaigrette and mayonnaise dressings are mixed with the other ingredients to "dress" them with flavor. Both of these dressings are described in detail in Chapter Five. The more you know about them, the better salads you can make.

□ *Seasonings*
Most seasonings are usually mixed into the dressing so that their flavors are distributed evenly throughout the salad. Some, such as pepper, paprika, or seeds, also make an attractive garnish. When you use a seasoning as a garnish, be sure to account for its flavors by using little or none of it in the dressing, or you might get too much.

□ *Garnish (Optional)*
Once you have put your salad together, you might want to top it off with a garnish. Green salads can be garnished with attractively cut pieces of fresh vegetables, fruits, sprouts, bread crumbs, croutons, grated hard cheeses, crumbled medium-hard cheeses, or combinations of these. Salads featuring a base food such as chicken can be garnished with herbs and spices, attractively sliced fresh vegetables or fruits, nuts, or combinations of these. Arrange the garnish attractively over the top of the salad.

How to Make It

The simplest way to make a salad is just to put all the ingredients in a large serving bowl and toss them together. To make your salads more elaborate, assemble or build them using the method described in the following "How to."

How to Make Salads

0. **Before you begin:** Read all the steps below. Review the description of salads above as well as the descriptions

of mayonnaise (pp. 164–172) and vinaigrette dressings (pp. 172–175) if necessary.

1. **Tear or cut base greens** and arrange them attractively on individual serving plates. This forms a bed for the other ingredients. To keep salad cool and fresh longer, use plates that have been chilled in the refrigerator or freezer.
2. **Cut fresh vegetables** such as celery, tomatoes, and onions into small, attractive pieces.
3. **Build the salad:**

   · *Fresh vegetable salads:* Arrange the cut vegetables attractively over the green base. Add garnish if you like and serve the salad without dressing. Accompany with separate containers of one or more vinaigrette or mayonnaise dressings for each diner to choose and add as he or she likes.
   · *Feature salads:* Cook the feature food (such as chicken, potatoes, or shellfish) and cool it thoroughly. Cut the food and fresh vegetables into bite-sized pieces. Mix all ingredients together with just enough mayonnaise to hold them together. Chill the mixture in the refrigerator for at least 1 hour before serving. Use a large spoon or ice cream scoop to place servings attractively onto the green base on the serving plates. Add garnish if desired.

■

Hash

Hash is a wonderful way to use leftovers, particularly chicken, turkey, and ham. That is probably why there are so many different versions of it. In fact, there are so many ways of making hash that it is difficult to define it, let alone come up with basic instructions for how to make it.

The Ingredients

Hash is made from any food that has been fully cooked and then cut or chopped into smaller pieces. Usually the food pieces are mixed with chopped potatoes and perhaps some other filler and fried or baked until brown. That isn't much of a definition, but it will have to do. Perhaps after making a more detailed study of this culinary mystery, you will be able to "hash out" a few good dishes for yourself, even if you aren't able to define them very well.

☐ *Base*

As with casseroles, many different foods can be used for making hash. Beef, turkey, and ham are three of the most popular. Whatever the food, at least half of the total amount of the hash should be the base.

☐ *Potatoes*

It is difficult to find a recipe for hash that does not include potatoes. In fact, potatoes may be served alone "hash browned." When another food is used as the base, as much as an equal amount of potatoes may be mixed with it to make hash.

☐ *Filler*

Again as with casseroles, other foods can be combined with the base food and potatoes to add flavor and texture as well as to make them go farther. Don't add too much, though, if you want the hash to maintain some integrity. As a guide, you might use as much filler as potato. Onions are by far the most popular filler; sweet bell peppers run a not too close second. Peas and chopped celery are also popular, and other vegetables that go well with the base food can be used as well. Mix different vegetables together for more interesting flavors and textures.

☐ *Seasonings*

In most cases, hash is made of foods that have already been cooked. Consequently, the foods may already be seasoned, and additional seasoning may not be needed. You might want to add just a little salt and pepper, but add them after the hash has cooked.

What to Cook In

Hash can be formed into individual patties and pan-fried. For a larger, more solid hash, coat a heavy metal pan with a thin layer of fat and fill it with the hash to a depth of one-half to three-fourths of an inch. You can then bake or fry the hash, afterward cutting it into individual portions for serving.

How to Make It

Hash patties can be browned in a little fat in a pan on top of a range burner or baked in an oven. Baking can be done without turning the hash; frying requires that it be turned. If the hash covers the entire bottom of the frying pan, turn it by first pressing the hash down firmly with a pancake turner. Then place a large plate over the top of the pan. Hold the plate down with one hand, and grasp the handle of the pan with the other. Quickly flip the hash over and onto the plate. Return the pan to the heat and slide the hash back into it.

How to Make Hash

Model for four servings
    Food base: 1 to 2 cups
    Potatoes: If no filler is used, potatoes can be added, up to an amount equal to that of the base food. If a filler is used, then the filler and potatoes should total no more than an amount equal to that of the base food.
    Optional filler: 1/4 the amount of the base food
    Vessels: 1 mixing bowl, 1 frying or baking pan

0. **Before you begin:** Read all the steps below. Review the description of hash above as well as the principles of frying (pp. 45–61) if necessary.
1. **Plan** 1/4 to 1/2 cup hash mix per serving. Allow about 15 minutes to prepare the mix and 15 to 20 minutes to cook it.
2. **Prepare the mix:** As a guide, use two parts of solid base food such as meat or poultry to one or two parts of potatoes. Or, for each two parts of base food, use one part potatoes and one part onions or other vegetable filler.

    a. Cut the foods into small pieces about the same size.

    b. Sauté or parboil any food pieces that are firm until they are tender. Leftovers that have been cooked need no further cooking.

    c. Mix the foods together.

    d. Season to taste, accounting for any seasonings that may already be in the foods.

    e. Form into individual patties about 1/2 to 3/4 inch thick.

3. **Prepare the vessel:**

    · *To sauté:* Add 1/16 to 1/8 inch cooking oil to a heavy pan. Heat the oil on a range burner until bubbles begin to come up around the sides.

    · *To bake:* Use a shallow pan and coat it lightly with shortening. Preheat the oven to 350–375 degrees F.

4. **Cook:**

    · *To fry:* Place individual patties separately into the hot oil, or spread the mix over the entire bottom of the cooking vessel to a depth of about 1/2 to 3/4 inch. As the hash cooks, gently press it down with the bottom of a wide spatula or pancake turner. When the bottom has browned, flip the hash over and brown the other side.

    · *To bake:* Add the hash to the prepared cooking vessel. Bake it for 15 to 20 minutes at 350 to 375 degrees F. There's no need to turn the hash.

5. **Remove the hash to a warm plate.** Serve it right away or hold it in a warm oven (150 degrees F.).

6. **Optional:** Many people enjoy hash topped with poached or soft-boiled eggs, or "country style" with a fried egg or two on top. Gravy and white sauce are also popular toppings.

(See "Country Style Eggs," p. 329.)

■

Croquettes

Croquettes are small pieces of one or more foods that are mixed with a thick white sauce, chilled until they are firm enough to hold some shape, coated with breading, and fried in deep fat. Croquettes are usually made with pieces of cooked meat, poultry, or fish, although vegetable or fruit croquettes are good also.

The Ingredients

The basic ingredients in croquettes are very much like those in a casserole: base, filler, sauce, and seasonings. The only ingredient beyond those is breading. Indeed, thick leftovers of casseroles can be shaped, breaded, and fried to make croquettes.

□ *Base*

Like the base food in a casserole, the base of croquettes should be present enough both in size and abundance that there can be no doubt it is the main ingredient. That means the base should account for at least half of all the ingredients. It should also be tender, which means it may require precooking at least partially before being combined with the other ingredients.

□ *Filler*

Onions, chopped celery, peas, rice, and mushrooms are popular ingredients that can be combined with the base food for added flavor and texture, and to make it go farther. The filler should not be so strongly flavored or so abundant that it overpowers the taste and texture of the base.

□ *Sauce*

A sauce is used to unify and bind the solid ingredients as well as to contribute its own flavor to the croquettes. A thick prepared white sauce enriched with egg is the most common, but thick, undiluted cream soups or even mashed potatoes can be used as well.

□ *Eggs*

To make croquettes more firm, add one beaten egg or two egg whites to each cup of sauce.

□ *Seasonings*

Since the base, filler, and sauce are usually prepared separately, any and all seasonings used for preparing them initially must be accounted for before adding more. Mix any additional seasonings into the sauce so that they become evenly distributed.

□ *Breading*

To give croquettes a crisp, brown surface texture, roll them in breading or breading mixed with flour (see p. 54).

How to Make It

The base food and filler should be chopped into small pieces of about equal size. Meats, poultry, and tougher vegetables should be precooked a bit so that they will cook fully in the time required for frying the croquettes.

Use enough sauce to bind the base and filler to make a thick batter. The batter must be chilled in the refrigerator or freezer until it is firm enough to hold a shape, usually from thirty to sixty minutes. Spoon out a portion of the batter and roll it into a ball or cylinder, or shape it into a small patty. Coat the croquette with breading and fry it until it is browned evenly all over.

How to Make Croquettes

Model for four servings

Thick white sauce: 1 cup liquid, 4 Tbsp. butter or margarine, 4 Tbsp. flour

Egg: 1 whole egg or 2 whites

Solid food: 2 cups food pieces

Breading: 1 cup

Vessels: 1 mixing bowl, 1 deep pot or pan or deep-fat fryer

0. **Before you begin:** Read all the steps below. Review the description of croquettes above as well as the principles of frying (pp. 45–61) if necessary.

1. **Plan** 1/2 cup food pieces and 1/2 cup white sauce per serving. Allow 15 to 30 minutes to prepare the batter and 1 to 2 hours to chill it. Total cooking time will be 4 to 10 minutes per batch.

2. **Prepare the base food and (optional) filler:**

   a. Meats, poultry, or rice should be fully cooked. Tougher vegetables should be sautéed or parboiled until tender. Tender vegetables, fish, or fruits need not be precooked.

   b. Chop the food into small pieces of about equal size.

3. **Prepare a thick white sauce** (see pp. 144–145): For each serving, allow 1/2 cup. Alternatively you can use thick mashed potatoes.

   a. Season the sauce, accounting for any salt or other seasonings used to prepare the other ingredients.

gloop   glop

Ball   Cylinder   Patty   1 1/2" Thick

Cookie Cutter or Knife

  b. Beat the egg and mix it thoroughly into the sauce.

  c. Heat the sauce over medium-high heat, stirring it constantly until it thickens enough to fall in "gloops" and "glops" from a spoon.

4. **Mix the dry ingredients with the sauce to make a thick batter.**

5. **Chill the batter:** Prepare the bottom and sides of a pan with a thin coating of shortening. Pour the batter into the pan. Coat the top of the batter with plastic wrap or buttered waxed paper to prevent a film from forming. Chill the batter for 1 hour in the freezer or for 2 hours or longer (up to 2 days) in the refrigerator.

6. **Shape the croquettes:** Scoop the chilled batter out of the pan with a large spoon and shape it into balls, cylinders, or patties, not more than 1 1/2 inch thick. Alternatively, dump the contents of the pan onto a piece of waxed paper and use a cookie cutter or knife to cut out individual shapes.

7. **Optional:** Stuff the croquettes with small pieces of mushroom, olive, nuts, pimiento, fruit, hominy, or whatever might go well with the food and give the croquettes added flavor and texture.

(See "Breading," p. 54.)

8. **Bread the croquettes:** Roll the croquettes in breading or in breading mixed with up to an equal part of flour, pressing the breading into the batter. For best texture, chill the croquettes for another half-hour before frying.

9. **Prepare the vessel:** Use a heavy pot or pan deep enough to hold enough cooking oil to float the croquettes. Add the cooking oil and heat it slowly until a bit of batter will sizzle when it hits the oil.

10. **Cook:**

    a. Use a spoon to carefully lower the croquettes into the hot oil one at a time. Leave space between them so that they can cook evenly.

    b. When the edges brown, turn the croquettes over so that they brown evenly all over.

    c. Remove the cooked croquettes to paper towels to drain. Clean scraps and crumbs out of the oil so that they do not burn.

    d. Repeat the cooking procedure until all croquettes are cooked.

11. **Serve hot** right away or hold for serving in a warm oven (150 degrees F.).

12. **Optional:** Top the croquettes with a hot white sauce or garnish. Parsley, paprika, grated cheese, pimiento, or other garnishes go well with croquettes made of meats, fish, or vegetables. Fruit croquettes can be dressed up with a sprinkle of confectioner's sugar.

■

Fritters

Fritters are fried pancake-like creations made by combining pieces of a firm food with a thick wet batter enriched with egg. Sometimes served as a side dish, fritters may also be used as a substitute for bread during a main meal, for toast at breakfast, or as a tasty snack.

The Ingredients

☐ *Base*

Pieces of firm fruits such as apples, peaches, or apricots make wonderful fritters for breakfast or snacks. Corn kernels, pieces of fish or shellfish, or chopped potatoes make fritters suited for serving at main meals or breakfast.

□ *Fritter batter*

Fritter batter is really just a basic wet batter that is very thick (see pp. 52–54). Use equal parts of flour and liquid (milk, broth, or beer). For really thick batter, mix it and let it sit in the refrigerator for an hour or longer. Pour off the excess liquid before mixing in the base food.

□ *Egg*

Use one whole egg or two whites for each cup of batter. To make the fritters lighter in texture, beat the egg well and fold it into the batter just before the fritters are fried. For really light fritters, beat the egg white until it peaks before incorporating it.

□ *Seasonings*

Herbs and spices that are compatible with the base food can be mixed into the sauce. Use salt and pepper only after frying the fritters.

How to Make It

About all there is to making fritters is mixing the batter, chopping the food, mixing the food into the batter, and frying the fritters.

How to Make Fritters

Model for four servings
  Batter: 1/2 cup flour, 1/2 cup liquid
  Egg: 1 whole egg or 2 egg whites
  Food base: 1 cup chopped food pieces
  Vessels: 1 mixing bowl, 1 frying pan

 0. **Before you begin:** Read all the steps below. Review the description of fritters above as well as the principles of frying (pp. 45–61) if necessary.
 1. **Plan** 1/4 cup solid food and 1/4 cup wet batter per serving. Allow 15 to 30 minutes to prepare the foods and the batter, plus at least 1 hour for the batter to set. The batter can be held for up to 48 hours.
 2. **Prepare the batter:** For each serving, use 1/4 cup batter (equal parts flour and liquid mixed together).
 3. **Prepare the food:** For each serving, use 1/4 cup chopped solid food.

a. You can use delicate, watery vegetables or fruits raw, but try to account for their moisture by using less liquid in the batter. Parboil or sauté firm vegetables until they are tender. Tender vegetables, fish, and fruits need not be precooked.

b. Chop the food into small pieces.

c. Drain the food thoroughly before mixing it into the batter.

4. **Combine the ingredients:** Pour the batter onto the solid food, stirring constantly to coat the food particles evenly.

5. **Season** the batter, accounting for any salt or other seasonings that have been used for preparing any of the ingredients.

6. **Chill the batter** to make it thicker before frying. Let it sit refrigerated for at least 1 to 2 hours. It will be good for as long as 48 hours. For really thick fritters, pour off excess liquid after the batter has chilled.

7. **Prepare the vessel:** Use a heavy pot or pan and put in enough cooking oil to pan-fry or deep fry the fritters, about 1/8 inch deep. Heat the oil slowly until a bit of batter will sizzle when it hits the oil.

8. **Incorporate the egg into the batter.** Use 1 whole egg or 2 whites per cup batter. Beat whole eggs slightly, whites until they peak, before incorporating them into the batter.

9. **Cook:**

a. Use a large spoon or ladle to lift the batter and gently pour it into the hot oil. Leave space between individual fritters so they can all cook evenly.

b. When the edges brown, use a pancake turner to turn the fritters so that they brown evenly all over.

    c. Remove cooked fritters to paper towels to drain.

    d. Clean scraps and crumbs out of the oil so that they do not burn.

    e. Repeat the cooking procedure until all fritters are cooked.

10. **Serve hot** right away or hold for serving in a warm oven (150 degrees F.).

11. **Optional garnish:** Parsley, paprika, grated cheese, pimiento, and other garnishes go well with fritters made with meats, fish, or vegetables. Dessert or fruit fritters may be dressed up with a sprinkle of confectioner's sugar.

■

*H*ot Sauces

CHAPTER FOUR

*T*he world of foods is enriched—literally and figuratively—by hot sauces. Whether as a topping for a meat, vegetable, crepe, or other food, or as the liquid ingredient in a casserole, timbale, or soufflé, a good hot sauce is a delectable addition to the flavor, texture, and appearance of many foods. Of course, hot sauces also add calories and cholesterol to the diet, so for the sake of good health and a good figure, they should be enjoyed infrequently and in moderation.

The subject of hot sauces can seem confusing and troublesome to understand if only because there are so many of them—or so their many names might make you think. There are more than two hundred names for sauces used for French cookery alone! To add to the confusion, any one hot sauce may be known by several different names. It's no help that these names are quite often used erroneously. The names "cream sauce," "white sauce," and "béchamel," for example, are used by many cooks and books as though they all meant the same thing. They do not. The bewildering subject of hot sauces will become a good deal simpler for you if you understand the essential principles involved in making them.

Basic Considerations

There are two terms that can be used to classify hot sauces and eliminate much of the confusion surrounding them. Those terms are *mother sauce* and *small sauce.* As you might guess, small sauces (of which there are hundreds) are all derived from mother sauces (of which, thank goodness, there are only a few). The most important mother sauces are those described in this chapter.

By adding flavorings to a mother sauce, you can change it into a small sauce. In other words, all those elegant-sounding names really denote one of the mother sauces with some special flavoring. Once you appreciate this fact and work accordingly, you can use the "How to" instructions in this chapter to make any number of small sauces. You can duplicate any of the sauces with the fancy names, or you can create your own sauces and call them whatever you like.

The Ingredients

Most hot sauces are made of a liquid, seasonings, thickener, and fat. Sometimes an "enricher" is added, and sometimes a "finishing" or "buttering" is added to white sauces, brown sauces, and gravies. Later in this chapter, we'll look at some of the specific ingredients for the main kinds of sauces. First, though, let's consider the general characteristics of the basic ingredients most of them share.

☐ Liquids

More than any other ingredient, the liquid determines the flavor of a hot sauce. In the case of some liquids, the manner in which they are cooked will determine success or failure. Milk products, for example, can scorch easily unless they are stirred almost constantly and removed from the heat frequently. All that was said about cooking liquids in Chapter Two applies especially to their use in sauces, so you may want to review those topics as needed. (See pp. 22–37.)

☐ Seasonings

A hot sauce can be something as simple as a reduced liquid to which seasonings and other flavoring ingredients are added—for example, the "au jus" sauce that sometimes accompanies roast beef. A good sauce should be seasoned just enough to have a flavor that is noticeable but subtle. The strength of seasonings can be tricky because the sauce will be reduced as it cooks, and that will make its flavors stronger. In addition, the strength of the seasonings varies with their form (fresh or dried) and their age (see pp. 305–311). The variability of seasonings is one reason why the amounts specified in recipes often require adjustments "to taste." The expression "to taste" means, in effect, that each sauce is unique. Sauces are made by persons of different tastes, with ingredients of various qualities, to be served with foods of various flavors. In other words, there is no way to account for things too exactly, not even when using a recipe.

□ *Thickeners*

Almost by definition, any hot sauce is simply a seasoned liquid that is thickened. The liquid used for cooking stews or braises, for example, is made not only less runny but also more flavorful with the addition of cornstarch or a roux. The liquid used in casseroles requires the addition of eggs, cornstarch, roux, or some other thickener in order to bind the ingredients to make what most of us would identify as a casserole. And of course, any liquid that is used as a topping for foods should be thickened in some way so that it can cling to the surface of foods and not soak into them.

The thickness of any hot sauce will be determined by the characteristics of the thickener as well as the amount, so you should know as much as you can about each one. Also, when making a hot sauce it is better to make it thicker than desired and then thin it if necessary. It is easier and takes less time to thin a thick sauce than to thicken one that is too thin. Remember, though, that any hot sauce will thicken as it cools.

Thickening by reducing the liquid.   Reducing is certainly the easiest way to thicken any liquid. Lately, more and more people, especially diet-conscious folk, have been using this method because it thickens liquids without adding calories or fats. The more a liquid is reduced, the less additional thickener it will require.

To reduce a liquid, simply simmer it in an uncovered container to evaporate some of its water content. The greater the surface area of the liquid, the faster it will be reduced. A major consideration with this method is that the flavors of the liquid become more concentrated as it is reduced.

Cooked and pureed vegetables.   Cooked and pureed vegetables, especially onions and potatoes, can be used to thicken liquids and give them more flavor. Brown sauces and sauces for braises and stews, for example, are often thickened with a puree of their flavoring vegetables. Since the thickening ability varies with the vegetable, it is best to start by using one tablespoon per cup of liquid, adding more as needed.

Starch thickeners.   Dry thickeners from the starch family—flour, cornstarch, potato starch, and arrowroot—are the thickeners that are used most often to thicken casseroles, stews, white sauces, brown sauces, and gravies. Flour is the most commonly used by far, but cornstarch, arrowroot, and potato starch can all be substituted for it. In fact, cornstarch has come to be favored over flour by many cooks because it doesn't have the starchy taste of flour. Consequently, it doesn't require cooking in added fat, as flour does to eliminate its starchy taste.

Starches other than flour all have about twice the thickening power of flour. If you want to substitute cornstarch or one of the other starches for flour, simply use half as much. For each cup of liquid, use flour in the following amounts (or half these amounts for other starches): *thin sauce*, 1 to 1 1/2 Tbsp. flour; *medium-thick sauce*, 1 1/2 to 3 Tbsp. flour; *thick sauce*, 3 to 4 Tbsp. flour.

(See the reference chart inside the front cover.)

Cooking Considerations for Starches

1. To avoid lumps, never add a dry starch directly to hot fat or liquid. Instead, dissolve the thickener in cool liquid to make what is called a *wash* or in warm fat to make what is called a *roux*. Then add the wash or roux to the remaining liquid. (See the discussion that follows.)

2. For maximum thickening, heat liquids containing starches to a slow simmer, stirring them frequently.

3. All-purpose flour and bread flour are the two most frequently used dry thickeners. Unless flour is cooked a long time in liquid, or first cooked in fat to make a roux, it will produce sauces with a starchy taste.

4. Cornstarch and arrowroot produce sauces that are clear and glossy without any starchy taste. They are best suited for sweet sauces and glazes but are also good for making gravy and for thickening casseroles, braises, and stews.

5. To substitute another starch for flour, use half the amount of flour called for.

6. High temperatures or excessive stirring will cause sauces thickened with arrowroot or potato starch to thin.

Wash or roux. Any starch will cook into lumps when added to a hot liquid or fat. To avoid lumps, do as professional chefs do: make a *wash* or a *roux*. A wash is simply a cool liquid in which a starch is dissolved before it is added to thicken a hot liquid. Cornstarch, arrowroot, and potato starch work nicely in a wash, but a wash made with flour can produce a sauce with a starchy taste.

To thicken sauces with flour, use a *roux:* equal parts of fat and flour cooked for three to five minutes over low heat to eliminate the starchy taste. If you do much cooking using flour-thickened sauces, you will find it convenient to make roux in large amounts and refrigerate or freeze it in ice cube trays, one tablespoon per cube. It will keep well for several weeks refrigerated, or up to eight months frozen.

There are two forms of roux. *Light roux* (also called *white, blonde,* or *pale* roux) is used for making white sauces, light-colored gravies, or for thickening any liquid. *Dark roux* (also called *brown* roux) is used for making brown sauces and dark-colored gravies. Dark roux has a distinctive color and a nutlike flavor that is different from that of light roux. It also does not absorb liquids as readily as light roux, so more of it (as much as three times more) will be needed to equal the thickening power of the same amount of light roux. Here's how to make both types.

How to Make Roux

White roux
1. **Heat the fat** (butter or margarine) until it foams.
2. **Cool the fat** for a minute or two.
3. **Add an equal amount of flour,** stirring the mixture constantly until the flour dissolves.
4. **Cook over low heat** for 3 to 5 minutes, stirring frequently.

Brown roux

Use browned butter or margarine (p. 291), or cook light roux long enough for it to turn a golden brown. Here's another way to make it:

1. **Pour** a thin layer of flour into a shallow pan.
2. **Bake the flour** until it browns.
3. **Mix the browned flour with an equal amount of plain butter or margarine,** or with browned butter or margarine.
4. Cook the mixture over low heat for 3 to 5 minutes, stirring frequently.

Amounts of roux to use

For white roux, use the amounts shown below. Use two to three times more brown roux for equal thickening.

· **Thin sauce:** 2 to 3 Tbsp. per cup liquid.
· **Medium-thick sauce:** 3 to 6 Tbsp. per cup liquid.
· **Thick sauce:** 6 to 8 Tbsp. per cup liquid.

■

Mannie butter. When only a little extra starch thickener is needed—usually in an emergency to thicken a sauce just before serving—roll equal amounts of butter or margarine and flour or other starch together and knead them in a ball to make a smooth paste before adding it to the sauce. (See the illustration on the next page.) This "kneaded butter," as many cooks call it, will prevent the starch from cooking into lumps. The French call this *beurre manié* (pronounced *burr mahn-yay*). Here in America, words like "burr mahn-yay" sound a bit pretentious, especially if one doesn't speak French, so many cooks call it simply "mannie butter." That is how it will be referred to throughout this book. Anything that can be done using mannie butter can be done better using prepared roux, which is less likely to impart a starchy taste to the sauce.

Cheese and other milk products.   Cheese, cream, sour cream, and plain yogurt will all thicken thinner liquids when they are combined with the liquids and heated. Cheese can separate and become stringy if it becomes too hot, and cream or sour cream can scorch. It is best, therefore, to cool hot liquid before adding any of these ingredients to it; and don't let any sauce in which they are included get too hot.

How much cheese and other milk products should you use? That's a difficult question to answer, because these milk products are usually added to liquids in which some other thickener is also used. It is best, therefore, to add these ingredients to taste, adding liquid or thickener to adjust the thickness of the sauce after the milk product has been incorporated.

Eggs.   Eggs are the primary thickening agent for casseroles, custard sauces, and egg yolk and butter sauces. To thicken liquids, as for making a casserole, use two whole eggs for each cup of thin liquid to make a medium-thick sauce. Two yolks can be substituted for each whole egg for extra richness, or two whites may be used to eliminate cholesterol.

Hot liquids can curdle eggs, so cook egg mixtures slowly and don't let them get too hot. When raw eggs are added to a cold liquid, there will be no problem so long as the mixture is heated slowly enough to cook the egg gradually. Before adding raw eggs to a hot liquid, cool the liquid until it feels comfortable on the underside of your wrist. Alternatively, add warm liquid to the egg, a tablespoon at a time, stirring the mixture constantly to cool it before adding more liquid. Once half the liquid has been incorporated in this way, the egg mixture can be added safely to the remainder of the hot liquid.

To raise the temperature at which eggs may be cooked in hot liquids as well as to add flavor and thickening power to them, mix eggs with heavy cream (whipping cream) to make what is called a *liaison* (pronounced *lee-ay-zohn*): three parts cream to one part egg. Any egg/cream liaison is very delicate and will cook quickly. If the liquid is very

Making mannie butter

(knead butter & flour...

roll into a ball....

add small pieces while stirring til sauce thickens.

hot (over 180 degrees F), cool it first and then add the liaison the same way you would add eggs to any warm liquid.

☐ *Fats*

Most often, fats are used in sauces to make a roux, which is used to eliminate the starchy taste of flour. Gravy uses the fat rendered from the meat or poultry with which it is to be served. White and brown sauces use a roux made with butter or margarine. Butter and margarine also serve as one of the primary ingredients in Hollandaise and the other egg yolk and butter sauces. Butter and margarine can also be used to "finish" gravies, white sauces, and brown sauces, giving them a glossy appearance and added flavor.

☐ *Optional Enricher*

An *enricher* can be used to add flavor and body to any white sauce, brown sauce, or gravy. Simply add cream, sour cream, or a liaison of egg yolk and cream to taste just before serving the sauce. For as much body and almost as much flavor, but fewer calories and less cholesterol, you can substitute half-and-half for cream or pureed low-fat cottage cheese or unflavored yogurt for sour cream.

☐ *Optional Finishing or Buttering*

A last step of *finishing* or *buttering* can add a gloss and extra richness to white sauces, brown sauces, and gravies. Simply float a pat of butter or margarine on the completed sauce. The fat will melt and spread, covering the surface and preventing film from forming. Just before serving, stir and blend the fat into the sauce. If the buttering separates and floats to the surface, blend it in again.

Cooking the Sauce

Liquid, of course, is the cooking medium for any sauce, and the cooking considerations for liquids (p. 36) certainly apply. You must also take care that ingredients such as eggs, cheese, and cream do not scorch, separate, or overcook. In a nutshell, the main precautions are to stir any hot sauce frequently and prevent it from getting too hot. Apart from these points, the "How to" instructions in this chapter should account for almost everything you need to know to make your sauces successfully.

What to Cook in

Part of what determines success or failure in making any hot sauce is the vessel in which it is cooked. Here are a few considerations to guide you.

1. *Use pots or pans that conduct heat evenly.* Pots or pans that are thin or warped, or that are made of materials that don't conduct heat evenly, can cause hot spots. Specially treated aluminum and lined copper are both excellent materials, but they are expensive. Aluminum coated with a non-stick inner lining is an economical substitute. Plain aluminum, while an excellent heat conductor, can react chemically with eggs, tomatoes, and certain other foods, affecting their flavor. A double boiler, preferably one made of heat-proof glass, is best for Hollandaise and other egg yolk and butter sauces.

2. *The size and shape of the vessel will affect the consistency of the sauce.* The broader the surface area and the shallower the liquid, the greater the evaporation and consequent reduction of the sauce. This is a principal reason why the cooking times given in recipes are far from absolute. For sauces especially, you need to use your own knowledge and judgment rather than the times given in recipes if the product is to turn out right.

3. *The cooking heat must be carefully controlled.* Even if a good pot is used, most hot sauces must be stirred frequently. It might also be necessary to remove the pot from the heat occasionally to keep the sauce from cooking too quickly. (This is especially true if eggs are used in the sauce.) If a lightweight vessel is used, it is a good practice to place a heat-retarding device between the vessel and the burner.

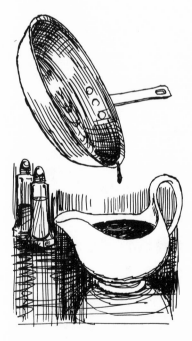

Gravy

Gravy is so basic to everyday cooking that some cooks won't think of it as being a sauce. It doesn't have a fancy name, nor are there any well-established variations of it that could be called small sauces. In fact, most cooks probably regard gravy as just what you get using the grease and pan drippings left in cooking pans to make something to serve with the meat or poultry that has been cooked. That is certainly true, but even with such a basic and pedestrian description, gravy is a sauce nonetheless, and one that most cooks would benefit from knowing more about.

Since gravy is so basic and common, I think it is the best example to use to begin our detailed consideration of sauces. Knowing more about gravy will help you to understand and appreciate the descriptions of the other sauces that follow.

The Ingredients

☐ Liquid

For planning, figure about 1/4 cup of liquid per serving. The pan in which meat or poultry has been cooked will usually contain some liquid as well as fat. That is usually not enough, so some other liquid must be added to it. Water and milk are most common, but broth or broth enriched with milk will make gravy with richer flavor. Wine and even beer can also be used but should be combined with at least an equal amount of another liquid to mellow their flavor.

☐ Seasonings

Most gravies are seasoned with only salt and pepper, although other seasonings that go well with the base food may be added to taste. For better appearance, use white pepper.

☐ Thickener

Flour and cornstarch are both used to thicken gravy. Either dissolve cornstarch into the liquid to make a wash (1/2 to 2 Tbsp. per cup liquid), or cook flour in fat to make a roux, using equal parts flour and fat from the food that was cooked (1 to 4 Tbsp. of each per cup liquid). If more fat is needed, use butter or margarine. Gravy thickened with roux is favored by most cooks for its flavor.

(See "How to Make Roux," p. 132.)

How to Make It

Making gravy is as easy as draining the pan in which meat or poultry has been cooked, adding liquid and a thickener, and cooking the gravy until it thickens.

How to Make Gravy

Model for four servings

Liquid: 1 cup (see step 4)

Fat: 1 to 4 Tbsp. (see step 4)

Thickener: Flour equal to the amount of fat, or half as much cornstarch (see step 5)

Seasonings: Salt and pepper to taste

Vessel: The vessel in which the food was cooked plus 1 heat-proof measuring cup

1. **Plan** about 1/4 cup gravy per serving.
2. **Remove cooked meat or poultry from the cooking vessel.** Hold the food in a container or serving plate in a warm oven (100 degrees F.).
3. **Deglaze the vessel.**
   a. Add liquid to the vessel and stir the pan drippings to dissolve them as much as possible.
   b. Strain the pan liquid into a heat-proof measuring cup.
4. **Prepare the fat and liquid:**
   a. *Fat:* Spoon off enough fat from the liquid to make roux, and put it into the cooled cooking vessel. Discard excess fat from the liquid. Add butter or margarine to the cooking fat if needed. For each four servings use:
      · *Thin gravy:* 1 to 1 1/2 Tbsp.
      · *Medium-thick:* 1 1/2 to 3 Tbsp.
      · *Thick:* 3 to 4 Tbsp.
   b. *Liquid:* To the liquid in the measuring cup, add enough warm water, broth, milk, or combinations of these to make the gravy (1/4 cup per serving).
5. **Prepare the roux:**
   a. To the fat in the cooking vessel, add an equal amount of flour or half as much cornstarch.
   b. Stir the starch and fat together until smooth.
   c. Return the vessel to a range burner and cook the roux over low heat for 3 to 5 minutes, stirring it frequently.
   d. Remove the vessel from the heat and cool the roux for 1 minute.
   e. Pour the liquid into the roux, all at once.
6. **Return the vessel to the burner** and slowly bring the gravy to a boil, stirring it constantly. Lower the heat

and simmer until the gravy thickens (3 to 10 minutes), stirring it frequently.

7. **Season to taste,** using salt, pepper, and any seasonings you like that go well with the base food.

8. **Optional:** Strain the gravy through a fine-mesh tea strainer to remove unattractive food particles.

9. **Optional:** Enrich the gravy, adding half-and-half, cream, sour cream, yogurt, or pureed low-fat cottage cheese.

10. **Make final adjustments:**
    - *To thin:* Add liquid.
    - *To thicken:* Add warmed roux or mannie butter, a tablespoon or less at a time, stirring constantly over medium-high heat. Allow a minute or two for the sauce to thicken before adding more.
    - *Adjust seasoning* if necessary.

11. **Optional finishing:** Float a pat of butter or margarine on the surface of the gravy. This will prevent a film from forming and will enrich the flavor. Stir the finishing into the gravy just before serving.

12. **Optional:** To hold for serving, place the pan in a container of warm water or refrigerate it. To prevent a film from forming on the surface, place plastic wrap or butter-coated waxed paper directly on the surface. Reheat the gravy over low heat, stirring it constantly. Make final adjustments before serving.

■

How to Deglaze a Cooking Vessel

Any cooking vessel in which meats or poultry are fried, roasted, or baked will contain tasty pan drippings. Those pan drippings as well as the fat and liquid in the vessel can be used to flavor gravy. All that is required is to dissolve the pan-drippings into the fat or the liquid that will be used to make the sauce. Here's how to do it.

1. To the liquid from the pan, add enough liquid to make the gravy. (Figure 1/4 cup liquid per serving.) Use broth, water, milk, wine, or combinations of these.

2. Pour the liquid into the pan and heat it, stirring the pan drippings to dissolve them.

3. Strain the liquid into a heat-proof container through a fine mesh tea strainer to remove unattractive food particles.

4. Remove any fat from the surface of the liquid and use it to make the roux to thicken the gravy.

■

White Sauce

White sauce is easily the most important sauce in all cookery. It serves as a topping for hot foods and as the base liquid for casseroles, croquettes, and soufflés. If you read recipes carefully and think about the procedures being described, you will find that a great proportion of them will have a "recipe within the recipe" for making a white sauce.

(See "Illustration of Recipes within a Recipe," pp. 14–15.)

The Ingredients

☐ Liquid

Depending on the way in which the sauce will be used, figure on 1/4 to 1/2 cup per serving; on 1/4 cup for use as a topping; and on 1/2 cup for use in casseroles. There are two different types of white mother sauce. The only difference between them is the liquid. *Béchamel* (pronounced *bay-shah-mel*) uses milk; *velouté (vehl-oo-tay)* uses broth. Béchamel is always called simply béchamel, but velouté sauces include the name of the food from which the broth is made—for example, veal velouté, chicken velouté, or fish velouté. You can combine broth with milk to make béchamel with richer flavor or véloute with milder flavor. If over half the liquid is milk, the sauce can still be called béchamel; if most of the liquid is broth, it will be velouté.

Many small sauces are flavored using a liquid such as sherry or some other wine, small amounts of a special broth, or tomato juice. The amounts of any flavoring liquids should be taken into account when making the mother sauce to achieve the thickness desired. Use less milk or broth in the mother sauce, in other words, to compensate for other liquids that may be added.

□ *Thickener*

The classic version of white sauce is thickened using a roux made of equal parts of butter or margarine and flour. (See "How to Make Roux," p. 132.) You can substitute other starches for flour, but use half as much. The butter or margarine may be whole or clarified, plain or flavored with onion, garlic, or other flavoring vegetables sautéed in the fat.

□ *Seasonings*

Basic white sauce is seasoned simply with a little salt and pepper to taste. If canned or powdered broth is used, salt may not be needed. White pepper will make a more attractive white sauce, without black specks. Beyond these basic seasonings, there are any number of ingredients that can be added to make a small sauce.

Small Sauces Made from a White Mother Sauce

A basic white sauce is good for many uses in its own right, but more often than not it is flavored with other ingredients to make a small sauce. Here are general descriptions of some typical small sauces. They are named according to their most prominent ingredients. Fancy names have not been used except in the case of fish sauces; those names are commonly used on the menus of restaurants.

These descriptions are intended to be used more as an inspiration than as a guide. Only the relationships of ingredients are specified, not exact amounts. Those are for you to experiment with, using recipes and the term "season to taste" as your guide. Again, it is the concept of making a basic white sauce and then flavoring it the way you want that is important, not the specific ingredients, their amounts, or the fancy names.

Caper sauce is traditional with mutton or lamb, but it also makes a delightful topping for poached fish. Simply add capers and a little caper juice to white sauce to taste.

Cheese sauce is one of the most popular of the small white sauces. It is used in casserole dishes as well as a topping for vegetables, shellfish, and eggs. To make it, simply add cheese to a white mother sauce: usually one part cheese to two parts white sauce. Hard cheeses such as American, Cheddar, Gruyère, Parmesan, and Swiss are the most popular. Use them individually or combine them for special flavors. The mother sauce should be rather thin, because cheese will thicken it. Take care not to overheat the sauce, or the cheese might become stringy. Stir the sauce frequently and remove the pot from the heat occasionally to prevent the cheese from getting too hot before it can melt and blend in smoothly.

(See "Cheeses," pp. 292–296, and "A Cook's Guide to Natural Cheeses," in the Appendix.)

Cream sauce is any white sauce to which cream (half-and-half or whipping cream) is added. The usual proportions are one part cream blended with two parts white sauce. Use cream sauce in casseroles or as a topping for vegetables, pasta, poultry, fish, and eggs.

Curry sauce is a white sauce or cream sauce seasoned with curry powder to make it hot and spicy. Use it as a topping for poultry or meats or in casseroles in which poultry or meats are the main ingredient.

Eggs can be added to any white sauce or cream sauce to make it richer and thicker. The customary ratio is two whole eggs per cup of thin white sauce. Beat whole eggs or egg whites and blend them smoothly into the sauce, or use hard-boiled eggs pressed through a fine-mesh tea strainer.

Herb sauce is any white mother sauce or cream sauce seasoned with an herb, such as dill weed or parsley, that goes well with the food with which the sauce is to be served. Use herb sauce in casseroles and as a topping for vegetables, meats, poultry, and fish.

(See "Herbs and Spices," pp. 308–311, and "A Cook's Guide to Herbs and Spices," in the Appendix.)

Horseradish sauce is a popular topping for meats and variety meats. Make a basic white sauce or cream sauce and add horseradish to taste.

Mustard sauce is any white sauce or cream sauce seasoned with dry or Dijon mustard. Use it as a topping for meats, variety meats, and poultry.

Onions, like eggs, can be added to any white sauce to make it thicker and enrich its flavor. Onion-flavored sauce is popular in casserole dishes and as a topping for vegetables, poultry, meats, and fish. To make it, sauté onions and puree them before adding them to the sauce. How much? One to two tablespoons of pureed onions per cup of thin white sauce.

Tomato sauce can be made either as a mother sauce in its own right or by adding tomato juice, tomato puree, or tomato paste to a white mother sauce. For a thin sauce, use tomato juice. For a thicker sauce, use tomato puree or paste. Use tomato sauce in casseroles and as a topping for pasta, vegetables, eggs, meat, and poultry.

(See "Tomato Sauce," pp. 150–153.)

The list that follows is for sauces that are served exclusively with fish and shellfish. The names used are those that might be used on the menus of fine restaurants.

Bercy sauce is fish velouté that is first reduced, thinned with white wine, and then seasoned with shallots and parsley.

Cardinale sauce is a béchamel or fish velouté flavored with mushroom essence, lobster puree, paprika, and red pepper.

Diplomat sauce is velouté made with the liquid inside mussels or clams combined with mushroom broth. The velouté is then enriched and thickened with a liaison of egg yolk and cream, thinned with brandy, and finished with lobster butter.

Nantua sauce is velouté made from crayfish or lobster broth that is thickened with tomato puree and thinned with white wine or brandy.

Newburg sauce is either a béchamel or a fish velouté that is thinned with sherry, enriched with cream, and flavored with red pepper and paprika.

Normande sauce is velouté made with the liquid inside mussels or clams combined with mushroom broth that is enriched with a liaison of egg yolks and cream.

How to Make It

When a recipe calls for a "white sauce," with no detailed description provided, it probably means a béchamel if it is to be served with a vegetable or eggs and a velouté if it is to be served with meat, poultry, or fish (the main food providing the broth). Beyond the basic sauce, you can add seasonings and other flavorings that are compatible with the food to make a small sauce.

How to Make White Sauce

Model for four servings

Liquid: 1 cup (see step 3)

Thickener: 2 to 8 Tbsp. roux (see step 2)

Seasonings: Salt and pepper to taste, plus any ingredients required to make a small sauce

Vessel: 1 pot large enough to contain the sauce at a depth of 1 to 2 inches

1. **Plan** 1/4 cup sauce per serving.

2. **Make a roux** of equal parts butter or margarine and flour. Set it aside to cool.

   (See "How to Make Roux," p. 132.)

   - *For thin sauce,* use 2 to 3 Tbsp. roux per cup liquid.
   - *For medium-thick sauce,* use 3 to 6 Tbsp. roux per cup liquid.
   - *For thick sauce,* use 6 to 8 Tbsp. roux per cup liquid.

3. **Prepare the liquid:** For classic béchamel, use milk. For classic velouté, use broth from the food. Alternatively, combine broth and milk to taste.

   a. Heat the liquid slowly over moderate heat until it is warm but not boiling.

   b. Allow the liquid to cool for one minute before combining it with the roux.

4. **Add the liquid to the cooled roux all at once,** stirring the mixture briskly to blend it smoothly.

5. **Season to taste,** using salt, pepper (preferably white pepper for better appearance), and other seasonings needed for a small sauce. (See description of small sauces, pp. 141–143.)

6. **Cook the sauce:**

   a. Heat the sauce over medium-high heat, stirring it constantly until it simmers. Simmer, stirring frequently, until it thickens (2 to 5 minutes).

   b. Optional: Add ingredients to make a small sauce. (Cream and milk products other than cheese should be added in step 7.)

   (See "Small Sauces Made from a White Mother Sauce," pp. 141–143.)

   c. Reduce the heat to low, cover the pot, and cook the sauce for an additional 5 to 10 minutes, stirring it frequently.

   d. Remove the sauce from the heat and stir it for about a minute to cool it evenly.

7. **Optional:** Enrich the sauce by adding half-and-half,

cream, sour cream, yogurt or pureed low-fat cottage cheese, or pureed onions.

8. **Make final adjustments.**

   · *To thin:* Add liquid.
   · *To thicken:* Add warmed roux or mannie butter—a tablespoon or less at a time—stirring the sauce constantly over medium-high heat. Allow two or three minutes for the sauce to thicken before adding more.
   · *Adjust seasonings* if necessary.

9. **Optional finishing:** Float a tablespoon of butter or margarine on the surface. This will enrich the color and flavor of the sauce and prevent a film from forming on its surface. Stir the finishing into the sauce just before serving.

10. **Optional:** To hold for serving, place the pot into a container of warm water or refrigerate it. To prevent a film from forming on the surface, place plastic wrap or butter-coated waxed paper directly on the surface. Reheat over low heat, stirring constantly, and make final adjustments just before serving.

■

Brown Sauce

Brown sauces are not nearly as popular in the United States as they once were. That's because they are served only with meats, and most Americans prefer their meats plain, with no sauce topping. The exception, of course, is the sauce that accompanies braises and stews, and that is basic brown sauce.

Like the term *white sauce,* the general term *brown sauce* does not apply to any one sauce in particular. Any sauce that is brown is correctly called "brown sauce." White sauce has its two basic types (béchamel and velouté), but there is no comparable agreement when it comes to brown sauce. Most cooks and most books do seem to have their own favorite recipes that they call "brown sauce," and even professional chefs commonly (and erroneously) refer to Sauce Espagnole as if it were the one basic brown sauce. The fact is, though, that different sources disagree about what goes into Sauce Espagnole as well as about how it should be made. In any case, while Sauce Espagnole is indeed a brown sauce, not all brown sauces are Sauce Espagnole.

The instructions given in this section are for a good basic mother sauce, the kind you get when you make meat braises and stews. It can be used in its own right or embellished with other ingredients to make any number of small sauces, including Sauce Espagnole.

The Ingredients

☐ Liquid

(See "How to Make Broth," p. 111.)

Broth generated from the meat being cooked is the primary liquid for any brown sauce. For planning, figure about 1/4 cup liquid per serving. To make broth thicker and more gelatinous, cook pigs' feet or pieces of veal in it.

☐ Thickener

Brown sauce is usually reduced quite a lot as it cooks, and that plus the incorporation of pureed flavoring vegetables can thicken it enough that additional thickener may not be needed. When more thickener is required, dark roux is a favorite, as is tomato paste. You can also use a combination of the two. It is difficult to determine how much dark roux might be needed, since its ability to thicken can vary depending on how it is made. It's a good idea to plan to have more than enough prepared; I suggest 2 to 4 Tbsp. light roux or 4 to 8 Tbsp. dark roux or tomato paste per cup liquid.

(See "How to Make Roux," p. 132.)

☐ Flavorings

In addition to salt, pepper, and other seasonings that go well with the meat, basic brown sauce uses a mirepoix of two parts onion, one part celery, and one part carrots or parsnips, all sautéed until tender and then cooked in the liquid. Garlic and mushrooms are often used as well. Additional ingredients can be added to make a small sauce, such as those described below.

Small Sauces Made from a Brown Mother Sauce

When it comes to the small sauces made from basic brown sauce, there is even less agreement among "authorities" about what they are called and how they should be made than with white sauces. Worse, these sauces can't be easily classified according to their main ingredients, as white sauces can. For that reason, the sauces described here are listed by fairly standard names such as those used in restaurants. The ingredients are those that seem to be favored by professional chefs.

These descriptions will give you some idea of the variety to be had just by adding ingredients. Use the basic mother sauce as a start, add your own imagination and knowledge of ingredients to flavor the sauce the way you like, and call the small sauces you create whatever you like.

Birgarde (*beer-gard*) is a basic brown or Espagnole sauce flavored with a reduced mixture of orange juice, lemon juice, and red wine. Currant jelly is a popular addition also.

Bourguignonne (*boor-gee-nyohn*) is a basic brown sauce thinned and flavored with red wine (usually burgundy). A dash of caramelized white sugar, and perhaps sautéed mushrooms, may be added also.

Champignon (*shahm-pee-nyohn*) is a basic brown or Espagnole sauce thinned with Madeira wine and flavored with sautéed mushrooms.

Chasseur (*shah-sur*) is an Espagnole sauce thickened with a puree of mushrooms and thinned with white wine.

Demiglaze (*dem-ee-glahz*) is a basic brown or Espagnole sauce flavored with sherry and reduced until it is one-tenth its original volume. As its name implies, demiglaze is used as a glaze for meats.

Duxelles (*duke-sell*) is Espagnole sauce flavored with mushrooms and parsley.

Espagnole (*ess-pan-yole*) is a basic brown sauce thickened with tomato paste instead of roux, or with equal parts of tomato paste and roux.

Madere or **Madeira** (*ma-dear-ah*) is a basic brown or Espagnole sauce flavored with Madeira wine.

Meyerbeer (*ma-yer-beer*) is a basic brown or Espagnole sauce flavored with sauteed chicken livers, onions, mushrooms, and sherry wine.

Perigueux (*pear-ee-go*) is a basic brown or Espagnole sauce to which mushrooms, truffles, red wine, and Madeira wine are added. The sauce is then reduced to about one-tenth its volume to make a demiglaze.

How to Make It

Since there is no agreement about any one basic brown sauce, the procedure that follows is based on what seem to be the most common ingredients. The resulting sauce can be used as a good serving sauce in its own right or as a sound mother from which small sauces can be made.

How to Make Brown Sauce

Model for four servings
   Liquid: 2 cups broth
   Thickener: 8 to 16 Tbsp. dark roux, tomato paste, or a combination of the two
   Chopped vegetables: 1/4 to 1/2 cup (see step 2)
   Seasonings: Salt and pepper to taste, plus ingredients to make a small sauce
   Vessel: 1 large pot or skillet with a broad surface area

   1. **Plan** 1/4 cup brown sauce per serving.
   2. **Prepare a mirepoix:** Chop vegetables to make 1/4 to 1/2 cup for each cup of sauce. A good combination is two parts onion, one part celery, and one part carrots or parsnips. Garlic, mushrooms, and sweet bell peppers are also popular flavorings.
   3. **Sauté the vegetables** for about 10 minutes. Drain off the fat and save it for making the roux.
   4. **Add broth.** (See "How to Make Broth," p. 111.) For best flavor, begin with 1/2 cup of meat broth for each serving. Add the broth to the vegetables and slowly bring the mixture to a simmer, stirring in any browned food particles to remove them from the bottom of the cooking vessel. Optional: For a thicker, more gelatinous sauce, add one or more pigs' feet or pieces of veal to the liquid.

5. **Cook uncovered** at a simmer until the liquid is reduced by half. Skim off any scum, fat, or skin as it accumulates on the surface.

6. **Prepare a dark roux.** Make 4 to 8 Tbsp. for each cup liquid. (See "How to Make Roux," p. 132.)

7. **Strain out the vegetables and any meat pieces.** Puree the vegetables in a food mill, blender, or food processor, and stir them into the sauce.

8. **Add thickener if needed:** Allow the sauce to cool for 2 to 3 minutes. If it is not thick enough after it has cooled, return the pot to medium-high heat and slowly add dark roux or tomato paste, a tablespoon at a time, stirring the sauce constantly. Allow 2 to 3 minutes for the sauce to thicken and add more thickener if needed until the sauce is slightly thinner than desired for serving.

9. **Season to taste.** Use salt, pepper, and any seasonings that go well with the meat.

10. **Optional:** Add special ingredients to make a small sauce. (See description of small sauces, p. 147.)

11. **Cook the flavored sauce** over low heat for another 10 to 15 minutes to allow the flavors to blend.

12. **De-fat the sauce.** (See "How to" instructions, p. 101.)

13. **Optional:** Enrich the sauce by adding half-and-half, cream, sour cream, yogurt, or pureed low-fat cottage cheese.

14. **Make final adjustments:**

· *To thin:* Add liquid.
· *To thicken:* Add warmed roux, mannie butter, or tomato paste, a tablespoon or less at a time, stirring the sauce constantly over medium-high heat. Allow 2 to 3 minutes for the sauce to thicken before adding more.
· *Adjust seasonings* if necessary.

15. **Optional finishing:** Float a tablespoon of butter or margarine on the surface. This will enrich the color and flavor of the sauce and prevent a film from forming on its surface. Stir the finishing into the sauce just before serving.

16. **Optional:** Flavors will be improved if the sauce is allowed to sit refrigerated for a few hours or longer and then reheated for serving. To prevent a film from forming, place plastic wrap or butter-coated waxed paper directly on the surface of the sauce. Reheat the sauce over low heat, stirring constantly, and make final adjustments just before serving.

■

Tomato Sauce

Tomato sauce is one of the handiest and most versatile of all sauces. Keep it on hand for making such dishes as stuffed peppers, stuffed cabbage, and pasta dishes such as lasagna and spaghetti, as well as to use as a topping for eggs, poultry, fish, meats, and many vegetables. Because it is needed often, and because it can take a good deal of time and work to prepare well, make it in large amounts and refrigerate, can, or freeze it. In fact, refrigeration or freezing seems to mellow its flavor and improve its taste.

The Ingredients

There are any number of prepared tomato sauces on the market, ranging from the plain, lightly seasoned, low-cost purees to fully seasoned sauces complete with meat. Using prepared sauces is certainly convenient; the tradeoff is the loss of originality and pride in making everything yourself. A fair middle ground between making tomato sauce from scratch and buying a finished product is to use a plain, inexpensive canned or bottled tomato sauce or puree as a base and then add your own ingredients to make the final sauce the way you like it.

□ Tomato Base

Any tomato liquid can be used alone or mixed with other liquids to serve as the base. Figure about one cup per serving. You can start with something as simple as tomato juice or canned tomatoes and add a thickener, or you can start with tomato puree or paste and thin it with tomato juice, stewed tomatoes, broth, wine, water, or combina-

(See "Tomatoes and Tomato Products," pp. 311–313.)

tions of these. Different methods and combinations will produce different flavors and textures. If you prefer a smooth sauce, use a tomato puree or paste and thin it. If you like lumps of tomato, use fresh or canned tomatoes and thicken them. When using whole tomatoes, it is preferable to remove the skins and seeds; skins can be tough, and seeds can make the sauce bitter. A very good liquid base is equal parts of tomato puree and canned stewed tomatoes.

□ *Thickener*

If the liquid base is thick enough, or if the sauce cooks long enough to reduce its liquid content, then additional thickener might not be needed. If thickener is needed, add tomato paste, roux, or mannie butter, stirring it in a little at a time until the sauce thickens to your liking.

□ *Flavorings*

This is where tomato sauce becomes really varied and interesting. Almost any good sauce uses fresh onions, celery, sweet bell peppers, and garlic, as well as salt, pepper, basil, and usually oregano or Italian seasonings. Those are only the start. You can include cooked chopped meat or shellfish, mushrooms, olives, or any number of other foods to make the sauce to your liking.

□ *How to Make It*

Opinions about how to make tomato sauce are about as varied as the ingredients that can be used. The following instructions are very broad and should provide a workable model for anyone. You can use ingredients as simple as canned sauce or make everything from scratch. Try using different ingredients until you arrive at a combination you like that distinguishes your style. If others enjoy it, then you might want to share your "secret" recipe with them.

How to Make Tomato Sauce

Model for four servings

Liquid: 4 cups (see step 5)

Flavoring vegetables: 1 cup (see step 3)

Optional: 1 cup chopped or ground meat

Seasonings: See step 7

Vessel: 1 pot or skillet with a broad surface area and a lid. Do not use a pot made of plain aluminum unless the inside is lined. Plain aluminum interacts chemically with tomatoes.

1. **Plan** 1 cup finished sauce per serving. Allow at least 60 to 90 minutes to make a good sauce. Flavor will be improved if the sauce is refrigerated overnight.

2. **Optional:** Prepare the meat. Allow 1/4 cup per serving. Pan-broil ground or chopped beef, pork, veal, sausage, or combinations of these until brown. Drain off fat and use it to sauté the vegetables and make roux.

3. **Prepare flavoring vegetables:** Allow 1/4 cup per serving. Use vegetables such as onions, celery, sweet bell peppers, mushrooms, and garlic. Sauté them in olive oil, butter or margarine, or in the rendered meat fat until soft but not browned. If garlic is used, mince it or press it through a garlic press *after* it has been sautéed.

4. **Deglaze the pan:** Pour off any fat from the pan and save it in case you need to make roux to thicken the sauce. Stir in a small amount of liquid to dissolve any browned food particles in the pan.

5. **Add tomato liquid:** Plan 1 cup per serving. Any of the following may be used alone or in combination with other liquids. (See "Tomatoes and Tomato Products," pp. 311–313.)

- *Tomato juice or stewed tomatoes:* Remove seeds.
- *Whole tomatoes with juice (canned or fresh):* If fresh, use very ripe tomatoes and parboil them until their skins peel easily. Remove the skin, seeds, and core and cut into pieces.
- *Tomato puree:* A mixture of tomato puree with tomato juice (for smooth sauce) or with tomato pieces (for chunky sauce) will produce a sauce with excellent flavor that will usually require no additional thickener.
- *Commercial tomato sauce:* Use a prepared sauce with few flavorings and no meat. This will usually not require any additional thickener.
- *Broth, red wine, or combinations of the two* can be mixed with any of the other liquids listed to mellow their flavor and thin the sauce. Dry red wine is preferred. A little lemon juice may also be used for extra flavor.

6. **Simmer the mixture** in an uncovered pot for 30 to 60 minutes to mellow the acid in the tomato and reduce the liquid.

7. **Season to taste:** Popular flavorings are salt, pepper, basil, Italian seasoning, paprika, oregano, bay leaf, fennel, sugar, garlic, onion, celery, pickled peppers, Worcester-

shire sauce, and Tabasco sauce. For best flavor, cook seasonings no longer than 30 minutes.

8. **Cover the pot and cook** over low heat an additional 30 minutes, stirring frequently. If the sauce is to be refrigerated before serving, save this step for reheating it.

9. **Add thickener if needed:** Use tomato paste, roux, or mannie butter, adding it to the sauce a tablespoon or less at a time. Allow the sauce to simmer 2 to 3 minutes before adding more. (See "Thickeners," pp. 130–135.)

10. **De-fat the sauce.** (See "How to" instructions, p. 101.)

11. **Make final adjustments:**

· *To thin:* Add liquid.
· *To thicken:* Add tomato paste, roux, or mannie butter— a teaspoon at a time—stirring the sauce constantly. Allow the sauce to simmer 2 to 3 minutes before adding more.
· *Adjust seasonings* if necessary.

12. **Optional:** Flavors will be improved if the sauce is refrigerated for a few hours or longer and reheated over low heat. Make final adjustments before serving.

■

Egg Yolk and Butter Sauces: Hollandaise, Maltaise, Béarnaise, Bordeaux, and Choron

These popular sauces are used most frequently as a topping for vegetables such as asparagus and broccoli. However, they also make a gracious and tasty accompaniment to meats and even eggs as well as specialty dishes such as timbales.

Egg yolk and butter sauces have a reputation for being difficult to make and easy to goof up. That is unfortunate because it discourages cooks from trying to make them. It is also true.

Unless they are used in moderation and properly cared for, egg yolk and butter sauces are potential health hazards. Not only are they loaded with fat and cholesterol, but they also can contain *Staphylococcus aureus*, a heat-resistant bacterium that can produce a dangerous toxin. Do not let an egg sauce sit out for longer than one hour, or it might "go bad," as they say, and make you ill. For safety's sake, it is best to throw out any leftover egg sauces rather than to try to save them for later use. If you reheat the sauce enough to destroy harmful bacteria, it will be ruined. If you heat it only enough to make it good, bacteria can survive and harm you. (See table on p. 242.)

The Ingredients

☐ *Liquid and Seasonings*

All of these sauces are made in exactly the same way. What differentiates them is the liquids and seasonings used. For lighter texture and milder flavor, substitute warm water for up to half the liquid specified. Plan 4 teaspoons liquid for each egg yolk, using no more than half at the start and saving the remainder to thin the sauce, if needed, later on. The amount of seasonings will vary according to taste.

Hollandaise: Lemon juice seasoned with salt and pepper.
Maltaise: Orange juice seasoned with salt and pepper.
Béarnaise: Vinegar flavored with shallots and tarragon.
Bordeaux: White wine seasoned with chives, tarragon, and either parsley or dill.
Choron: Béarnaise sauce with tomato puree added.

☐ *Fat*

(See "How to Clarify Butter," p. 291.)

The fat used in all these sauces is butter. You can use margarine, but it just isn't the same. If the butter is clarified, it gives a different flavor and a slightly thicker sauce.

Because egg yolks can hold only so much butter, and because the method used to incorporate the butter into the yolks determines, to some extent, the amount of butter the yolk can hold, the amount of butter used in the sauce will vary as a function both of the number of yolks and the method. Using the chef's method, you can safely use as many as 4 Tbsp. (1/2 stick) butter per. egg yolk. The blender method whips the yolks, so they can hold no more than 2 Tbsp. butter per yolk.

☐ *Thickener*

Egg yolks thicken the sauce as well as determine the amount of all the other ingredients used. For planning, figure that each egg yolk will produce enough sauce for two to three servings. Use the yolks of large or extra large eggs.

To cook these sauces successfully requires some basic knowledge of egg yolks. Here are some pointers.

1. *Egg yolks cook very easily and quickly.* If they become too hot (over 180 degrees F.), they separate and curdle. If they are heated too quickly, they become grainy. The result

in either case may be a ruined sauce. It is safest, therefore, to heat egg yolks slowly, stirring them constantly to distribute the heat evenly. Don't let them get too hot.

2. *Egg yolks can hold only so much butter at a time.* If the butter is added to the yolks too quickly for them to absorb it, especially in the early stage, the sauce will not thicken. If too much butter is added, the sauce will separate. To be really safe making egg yolk and butter sauces, use no more than 2 Tbsp. butter for each egg yolk when using the blender method and no more than 4 Tbsp. butter per yolk for the chef's method. Also, blend the butter into the eggs very slowly—no more than a teaspoon at a time.

3. *Egg sauces have a limited holding ability.* For this reason, make egg sauces as close to serving time as possible. If they are kept too hot, they will curdle. If they are kept too cold, dangerous bacteria will grow and the butter will stiffen. Rewarming them is difficult at best, and hazardous to your health at worst.

How to Make It

There are two ways to make these sauces: the chef's method and the blender method. The blender method is virtually foolproof. It also has the advantage of using less butter than is required for the chef's method, which means it has fewer calories and less cholesterol. The tradeoff is taste. Egg yolk and butter sauces made using the chef's method taste better.

□ *Blender Method*

With the blender method, the heat from the butter cooks the egg yolks to thicken the sauce. There is virtually no danger of curdling the eggs. However, if either the eggs or the liquid is too cold, or if the butter is not hot enough, the eggs won't cook enough to thicken the sauce. In that case, the sauce must be heated on a range burner to thicken it.

How to Make Egg Yolk and Butter Sauces: Blender Method

Model for four servings
(For some blenders, these amounts might have to be increased in order for the mixture to reach the blades of the blender.)

Egg yolks: 2
Liquid: 8 tsp. (see step 3)
Butter: 4 Tbsp. (1/2 stick)
Seasonings: See step 3
Vessels: Food blender, 2 bowls for holding eggs and liquid, 1 pot for melting the butter

1. **Plan** 1 egg yolk for every 2 to 3 servings. Allow time to bring all ingredients to room temperature (see p. 317), plus 15 to 20 minutes to make the sauce.

2. **Prepare the egg yolks:** Use large or extra large eggs. Separate the eggs cold, putting the yolks in a warm bowl. (Save the whites for other uses.) Bring the yolks to room temperature.

3. **Prepare the liquid and seasonings:** For each yolk, use 4 Tbsp. liquid plus seasonings to taste mixing them together in a warm bowl. Bring the mixture to room temperature. (Optional: For a lighter flavor and texture, substitute warm water for up to half the liquid specified.)

- *Hollandaise:* lemon juice, salt, and white or red pepper.
- *Maltaise:* orange juice, salt, and white or red pepper.
- *Bordeaux:* white wine, salt, white or red pepper, tarragon, chives, and either parsley or dill.
- *Béarnaise:* vinegar, salt, black pepper, and tarragon. Use twice the amount of vinegar called for, and cook the seasonings in it until the liquid is reduced by half.
- *Choron:* Béarnaise sauce with 1 Tbsp. tomato puree added per cup of sauce.

4. **Prepare the butter:** Use 2 Tbsp. butter per egg yolk. Heat the butter slowly over low heat until it is fully melted and begins to bubble. Set aside to cool, and spoon any foam off the top.

5. **Rinse the bowl of a food blender in hot water.** (The heat from it will warm the eggs and the liquid.)

6. **Pour the egg yolks into the warmed blender bowl.** Cover the bowl and blend on low speed for 10 seconds. Add half the liquid and blend for 10 seconds.

7. **Reheat the butter until it bubbles.**

8. **Add the butter:** Turn the blender on high and slowly pour in the hot butter a drop at a time until the sauce thickens. Stop adding butter when the sauce is thick. (The sauce may become very thick before all the butter is used.) Try to keep any white milk particles from the butter out of the sauce.

9. **Make final adjustments:**

· *To thin:* Add more liquid, whisking it in a little at a time.

· *To enrich with more butter:* Pour the sauce into a mixing bowl or pot so you can work with it more easily. Add hot butter, whisking it in a little at a time.

· *To thicken or reheat:* Pour the sauce into a heavy pot or double boiler and heat it over low heat, whisking it constantly until it thickens. If the pot gets too hot for your fingers to touch, it is too hot for the sauce.

10. **Optional:** To hold before serving, cover the top of the vessel and place it into a container of warm (not hot) water. Stir the sauce occasionally to distribute the heat evenly. Do not try to hold any longer than one hour without refrigeration. *Any egg yolk and butter sauce that is left at room temperature for over one hour can contain bacteria that can make you very ill.* (See "Bacterial Foodborne Illness," p. 242.)

■

□ *Chef's Method*

The chef's method calls for the sauce mixture to be heated on a range burner. If the sauce gets too hot, the eggs will curdle. The key to success is keeping the sauce from getting too hot, and that is sometimes difficult to do. To do it, remove the pot from the heat once a minute and test the temperature of the bottom. If it is too hot for your finger to touch, it is too hot for the sauce.

How to Make Egg Yolk and Butter Sauces: Chef's Method

Model for four servings
  Egg yolks: 2
  Liquid: 8 tsp. (see step 3)
  Butter: 8 Tbsp. (1 stick)
  Seasonings: See step 3
  Vessel: 1 double boiler (preferred), or 1 lined copper or coated aluminum sauce pot

1. **Plan** 1 egg yolk for every 2 to 3 servings. Allow time to bring all ingredients to room temperature plus 15 to 20 minutes to make the sauce.

2. **Prepare the egg yolks:** Use large or extra large eggs. Separate the eggs cold, putting the yolks into a double boiler or sauce pot. (Save the whites for other uses.) Bring

the yolks to room temperature. Beat them until smooth before adding the liquid.

3. **Prepare the liquid and seasonings:** For each egg yolk, use 4 tsp. liquid. (Optional: For a lighter flavor and texture, substitute warm water for up to half the liquid specified.)

- *Hollandaise:* lemon juice, salt, and white or red pepper.
- *Maltaise:* orange juice, salt, and white or red pepper.
- *Bordeaux:* white wine, salt, white or red pepper, tarragon, chives, and either parsley or dill.
- *Béarnaise:* vinegar, salt, black pepper, and tarragon. Use twice the amount of vinegar called for, and cook the seasonings in it until the liquid is reduced by half.
- *Choron:* Béarnaise sauce with 1 Tbsp. tomato puree added per cup sauce.

4. **Prepare the butter:** Use 4 Tbsp. (1/2 stick) per egg yolk of either warm clarified butter or whole butter. If whole, cut butter into small pieces (about a teaspoon each), and place it on a warm plate long enough to soften but not melt.

5. **Blend half the liquid into the egg yolks.** Save the remainder to thin the sauce later on if necessary.

6. **Heat the mixture:** Use low heat and stir constantly until the mixture thickens to the consistency of heavy cream. The sauce should be thick enough that you can see the bottom of the pot between strokes. If a double boiler is used, the water should not be boiling, and the top pot must not touch the hot water. If a sauce pot is used, lift it off the burner frequently to check the temperature of the bottom. If it is too hot for your finger to touch, then it is too hot for the sauce.

7. **Add the butter:** Slowly add the butter—a teaspoon at a time—whisking the mixture constantly. Blend in each bit of butter thoroughly before adding the next. Continue to check the bottom of the pot to be sure it does not get too hot.

8. **If the sauce curdles:** The sauce will curdle if it is too hot. If this happens, remove the pot from the heat and quickly plunge its bottom into cold water. Toss in an ice cube or 1 tablespoon of cold water, milk, or cream, whisking the sauce briskly until it no longer appears curdled. If that doesn't work, leave the sauce pot in the cool water and follow the instructions for thickening below.

9. **Make final adjustments:**

- *To thin:* Add liquid, stirring the mixture constantly.

· *To thicken:* Continue cooking the sauce over low heat, stirring it constantly. If that doesn't work, it means that too much butter was added too quickly. Remove the pot from the heat. Rinse a small mixing bowl with hot water to heat it. Separate an egg and place the yolk into the warmed bowl. Beat the yolk until it thickens slightly. Slowly add the sauce—a tablespoon at a time—whisking the mixture constantly until all the sauce has been incorporated into the yolk and the mixture is smooth. Return the pot to the heat and reheat the sauce slowly, whisking it constantly.

10. **Reheat, if necessary,** and make final adjustments before serving. These sauces should be served warm, not hot.

11. **Optional:** To hold before serving, cover the top of the pot and place it in a container of warm (not hot) water. Stir the sauce occasionally to distribute the heat evenly. Do not try to hold any longer than one hour without refrigeration. *Any egg yolk and butter sauce that is left at room temperature for over one hour can contain bacteria that can make you very ill.*

(See "Bacterial Foodborne Illness," p. 242.)

■

Custard Sauce or Baked Custard

Custard sauce is blended with many different foods to make quiches, puddings, and timbales that can be served as main dishes, side dishes, or hors d'oeuvres. Custard sauce can also be used to make wonderful dessert dishes. The elegant flans so popular in France, Spain, and other Latin countries, for example, are just sweet custard sauce with a caramel topping. Rice pudding, bread pudding, and tapioca pudding, among others, are all made using a sweet custard sauce with special ingredients mixed in. Here again, you can use the simple idea of adding ingredients to a basic mother sauce to make any number of dishes.

The Ingredients

☐ Liquid
One cup liquid will make enough custard for three to four servings. Broth, or broth mixed with milk or half-and-half, is suitable for main and side dishes such as quiche, but

not for sweet desserts. Cream or half-and-half are suitable for any dishes, especially desserts. Fruit juices can be used alone for making dessert custards, but they are usually mixed with at least an equal amount of milk, half-and-half, or cream.

□ *Thickener*

Eggs provide the thickener. Two to three eggs per cup of liquid is the customary ratio, depending on the thickness desired. Whole eggs alone are fine, but for a richer sauce use extra yolks. For a really rich custard, use only yolks. (Two yolks equal one whole egg.)

□ *Seasonings*

Salt and pepper in small amounts are used for making quiche and other main and side dishes. (Either white or cayenne pepper is preferred for better appearance.) Nutmeg is called for in almost any custard, whether it is used for a main dish, side dish, or dessert. Sugar, of course, is used for making dessert custard. Cinnamon, allspice, vanilla, and almond or other fruit extracts are also popular flavorings for dessert custards.

How to Make It

Making custard sauce is different from making the other hot sauces covered in this chapter. Instead of cooking the sauce on a range burner and then adding it to another food, you mix cold custard sauce with the food and then bake the entire mixture. The sauce thickens and binds everything together as it cooks.

Because custard sauces are used largely for making quiches, timbales, and puddings, it might help you to understand the procedure described here if you review the cooking considerations and "How to" instructions for cooking those special casserole dishes (see pp. 85–87).

How to Make Custard Sauce

Model for four servings
   Eggs: 4 to 6 whole eggs (see step 2)
   Liquid: 1 cup (see step 3)
   Seasonings: See step 4
   Vessel: 1 mixing bowl, 1 or more baking dishes

1. **Plan** about 1/2 cup of sauce per serving. When the sauce is mixed with other foods (such as for making quiche), you will need enough to cover the food plus 1/8 to 1/4 inch. Allow 15 minutes to preheat the oven and make the sauce plus 20 to 60 minutes to cook the custard.

2. **Prepare the eggs:** Use 2 to 3 whole eggs per cup of liquid depending on the thickness desired. For a richer sauce, substitute extra yolks for some of the whites. For extra rich sauce, use only egg yolks. (Two yolks equal one whole egg.) Break cold eggs into a mixing bowl and bring them to room temperature.

3. **Stir in the liquid:** Use 1/4 to 1/2 cup per serving. Milk products (milk, half-and-half, or cream) are used for dessert and many main and side dishes. Broth, or equal parts of broth and a milk product, is good for making main and side dishes. Fruit juices can be mixed with milk products (up to equal amounts) for making dessert custards.

4. **Season to taste:** *For main and side dishes:* Use salt and pepper (preferably white or red pepper) plus whatever seasonings might go well with the food ingredients. Nutmeg is usually used, a pinch or two per cup liquid. A light garnish of nutmeg on the top also makes the custard more attractive.

For dessert custards: Use a dash of salt and 1 to 2 Tbsp. sugar per cup liquid. Add nutmeg, cinnamon, allspice, vanilla, almond extract, fruit juice, fruit liqueur, or other ingredients to taste.

5. **Mix the ingredients well until blended.**

6. **Prepare a baking dish or dishes:** Coat the inside lightly with shortening. Distribute any precooked solid foods that might be called for evenly across the bottom.

7. **Pour the sauce into the baking dish:** Use enough to cover any solid food by 1/8 to 1/4 inch.

8. **Optional:** To hold the sauce before baking, place plastic wrap or butter-coated waxed paper on the surface to prevent a film from forming and refrigerate the sauce.

9. **Bake in a preheated oven** (325 to 350 degrees F.) until a toothpick or knife blade inserted into the center comes out almost dry. That will be about 20 to 30 minutes for small dishes and 30 to 60 minutes for large ones. For large dishes, place the baking dish in a pan of hot water (a "Mary's bath") and cook on the bottom rack of the oven.

10. **Serve hot or cold.**

■

*C*old Sauces or Dressings

CHAPTER FIVE

*C*old sauces can include an enormous number of things, from basic French dressing to walnut-flavored butter. If we think of them as all being different, their number is probably endless. However, if we again use the notion of *mother sauce* to simplify things, as we did with hot sauces in Chapter Four, then the number of basic cold sauces is only three: mayonnaise, vinaigrette dressing, and cold butter sauce.

Mayonnaise

Mayonnaise is used mostly in sandwiches and as a dressing for salads. It is also popular as a topping for cooked vegetables such as asparagus and broccoli, as well as for fish and beef steaks.

Mayonnaise is as common to most kitchens as butter or margarine and just as convenient to use, because prepared mayonnaise is readily available. Since commercial mayonnaise is good as well as convenient, many cooks never bother to try making fresh mayonnaise for themselves. Perhaps after reading this section and considering the variety of flavors that can be had with homemade mayonnaise, you will be tempted to make it yourself. Even if you stick with commercial mayonnaise, however, you can at least add seasonings to make any of the small sauces described here.

The Ingredients

Basic mayonnaise is made using an oil base, seasonings, acidic liquid, and thickener: eggs or egg yolks. Other ingredients can be added to basic mayonnaise to make any number of small-sauce variations.

□ Oil

Oil forms the greatest part of mayonnaise. The amount of oil is determined by the number of egg yolks, because an egg yolk can hold only so much oil—a maximum of three-

fourths cup. If that amount is exceeded, the emulsion will break down and the mayonnaise will separate. To be really safe, use as little as one-half cup of oil per egg yolk, and never more than two-thirds cup.

What kind of oil? That depends on what you like and how much you are willing to pay. Olive oil and peanut oil are used most often, but both are expensive. Less expensive vegetable oils just don't seem to taste quite as good. A fair compromise may be to mix two oils to suit your own taste and budget. For example, mix olive or peanut oil with an equal amount of safflower or corn oil.

□ *Acidic Liquid*

Lemon juice and vinegar (preferably white-wine vinegar), used alone or mixed together, thin the oil and give it flavor. Prepare two tablespoons liquid per egg yolk, using half of it in the basic preparation and the remainder to thin the mayonnaise if needed. For milder flavor, substitute water or a dry white wine such as vermouth for up to half the acidic liquid.

(See "Acidic Liquids," pp. 284–287.)

□ *Thickener*

The oil and liquids will not mix without something to hold them in suspension. That something is called an *emulsifier*, which in this case is egg yolk. What happens is this: As the ingredients are beaten together, the oil is broken down into tiny globules that spread evenly throughout the egg and the liquid. The liquefied egg yolk then holds everything in suspension. The balance is a delicate one, however, and the ingredients can become separated unless you take the following precautions:

1. Make sure that the egg yolks and all other ingredients are at room temperature: 65 to 75 degrees F.

2. Use no more than two-thirds cup of oil per egg yolk.

3. Add the oil to the egg yolk *very slowly,* beating the mixture constantly until it thickens, or "sets."

□ *Seasonings*

The oils and liquids used determine the basic flavor of the mayonnaise. Beyond those basic ingredients, classic mayonnaise is usually flavored simply with salt and pepper (preferably white pepper for better appearance) and perhaps with a little sugar or honey for sweetness. A bit of mustard can give it some bite. Other flavorings can be added to make one of the small sauces described below. Use small amounts of seasonings at first, incorporating them into the oil so they mix evenly in the sauce. Add more seasonings to suit your taste after the mayonnaise is made.

Some Small Sauces Made from a Mayonnaise Mother Sauce

Here is a partial list of small sauces that you can make simply by adding flavorings to either commercial or homemade mayonnaise. Only the most commonly used ingredients are given. "Season to taste."

Basic mayonnaise: For each egg yolk (or for each whole egg, in the blender method), mix in 1/2 to 2/3 cup oil and 1 to 2 Tbsp. acidic liquid, plus a dash of salt and a pinch of white pepper.

Creamy mayonnaise: Start with a thick basic mayonnaise and blend in up to an equal amount of cream, sour cream, plain yogurt, or buttermilk. Cream or buttermilk will thin the mayonnaise.

Garlic mayonnaise ("Aioli"): Use either garlic-flavored oil to make a basic or creamy mayonnaise, or add garlic pieces (finely minced or parboiled or sautéed and pressed) or garlic juice to prepared mayonnaise.

Green ("herbed") mayonnaise: To basic or creamy mayonnaise, add a puree of green leaves from vegetables such as chives, scallions, parsley, or spinach. Use two tablespoons or so of chopped fresh leaves per cup of mayonnaise. Mix the green leaves with an equal amount of lemon juice and puree and drain them before mixing them into the mayonnaise.

Horseradish mayonnaise: To basic or creamy mayonnaise, add prepared horseradish and finely chopped onion or shallots to taste.

Mustard mayonnaise: Flavor basic or creamy mayonnaise with a little dry mustard or Dijon mustard; about 1 tsp. mustard per cup of mayonnaise.

Roquefort dressing: Mix Roquefort, blue, or other semi-hard cheese with basic or creamy mayonnaise to taste.

Tartar sauce: To a thick plain or mustard mayonnaise, add finely chopped pickles—1 Tbsp. per cup—together with about half as much finely chopped onion or shallots. Other popular additions include finely chopped parsley or tarragon and hard-cooked egg chopped into fine pieces. Add lemon juice to thin if needed.

Thousand Island dressing: To basic or creamy mayonnaise, add a little chili sauce together with pimiento and minced sweet bell peppers, onions, or shallots. Hard-cooked egg yolk, finely chopped, is another popular addition. Add liquid to thin the dressing if needed.

How to Make It

There are two ways to make mayonnaise: the chef's method and the blender method. The blender method is by far the easier, and it also makes mayonnaise that has a lighter texture and is better for your health.

In the *blender method*, an electric food blender or food processor does most of the work. Because the rapid blender action sets the mixture very quickly, it is best to use whole eggs instead of egg yolks alone. Whole eggs produce mayonnaise that has a fluffier texture, less cholesterol, and lighter taste than mayonnaise made by the chef's method.

Unless you use an electric mixer, the *chef's method* can be a two-person operation. One person beats the mixture with a whisk or rotary beater as the other pours the oil. Even if two people do it, the process is tiring because it can take as long as five minutes of constant beating before the emulsion sets. With an electric mixer, the machine does the work while you simply control the flow of the oil.

Whichever method you use, for best results combine the

ingredients in the following order: eggs + seasoned oil + liquid + optional ingredients. Here are some other pointers:

1. Have all ingredients at room temperature.

2. Arrange correct amounts of all the ingredients in separate containers with the seasonings mixed into the oil. That way, once the blending process is begun it can be continued without interruption.

3. Beat the egg yolks well before adding anything to them.

4. Incorporate the oil into the egg *very slowly* (literally drop by drop), beating the mixture constantly until the emulsion "sets" and the mixture firms up. This is crucial to making mayonnaise successfully, for unless it is done right, the oil and egg can separate. The easiest way to control the flow of the oil is to use a bulb baster.

5. When the oil and egg mixture is firm, gradually add some of the acidic liquid to thin it. Alternate the oil and the liquid until all of the oil has been used. Use remaining liquid to thin the mayonnaise later if needed.

6. Once the mayonnaise is completed to your liking, refrigerate it in a covered container until it is well chilled. It will thicken more as it cools.

7. For safety, let mayonnaise stand at room temperature for no longer than one hour, and keep it no more than one week. Mayonnaise that has warmed, or that is more than one week old, is likely to break down and separate. Even if it has not separated, it just might contain bacterial growths that can cause food poisoning. (See table on p. 242.)

How to Make Mayonnaise: Blender Method

Model for one cup
Note: Depending on the blender, you might have to double these amounts in order for the mixture to reach the blades of the blender.

> **Whole egg:** 1
> **Oil:** 2/3 cup (see step 4, below)
> **Acidic liquid:** 2 Tbsp. (see step 6, below)
> **Seasonings:** See step 5, below
> **Vessels:** Food blender, 2 mixing bowls

1. **Plan** 1/2 hour to make the mayonnaise, plus at least 1 hour to chill it before serving. Make no more than you are likely to use in a week. For use as a topping

or for making potato salad and such, figure 5 to 10 servings per cup. For use in making sandwiches, figure 10 to 15 sandwiches per cup.

2. **Prepare the bowl:** Rinse the bowl of a food blender or food processor in warm water and dry it thoroughly.

3. **Prepare the eggs:** Use 1 whole large or extra large egg for each cup of mayonnaise. Break the eggs into the warmed blender bowl and blend on low speed for about 10 seconds. Bring to room temperature.

4. **Prepare the oil:** For each egg, use 2/3 cup olive oil or peanut oil alone or mixed with up to an equal amount of another vegetable oil. Measure the oil into a separate bowl and bring it to room temperature.

5. **Season the oil:** For each 2/3 cup oil, use 1/4 to 1/2 tsp. salt, half as much white pepper, a pinch of sugar, and any other seasonings required for making a small sauce, to taste. (See pp. 166–167.)

6. **Prepare the liquid:** For each egg, measure and hold in a separate bowl 2 Tbsp. acidic liquid: lemon juice, vinegar, or a combination of the two. For milder flavor, substitute water or dry white wine such as vermouth for up to half the acidic liquid. Bring to room temperature.

7. **Mix the ingredients:**

   a. Pour half the liquid into the eggs.

   b. Blend at high speed for about ten seconds.

   c. Reduce the speed to low and begin adding the oil *very slowly*—drop by drop—until the mixture becomes thick and creamy. To be really safe, pause at intervals of ten seconds or so for two or three seconds. When the emulsion firms up ("sets"), you can begin pouring the oil at a faster rate—a tablespoon at a time—until half the oil is used.

   d. Alternate adding the remaining oil and liquid, using twice as much oil as liquid, until all the oil has been used. Save the remaining liquid to make final adjustments later on.

8. **Optional:** Add special ingredients to make a small sauce. (See pp. 166–167.)

9. **Make final adjustments.** If the sauce is *too thick*, add liquid. If the mixture is *too thin or separates* ("turns"):

   a. Rinse a bowl with warm water and dry it.

   b. Add 1 egg yolk to the bowl and beat until smooth.

   c. Slowly pour the mayonnaise into the egg—one

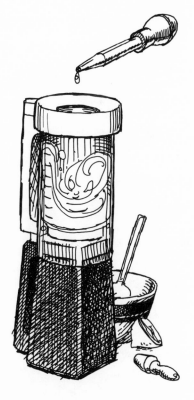

tablespoon at a time—beating the mixture constantly until it blends smoothly before adding more. Repeat until all of the mayonnaise has been incorporated into the egg yolk.

10. **Cover and refrigerate the mayonnaise for at least one hour before serving.** The mayonnaise will thicken more as it chills. Keep well refrigerated for safety.

■

How to Make Mayonnaise: Chef's Method

Model for one cup
Egg yolk: 1
Oil: 2/3 cup (see step 4, below)
Acidic liquid: 2 Tbsp. (see step 6, below)
Seasonings: See step 5, below
Vessels: 3 mixing bowls

1. **Plan** 1/2 hour to make the mayonnaise, plus at least 1 hour to chill it before serving. Make no more than you are likely to use in a week. For use as a topping, or for making potato salad and such, figure 5 to 10 servings per cup. For use in making sandwiches, figure 10 to 15 sandwiches per cup.

2. **Prepare the bowl:** Rinse a mixing bowl in warm water and dry it thoroughly.

3. **Prepare the egg yolks:** Use the yolk of 1 large or extra large egg for each cup of mayonnaise. Separate the eggs and put the yolks into the warmed bowl. Save the whites for other uses. Beat the yolks until they are smooth and bring them to room temperature.

4. **Prepare the oil:** Use 2/3 cup oil for each egg yolk. Use olive or peanut oil alone or mixed with an equal amount of another vegetable oil. Measure the oil into a separate bowl and bring it to room temperature.

5. **Season the oil:** For each 2/3 cup oil, use 1/4 to 1/2 tsp. salt and half as much white pepper, a pinch of sugar, and any other seasonings required for making a small sauce, to taste. (See pp. 166–167.)

6. **Prepare the liquid:** For each yolk, measure and hold in a separate bowl 2 Tbsp. acidic liquid: lemon juice,

vinegar, or a combination of the two. For milder flavor, substitute water or a dry white wine such as vermouth for up to half the acidic liquid. Bring to room temperature.

7. **Mix the ingredients:**

    a. Beat the yolks and add the oil slowly—drop by drop—beating the mixture constantly until it becomes thick and creamy. To be really safe, stop pouring the oil at intervals of ten seconds or so for two or three seconds. When the emulsion firms up ("sets"), you can stop beating, but not before. You can then add oil at a faster rate—a tablespoon at a time—until half the oil is used.

    b. When half the oil is used, thin the mayonnaise with a little liquid. Add the liquid slowly, alternating between the liquid and the oil until all the oil and half the liquid are used. Save the remaining liquid to thin the mayonnaise later if necessary.

8. **Optional:** Add special ingredients to make a small sauce. (See pp. 166–167.)

9. **Make final adjustments.** If the sauce is *too thick*, add liquid. If the mixture is *too thin or separates* ("turns"):

    a. Rinse a bowl with warm water and dry it.

    b. Add 1 egg yolk to the bowl and beat until smooth.

    c. Slowly pour the mayonnaise into the egg yolk—one tablespoon at a time—beating the mixture constantly until it blends smoothly before adding more.

Repeat until all of the mayonnaise has been incorporated into the egg yolk.

10. **Cover and refrigerate the mayonnaise for at least one hour before serving.** The mayonnaise will thicken more as it chills. Keep well refrigerated for safety.

■

Vinaigrette Dressing

"Vinaigrette" is a general term for any dressing made with a lot of oil, a little acidic liquid, and flavorings. A classic vinaigrette dressing is one part vinegar and/or lemon juice to three or four parts oil, flavored with a little salt and pepper. That is what many cooks and books call "French dressing." Others call it "Italian dressing," and still others call it "oil and vinegar dressing." So it goes with the language of cookery. Whatever you might call it, vinaigrette dressing is used most often as a topping for salads. It also (See "Marinades", p. 102.) makes a wonderful marinade for vegetables, poultry, fish, and meats.

The Ingredients

"A fool with the oil, a miser with the vinegar" is an expression many cooks use as a guide for making basic vinaigrette dressing. Various recipes call for a ratio of one part acidic liquid to three parts, four parts, and even five parts oil. The ratio of oil to acidic liquid should be varied to suit your own taste as well as to accommodate the flavors of the oil and other ingredients.

□ *Oil*

Since oil is the most prominent ingredient, it should be selected for its flavor. Any vegetable oil will do, but olive oil of the highest quality ("extra virgin") and peanut oil are most preferred for their fine flavors. Tahini oil, walnut oil, and other special oils have become very popular as well. Any of these oils is expensive, however, so you might want to mix one of them with one of the less expensive but less flavorful oils such as corn oil, safflower oil, or soybean oil. If you use garlic or some herb flavoring for most of your dressings, it may be convenient to flavor an entire bottle of oil with it. Label the bottle so you won't use it for something in which that flavor is not desired.

□ *Acidic Liquid*

Vinegar is used most often as the acidic liquid, but lemon juice is another favorite. The two are often mixed together. Any vinegar will do, but wine vinegar is preferred for its more delicate flavor. For a milder flavor, substitute water, fruit juice, or white wine for up to half the acidic liquid.

(See "Acidic Liquids," pp. 284–287.)

□ *Seasonings*

Other than the primary ingredients—oil and vinegar—the only seasonings needed for a basic vinaigrette dressing are a little salt and pepper with perhaps a pinch of sugar or a drop of honey for sweetness. For better appearance, use white pepper with white vinegar, white or black pepper with red vinegar.

Some Small Sauces Made from a Vinaigrette Mother Sauce

You can add any number of flavorings to basic vinaigrette dressing to make one of the small sauces described below or another of your own invention.

Cheese dressing: Mix any of the semi-hard cheeses, especially Roquefort, Danish blue, or feta, with basic or creamy vinaigrette. The amount of cheese to use depends on the strength of the cheese and the consistency desired.

Creamy vinaigrette: Thicken a basic vinaigrette with up to an equal amount of cream, buttermilk, sour cream, plain yogurt, or pureed cottage cheese.

"French" dressing: To many cooks, this is simply a basic vinaigrette. To others, it is a basic vinaigrette to which some tomato product is added, usually catsup, chili sauce, or tomato juice. Other flavorings such as Worcestershire sauce, Tabasco sauce, and paprika add color and flavor, but a little of those flavorings goes a long way.

Herb dressing: You can flavor a basic or creamy vinaigrette dressing with one or more special herbs, naming the resulting dressing for the predominant herb used ("tarragon dressing," "dill dressing," "garlic dressing," and so forth). Depending on the strength of the herb(s), use about one tablespoon fresh or one teaspoon dried herb per half-cup of dressing. Use no more than three herbs at a time so that their flavors remain distinct.

(See "Herbs and Spices," pp. 308–311.)

"Italian" dressing: Like French dressing, this is defined differently by different people. Most cooks would probably say it is a basic vinaigrette dressing flavored with garlic, oregano, and other "Italian" seasonings.

Vegetable or fruit dressings: You can flavor basic or creamy vinaigrette dressing with a puree of a vegetable or fruit such as avocado, cucumber, onion, or orange. (Grated fruit peel adds to the flavor.) Choose the vegetable or fruit to go along with the food with which the dressing will be served.

How to Make It

About all there is to making any vinaigrette dressing is combining the ingredients and shaking them in a small bottle (called a *cruet*) or blending them in a food blender. Because there is no emulsifier to hold the ingredients in suspension, they will separate. Consequently, the dressing must be mixed well before each use.

Any dressing tastes better the fresher it is. It is best, therefore, to make dressings in small amounts and make them frequently. That also allows you to change the ingredients to provide interesting variety.

It is not necessary to refrigerate a vinaigrette dressing if it will be used within a week. The acid in the liquid will prevent bacterial growth. It will keep just as well and will be easier to pour if it is left at room temperature.

How to Make Vinaigrette Dressing

Model for one cup

Oil: 3/4 cup

Acidic liquid: 1/4 cup vinegar, lemon juice, or a combination of the two (for a milder flavor, substitute water or white wine for up to half the acidic liquid)

Seasonings: Dash of salt and pepper plus other flavorings, to taste

Vessel: 1 cruet, jar, or bowl

1. **Plan** 1 cup to last three or four people for three to five meals. The fresher the dressing, the better it will be, so make it in small amounts.
2. **Combine all ingredients and mix well.**
3. **Store** at room temperature for easier pouring.
4. **Mix well** before each use.

■

Cold Butter Sauce

Butter and margarine are both used to flavor foods as they cook as well as to top vegetables, pasta, rice, fish, poultry, and meats. Butter that is used to sauté onions, garlic, and other foods becomes infused with their flavors, which are then passed along with the flavor of the butter in whatever way it is used: hot for sautéing or basting foods, or cold as a topping called *cold butter sauce*. You can also add seasonings and other flavorings to cold butter to make cold butter sauce. If you use one cold butter sauce a great deal—lemon, garlic, or onion, for example—you will find it convenient to make it in larger amounts and refrigerate or freeze it to have on hand when you need it. That saves time when you're cooking and usually produces a better product because you take the time to make it right.

The Ingredients

The primary ingredient, of course, is butter, or, if you prefer, clarified butter or margarine. Add to any of these whatever flavorings you like. Garlic butter and lemon butter are probably the most common varieties, but have you ever

(See "Butter and Margarine," pp. 290–292.)

tried orange butter or butter flavored with fresh parsley, dill, or other herbs? What about butter flavored with ground walnuts or cheese? The number of possible ingredients and their combinations is enormous, and part of the fun of making flavored butters is experimenting with different ones.

How much flavoring do you add to the butter? That depends on the strength of the basic flavoring and the strength you want the butter to be. For a strong flavoring such as anchovy, you may need as little as one teaspoon per one-fourth to one-half cup of butter. For nuts or weaker herbs, you might use as much as equal parts of butter and flavoring. When using pureed fruits or fruit juices, remember that the grated outer rind of the fruit will add to the flavor.

How to Make It

Simply warm butter at room temperature until it softens. Beat it into a thin paste with a fork or whisk and then blend in one or more flavorings. If it is to be served as a topping, put the butter sauce in an attractive container, cover it, and refrigerate it for one hour or longer before serving. For individual servings, mold the butter into balls, patties, or cylinders and drop them into iced water to firm them quickly so they hold their shape. Cover and chill the butter for 1 hour or longer before serving.

How to Make Cold Butter Sauce

Model for four servings
  Butter or margarine: 8 Tbsp. (1 stick)
  Seasonings: See step 5, below
  Vessels: 1 mixing bowl or serving bowl

1. **Plan** 1 to 2 Tbsp. per serving.
2. **Prepare the butter:** Warm the butter at room temperature until it softens. Caution: If it becomes too warm, it might become oily.
3. **Prepare the seasonings:** Some popular ingredients are garlic, shallots, chives, onion, lemon, orange, parsley, or finely chopped nuts such as walnuts or almonds. Fresh herbs are not nearly as strong as dried ones. Chop fresh

herbs, fruits, vegetables, or nuts very fine. Fresh garlic can
be chopped very fine or pressed in a garlic press. It will be
better if it is sautéed or parboiled before being incorporated into the butter.

4. **Whip the butter:** Use a fork or whisk to whip the
softened butter into a thin paste.

5. **Season:** Add the prepared seasonings to taste.

6. **Prepare for serving:** Place the butter in a container
and cover. For individual servings, form balls, patties, or
cylinders and drop them into iced water to firm them up.

7. **Cover the butter and chill for 1 hour before serving.**

O*ther Facts of Life*

PART TWO

The "facts of life" to be discussed here might not be the ones you were thinking of. Like those other facts of life, though, they are very important and rather personal—so they are treated in more personal language than I have used so far.

If you've read Chapter Zero, you've seen a basic, functional definition of cooking. To illustrate why good cooks should master the topics in this part of the book, let's review that definition. The basic craft of cooking includes the following steps:

1. **Planning** what to cook and when to cook it. This step includes diet and nutrition (see Chapter Six) and the process of planning (see Chapter Seven).

2. **Selecting** foods and ingredients. This includes shopping (see Chapter Eight).

3. **Storing** foods and ingredients to preserve their flavor, texture, and appearance. Some general considerations for storing foods are given in Chapter Eight.

4. **Preparing** foods for a particular recipe or cooking method. This step requires kitchen tools (see Chapter Eleven).

5. **Combining** foods for special effects. This process not only requires kitchen tools, but also involves considerations of kitchen efficiency, sanitation, and safety, the topics of Chapter Ten.

6. **Seasoning** the food (see Part Three).

7. **Cooking** the food (see Part One).

8. **Serving** the food (see Chapter Nine).

9. **Dining** (see Chapter Nine).

10. **Cleaning up** (see Chapter Ten).

*E*ating Smart
Diet and Nutrition

CHAPTER SIX

The Smart Person's Diet
Good Nutrition: Four Basic Rules

*T*o serve meals that are healthy as well as tasty, good cooks need to know and account for basic principles of nutrition. After all, you don't want to make yourself or your family or guests fat or unhealthy with your cooking. Good nutrition is also fundamental to a topic that is usually more interesting to most people: diet and dieting.

Diets are a preoccupation for many people today, whether it's simply because they want to be slender and attractive or because they have high blood pressure or other health problems related to being overweight. What about all those lucky folk who never seem to have such health problems or who never have to worry about going on a diet to regain their figures? They don't get overweight in the first place. How do they do it? A large part of the answer is that they eat the right things and avoid eating the wrong things. In other words, they eat smart.

The Smart Person's Diet

Whether you want to lose weight or simply avoid getting to the point where losing weight is a concern, the best way to do it is to eat smart. Here's how.

1. Follow the four basic rules of good nutrition (pp. 189–197).
2. Don't overeat.
3. Eat a variety of foods in small to moderate amounts three to six times a day.
4. Stay away from pastries and desserts, sauces, junk foods, soft drinks, prepackaged "factory foods," and fast-food eateries.
5. Drink plenty of water instead of soft drinks and hard drinks.
6. Exercise.

Six easy steps—that's all there is to the smart person's diet. Like most good diets, this one sounds a lot like what is (or should be) common sense. Unlike many popular or fad diets, it is based on fundamental, sound, recognized principles of good nutrition. To better understand those principles of nutrition as well as the rules of the smart person's diet, you should first know some things about how your body uses the foods you eat.

Calories are a measure of the energy or fuel contained in foods. Your body requires a certain number of calories in order to function properly. If you take in more calories than you need, you gain weight. If you take in fewer calories than you need, or if you burn off excess calories through work or exercise, then you lose weight. There are exceptions to this simple scheme, of course, but for most normal adults that is how things work. A basic rule of the smart person's diet, then, is *don't overeat.* The table on the next page shows the calorie content of many common, high-calorie foods.

As a rule of thumb, figure that 3,500 calories equals one pound. If you want to lose a pound, you need to burn up 3,500 more calories than you consume, or consume 3,500 fewer calories than you use. Conversely, if you consume 3,500 calories more than you burn off, you'll gain a pound.

If you are a normal adult with no unusual health problems, your daily caloric intake should average around 1,500 to 2,000 calories if you are a woman, or 2,000 to 2,500 calories if you are a man. Most people who stay within this range most of the time will have no problems being overweight. If you do become overweight, reduce your daily caloric intake so that it falls within this range or slightly below. At no time, however, should you consume fewer than 1,000 calories a day. That isn't healthy.

It is possible to get all the calories you need in one day from a couple of fast food hamburgers, fries, and a milk shake. And you can easily consume that in only one meal. So should you "pig out" on one big meal and starve yourself the rest of the day? No! When you eat only one meal a day, your body converts those calories into fat, which it then stores to burn off slowly during the rest of the day when you are not eating. That is why you can get fat eating only one meal a day. That is also why so many starvation diets don't work, and why you should avoid eating only one meal a day even when you are trying to lose weight.

You will be a lot happier, a lot less hungry, and a lot healthier if instead of eating just one meal and then starving yourself for the rest of the day, you eat moderate amounts of low-calorie foods several times a day. Consequently, the smart person's diet calls for eating *three to six times a day.*

High-calorie foods

Food	Amount	Approximate Number of Calories
Desserts and treats		
pies and pastries	1 serving	250–400
ice cream	1 cup	250–400
doughnuts	1	150–300
cookies	1 small	50–100
Fats		
cooking oil	1 Tbsp.	115
shortening or lard	1 Tbsp.	115
butter or margarine	1 Tbsp.	100
Meats		
roasts or steaks	8 oz.	350–750
hamburger	4 oz.	200–250
ham	3 oz.	150–250
luncheon meats	2 oz.	150–200
sausage	2 oz.	150–200
bacon	2 slices	60–90
Milk products		
condensed milk	1 cup	1,000
cream	1 cup	500
sour cream	1 cup	400
evaporated milk	1 cup	350
half-and-half	1 cup	300
yogurt	1 cup	125–250
cheeses	1 oz.	50–100
Beverages		
milk shakes	12 oz.	300–500
liquor	1 1/2 oz.	100–250
beer	12 oz.	100–150
soft drinks	12 oz.	150
whole milk	8 oz.	150
wine	4 oz.	100

That way you won't be forcing your body to convert the food it does get into fat.

Eating smart involves *avoiding foods that contain large amounts of fats, sodium, and sugar.* Pastries and desserts, sauces, junk foods, soft drinks, prepackaged "factory foods," and foods served in most fast-food eateries are usually loaded with one or more of these, and quite often with all three. That is why smart people do what they can to avoid them.

Eating smart calls for *drinking plenty of water:* six to ten eight-ounce glasses a day. Water plays an important part in the diet by oxidizing with food, allowing your body to burn calories efficiently. Notice that what is called for is water, not just liquids of any kind. Soft drinks, alcoholic beverages, and even milk all contain too many calories and potentially harmful ingredients to be drunk in anything but moderate amounts if you want to stay trim. Looking at this another way, a single serving of anything other than water can supply as much as 5 to 10 percent of the total number of calories you should have in an entire day!

Finally, eating smart calls for getting a fair amount of *exercise*—at least enough exercise to burn off any calories your body doesn't need and to enable it to operate efficiently. The more fit your body is, the more efficiently it will burn the calories you take in. Flabby, overweight, out of shape bodies don't process foods very efficiently, and so to some degree they are part of the cause for maintaining their predicament. Trim and healthy bodies, on the other hand, are partly responsible for staying the way they are. Health begets health, it seems, but you have to work at it to have it.

Depending on your lifestyle and the amount of physical labor you do, you may or may not have to exercise more in order to stay fit and trim or to lose weight. A person who works hard out of doors certainly doesn't need much additional physical activity. Someone who sits behind a desk all day, on the other hand, probably does.

Many simple daily activities can be used as part of a basic exercise program without being strenuous or requiring special apparatus, or even taking too much time. Walking—walking briskly, that is—instead of riding in a car is something most of us can do a lot more of. Stairs also afford a wonderful opportunity for exercise. Two flights of stairs taken two at a time can burn as many calories as a brisk walk of one full city block! A few morning sit-ups and

Calories expended in various types of activities

Type of Activity	Calories per Hour
Sedentary activities, such as reading; writing; eating; watching television or movies; listening to the radio; sewing; playing cards; and typing, office work, and other activities done while sitting that require little or no arm movement.	80 to 100
Light activities, such as preparing and cooking food; doing dishes; dusting; handwashing small articles of clothing; ironing; walking slowly; personal care; office work and other activities done while standing that require some arm movement; and rapid typing and other activities done while sitting that are more strenuous.	110 to 160
Moderate activities, such as making beds; mopping and scrubbing; sweeping; light polishing and waxing; laundering by machine; light gardening and carpentry work; walking moderately fast; other activities done while standing that require moderate arm movement; and activities done while sitting that require more vigorous arm movement.	170 to 240
Vigorous activities, such as heavy scrubbing and waxing; handwashing large articles of clothing; hanging out clothes; stripping beds; walking fast; bowling; golfing; and gardening.	250 to 350
Strenuous activities, such as swimming; playing tennis; running; bicycling; dancing; skiing; and playing football.	350 or more

Source: *Psychology Applied to Modern Life,* 2nd ed., by Wayne Weiten. Monterey, Calif.: Brooks/Cole.

"touch me toes" will not only burn calories but firm up some neglected muscles as well. Even such daily activities as showering and toweling off can be an important part of a simple exercise program if they are done with vigor. In short, exercise can be a simple thing. The more of it you do, the better your body will look, and the more efficiently it will work for you.

Many people who lose weight on a diet program will pat themselves on the back, boast of how many pounds they have lost, and promptly return to their old way of life. The result, of course, is that those lost pounds come right back. If you lose weight by following the smart person's diet or

Are You Overweight?

A study released in 1978 by the National Center for Health Statistics indicated that fully one-third of the population in the United States is overweight! Are you?

The National Institutes of Health have determined that being overweight is hazardous to your health. Now if only someone could determine whether you're fat.

The NIH panel of experts, who recently proclaimed obesity a "killer disease" linked to cancer and heart problems, debated the merits of the familiar charts of "desirable weights." The charts are based on insurance companies' analyses of which policyholders lived longest. The chart made in 1959 was revised upward in 1983 to reflect changes in mortality statistics. Some of the NIH experts accept the 1983 chart, but others think it's too liberal. They suggest that a person with other risk factors—such as diabetes or hypertension—go by the 1959 chart.

Desirable weights for ages 25 to 59 (Metropolitan Life Insurance Company)

Height	1959 Table Men	1959 Table Women	1983 Table Men	1983 Table Women
4'10"		91–119		100–131
4'11"		93–122		101–134
5'0"		96–125		103–137
5'1"	107–136	99–128	123–145	105–140
5'2"	110–139	102–131	125–148	108–144
5'3"	113–143	105–135	127–151	111–148
5'4"	116–147	108–139	129–155	114–152
5'5"	119–151	111–143	131–159	117–156
5'6"	123–156	115–147	133–163	120–160
5'7"	127–161	119–151	135–167	123–164
5'8"	131–165	123–155	137–171	126–167
5'9"	135–169	127–160	139–175	129–170
5'10"	139–174	131–165	141–179	132–173
5'11"	143–179	135–170	144–183	135–176
6'0"	147–184		147–187	
6'1"	151–189		150–192	
6'2"	155–194		153–197	
6'3"	159–199		157–202	

continued

Reubin Andres faults *both* charts. Andres, clinical director of the Gerontology Research Center of the National Institute of Aging, did his own analysis of the insurance data to see who lived longest. He was surprised to find that ideal weights were the same for men and women. More important, the weights rose with age.

Recommended weights for both sexes (Gerontology Research Center)

Height	1985 Table by Age				
	20–29 yr	30–39 yr	40–49 yr	50–59 yr	60–69 yr
4'10"	84–111	92–119	99–127	107–135	115–142
4'11"	87–115	95–123	103–131	111–139	119–147
5'0"	90–119	98–127	106–135	114–143	123–152
5'1"	93–123	101–131	110–140	118–148	127–157
5'2"	96–127	105–136	113–144	122–153	131–163
5'3"	99–131	108–140	117–149	126–158	135–168
5'4"	102–135	112–145	121–154	130–163	140–173
5'5"	106–140	115–149	125–159	134–168	114–179
5'6"	109–144	119–154	129–164	138–174	148–184
5'7"	112–148	122–159	133–169	143–179	153–190
5'8"	116–153	126–163	137–174	147–184	158–196
5'9"	119–157	130–168	141–179	151–190	162–201
5'10"	122–162	134–173	145–184	156–195	167–207
5'11"	126–167	137–178	149–190	160–201	172–213
6'0"	129–171	141–183	153–195	165–207	177–219
6'1"	133–176	145–188	157–200	169–213	182–225
6'2"	137–181	149–194	162–206	174–219	187–232
6'3"	141–186	153–199	166–212	179–225	192–238
6'4"	144–191	157–205	171–218	184–231	197–244

All weight ranges are in pounds, for a person not wearing clothing or shoes.

Adapted from *Science*, May 1985.

Confused? Here are two other guidelines—one complicated, one nice and simple.

First the complicated. Multiply your weight (in pounds) by 703. Divide the answer by your height (in inches). Now divide that answer again by your height. The result is your Body Mass Index, which the NIH panel regards as a good indicator of fatness. A value of 20 to 25 is often considered

continued

normal. If it's between 26 and 30, many experts advise losing weight. A value over 30 is commonly considered a sign of "medically significant obesity," a condition of perhaps 34 million Americans.

Now for the simple test. Measure the circumference of your waist and your hips. Studies have shown that having a pot belly is more dangerous than having fat in the lower body. The risk of heart disease goes up if a woman's waist-to-hips ratio is above .8, and if a man's waist is bigger than his hips.

some other plan, the way to keep it off is by maintaining a consistently smart lifestyle. Just practice the six rules of the smart person's diet and don't stray from them too often, and your health and figure will both be better off. Maintain a balanced diet of the right foods in moderate amounts, and remember such slogans as: "All things in moderation," "Booze and beer may be great, but they sure do add weight," and "A moment of abstinence is worth a week of dieting."

Good Nutrition: Four Basic Rules

Controlling calories alone does not a good diet make. Eating smart requires accounting for the basic principles of good nutrition. All you need to know is covered in four basic rules:

1. Establish and maintain a balanced diet.
2. Minimize consumption of fats, salts, and sugars.
3. Eat plenty of fresh fruits, vegetables, and whole-grain cereals.
4. Eat a varied diet.

Let's consider each of these rules in detail.

1. Establish and Maintain a Balanced Diet

In essence, a good diet should include the following each day: milk and milk products; fruits and vegetables; meat, poultry, fish, eggs, or other high-protein foods; bread and cereal products (preferably enriched or whole grain). These are the "basic four" food groups that for almost twenty-five years served as a fundamental guide to good nutrition. However, studies have shown that many of the foods in the basic four groups contain levels of fats, cholesterol, salts, sugars, and other ingredients that are bad for your health. The "New American Eating Guide" shown in the accompanying table was developed to account for such considerations, and now may be the best guide to follow for maintaining the healthiest diet.

2. Minimize Consumption of Fats, Salts, and Sugars

Today, when doctors and nutritionists in the United States speak of "malnutrition," more often than not they are referring to *excessive* intake of the wrong things—calories, sugars, fats (especially saturated fats), salt and other high-sodium products, chemical preservatives, and cholesterol. The "in moderation" and "now and then" columns in the New American Eating Guide show many of the sources of these substances. Besides contributing to overweight, excessive amounts of fats, salts, and sugars are said to contribute to such health problems as heart disease, high blood pressure, strokes, and even cancer. In other words, *not* eating smart can kill you.

It's not an easy job for most of us to regulate our consumption of these things, if only because we have little control over what goes into much of the food we eat. As a nation, we eat quite a few of our meals in restaurants, and restaurants (especially fast-food eateries) serve a great many fried foods as well as other foods containing large amounts of salts, sugars, and fats. When we eat at home, more and more of us have come to rely on prepackaged, processed "factory foods" such as frozen dinners, canned vegetables, and dried prepared foods and ingredients from boxes. Almost half of all the foods sold by grocers in the United States today are processed, and most of them contain large amounts of salts, sugars, and fats. Just read a few labels on food packages and you will learn just how true this is.

(See "How to Read a Label," p. 215.)

What to do? For one thing, you can *eat defensively.* Avoid high-calorie, low-nutrition junk foods such as candy, potato chips, and soft drinks. When you eat away from home, try to avoid foods that are high in calories, fat, and sodium, such as the fried foods that make up the vast majority of items sold in fast-food eateries. When you eat at home, be attentive to the ingredients in prepackaged, processed foods and use them with restraint. Choose other methods of cooking in preference to frying, and when you

New American eating guide

	Anytime	In Moderation	Now and Then
Group 1: beans, grains, and nuts (Four or more servings per day)	bread and rolls (whole grain) bulgur dried beans and peas (legumes) lentils oatmeal pasta, whole wheat rice, brown rye bread sprouts whole grain hot and cold cereals whole-wheat matzoh	cornbread[8] flour tortilla[8] granola cereals [1 or 2] hominy grits[8] macaroni and cheese[1, (6), 8] matzoh[8] nuts[3] pasta, except whole wheat[8] peanut butter[3] pizza[6, 8] refined, unsweetened cereals[8] refried beans, commercial,[1] or homemade in oil[2] seeds[3] soybeans[2] tofu[2] waffles or pancakes with syrup[5, (6), 8] white bread and rolls[8] white rice[8]	croissant[4, 8] doughnut (yeast leavened)[3 or 4, 5, 8] presweetened breakfast cereals[5, 8] sticky buns[1 or 2, 5, 8] stuffing (made with butter[4, (6), 8]

[1]Moderate fat, saturated.
[2]Moderate fat, unsaturated.
[3]High fat, unsaturated.
[4]High fat, saturated.
[5]High in added sugar.

[6]High in salt or sodium.
[(6)]May be high in salt or sodium.
[7]High in cholesterol.
[8]Refined grains.
[9]Vegetarians: Nutrients in these foods can be obtained by eating more foods in groups 1, 2, and 3.

"Anytime" foods contain less than 30 percent of calories from fat and are usually low in salt and sugar. Most of the "now and then" foods contain at least 50 percent of calories from fat—*and* a large amount of saturated fat. Foods to eat "in moderation" have medium amounts of total fat and low to moderate amounts of saturated fat or large amounts of total fat that is mostly unsaturated. Foods meeting the standards for fat, but containing large amounts of salt or sugar, are usually moved into a more restricted category, as are refined cereal products. For example, pickles have little fat, but are so high in sodium that they fall in the "now and then" category.

Important: To cut down on salt intake, choose varieties of the foods listed here that do not have added salt, such as no-salt cottage cheese, rather than the regular varieties. The guide is not appropriate for individuals needing very low-salt diets.

continued

New American eating guide (continued)

	Anytime	In Moderation	Now and Then
Group 2: fruits and vegetables (four or more servings per day)	all fruits and vegetables except those listed at right applesauce (unsweetened) fruit juices (unsweetened) potatoes, white or sweet vegetable juices (unsalted)	avocado[3] cole slaw[3] cranberry sauce (canned)[5] dried fruit french fries, homemade in vegetable oil,[2] commercial[1] fried eggplant (vegetable oil)[2] fruit juices, sweetened[5] fruits canned in syrup[5] gazpacho[2,(6)] glazed carrots[5,(6)] guacamole[3] potatoes au gratin[1,(6)] vegetables canned with salt[6] vegetable juices, salted[6]	coconut[4] pickles[6]
Group 3: milk products (children, 3 to 4 servings per day; adults, 2 servings per day)	buttermilk made from skim milk lassi (low-fat yogurt and fruit juice drink) low-fat cottage cheese low-fat milk, 1 percent milkfat low-fat yogurt non-fat dry milk skim milk skim milk and banana shake skim milk cheeses	cocoa made with skim milk[5] cottage cheese, regular, 4 percent milk fat[1] frozen low-fat yogurt[5] ice milk[5] low-fat milk, 2 percent milk fat[1] low-fat yogurt, sweetened[5] mozzarella cheese, part skim-type only[1,(6)]	cheesecake[4,5] cheese fondue[4,(6)] cheese soufflé[4,(6),7] eggnog[1,5,7] hard cheeses: bleu, brick, Camembert, cheddar, Muenster, Swiss[4,(6)] ice cream[4,5] processed cheeses[4,6] whole milk[4] whole milk yogurt[4]
Group 4: poultry, fish, meat, and eggs (two servings per day)[9]	fish cod flounder gefilte fish[(6)] haddock	fish (drained well, if canned) fried fish[1 or 2] herring[3,6] mackerel, canned[2,(6)] salmon, pink, canned[2,(6)]	poultry fried chicken, commercially prepared[4] egg cheese omelet[4,7]

192

Anytime	In Moderation	Now and Then
halibut	sardines[2,(6)]	egg yolk or whole egg
perch	shrimp[7]	(about 3 per week)[3,7]
pollock	tuna, oil packed[2,(6)]	red meats
rockfish	poultry	bacon[4,(6)]
shellfish, except shrimp	chicken liver, baked or	beef liver, fried[1,7]
sole	broiled,[7] (just one)	bologna[4,6]
tuna, water packed[(6)]	fried chicken, homemade	corned beef[4,6]
egg products	in vegetable oil[3]	ground beef[4]
egg whites only	chicken or turkey, boiled,	ham, trimmed well[1,6]
poultry	baked, or roasted (with	hot dogs[4,6]
chicken or turkey—boiled,	skin)[2]	liverwurst[4,6]
baked, or roasted (no	red meats (trimmed of all	pig's feet[4]
skin)	outside fat)	salami[4,6]
	flank steak[1]	sausage[4,6]
	leg or loin of lamb[1]	spareribs[4]
	pork shoulder or loin,	untrimmed red meats[4]
	lean[1]	
	round steak or ground	
	round[1]	
	rump roast[1]	
	sirloin steak, lean[1]	
	veal[1]	

[1]Moderate fat, saturated.
[2]Moderate fat, unsaturated.
[3]High fat, unsaturated.
[4]High fat, saturated.
[5]High in added sugar.

[6]High in salt or sodium.
[(6)]May be high in salt or sodium.
[7]High in cholesterol.
[8]Refined grains.
[9]Vegetarians: Nutrients in these foods can be obtained by eating more foods in groups 1, 2, and 3.

"Anytime" foods contain less than 30 percent of calories from fat and are usually low in salt and sugar. Most of the "now and then" foods contain at least 50 percent of calories from fat—*and* a large amount of saturated fat. Foods to eat "in moderation" have medium amounts of total fat and low to moderate amounts of saturated fat or large amounts of total fat that is mostly unsaturated. Foods meeting the standards for fat, but containing large amounts of salt or sugar, are usually moved into a more restricted category, as are refined cereal products. For example, pickles have little fat, but are so high in sodium that they fall in the "now and then" category.

Important: To cut down on salt intake, choose varieties of the foods listed here that do not have added salt, such as no-salt cottage cheese, rather than the regular varieties. The guide is not appropriate for individuals needing very low-salt diets.

Reprinted from *Nutrition Action Healthletter*, which is available from the Center for Science in the Public Interest, 1501 16 St., NW, Washington, DC 20036, for $19.95 for 10 issues. Copyright January 1979.

do fry, use cholesterol-free oils instead of animal fats. Finally, use as little salt and sugar as you can. You'll find that many foods taste just as good—or even better—when you reduce the amount of salt and sugar you use in preparing them.

Perhaps if you know more about fats, salts, and sugars, you will have a better understanding of the reasons why you need to control your consumption of them. Let's consider each in detail.

□ *Fats*

(See "Cooking in Fats," pp. 45–48.)

At nine calories per gram, fat has more than twice as many calories as proteins or carbohydrates do! In the United States, the average person gets 40 percent of his or her daily calories from fats. The American Heart Association has recommended that that amount be no more than 30 percent, and many doctors recommend that it be no more than 20 percent. The most common sources of fats are fried foods, meats, butter, margarine, cooking oils, milk and milk products, and combination foods such as pastries, sauces, and desserts in which fats are used.

More than any other food group, fats cause overweight. Overweight is a major health problem in its own right, but fats are associated with other health problems as well. A great deal of medical evidence has been compiled associating fats directly with high blood pressure and heart disease. Recent medical evidence has also linked fats to cancer—particularly breast cancer, cancer of the colon, and prostate cancer—regardless of the type of fats or whether they contain cholesterol. As far as cancer is concerned, consumption of fats of all kinds increases your risk of developing it.

There are three types of fats: saturated, polyunsaturated, and monosaturated. Saturated fats do you the greatest harm. They contain cholesterol, and it is cholesterol that medical scientists believe can build up in your blood vessels until they literally become clogged. That leads to such medical problems as hardening of the arteries, high blood pressure, strokes, and heart attacks. A ten-year study (costing some $150 million) conducted by the National Heart, Lung, and Blood Institute concluded the following about cholesterol:

1. Heart disease is linked directly to the level of cholesterol in the blood.
2. Lowering cholesterol levels markedly reduces the incidence of fatal heart attacks.

Focus on Fats

Saturated fats are contained in animal products (butter, cheese, cream, eggs, milk, meat fat), shortening, margarine, poultry fat, oysters and other shellfish, chocolate, lard, and some vegetable oils, notably coconut oil and palm oil. (Many people believe that *all* vegetable oils are low in saturated fats and cholesterol. They are wrong.)

Polyunsaturated fats are believed to offset the effects of cholesterol and reduce its presence in the blood. In fact, recent studies have suggested that eating a great deal of sea fish (other than shellfish) can lessen the risks of heart problems because the fats in fish are polyunsaturated. Polyunsaturated fats are also found in oils from many vegetables, and in products such as shortening and margarine made from them. The oils highest in polyunsaturated fat content are safflower oil and corn oil, in that order. Remember, not all vegetable oils are polyunsaturated. Coconut oil and palm oil have about twice as much saturated fat content as an equal amount of beef.

Monosaturated fats do not contribute to and may take away from cholesterol in the blood. Olive oil and peanut oil are the two most common monosaturated fats.

3. The more you lower cholesterol and fat in your diet, the more you reduce your risk of heart disease.

But cholesterol is all around us. Some of its sources are hydrogenated fats and shortenings, animal fats, some vegetable oils such as coconut oil and palm oil, and any cooked or processed foods in which these products are used. Meats, baked products (cakes, cookies, pastries, doughnuts, biscuits, croissants, and so on), and the fried foods served in fast-food eateries all are common sources of cholesterol.

You can reduce your consumption of fats by substituting chicken or fish for red meats and by minimizing or eliminating your consumption of fried foods and baked goods. You can reduce your cholesterol intake by substituting polyunsaturated or monosaturated fats for saturated fats whenever possible. The table on page 196 gives some specific suggestions.

□ *Salts and Sugars*

Nutritionists may disagree on many things, but this is one issue on which there is virtually no disagreement: we in the United States eat entirely too much salt and other sodium products as well as sugar. A select committee of

Substitutes for survival

Foods High in Fats	Substitutes
Dairy products	
milk and cheese products	Low-fat milk and cheese; "imitation" cheese
sour cream	low-fat cottage cheese smoothed in a food blender; plain yogurt
Eggs	
whole eggs or egg yolks[1]	egg whites alone (two whites equal one egg)
Fats	
rendered meat fats, vegetable oils or shortening with saturated or hydrogenated fats	polyunsaturated oils such as safflower oil and corn oil; monosaturated vegetable oils such as peanut oil and olive oil
Meats	
bacon, sausage	Canadian-style bacon; breakfast beef
fatty red meats[2]	lean red meats, chicken, fish

[1]Eat no more than three egg yolks per week, including those used in sauces, mayonnaise, pastries, and prepackaged food products.
[2]Eat no more than six ounces of red meats per day.

the United States Senate in 1977 recommended that as a nation we should cut down on salt and sugar consumption by half! Even that amount would not satisfy many nutritionists. Both salt and sugar contribute to overweight—sugar because of its calories, salt because it causes the body to retain fluids. Salt and other sodium products also raise blood pressure, and that contributes to many problems, including heart disease.

As with fats, though, it is virtually impossible to avoid sugar and salt altogether, even if you try. It is really insidious how they slip into our diets without our being aware of them. For example, some non-dairy creamers are more than half sugar. Mayonnaise and mustard—and the foods that use them as ingredients—contain large amounts of sodium and sugar as well as egg yolks, with their cholesterol. Catsup and meat sauces are loaded with sugar and sodium. Many prepackaged "factory foods" list sugar or salt, or some other sodium product, in the top half of their (See "How to Read a Label," p. 215.) ingredients. Just read a few labels and you will see.

If you really want to cut down on sugar, salt, and sodium, the best place to begin is with junk foods: candy, soft drinks, potato chips and other snack foods, presweetened cereals, and prepared foods and ingredients in boxes. They may have lots of taste (lots of calories, too), but they don't have much nutritional value. Next, try to avoid buying any canned, bottled, or processed foods in which sugar, salt, MSG, sodium, soy sauce, glucose, fructose, and so on appear in the top one-fourth to one-half of the list of ingredients. Beyond those two major things, many nutritionists and dieticians recommend that we simply leave the salt and sugar off the dining table and minimize their use in cooking.

3. Eat Plenty of Fresh Fruits, Vegetables, and Whole-Grain Cereals

This is one recommendation most people will really like. If you enjoy snacking between meals, eat fresh or dried fruits and raw vegetables instead of sweets and junk food. They are low in calories and quite tasty. Besides, they are good for you. The American Cancer Society, for example, has stated that diets containing a good bit of fruits, vegetables, and whole-grain cereals may be good protection against cancer. Most of us don't eat enough of these foods.

Fruits and whole grains are both easily accounted for. At breakfast, fresh fruits and fruit juices go well with whole-grain cereals and bread or toast made of whole grains. For lunch, pack a sandwich made with whole-grain bread and accompany it with some crunchy raw vegetables or fresh fruit. Your lunch will be nourishing, and "brown-bagging" it will keep you out of fattening restaurants and fast-food eateries. For desserts, substitute fresh fruits for pies, cakes, puddings, and pastries.

Vegetables are not so easily accounted for as fruits and whole grains, especially if you eat out a great deal. Most restaurants seem to think the spectrum of vegetables begins with salad bars and ends with baked or French-fried potatoes, with nothing in between. Neither man nor woman can live well by potatoes and salad bars alone, so it is best, when you can, to try to have at least one meal a day at which two or more vegetables are featured.

4. Eat a Varied Diet

The greater your choice of foods, the greater your chances for getting all the nutrients your body needs. That statement just about sums up almost all you need to know about nutrition and eating smart.

(See "Just Desserts," p. 232.)

*P*lanning
The Key to Success

CHAPTER SEVEN

Planning for Nutrition
Planning for Variety
Planning for Using Leftovers
Planning Timing

*P*lanning—good meal planning, especially—really begins at the end. You must know *what* you want in order to get it, and you must know *when* you want it in order to have it on time. When it comes to cooking, knowing what you want and when you want it means planning for nutrition, variety, what to do with leftovers, and timing. All of this requires practice and experience as much as knowledge; there is no magic formula or easy path.

Planning for Nutrition

Many people eat or cook only what they like without adequate regard for what might be good or bad for their figures or their health. Unless your meal planning accounts for the fundamentals of health and nutrition, though, you might end up having to go on a diet or otherwise change your eating habits for health reasons. The principles of nutrition that should be accounted for in meal planning are very simple. They are just the four basic principles described in Chapter Six: (1) establish and maintain a balanced diet; (2) minimize consumption of fats, salts, and sugars; (3) eat plenty of fresh fruits, vegetables, and whole-grain cereals; (4) eat a varied diet.

Personal tastes and preferences for foods vary enormously and simply cannot be accounted for in any menu guide. Here, though, are some considerations and suggestions for planning your menus so they will be healthy and nutritious. These suggestions reflect conventions that are common throughout the United States.

Breakfast

Personal preferences for the day's first meal range from a "cuppa coffee ana cigarette" to "bacon 'n eggs with lots of biscuits and grits with redeye gravy." Unfortunately, either of these extremes is likely to be unhealthy. You should consider taking a more moderate and smarter course. A breakfast that conforms to the smart person's diet will provide some important basic foods that many people are likely to neglect. Here is an example of a good, nutritious breakfast:

· Fresh fruit and/or juice
· Whole-grain cereal and/or whole-grain toast or muffins
· Milk (preferably low-fat)
· Beverage (preferably decaffeinated)

Eating light, low-calorie breakfasts such as this one leaves room to accommodate richer, higher-calorie foods during the rest of the day. For a varied breakfast menu, serve different kinds of fresh fruits as they come in season. Serve cold cereals on some mornings and hot cereals on others. An occasional breakfast of bacon and eggs, French toast, or pancakes will add variety and will be a welcome treat because it is unusual.

The "Heavy" Meal

The day's heavy meal is the one you will spend the greatest amount of time and effort planning and preparing. Indeed, for most of us it is and should be a major part of our social lives as well as the principal source of daily nutrients. It deserves to receive a great deal of attention.

Whether you serve your heavy meal in a formal or an informal style, at midday or in the evening, it will usually include the following:

· Soup (optional)
· Salad (optional)
· Main dish: meat, fish, or poultry
· One or two side dishes: vegetables or foods called vegetables
· Bread
· Beverage
· Dessert (optional)

Such a meal can be heavy indeed, especially with fats and calories, unless you plan carefully. In particular, it is important to balance the heavy meal against the other meals and snacks of the day. For example, if you have pancakes or waffles for breakfast, a milk shake for lunch, or pastries, snack foods, or soft drinks in between, then it would be best to eat smaller portions in the heavy meal and to do without dessert. That does not mean, however, that if you starve yourself all day you can stuff yourself during the heavy meal. Maintaining a balanced diet includes distributing the amount of food you eat throughout the day.

The "Light" Meal

More than one heavy meal in a day isn't good for either your health or your figure—too many calories, to say nothing of fats, salts, and sugars. To make the heavy meal healthier and more enjoyable, try to balance it by eating lighter, less fattening foods for your breakfast and light meal of the day.

Soups, salads, and sandwiches are perfect for light meals. They are great sources of nutrients and are usually (but not always) low in calories. If they contain large amounts of fats or salt, however, or if you eat too much of them, they can be bad for you. Sandwiches, especially, are potential sources of fats and cholesterol. Hamburgers, liverwurst, and many processed luncheon meats can contain large amounts of both. Fried sandwiches, french fries, soft drinks, milk shakes, and other common accompaniments served up in fast-food eateries are also major sources of fats, sugar, and salt. You don't need to eliminate such foods from your diet altogether, but you should enjoy them infrequently and always in moderation.

(See the "New American Eating Guide," p. 191.)

Snacks

Believe it or not, many nutritionists have come to favor snacking between meals. The body functions best if it is refueled frequently in small amounts rather than in the traditional three meals per day, let alone in two meals or one major meal. If you are hungry, snack. Just snack on nutritious, low-calorie foods such as fruits and fresh vegetables in moderate amounts, and then compensate for them by eating less at the day's heavy and light meals.

Planning for Variety

Whatever the meal, variety is important: variety in tastes, variety in colors, variety in textures. Even if the meal consists of the best of foods all prepared well, it will be dull and uninteresting if the foods are all alike. You wouldn't want to serve a main meal of potato soup, chicken casserole made with white sauce, and vanilla ice cream, for example. It would have no crunch, no color, no pizzazz—in short, no variety. Similarly, a meal of foods all cooked the same way—all fried foods or casseroles, for instance—won't win much applause in most homes.

Variety within meals is not difficult to achieve. Select foods for variety of color, texture, nutritional value, and method of preparation. Fresh vegetables, rice, or pasta are good accompaniments for meats, fish, or poultry. If two of these accompaniments are used, then one should be green and the other white or yellow to provide a balance of color as well as nutrition. Dark beef goes nicely with white potatoes or cauliflower, while fish or chicken looks better with broccoli or green beans. Crunchy vegetables such as peas or carrots go well with the softer textures of meats, fish, poultry, casseroles, and stews. The same is true of an accompanying crisp, fresh bread or a garden salad. In terms of cooking methods, a main dish prepared according to a basic cooking method can be balanced by a casserole, soufflé, or other dish cooked by one of the combination methods described in Chapter Three.

Adding garnishes is another way to create variety within a meal and dress up foods. Grated cheeses and spices such as paprika and freshly ground pepper sprinkled lightly over main or side dishes contribute their own special colors and flavors while making the dishes look more interesting. Chopped fresh vegetables, such as parsley, scallions, and sweet bell peppers, also make attractive garnishes that add flavor, texture, and color to foods. Sliced tomatoes or other fruits such as peaches on a small piece of lettuce give a dish an accent of color. None of these things is fancy, necessarily. All they involve is a little foresight and planning with variety in mind.

(See "Garnishes," pp. 74–75.)

Variety across meals is at least as important as variety within them. "Ah, shucks! Meat loaf again?!" Exclamations such as this are all too common in too many homes. Many cooks do get into a rut with one basic food, particularly with a type of main dish. Others use the same cooking method too frequently—constantly serving fried foods or casseroles, for example. To avoid such ruts, experiment with different cooking methods and try to plan your meals a week or even two weeks in advance, accounting for leftovers as well as meals that might be eaten away from home. That kind of advance planning is a difficult thing for many people to do, especially those who have families. Even if you cannot do it all the time, however, careful planning will go a long way toward creating healthful and appealing variety in your meals.

Planning for Using Leftovers

No matter how well you plan your meals, you are likely to have leftovers. That can be bad if all you do is either throw them out or store and reheat them in ways that make them look and taste like leftovers. You can serve leftovers with imagination and flair, however, simply by using them in a dish made with one of the methods of combination cookery described in Chapter Three. You can use leftover turkey or chicken pieces, for example, to make sandwiches, casseroles, croquettes, hash, quiches, or even soufflés. Then the remaining bones can be boiled to make broth for soups. Beef can be used to make sandwiches, hash, croquettes, soups, and casseroles. Vegetables of almost any kind can be frozen and saved for making soup. You can also use vegetables to make fritters or as a filler in casseroles, hash, or croquettes.

(See "Old-Fashioned Stock Pot Soup," p. 110.)

If you plan meals a week in advance, you can account for leftovers more easily. Simply plan two or three main dishes for alternate days using meat, poultry, and fish cooked and served by different basic cooking methods. For example, try having roast beef on Sunday, baked chicken on Wednesday, and broiled fish on Friday. Store the leftovers in the refrigerator or freezer and use them to make combination dishes such as croquettes, casseroles, or soups to serve as main or side dishes on Tuesday, Thursday, and Saturday. Even with leftovers, every meal for a week can be different, and they can all be good if you plan them right.

Planning Timing

The first thing you need to settle in planning meal timing is what you should do last. Working backwards, in other words, is what timing is all about. Know when you want to serve the food and figure the preparation time backwards, giving your greatest attention to the part of the meal that will require the longest time to prepare and cook.

As soon as you have planned your menu, write down how long each dish will take to cook. Then figure the time that each dish should begin cooking. Working back from that, estimate the amount of time required to prepare the food for cooking (to "prep" it, as professional cooks say). The prepping sometimes requires the most time and work, but prep times are seldom accounted for in recipes. The times given in recipes usually are based only on the amount of time required to actually cook the food.

To be really safe and to control your timing best, prepare as many dishes as you can ahead of time, either all the way or as much as you can. That way when the unexpected occurs, as it usually does, you'll have time to account for it.

Three Tips for Timing

1. Prepare foods in advance. The best way to time an individual dish or an entire meal is to prepare as much of it as possible well before the time it is to be served. Desserts usually require a great deal of work as well as special cooking conditions and often require time to cool. Make them up hours or even a day or two in advance so that they don't get in the way when you prepare the rest of the meal. Clean vegetables before storing so they will be ready when needed. Casseroles and braised dishes not only are easier to account for if they are prepared and cooked in advance, but will actually taste better if they are cooked, cooled, and reheated for serving. Foods to be fried in a dry coating may be made up in advance and refrigerated for as long as two days before they are cooked.

2. Measure ingredients in advance. Many dishes (cakes and pastries, especially) are much easier to put together if all the ingredients are measured into individual containers before the mixing begins. The mixing can then be done in a minimum of time with very little mess or bother. This saves a great deal of rereading the recipe as you go, too.

3. Prepare and store basic ingredients in bulk for later use. There are a number of things used almost daily by many cooks that require a good deal of time to prepare. It takes little more time to make them up in larger amounts and store them for quick and easy use later on. Here is a list of some of the most common ingredients that can be prepared and stored:

· *Boiled chicken pieces:* Used in casseroles, salads, and sandwiches.
· *Broth:* Used in soups and sauces, and as a liquid for cooking vegetables and other foods.
· *Chopped or diced onions:* Used to flavor sauces and foods.
· *Clarified butter:* Used for sautéing, as a topping for fish and shellfish, and for making sauces.
· *Roux:* Used to thicken liquids to make sauces.
· *Tomato sauce:* Used as an ingredient in stuffed cabbage or peppers, and as a serving sauce for pasta dishes.
· *White sauce:* Whether alone or as the mother sauce for many small sauces, used in casserole dishes or as a topping for vegetables, poultry, meats, and fish. (Note: Do not freeze white or brown sauces made with flour; they are likely to separate if they are frozen.)

Even the most inexperienced cook can estimate the total time needed for the entire process of preparing, cooking, and serving a meal. To avoid disaster, though, allow more than enough time to account for everything and then add fifteen to thirty minutes to that. You'll then be likely to come out all right even if things don't go exactly as planned. The accompanying box contains some other tips to help you plan your timing.

Shopping
A Guide to Saving Money, Time, and Aggravation

CHAPTER EIGHT

*S*hopping is fundamental to the cooking process, and yet it is seldom discussed in books. It doesn't require much knowledge to do, but a little consideration and thought will enable you to do it well and save time, money, and considerable aggravation.

A Guide to Smart Shopping

Smart shopping can be summed up in the ten basic steps listed below. The rest of this chapter develops these ideas in detail.

1. Pick one food store and stick with it.
2. Plan one major shopping trip each week, and use a shopping list.
3. Save and use discount coupons for foods you need.
4. Compare prices and read labels.
5. Ask questions of other shoppers and store personnel.
6. Avoid buying anything except what you have planned to buy.
7. Use store brands whenever possible.
8. Look for unadvertised specials.
9. Buy nonperishable items in bulk when they are on sale.
10. Store foods properly as soon as you get them home.

Two Ways to Shop

If you are like most people, you want to get the most for your money with the least amount of work. To do that, you should choose an efficient way to shop.

One way to shop is to go to the store whenever you need something and buy what looks good or whatever you think you need at the time. This is the "I'll know what I want when I see it" school of thought, and a lot of people practice it regularly. It is also the kind of shopping that usually leaves shoppers coming out of the store a lot poorer with many things they don't need and quite often without the things they went shopping for to begin with. This is the result of what is known as "impulse buying," and every store does what it can to encourage it. That's what those imposing and tempting displays at the ends of aisles and at checkout counters are for.

Studies have shown that people who shop without a shopping list are more susceptible to impulse buying and buy more than they ordinarily would. All too frequently, what they buy are things they don't really need and may never even use. Any possible advantages to be had from this kind of shopping are far outweighed by its many disadvantages.

The second and much more practical way to shop is to plan ahead. Know what you want before you go to the store, and stick to your shopping list.

Don't wait until it's time to go to the store to make your list. As you work in your kitchen, keep notes of foods and staple items that are getting low or have run out. When it's time to shop, add to that list the things you will need for the next week or so. Try to account for the specific dishes you'll be preparing (including leftovers), checking your recipes to be sure your list is complete. Having everything you need when you need it will save a great deal of aggravation, not to mention extra trips to the store.

Plan to shop when you're not hungry. When you're hungry, everything looks good. Hungry shoppers are likely to buy more than they need, especially tempting foods such as relishes, nuts, desserts, and other "goodies" that aren't good for their diet.

Where to Shop

Some shoppers arm themselves with coupons and go from store to store hunting down specials and stocking up on anything and everything that looks like a bargain. They might save some money that way, but is it really worth the effort? Reading all the store ads in newspapers and running from one store to another involves a lot of work and time, to say nothing of the automobile expense. Even at that, such shoppers aren't always getting bargains. "A bargain is no bargain if you don't need it," the saying goes, and a lot of bargain shoppers end up buying things they don't need and probably won't use.

Instead of shopping at different stores from trip to trip just to take advantage of special offers, you will probably do better selecting one store and sticking with it. By shopping in one store, you will come to know the times when it will be less crowded, and that will save you time and aggravation. You will also get to know the systems used at your store, and that will enable you to save money over and above the advertised bargains. Most major food stores have their own special bargain sections, house brands, and unadvertised specials, and the more you know about how your store operates, the more money you can save.

There are several things to consider when selecting your store. Quality should be a primary consideration—quality of produce, meats, and other fresh foods, especially. Other things to look at are overall prices, quality and price of house brands, and types of weekly specials. Convenient location, helpfulness of store personnel, attractiveness of the food displays, and other niceties are all important too. Above all, shop in a store you can be happy with so that you will be able to stick with it.

Comparison Shopping

Comparison shopping is an easy and effective way to save money and ensure that you get what you want. As you shop take some time to compare different versions of the items on your shopping list. Compare prices, compare quality, compare dates, compare sizes, and compare labels.

Compare Prices

Not only brand products, but basic foods such as milk and eggs often vary widely in price. For example, the same shelf might have four different brands of eggs, all the same size and grade. Their prices, though, can vary by as much as 40 percent! "Eggs is eggs," and it isn't likely that one brand will be much better than another, but it certainly can be more expensive.

House brands and store specials are usually the best places to start looking for low prices. A study conducted in 1983 for the Private Label Manufacturers Association showed that shoppers can save about 35 percent by buying house brands. But even house brands can sometimes be more expensive than comparable products, so do check the prices as you shop.

There are also the generic or "no name" products. Those usually are the lowest in price, but their quality is usually the lowest also. That's fine if the product serves your needs, but do compare labels so that you know just what you're getting.

(See "How to Read a Label," p. 215.)

Compare Unit Prices

Many stores have labels mounted on display racks to show how prices compare according to a standard unit of measure—so many cents per ounce for liquid or solid foods, so many cents per square foot for paper towels, and so on. These unit prices enable shoppers to compare the true prices of products packaged in different sizes. Using canned beans as an example, you might find that a large size of one major brand costs ten cents an ounce, while a smaller size of another major brand advertised as a store special costs twelve cents an ounce and the same size of the store brand only seven cents an ounce.

It's often surprising to see what comparisons of unit prices reveal. Featured specials, for example, might not really be the best buys, as in the case of our canned beans; or a larger size of a major brand may actually be more economical than a smaller size of the house brand. Only by comparing unit prices can you know what really costs the least.

Compare Quality

Price, of course, is only one factor to consider when shopping. Quality and getting what you want are major considerations as well. It can take a great deal of trial and error to determine what you like best and what really is the best buy. (All the more reason for selecting one store and sticking with it. That will narrow the range of selection.) Experimentation, though, is an important part of smart shopping. By doing enough of it, you'll be able to settle on products that satisfy you at prices that will save you money.

Compare Dates

Most perishable products such as milk, eggs, and meats are required to be stamped with the date beyond which they are not to be sold. That is not to say they won't be good after that date, but it is best to use them as soon thereafter as possible to be sure of their freshness and flavor. Unless you plan to use perishable foods right away, buy those marked with a date that is as far in the future as you can get. They are usually placed at the back of the shelf, behind the older foods that have been moved forward so that they will sell faster.

Many stores mark down their prices on dated foods the day before their freshness dates expire. For example, some stores get their fresh meats out on Friday mornings. On Thursday afternoons, they may take many meats that have been on display for two to three days and reduce their prices by as much as half! Such bargains are often placed in special sections so that regular customers can find them. You might have to ask to know where and when to find bargain-priced foods, but asking questions is a basic part of smart shopping.

Compare Sizes

Most often (but not always), the larger the package, the lower the unit cost of the product. You really can save money by buying larger packages—if you need the larger amount, that is. Buy large amounts of any food only if you will use all of it within a reasonable period of time. There won't be any savings if the contents spoil and have to be thrown out before they are used.

Compare Labels

Different brands of the same product can vary enormously in price, even though the amount and quality are virtually the same. The key word, of course, is "same." Don't compare Grade C canned vegetables with Grade A just for price any more than you would compare apples with oranges.

The degree of sameness between products can be determined only by reading their labels. Many prepackaged and processed canned or frozen foods have added ingredients, including salt and other sodium products, sugar, chemical preservatives, or artificial flavorings. Nothing is free, and you may be paying a high price for those things even if you don't want them. Read labels and compare to know what you are really getting.

How to Read a Label

The Food and Drug Administration (FDA) requires certain information to be included on the labels of many canned and prepackaged foods. Information printed on labels typically includes the name of the product, the net contents or net weight (canned food weight includes the weight of any packing liquid), the name and place of business of the manufacturer, packer, or distributor, and the ingredients. Additional information such as whether the food meets kosher standards may be present also, and some labels carry discount coupons or recipes.

The following is an example of a typical food label. The numbers on the illustration correspond to the detailed descriptions given below of the kinds of information many labels display.

1. **Ingredients** must be listed in descending order according to their amounts, beginning with the most abundant. Manufacturers list any colors and flavorings, however, simply as "artificial color" or "natural flavor" without specifying the exact makeup of these ingredients. Certain foods—mayonnaise and catsup, for example—are made according to specified standards. If these foods are used in other products, they are listed only by their standard names, such as "mayonnaise."

2. **Nutrition** information tells the number of calories and the amount of protein, carbohydrates, and fats contained in a single serving, as well as the percentage of U.S. Recommended Daily Allowance (U.S. RDA) of protein and seven

important vitamins and minerals. A "serving" is one standard measure commonly used for the food, such as one cup, four ounces, or one tablespoon. Some products carry a statement like "This product meets the U.S. nutritional quality guidelines for [name of the product]." That means just what it says. The FDA has minimum standards and guidelines for some foods that must be met in order for the food to be called by its standard name. "Mayonnaise," for example, must contain a certain amount of eggs; "peanut butter" must have a certain amount of peanuts.

3. The **grade designation** indicates that the product conforms to some standard established by the U.S. Department of Agriculture (USDA). Some fresh foods, such as dairy products, meats, and poultry, must have the grade quality displayed on their labels. Canned, frozen, and prepackaged foods may or may not be required to display the grade quality. The grade designations for different food groups vary, but U.S. Grade AA and A generally designate the highest quality. The letter designation goes down along with the quality in whatever way quality is measured for a particular food group. The lower the quality, the lower the grade and (usually) the lower the price. Quality standards, though, are based on appearance as much as flavor. If appearance is not an important consideration (as with some ingredients to be used in a casserole or stew, for example), you might save some money by using a lower grade.

4. **Open dating** is required by the FDA on most perishable food products to protect shoppers and assure them that the foods they buy are fresh and wholesome. There are different kinds of dates on food packages. The **pull** or **sell date** is now being used most often. It means simply that the product is to be pulled off the shelf if it is not sold by that date. The food will still be good for a short time after the pull date. Some products have an **expiration date** to tell the consumer the time after which the product is likely to be no good. Yeast, for example, has a certain lifetime after which it is not likely to work. You should always check expiration dates before using a product. A **pack date** tells when the food was packed, information that will tell you just how fresh the food really is. Unfortunately, many food manufacturers and packers put this date in code intended for use by store operators but not consumers. You can inquire about the codes where you shop, and store personnel should tell you how to read them. A **freshness**

date is used mostly with breads, pastries, and other highly perishable products. Like the pull or sell date, it tells the consumer that the closer the time before that date, or the longer the time after it, the less fresh and tasty the product will be.

5. The word **imitation** on a label means that in some way the product does not meet the FDA's nutritional standards for the food in that category. Imitation ham, for example, is real ham that has been treated with more water than the FDA allows for the thing to be called simply "ham." That is not to say that foods labeled "imitation" are not good or that they are not good for you. Quite the contrary, many "imitation" food products might taste just as good as or even better than the "real" thing. They might also be better for your health, because many "imitation" foods, such as cheeses, ham, and mayonnaise, leave out fats. Consequently, they have fewer calories and cholesterol than their "real" counterparts.

6. The **universal product code (UPC)** is the block of peculiar-looking lines now being used on many food packages. It is a standardized code designed to be read by a computer. Stores with special equipment use these codes to maintain pricing and inventory controls that enable them to operate more economically. The consumer may benefit by having lower food costs as well as itemized receipts listing individual food items in English beside their prices. Universal product codes can also be used to automate the checkout counter, leaving less room for human mistakes.

7. **Premiums and coupons** offering discount or refund savings are printed on many labels. They can be sources of considerable savings if you save and use them. Remember, though, to compare the original price of the item you're buying with the price of other brands so that you can determine whether the savings are real.

■

About Coupons

Too often, shoppers seem to feel compelled to use coupons because they think they will be saving money. "It ain't necessarily so." Depending on the product, even with the discount price you might be paying more than you would pay for a similar product of equal or even higher quality. For example, the unit price of a box of cereal with a fifty-cent discount coupon might still be higher than the price of comparable cereals from other food packagers. It pays to compare.

Keep in mind that need is even more important than price and discount savings. By far the great majority of discount coupons are for prepackaged convenience foods, many of which contain a great deal of sugar, salt, and fat that you will be better off without. Bad nutrition is no bargain, even if it is sold at a discount.

About Those Prepackaged "Convenience" Foods

(See "Unnatural Food Forms," pp. 275–281.)

When you get right down to it, smart shopping means getting what you like at a price you are willing to pay. What you like and what you want might be convenience as much as anything else, and that can mean prepackaged food products: canned and frozen vegetables, dried casserole mixes, prepared frozen dinners and desserts, and other foods that might otherwise be purchased fresh and cooked from scratch. (This does not include foods such as rice, dried beans, and pasta that, while prepackaged and convenient, are usually not available fresh.)

Convenience foods are available in such variety and abundance that there is virtually no need for you to use fresh foods unless you want to. In fact, over 50 percent of the foods sold in groceries today are prepackaged in one form or another.

Many prepackaged foods can be quite tasty. They may even taste better than what you might be willing to take the time to prepare for yourself. Because they are easier to ship and store, many might actually be cheaper than fresh, depending on the time of year. In season, fresh foods are usually cheaper than the prepackaged varieties, but when out of season, fresh foods must be imported and thus go up in price. Also, because there is virtually no waste with prepackaged foods, they may well be more economical than fresh foods, even though the package price might be higher. For example, a pound of frozen broccoli (with no hard stalks) can yield as many servings as two pounds of fresh broccoli with stalks that can't be used. On the other hand, when all factors are considered, prepackaged foods are usually more expensive. So the question is not so much what you like, or whether the prepackaged food is more convenient than fresh, but whether you are willing to pay for that convenience.

Leaving the issue of price, consider the questions "What do you like?" and "What do you want?" Answers to both of these questions should pay due attention to health and nutritional considerations as well as taste. Many convenience foods contain large amounts of fats, salt or MSG or other high-sodium products, sugar, and chemical preservatives. Sugar is fattening and has very little food value. MSG and many chemical colorings are suspected of being carcinogenic (cancer causing). Saturated fats and cholesterol are major contributors to heart disease. Salt and other products containing sodium can quite literally raise your blood pressure. In short, there are usually a lot of things in convenience foods that are not good for you. (See Chapter Six, "Eating Smart.")

You can't control the ingredients in prepackaged foods, but you can know what they are and account for them in your diet and your cooking. The only way to do that is to take the time to read labels. (See "How to Read a Label," p. 215.)

Storing Foods

Proper food storage begins with planning and timing the shopping trip. Being left in hot cars does little for foods, especially those that need refrigeration. Ice cream and frozen foods are not much good if they have melted, and they might just do that unless you time your trip to the store to get them home as quickly as possible. It's a good practice to carry a small ice chest in the trunk of your car to store frozen foods just in case you get delayed somewhere between the store and home.

Plan time to store foods properly as soon as you get them home. Begin with the frozen foods; then meats, milk, and other perishables; then fruits and vegetables; and finally canned goods and other nonperishable items. Vegetables and fruits should be cleaned and prepared for storing. All of this, of course, takes time and plenty of it—as much as an hour or more for a major shopping trip. It probably won't happen unless you plan your timing for your shopping trip accordingly.

For efficiency, store all foods of the same type together so that you always know how much you have on hand. But when you add to your stock of stores, do you put the new items in front of the old ones, or behind? On top, or on the bottom? If the foods may be stored for any length of time, put the new ones on the bottom or behind the older ones so that previously stored foods will be used first.

Vegetables and fruits require the longest time to prepare for storage—if they are stored properly. Perhaps that is why so many people never bother to do it. Too often, these foods are simply tossed into the vegetable bin and left until they are used or rot, and they rot faster if they are not prepared and stored properly. For example, sorting them separately in individual plastic bags can double the storage life of some fruits and vegetables. To save time and money, and to improve the taste and longevity of vegetables and fruits, take the time to store these foods properly. The following "How to" explains what you need to do. (Proper storage techniques for individual foods are described in Part Three.)

How to Store Vegetables and Fruits

Green leafy vegetables should be soaked for ten minutes in cold, salty water to destroy bugs and bacteria. (Lettuce may be broken up, and celery should be broken into individual ribs.) Rinse the vegetables under cold running water. Drain them thoroughly and store them separately in plastic bags to keep them moist. Cleaned and properly stored, they will stay fresher longer, and they will be clean, crisp, and ready for use when you need them. You won't have to duplicate the whole cleaning process each time some are used.

Fruits and seed-bearing "vegetables" with a skin (such as tomatoes) should be washed in cold, soapy water to remove pesticides, dirt, chemicals, and bacteria on their skins. Rub the surface gently between your fingers to clean the skins. Rinse the foods thoroughly under cold running water to remove the soap. These foods keep best if they are cool and a little moist, so store them separately in the refrigerator in the vegetable drawer and/or in plastic bags.

Potatoes, onions, and garlic keep best in a dry place with good air circulation and some light. Wash potatoes and peel bulbs just before using them.

Tubers such as beets and turnips should not be washed until you are ready to use them. Most have either a natural or an added film on their surface to protect them and retard decay. Before storage, cut off any leaves so they won't draw

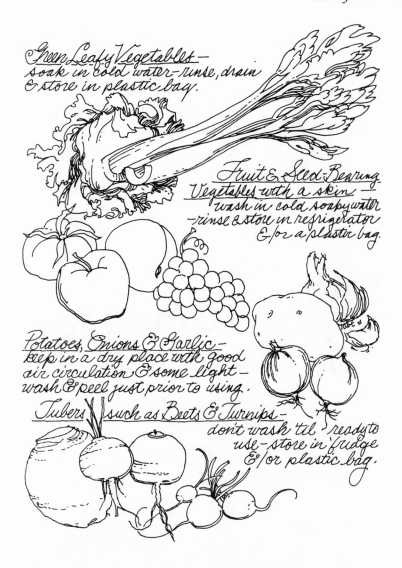

Green Leafy Vegetables — soak in cold water — rinse, drain & store in plastic bag.

Fruit & Seed-Bearing Vegetables with a skin — wash in cold soapy water — rinse & store in refrigerator &/or a plastic bag.

Potatoes, Onions & Garlic — keep in a dry place with good air circulation & some light — wash & peel just prior to using.

Tubers such as Beets & Turnips — don't wash 'til ready to use — store in fridge &/or plastic bag.

off nutrients from the root. A little moisture will help keep tubers fresh, so refrigerate them in the vegetable drawer and/or in plastic bags.

"One rotten apple will spoil the whole bunch." That old saying applies to many foods besides apples. Bruised or soft vegetables and fruits should not be stored with good ones. Store all fruits and vegetables of the same type in their own plastic bags. All of your fruits and vegetables will keep fresher longer if you throw out bad ones and clean vegetable storage bins every few days.

*D*ining
Serving What You Have Cooked
So It Tastes Even Better

CHAPTER NINE

*N*o matter how good the food, it can be even better if it is enjoyed in a dining atmosphere. The atmosphere doesn't have to be formal, just special. Special because it is a joining together of the diners to enjoy the foods someone has worked hard to prepare. Special because it is a well defined social experience complete with its designated place, time, and conditions, free from television and other distractions.

Setting the Table

A dining table does not have to be formal or fancy. At the very least, though, it should be clean and free of papers, sewing, books, and other objects that are likely to accumulate on a tabletop.

A tablecloth or an attractive centerpiece is always a nice touch for a dining table, and flowers or a pretty vase or pottery piece can play a part in setting the stage for dining.

Plates and utensils also have their roles in making dining special. When they are arranged properly, each has a place that is as practical as it is attractive. The illustrations

Informal

Very Formal

on these pages show some examples of table settings on different levels of formality.

1. **The dinner plate or service plate** should be centered in front of the diner, with its nearest edge about one inch from the edge of the table.

2. **Utensils** are arranged with the forks to the left and the knife and spoon(s) to the right, with the knife blade towards the plate.

3. **Glasses** should be placed directly above the dinner knife, with the water goblet centered on its tip. If more glasses are used, place them an inch or two apart in the order in which they are likely to be used, starting at the right.

4. **Coffee cup and saucer**, if they are used, go to the right of the knife and spoon(s), centered on the dinner plate.

5. **The salad plate**, if used, should be to the left of the fork(s), placed so that it is centered on the dinner plate.

6. **The bread plate**, if used, should be to the upper left, centered above the fork(s) an inch or two from the dinner plate and in line with the water goblet.

Notice that the placement of the various articles remains the same regardless of the level of formality. Only their number varies. Also notice that all of the articles are spaced

Formal

evenly apart and in line with each other, so that an invisible line could be drawn through their centers—neat and attractive.

Let's consider the functions of the various articles in detail, focusing on the most formal arrangement so that nothing is left out.

Service Plates

If one or more dishes are to precede the entrée, it is not only correct but downright practical to use a special service plate to protect the table or tablecloth from spills. Save the dinner plates so that they can be clean and heated for serving the main course. Appetizer and soup plates are placed on the service plate as they are served. The service plate is removed along with whatever is the last plate on it and replaced with the dinner plate. Service plates don't all have to match. In fact, you can make a table setting more interesting by using a variety of service plates obtained at crafts fairs, flea markets, or antique shops.

Dinner Plates

At the very least, dinner plates should all be the same color and pattern. For formal dining, white is most elegant and proper. For serving hot main courses, dinner plates should always be heated. You can heat them in a warm oven or in hot water. It's easiest, of course, to have them warming as appetizers and soups are served on service plates. However, if dinner plates are used as service plates, then when you are ready to serve the entrée, remove the dinner plates along with the plates for the previous course, heat the dinner plates quickly in warm water, dry them, and then return them to the table.

Utensils

Having forks to the left and the knife and spoons to the right of the dinner plate is based on the European style of eating in which the fork is held in the left hand and the knife in the right hand for carving. That's a practical and convenient way to hold them.

Notice in the illustration of table settings that the arrangement of the utensils coincides with the order in which they are typically used: soup, salad, entrée, dessert. In this way, they can be removed as they are used, with each removal leaving an orderly and attractive arrangement.

Napkins

Although paper napkins are fine for everyday use, more formal dining really calls for cloth napkins. Cloth napkins can also spruce up an everyday meal setting. Napkins made of "wash and wear" materials are the most practical, because they don't require ironing.

Matching white napkins are usually used only for more formal occasions. For less formal dining, colored napkins are perfectly proper, but they should all match. For everyday family dining, it might be more practical as well as more colorful and interesting to have napkins that are mixed rather than matched.

Napkins can be placed on the table in any number of ways and places: on the service plate, to the left of the forks, or under the forks. For formal dining, they can be folded in a fancy way and placed on the service plate or in the water goblet.

Napkin rings are practical for holding cloth napkins. Individual rings of different designs add variety and interest to the table setting and can also be used to distinguish whose napkin is whose. Many people collect napkin rings, and their table settings always seem to gain interest from the variety and the stories that can accompany each one.

Glasses

Glasses seem to brighten a table just as a spotlight brightens a stage. Their number, shape, color, and variety can be used to highlight the table setting. Mixed or matched, attractive glasses make any meal more special. For more formal dining, all glasses should be of the same color and pattern.

Serving Vessels

Plates, bowls, and platters used for serving foods may be placed on the table before or after the diners are seated. The most formal table settings require serving vessels to match the dinner plates (a practice that seems to have started as a display of wealth). For less formal dining, it is perfectly proper to use vessels of different and varied patterns. Colorful pottery, porcelain, or china vessels not only brighten the table but also serve as conversation pieces. You can find wonderful vessels suitable for serving at crafts fairs, antique shops, and flea markets.

Serving the Meal

Meals can be served in a number of ways. Some considerations, though, apply to all styles of serving.

Except for buffet service, service plates and dining utensils should be placed at individual settings ahead of time. Bread, butter, salt, sugar, sauces, and condiments also should be on the table well in advance. Dining plates and serving vessels should be heated and placed on the table just before the diners are seated or the food is served so that they keep foods warm. You can heat them in a warm oven, in the dishwasher, or in a sink of hot water. If they are wet, dry them off before use.

Some individuals prefer to eat their salad before the meal, others after it. Many people enjoy munching on the salad throughout the meal. All these preferences are quite acceptable. So that guests can eat their salads as they like, have the salad beside the dinner plate before the diners are seated.

Appetizers may be placed at the individual settings before the diners are seated. Plates for appetizer and soup courses may remain on the table for informal dining but should be removed before the main course if the occasion is more formal.

Minding Your Manners

The topic of manners might seem a bit odd or out of place for a book about cooking, but good manners are as much a part of dining as serving foods. The bad manners of one or more persons at a dining table can do as much or more to spoil the pleasure of others as food that is poorly prepared or not served well.

It used to be that children were taught table manners before they were allowed to eat in the homes of others or in public places. That doesn't seem to be true in today's world, judging by the lack of table manners displayed by many diners in restaurants. Even the most conscientious of us could probably benefit from a quick refresher course in table manners. Here are four basic reminders (if they don't apply to you, share them with someone you care about).

1. *Respecting the rights of others* is the basis for all good manners, table manners included. Anything you do or say while dining should reflect your consideration for others who are present.

2. *Avoid making loud noises* of any kind. Don't talk with food in your mouth, and keep your lips closed as you chew. Speak softly, and don't clank plates, glasses, and eating utensils together.

3. *Sit erect and don't rest your elbow on the table.* It is acceptable in all but the most formal dining situations to brace the forearm against the table, but even that is frowned on by some.

4. *If you must smoke while others are dining, excuse yourself and do it elsewhere.* If you want to smoke after all others at your table have completed their meal, then do so only with *everyone's* permission. If anyone even looks like he or she would be offended, excuse yourself and smoke elsewhere. Cigar smoke is offensive to most persons, so don't smoke cigars in restaurants, public places, or in other people's homes.

To be really formal, each course should be served separately and the plates removed only after all diners have eaten their fill of each course. Dessert should be served only after all other plates have been removed.

Serving the meal is a great deal of work for the cook to do alone, and that is no doubt why there are several ways it can be done. Here are the four most popular styles for serving meals in most American homes. The very formal Russian and French styles are not covered here because they both require servants.

Buffet style is the least formal way to serve. Foods are placed along a serving table, and diners serve themselves. The advantages are that diners get what they want in the amounts they want and that more people can be served in less time. The disadvantages are that this method requires more room and may require special serving apparatus such as hot plates or ice trays to ensure that foods remain hot or cold.

In **family style** serving, fully prepared foods in hot serving bowls or dishes are placed on the table for diners to serve themselves. (Hot pads may be needed to protect the table and the diners from burns.) The serving bowls are passed to the left from one diner to the next. This is perhaps the easiest serving style. Like buffet style, it has the advantage of allowing diners to establish the size of their own portions. One disadvantage is that as the food is passed, portions may become small or the food may run out. A second disadvantage is that the service vessels add to the dishes you have to wash.

Serving foods **American style** requires putting food portions on heated plates in the kitchen and then carrying the plates to diners at the table, just as it is done in most restaurants. The advantages are that there are no serving dishes to wash and that all diners receive portions of about the same size. The disadvantages are that this procedure creates more work for the cook and that some diners may get more or less than they want of some foods.

In the old-fashioned **English style** of serving, all the foods are placed along with hot dinner plates before the host or the head of the family, who then serves up individual portions. The plates are passed to the left around the table until all diners have been served. This method has the advantage that the diners can each tell the host what foods they want and how much. The disadvantage is that this method is time-consuming, and foods may get cold by the time all the diners have been served.

Gilding the Lily

You can make even the simplest of meals and plainest of dishes special just by dressing them up a bit—"gilding the lily," as they say. Dressing things up can mean something as simple as arranging the foods pleasingly on the dinner plate or garnishing the food or plate with fresh herbs, fruits, vegetables, or nuts. These little touches are all a part of the craft of cooking. After all, the more attractive the food, the more it will be enjoyed.

(See "Garnishes," pp. 74–75.)

If you want to get really fancy with your serving, you might want to try flaming foods. The French call this technique "flambé." Flaming can be done with many foods, especially with fowl, and with many desserts, including ice cream. Flaming adds flavor to foods as well as heating them, and so it's not only fancy but practical, too. Be careful, though; you don't want to set anything on fire. Here's how to do it safely.

How to Flame (Flambé) Foods

Flaming is done with the help of the alcohol in a liquor such as brandy or whisky. It is a good practice to keep the flame at a distance, especially from your face. For safety, have a damp cloth or other cover nearby to extinguish the liquor in case of accidental spills and place the liquor bottle away from any flame. Do not pour liquor directly from the bottle over flames, because the gases in the bottle might ignite and burst the bottle.

1. Foods to be flamed must be warm, at least 75 degrees F.

2. Use a liquor whose taste is compatible with the flavor of the food. Brandy, vodka, whiskies, and rum are good with main dishes. Liqueurs and brandy go well with fruits and desserts.

3. Place the food close to where the liquor will be heated.

4. Pour two to four ounces of the liquor into a metal spoon or small pot and heat it over a range burner or a candle until you can see vapors rising from its surface.

5. Ignite the liquor, using one of the following methods:

· Pour the warmed liquor over the food and light it with a long-handled match.
· Light the liquor in its heating spoon or pot and then slowly pour the flaming liquid over the food.
· If the food is in a chafing dish over an open flame, gently pour the liquor onto the food while tilting the edge of the dish over the flame so that the liquor catches fire.

6. Allow the liquor to burn off completely, and let the flame go out by itself. The food may be served while still aflame, but do be careful.

■

Just Desserts

What's this? A collection of recipes for naughty things you can make and serve as desserts? No, I'm afraid not. In this case, I use the phrase "just" to mean "deserved," as in justice. Here we will give desserts the justice they deserve: short and sweet.

A good dessert is a treat and a pleasure most of us enjoy too much of too often for our own good. The only way to "have your cake and eat it too" is to have it infrequently and to enjoy it in moderation.

Desserts can and should be special. Really good ones—pastries and cakes, especially—require a lot of time and cooking expertise to make well. If you have the time and want to develop the expertise, there are thousands of recipes available to guide you. A much easier course is to buy desserts from bakeries or eat them only in good restaurants. Since desserts made by experts are more expensive, that provides another good reason for eating fewer of them. Because you eat fewer of them, the desserts you do eat will be all the more special.

To see why most desserts should be infrequent treats, let's consider them in light of the four rules of good nutrition discussed in Chapter Six.

Rule number one: *establish and maintain a balanced diet.* Desserts are not necessarily incompatible with good nutrition, especially if they include fresh fruits. However, too often so much emphasis is placed on desserts that the other parts of the meal are neglected at the expense of a truly balanced diet. That is especially true if "leaving room for dessert" means not eating other foods, or if eating too much of everything causes consumption of too much fat, salt, and sugar.

That leads to rule number two: *minimize consumption of fats, salts, and sugars.* Most desserts contain large amounts of all of these, especially sugar. Here again, for good diet and improved health, we will do well to minimize the number of desserts we eat.

Rule number three: *eat plenty of fresh fruits, vegetables, and whole-grain cereals.* Desserts *can* be good for you, and you *can* have them frequently—if you substitute fresh fruits for pies, cakes, puddings, and pastries. In fact, fresh fruits are considered an elegant, fancy dessert at some of the most fashionable restaurants in the world.

Rule number four: *eat a varied diet.* All right. In one sense, a varied diet can include pies, cakes, puddings, pastries, and other rich desserts. On the other hand, the real point of this rule is to be sure of getting all the nutrients you need. Most desserts are nutrient-poor at best, and what little nutrition they do provide can be obtained from other foods without the accompanying "empty" calories.

Finally, I should add a basic rule of the smart person's diet: *don't overeat.* Overeating means taking in more calories than your body burns, resulting in overweight. Most desserts contain an enormous number of calories. A piece of pie, for example, can contain from 300 to 500 calories, which is as much as one-fifth to one-third of the total caloric intake most people should have in an entire day! If you want to maintain a good figure and good health, or if you want to lose weight, then eliminating or minimizing desserts is the best place to begin.

Cleaning Up
A Guide to Kitchen Efficiency, Sanitation, and Safety

CHAPTER TEN

*I*f you enjoy having your pets around you to play with as you cook, or if you find the seat of your trousers or skirt a perfectly acceptable apron for wiping your hands, or if you don't believe in washing dishes until they really get in your way, then you might want to skip this chapter. Reading it will likely make you uncomfortable with your lifestyle or with mine.

Keeping It Clean: A Vital Subject

Why should the subject of keeping a kitchen clean be called "vital"? Because a clean kitchen is efficient, practical, economical, safe, and appetizing. First, a clean kitchen is efficient and practical because it is a lot easier to work in than one that is cluttered or dirty. Second, a kitchen that is not clean is usually an expensive one. A great deal of food can go to waste in a dirty kitchen because it gets lost in the mess and spoils before its time. Third, a kitchen that is not clean is not safe. Cuts, burns, and bruises occur most often in kitchens because someone is trying to move around in space that is congested with things that shouldn't be where they are. Also, illnesses can be caused by foods that have spoiled or become contaminated. Sickness can also be caused or spread by dirty dishes, eating utensils, aprons, and washcloths. Last but certainly not least, a dirty kitchen is an unappetizing kitchen. No matter how good the recipe or accomplished the cook, no matter how good the food or how well it might be served, it won't be enjoyed nearly as much if the diners know it was prepared in a kitchen that is not clean.

The practical efficiency of having a kitchen well organized, neat, and clean became apparent to me from a living relationship I once had with some friends. I will digress for a moment to relate that story, because it explains one of this chapter's principal suggestions.

Back in the early seventies, I shared a house with two friends: Ned and Jim. We shared expenses. We shared good times. And we shared the work. I did the general house

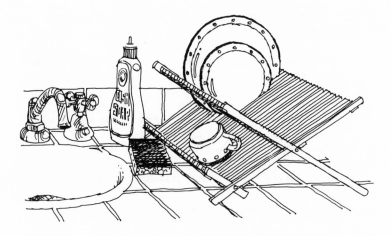

cleaning. Jim did the laundry and washed the dinner dishes. Ned did all of the cooking, and a great cook he was. Unfortunately, Ned was the kind of cook who could not make anything without messing up the kitchen and everything in it in the process. Worse, he would never clean anything (unless *he* needed it), let alone put it away.

Ned subscribed to what I call the "Need a Dish/Wash a Dish" school of thought. A very popular school it seems to be, too, judging by the number of cooks who work that way. Well, Ned ruled the kitchen while he was cooking, and Jim and I stayed out. Jim would go in after our evening meal and try to restore some order to the chaos that Ned, our chef, had wrought.

The three of us got along just fine until I decided to try this cooking thing for myself. At that point I discovered that not only could I never find anything when I needed it, but our little kitchen was dirty to the point of being unsanitary. Alas, our happy home was rapidly becoming unhappy. Jim didn't have time to clean up after Ned, and Ned couldn't have cared less about having things clean, to say nothing of neat and orderly. I wanted things to be neat and clean, and I also wanted to learn how to cook. The result was that I developed what I call the "Use a Dish/Wash a Dish" approach, which I tried to get all three of us to use. It does save time and work in the long run, and it can prevent a lot of domestic conflict if everyone who works in the same kitchen uses it. I never could get Ned to adopt it. Perhaps you will have more success getting others to use it in your kitchen.

Use a Dish/Wash a Dish

1. Keep a sponge or dishcloth on the sink at all times and use it *only* for washing dishes, glasses, and other eating utensils. For sanitary reasons, don't use it for scrubbing the counters, range, or floor, nor for washing the car, the dog, or anything else. Keep it clean and sanitary by pouring boiling water over it once a day.
2. Wash dishes, glasses, and utensils *as you use them* instead of letting them stack up.
3. Apply a few drops of liquid dish soap to the sponge or cloth.
4. Scrub objects to be cleaned with the soapy sponge or cloth.
5. Rinse the scrubbed objects thoroughly under hot running water.
6. Stack them in a rack to dry. If they dry in a rack, there is no chance of contamination from a dirty dish towel. Allowing them to dry by themselves saves a great deal of work too.

If you think of cleaning as an ongoing process rather than as a never-ending one, it might not seem quite so tedious or futile. The Use a Dish/Wash a Dish idea goes along with the ongoing nature of kitchen cleaning. Use the two ideas together, and your cleaning tasks will seem like a lot less work.

Keeping a kitchen clean begins with having it well organized. Professional chefs use a French expression as a basic guide to kitchen organization, *mise en place.* What it means is something like "a place for everything, and everything in its place." There is no more sound advice for keeping a kitchen neat, orderly, workable, and clean. When a dish or utensil is not being used, it should be in the sink or dishwasher ready for cleaning, or already clean and in the drying rack, or back in its place so that it is out of the way and can be located when needed. Here are some other practical sugestions for cleaning particular things.

Pots, pans, and other cooking tools may be needed more than once for preparing one meal and certainly for preparing several meals during the day or week. It is with them that the Use a Dish/Wash a Dish technique is most helpful. You don't want to put pots, pans, and tools into the dishwasher if you have one, because they take up a great deal of space—space that can be better used to wash a greater number of dishes and glasses. Besides, you are likely to need pots, pans, and tools for preparing other meals before it is time to run the dishwasher.

As you use cooking tools, put them into or near the wash sink and use your soapy sponge or cloth to wash them as soon as you have time. Not only will you have clean tools when you need them, but you will have more room and time for cleaning dishes, glasses, and eating utensils when you need to.

Dishes, glasses, and eating utensils are used all at the same time, and so they can usually be cleaned at the same time. For one or two persons, the Use a Dish/Wash a Dish technique might be the easiest, quickest, and cheapest way to clean them. If there are a lot of dishes, though, it is usually better to wash them all at once in a clean sink or bowl of hot soapy water and then rinse them under hot running water.

If you are fortunate enough to have a dishwasher, rinse and load dirty dishes right away so that they are out of sight and out of the way. Run the dishwasher only when it is full to save water, electricity, time, and money.

It's best to hold off cleaning the **counters, range top, floor,** and so on until everything else has been cleaned and put away. If you try to keep them too clean as you work, you might be wasting time and energy. That is not to say you should allow them to become messy or cluttered. Spills and spots should be cleaned up right away so that they

---

What to Use to Clean What

- *Hands:* Soap and warm water. Dry on paper towels.
- *General kitchen cleaning:* Warm soapy water, ammonia, or a commercial cleaner and a clean cloth or sponge.
- *Grease and stains:* Liquid spray cleaner or a mix of vinegar and warm water.
- *Stains on china or Formica:* Vinegar or a paste made of baking soda and warm water.
- *Severe stains on china or Formica,* or stains or burned spots in enameled iron: Soak in a solution of one part chlorine bleach to four parts water.
- *Stainless steel:* Rub with a cloth saturated with distilled vinegar.
- *Copper or silver:* Special cleaning liquids, powders, and pastes are made for cleaning these metals.

don't spread to become a bigger mess. Jars, cans, and other containers should be put back into their proper places right away so that they don't get in your way.

When the cooking chores are done and everything else has been cleaned and put away, then dig out the cleaning aids and go to work to clean the range, counter tops, and even the floor if needed. A kitchen left dirty will (and should) haunt you with thoughts of having to clean it, so you might as well do it and get it over with. On the other hand, a kitchen that is left clean is always inviting for anyone to go into at any time.

Keeping It Sanitary: A Dirty Subject

Sanitation is a dirty subject. It has to do with germs, sickness, and other unpleasant topics most of us would rather not think about. Unfortunately, not thinking about them doesn't make them go away.

Many people seem to believe that what they can't see won't hurt them. But when it comes to sanitation, it is precisely what you can't see that *can* hurt you—bacteria. Preventing the growth and spread of bacteria that can cause undesirable odors, food spoilage, and illness is what sanitation is all about.

The table on page 242 shows how various—and how serious—bacterial foodborne illnesses are. It is worth paying careful attention to, because many of us have never learned what we need to know about this important subject.

Take a look around your kitchen. Does it look dirty? Then it probably is not sanitary. Does it look clean? Then it still might not be sanitary, because bacteria are invisible to the unaided eye. Smell a few things: the dishcloth or sponge, the vegetable bin in the refrigerator, the cutting board, the wooden spoons, the garbage pail. If they smell dirty, they are. Invisible bacteria have been doing their job better than you have been doing yours.

Bacteria like the same things as you and I: good foods and a warm place to sleep. They especially like meats, poultry, fish, eggs, and milk—foods rich in protein and fat. Their greatest enemy is heat in the form of cooking temperatures and cleaning water hot enough to destroy them.

The thermometer chart shows the temperature range within which bacteria thrive, become dormant, or die. It pretty well says all you need to know to control the growth of bacteria in foods that are cooked. But what about foods that are not cooked? What about the utensils and other objects that sit out at room temperature for hours or even days with which foods might have come in contact? Using chicken as an example, let's consider a few common situations in which harmful bacteria might grow and spread.

If you handle chicken or things that have come into contact with it and then handle other objects—including knives, cutting boards, cloth towels, and aprons—those objects can become contaminated with bacteria from the chicken. Then they spread the bacteria to anything they touch. Since towels and aprons are usually slightly damp and don't get washed every few hours, they make especially good homes in which bacteria grow and multiply.

If you marinate raw chicken in a barbecue sauce, or even just hold it in a pan or on a plate, and then leave the pan or sauce out at room temperature while the chicken cooks, the bacteria from the chicken will grow and contaminate anything with which they come into contact.

Temperatures of Foods for Control of Bacteria

°F		°F
250	Canning temperatures for low-acid vegetables, meat, and poultry in pressure canner.	250
240	Canning temperatures for fruits, tomatoes, and pickles in water-bath canner.	240
212	Cooking temperatures destroy most bacteria. Time required to kill bacteria decreases as temperature is increased.	212
165	Warming temperatures prevent growth but allow survival of some bacteria.	165
140	Some bacterial growth may occur. Many bacteria survive.	140
125	**DANGER ZONE!** Temperatures in this zone allow rapid growth of bacteria and production of toxins by some bacteria. (Do not hold foods in this temperature zone for more than 2 or 3 hours.)	125
60	Some growth of food poisoning bacteria may occur.	60
40	Cold temperatures permit slow growth of some bacteria that cause food spoilage.*	40
32	Freezing temperatures stop growth of bacteria, but may allow bacteria to survive. (Do not store food above 10°F for more than a few weeks.)	32
0	* Do not store raw meats for more than 5 days or poultry, fish, or ground meat for more than 2 days in the refrigerator.)	0

From Keeping Food Safe to Eat: A Guide for Homemakers. *United States Department of Agriculture, Home and Garden Bulletin no. 162.*

Bacterial foodborne illness: Causes, symptoms, and prevention

Name of Illness	What Causes It	Symptoms	Characteristics of Illness	Preventive Measures
Salmonellosis. Examples of foods involved: poultry, red meats, eggs, dried foods, dairy products.	*Salmonellae.* Bacteria widespread in nature, live and grow in intestinal tracts of human beings and animals.	Severe headache, followed by vomiting, diarrhea, abdominal cramps, and fever. Infants, elderly, and persons with low resistance are most susceptible. Severe infections cause high fever and may even cause death.	Transmitted by eating contaminated food, or by contact with infected persons or carriers of the infection. Also transmitted by insects, rodents, and pets. Onset: Usually within 12 to 36 hours. Duration: 2 to 7 days.	Salmonellae in food are destroyed by heating the food to 140° F. and holding for 10 minutes or to higher temperatures for less time; for instance, 155° F. for a few seconds. Refrigeration at 40° F. inhibits the increase of Salmonellae, but they remain alive in foods in the refrigerator or freezer, and even in dried foods.
Perfringens poisoning. Examples of foods involved: stews, soups, or gravies made from poultry or red meat.	*Clostridium perfringens.* Spore-forming bacteria that grow in the absence of oxygen. Temperatures reached in thorough cooking of most foods are sufficient to destroy vegetative cells, but heat-resistant spores can survive.	Nausea without vomiting, diarrhea, acute inflammation of stomach and intestines.	Transmitted by eating food contaminated with abnormally large numbers of the bacteria. Onset: Usually within 8 to 20 hours. Duration: May persist for 24 hours.	To prevent growth of surviving bacteria in cooked meats, gravies, and meat casseroles that are to be eaten later, cool foods rapidly and refrigerate promptly at 40° F. or below, or hold them above 140° F.

Name of Illness	What Causes It	Symptoms	Characteristics of Illness	Preventive Measures
Staphylococcal poisoning (frequently called staph). Examples of foods involved: custards, egg salad, potato salad, chicken salad, macaroni salad, ham, salami, cheese.	*Staphylococcus aureus.* Bacteria fairly resistant to heat. Bacteria growing in food produce a toxin that is extremely resistant to heat.	Vomiting, diarrhea, prostration, abdominal cramps. Generally mild and often attributed to other causes.	Transmitted by food handlers who carry the bacteria and by eating food containing the toxin. Onset: Usually within 3 to 8 hours. Duration: 1 to 2 days.	Growth of bacteria that produce toxin is inhibited by keeping hot foods above 140° F. and cold foods at or below 40° F. Toxin is destroyed by boiling for several hours or heating the food in a pressure cooker at 240° F. for 30 minutes.
Botulism. Examples of foods involved: canned low-acid foods, smoked fish.	*Clostridium botulinum.* Spore-forming organisms that grow and produce toxin in the absence of oxygen, as in a sealed container.	Double vision, inability to swallow, speech difficulty, progressive respiratory paralysis. Fatality rate is high, in the United States about 65 percent.	Transmitted by eating food containing the toxin. Onset: Usually within 12 to 36 hours or longer. Duration: 3 to 6 days.	Bacterial spores in food are destroyed by high temperatures obtained only in the pressure canner. More than 6 hours is needed to kill the spores at boiling temperature (212° F.). The toxin is destroyed by boiling for 10 to 20 minutes; time required depends on kind of food.

From *Keeping Food Safe to Eat: A Guide for Homemakers.* United States Department of Agriculture, Home and Garden Bulletin no. 162.

Another way bacteria are commonly spread is from the handling of fruits and vegetables. Many people seem to think that foods are clean just because they are fresh from the store. Some even believe that washing fruits and vegetables might damage them. Wrong on both counts. Consider the dirty hands of the workers who pick fruits and vegetables. What about the dirty hands of the people who pack them or who paw and pick over them in the food store? What about people who might have sneezed on them between the time they were picked and the time you handle them?

(See "How to Store Vegetables and Fruits," pp. 220–221.)

Consider also the chemicals, insecticides, and other poisons that probably were sprayed on the foods somewhere between their source and you. Consider your own hands and the fact that each time you handle a food, or even food packages, your hands may become contaminated and then spread that contamination to anything else they touch. Suffice it to say that it's a very good idea to wash fruits and vegetables before eating them and to wash your hands frequently with soap and water as you handle any foods.

The following "How to" summarizes the basic steps in maintaining a sanitary kitchen. Few people do them all. Do you?

How to Keep Your Kitchen Sanitary

1. **Keep it clean.** Your foods, utensils, dishes, appliances, and work area are only as clean as the dirtiest thing they touch.

- *Yourself:* Always wash your hands with soap and water before handling foods and utensils and after handling meats, poultry, or fish. Dry them on paper towels to avoid contamination from cloth towels or aprons. If you have open cuts, sores, or boils on your hands, wear rubber gloves to avoid infection as well as to prevent spreading any contamination to others.
- *Sponges, washcloths, and dish towels* are often dirtier than the things they are used to clean. Change them often, and keep them sanitary by washing them frequently in soap and hot water.
- *Foods and food packages* often are coated with chemicals or insecticides. Wash fruits in warm soapy water. Soak vegetables in cool water with some salt, lemon juice,

or vinegar. Wash the lids of cans before opening them so that if the lid drops into the can, the contents won't be contaminated. Wash your hands with soap and hot water after handling packages, cans, and other containers.

· *Knives and other utensils* used for food preparation should be washed immediately after each use with soap and hot water, especially if they have come into contact with meats, poultry, or fish.

· *Wooden cutting boards, wooden spoons, and other porous objects* may have bacteria deep in their surfaces where soap and hot water cannot reach. Sterilize them frequently, using boiling water and/or chlorinated cleaning liquid. Washing in a dishwasher works also, provided the water temperature is at least 140 degrees F.

· *Drinking glasses and eating utensils* should be handled by their handles. Hands pick up bacteria from foods and other objects and then spread them around. If you sneeze on your hand, for example, and then handle a drinking glass by its rim, the contamination is the same as if you had sneezed directly on the glass. (You might notice waiters and waitresses in restaurants handling drinking glasses by their rims. As far as sanitation is concerned, that's just one step short of dipping their fingers into the drink.)

2. **Keep all foods at temperatures below 40 or above 140 degrees F.** The shorter the period a food sits out at a temperature within 40 and 140 degrees, the safer it will be and the longer it will last. The total accumulated time any food should be exposed to temperatures within that range is four hours.

3. **Never use foods from bulging cans.** They are likely to be contaminated with poisonous bacteria.

4. **Consume or freeze leftovers within forty-eight hours.** Not only will they be safe, but they will taste better.

5. **Do not refreeze foods that have fully thawed.** Cook them first to destroy any bacterial growth, and then refreeze them. If a partially thawed food still contains ice crystals, it has not thawed so much that it cannot be refrozen safely.

6. **When in doubt, throw it out!** If a food smells bad, it probably will taste bad, and it could well poison you.

7. **Keep foods covered to prevent contamination.** One sneeze and . . . .

8. **Buy only meats and poultry that have been federally inspected.** Use them as quickly as possible. If they smell bad, they probably are.

9. **Buy only pasteurized milk and keep it fresh.** Powdered and canned milk are also safe.

10. **Keep only the smallest amounts of foods needed.** Whatever you eat will then be as fresh, tasty, and safe as it can be.

■

Keeping It Safe: A Practical Subject

My, my. With all this discussion of bacteria and insecticides, contamination and poisons, it's beginning to sound as if kitchens are dangerous places. Indeed, many are. Your kitchen can be safe, though, and it will be if you keep it sanitary and practice a few simple rules to prevent accidents.

"More accidents occur in the kitchen than any other place in the home." You've probably heard that before. Now it is time to pay attention to it and do something about it; it's true.

The sad thing about kitchen accidents is that most of them can be prevented if only a few precautions are taken. The table that follows shows common kitchen accidents and how to avoid them. If you study it and operate your kitchen accordingly, then your kitchen should be accident free.

Kitchen accidents and how they can be avoided

Types of Accidents	How to Avoid
Cuts from knives	1. Keep knives in plain sight or stored in their special place. Never leave them to soak in dishwater, for example.
	2. If a knife is dropped, don't try to catch it. Get out of its way.
	3. Cut with the point of the knife away from yourself and anyone else.
	4. Keep the sharp edge pointing away from you while drying a knife with a towel.
	5. A sharp knife is safer than a dull one; there is less chance that it will slip while you're cutting.
	6. Never attempt to open a bottle or can with a knife or use it for anything other than cutting foods.
from glass	7. Pick up broken glass using a broom and dust pan for larger pieces and a dampened paper towel for slivers. Don't pick up shards with your fingers.
	8. Discard chipped glassware or china.
	9. If glass breaks in the sink, drain the water. Don't "fish" for it.

Kitchen accidents and how they can be avoided (continued)

Types of Accidents	How to Avoid
	10. Sudden changes in temperature may shatter glass. Put hot glass on a cloth or hot pad. Never put cold glass (even Pyrex) on a hot range burner or hot glass on a cold surface.
Burns from pots and pans	1. Always assume that every pot or pan is hot and treat it that way until you know it's not. 2. Use *dry* towels or cloths to handle hot pots and pans. Wet cloth conducts heat. 3. Keep handles turned away from the work area and range burners. 4. Tip pot covers from the rear so that steam escapes *away* from you.
from ranges	5. In case of fire, cover it with a pot lid, baking soda, or salt, or use a fire extinguisher. *Never use water around any fire in which grease may be involved.* Water will only spread it. 6. Keep grease, chemicals, and cloth articles away from cooking surfaces at all times. 7. Keep ranges and ventilators clean and free of grease. 8. When lighting a gas burner, place the match at the gas jet before turning the jet on. Open the jet gradually to avoid blowing out the match. 9. Ventilate a gas oven several minutes before attempting to light it.
from appliances	10. Always turn electrical appliances off or unplug them when not in use.
Falls	1. Keep floors clean. Wipe up spilled foods, grease, and the like right away. 2. Keep the kitchen area clear of obstructions of all kinds, including open doors of cabinets, drawers, ovens, etc. 3. Don't stand on boxes or chairs. Use a ladder. 4. Don't try to overreach. Use a ladder.
Strains	1. Don't try to carry loads that are too heavy. 2. Lift with your leg muscles, not your back. 3. Don't turn or twist your body while lifting heavy objects.

Kitchen Tools
Their Selection and Use

CHAPTER ELEVEN

*E*very kitchen requires certain tools. The chart on pages 254–256 lists kitchen tools that can be considered basic, desirable, and luxurious to have. You might want to review it briefly before reading further.

No matter how limited your budget, it will pay you to invest in good kitchen tools and stay away from the cheap junk. A dull knife can be a real safety hazard. The wrong pot can ruin a delicate sauce. A warped frying pan will have hot spots that will burn foods if you are not careful. And few things are as aggravating as having a tool break just when you need it. Instead of "economizing" by purchasing inadequate tools, start by stocking your kitchen with good basic tools, and work your way up to those that are desirable and finally to those that are luxurious. That way you'll gradually build a solid collection of tools you can be happy to own and to use.

Cooking Vessels

Whatever the cooking task, you will be wise to match the pot, pan, or plate to it. Because some materials are better for some purposes than others, it might be better to avoid matched sets of cookware and instead select each vessel for its special job. What those jobs are and what vessels are best suited to them are described in more detail in Chapters Two and Three. Here, though, are some general considerations.

Range-top Vessels

Pots and pans that will be used on top of the range should be heavy enough to rest evenly and flat on the burner. If they rock or tilt, hot and cold spots will occur, causing foods to cook unevenly and possibly to scorch or burn. Even the weight of the handles on lightweight pots and pans can tip them enough to cause uneven cooking. Lightweight metals are also likely to warp when exposed to high temperatures or to rapid changes in temperature caused by such things as placing a hot vessel on a cold surface or in cold water. This is especially true of lightweight pans used for frying. (Tip: To test whether the bottom of a pan or pot is flat, roll a pencil in the vessel. If the bottom is flat, the pencil will roll evenly in all directions.)

The ability of a material to retain or lose heat is the second most important consideration for range-top vessels. Braises and stews require long, slow cooking; the more evenly the vessel distributes the heat, the more evenly it will cook the food. Coated or clad aluminum, treated aluminum, lined copper, and enameled iron are the best materials for long, slow range-top cooking.

Delicate foods such as egg dishes and many sauces are best cooked in vessels that will lose heat rapidly so that their delicate contents do not overcook. Lined copper and coated or treated aluminum are the best materials for cooking delicate, heat-sensitive foods.

Frying is done at high temperatures, and the best materials for it are heavy, commercial-weight treated or clad aluminum, heavy stainless steel, and enameled iron.

As a rule, glass, ceramic, earthenware, and porcelain materials should never be used on a range burner. The rapid temperature changes can cause these materials to break. There are some ceramic materials that are supposed to be safe for range-top use, but even they should be treated with care and not subjected to rapid temperature changes.

Oven-cooking Vessels

The better a material conducts heat, the faster it will cook foods. Cakes and most pastries require a vessel that is a good heat conductor. Lightweight aluminum pans are best for cooking cakes and pastries so that their outer surface is dry and crusty while the center remains moist and soft. Glass, ceramic, and earthenware vessels are poor heat conductors and are therefore best for cooking pies, casseroles, and other foods that must cook thoroughly and evenly throughout before the outer surface gets too brown.

The size and shape of oven cookware are also important considerations. The vessel should be large enough to contain the food, but not so large that its sides extend too far above the food; otherwise the oven's heated air will be prevented from reaching the food's surface, and the surface will not brown evenly. If the vessel is round, the surface of a food cooked in it will brown more evenly. The corners of foods cooked in square or rectangular pans will be darker than the edges or center of the top.

Materials Used for Cooking Vessels

Copper, for some cooks, is the ultimate material for pots and pans. With its great sensitivity to rapid changes in temperature, copper is particularly well suited for vessels used to make delicate sauces. But good copper cookware is prohibitively expensive, it requires an extraordinary amount of cleaning, and it dents, bends, and warps with the greatest of ease. Add to these drawbacks the fact that the tin lining is easily scratched and will separate if the copper gets too hot, and you will know why copper is not used by most cooks. Many copper utensils being sold today are good for kitchen decorations, but not for cooking. They are so light that they warp easily, their tin lining comes off in a very short time, and they have a protective coating that keeps them shiny only if they are not used for cooking. The protective coating is practically impossible to remove.

Aluminum is inexpensive, heats quickly, and distributes heat evenly. Aluminum responds quickly to temperature changes, and it is easy to clean and maintain. For baking pans, bare aluminum is fine. Bare aluminum, however, will react chemically with some foods, such as egg whites and tomatoes, causing them to discolor and affecting their taste. It is therefore not a good choice for mixing bowls or for pots and pans used for range-top cooking. Aluminum that has been chemically treated, or that is coated with a non-stick inner surface, or that is clad with a stainless steel inner lining makes the most practical all-purpose material for pots. If it is really heavy, coated or chemically treated aluminum is an excellent material for frying pans.

Stainless steel is virtually maintenance-free and not too expensive. It is unlikely to warp unless it is really lightweight, and it doesn't easily stain or discolor. On the negative side, it is a poor heat conductor, it heats slowly, and it does not distribute heat evenly or respond rapidly to temperature changes. Being a poor heat conductor, it requires more energy to reach and hold cooking temperatures than other materials, and it tends to scorch foods easily. Stainless steel is best suited for small pots and for pans used to pan-fry or deep-fat-fry.

Clad combinations are made of stainless steel coated with either copper or aluminum for high heat conductivity and

continued

low maintenance. This kind of cookware is usually expensive, but very, very practical. The inner surface is lined with stainless steel so that it does not react chemically with foods and is easy to clean. The outer bottom, or the bottom and sides, are clad with either copper or aluminum for more even and responsive heat distribution than stainless steel alone can provide. To be any good, however, the copper or aluminum must be at least one-eighth of an inch thick. Lightweight copper or aluminum pots and pans will warp easily even if they are lined with stainless steel. Heavyweight clad combinations make the best frying pans and pots used for cooking stews and braises.

Cast iron is still the favorite of many cooks, especially for frying pans. It retains heat longer but requires more energy and more time to heat than other materials. Iron diffuses heat rather evenly at low temperatures, but not at high temperatures. It is ideal, therefore, for Dutch ovens, grills, gratin dishes, and other vessels used for long, slow cooking. Because they do retain heat well, it is best not to use vessels made of cast iron for cooking delicate foods such as eggs and sauces in which eggs are used.

Plain cast iron is inexpensive, and that is good. But it is heavy, and it can interact chemically with and discolor some foods, such as tomatoes, that contain a good deal of acid. Also, plain iron cooking vessels retain the flavors of foods that have been cooked in them. One food that is cooked in a plain iron pot or pan might end up tasting like another. Last but not least, plain iron rusts easily unless it is kept well oiled and dry.

Enameled iron does not have the drawbacks of plain iron, but it is quite expensive, and care must be taken not to scratch it. The enamel can also crack if it is exposed to high temperatures or to rapid changes in temperature, or if it is dropped. Cracks in the enamel provide good hiding places for bacteria as well as rust.

Glass, earthenware, porcelain, and ceramic vessels are used almost exclusively for oven cooking. With the exception of some modern ceramics, vessels made of these materials should never be used on a range burner, because they are likely to break. They will also break when subjected to rapid temperature changes—for example, when a hot plate is put on a cold counter or in cold water, or a cold plate on a hot range burner. Earthenware is not homogeneous, and vessels made of it may have hot spots. It should not be used for baking at high temperatures. Clear, heat-proof glass cooks evenly and has the advantage of allowing the surface of the food to be seen, so that it is more difficult to burn the surface if you pay attention to it as it cooks.

A cook's guide to kitchen tools

Function	Basic	Desirable	Luxurious
Cutting	1 cutting board 1 6–8-inch utility knife 1 6–8-inch slicing knife 1 4-inch paring knife 1 9–12-inch carving knife 1 vegetable peeler 1 sharpening steel 1 box-type grater	1 boning knife 1 10–12-inch slicing knife 1 8–10-inch chef's knife 1 pair kitchen shears 1 rotary grater 1 or more cookie/biscuit cutters 1 grapefruit knife Extra knives of different sizes	1 electric carving knife 1 food processor 1 food mill
Measuring	1 glass liquid measuring cup of 2-cup capacity 1 set of 4 cups for dry measures 1 set of measuring spoons 1 slow-response meat thermometer 1 oven thermometer	1 glass liquid measuring cup of 1-cup capacity 1 glass mixing bowl of 2-qt. capacity with cup and weight measures 1 rapid-response meat thermometer Extra measuring spoons	1 set kitchen scales 1 frying thermometer
Mixing	3 stainless steel mixing bowls in graded sizes 3 mixing spoons in graded sizes (plastic) 1 loop and/or wire whisk of medium size 1 hand rotary beater 1 rubber spatula	3 whisks in graded sizes 1 rolling pin 1 hand-held electric mixer 1 food blender 1 pastry blender Extra spoons and spatulas	1 unlined copper bowl 1 standing electric mixer 1 food processor 1 pastry board
Straining	1 to 3 slotted spoons in different sizes 1 colander 1 5-inch medium-mesh tea strainer 1 3–5-inch fine-mesh tea strainer Cheesecloth	1 flour sifter 1 3–4-inch fine-mesh skimmer	1 China cap ("Chinois") 1 4–5 inch fine-mesh skimmer

Function	Basic	Desirable	Luxurious
General Cooking	1 timer 1 set of tongs 1 slotted, long-handled "pan-cake turner" 1 basting brush 1 large ladle 1 short-handled 2–3-tine fork 1 long-handled 2–3-tine fork 1 bulb baster	1 short, narrow, hard spatula 1 long, narrow, hard spatula	1 trowel-shaped spatula
Cooking with Liquids	1 1–1½-qt. metal pot with cover 1 2–2½-qt. metal pot with cover 1 4–5-qt. metal pot or "Dutch oven" with cover 1 French steamer	1 3-qt. metal pot with cover 1 6–8 qt. metal pot with cover 1 tea kettle 1 coffee pot 1 double boiler 1 extra French steamer	1 10–12-qt. metal pot with cover 1 copper saucepot 1 crock pot 1 pressure cooker Extra pots with covers
Cooking with Dry Heat	1 1½–2-qt. rectangular deep casserole 1 1½–2-qt. rectangular or square shallow casserole 1 aluminum loaf pan, 9 × 5 × 3 inches 1 broiler pan with rack 1 flat aluminum cookie sheet 1 8–9-inch glass pie plate 1 aluminum cake pan, 9 × 13 × 2 inches 1 or 2 cake and cookie racks	1 1½–2-qt. round or oval casserole or soufflé dish 2 to 3 extra loaf pans 2 to 3 round aluminum cake pans, 8–9 inches 1 tube pan, 10 × 4 inches 1 aluminum muffin or cupcake pan with 2½-inch cups 2 square aluminum cake pans 6 to 8 custard cups or ramekins Extra casseroles or cake pans	6 to 8 individual-serving casseroles 1 or more spring-form pans 1 or more pizza pans 6 to 8 individual-serving loaf pans 1 aluminum angel-food-cake pan 1 toaster oven 1 convection oven 1 waffle iron
Frying	1 10-inch heavy fry pan with cover 1 12-inch heavy fry pan with cover 1 4–6-inch sauté pan	1 6–7-inch aluminum or lined copper omelet pan 1 10–12-inch griddle pan Extra fry pans with covers	1 electric skillet or fry pan 1 deep-fat fryer with thermostat

A cook's guide to kitchen tools (continued)

Function	Basic	Desirable	Luxurious
Storing	1 box 12-inch aluminum foil 1 box large, heavy-duty sealable plastic storage bags 1 box medium-size, heavy-duty sealable plastic storage bags 1 box 12-inch plastic wrap 6 to 10 1-qt. freezer containers with lids 6 to 10 1-pt. freezer containers with lids 6 to 10 ½-pt. freezer containers with lids Containers with tight-fitting lids for storing sugar, flour, etc. Jars with screw-top lids	Extra of everything	
Miscellaneous	1 can opener/bottle opener 1 corkscrew 1 pair salt and pepper shakers 4 to 5 dish towels 1 to 3 aprons 2 to 4 hot pads 1 funnel 1 vegetable brush 1 ABC fire extinguisher 1 dish sponge 1 soup ladle 1 pepper mill Rags for wiping spills	1 mortar and pestle 1 meat mallet 1 garlic press 1 salad spinner 1 potato masher 1 nutcracker	1 larding needle 1 ice-cream scoop

Tools for Cutting

Knives

Knives really are a cook's "tools of the trade," the most important tools you will use. The better your knives are, the better you care for them, and the more you know about how to work with them, the better they will serve you.

☐ *Types of Kitchen Knives*

There is a length and shape of knife for almost any purpose. You can work with as many or as few as you like. It is better to have a few really good ones, even if they don't match, than a number of matching knives that are not very good. Select each knife on the basis of the purpose for which it will be used.

For most slicing, chopping, or dicing, use an all-purpose **utility knife** with a blade from six to eight inches in length and triangular in shape so that you can rock the blade from the point back to the handle without banging your knuckles. This knife should balance at a point just behind the bolster. If you can afford only one really good knife, it should be this one. A good utility knife is used more than any other single kitchen tool, including other knives.

A **chef's knife** is shaped like a utility knife, but the blade is eight to ten inches long. It is used for chopping, slicing, or dicing larger pieces. The balance point is on the blade slightly beyond the bolster. This may also be called a "utility knife," and what I have described as a utility knife may be called a "chef's knife" by some cooks and books.

A **paring knife** is used mostly for trimming vegetables, which is why it is also called a vegetable knife. Whatever you call it, this knife should have a blade three to six inches long. It is used for peeling, paring, or cutting smaller pieces. The balance point is on the handle, an inch to an inch and a half behind the bolster.

A good **carving knife** has a blade that is from nine to twelve inches long. It is used for carving warm meats and poultry. The balance point is the bolster. A luxurious version is the electric carving knife. A slicing knife may also be used for carving.

Slicing can be done with any of the knives listed above. For slicing warm bread or soft foods such as tomatoes, however, a **slicing knife with scalloped edges** does a better job. Slicing knives come in lengths from six to twelve

Tools for Cutting

Knives

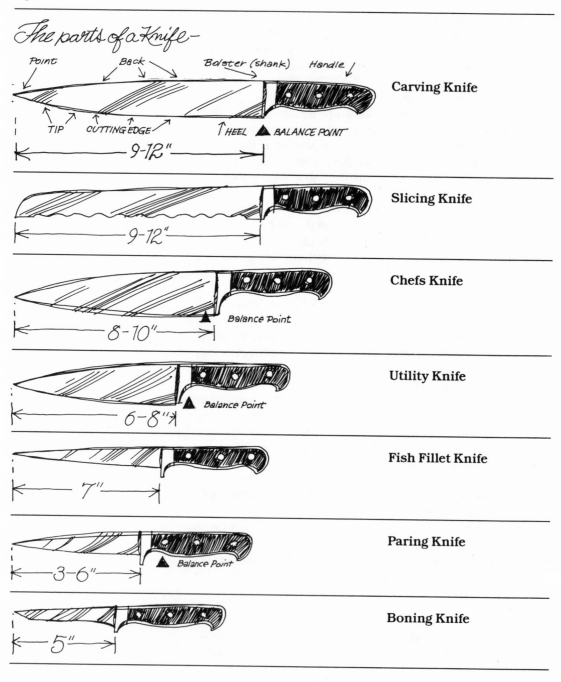

The parts of a Knife —

Point Back Bolster (shank) Handle

TIP CUTTING EDGE HEEL ▲ BALANCE POINT

9-12" **Carving Knife**

9-12" **Slicing Knife**

8-10" Balance Point **Chefs Knife**

6-8" ▲ Balance Point **Utility Knife**

7" **Fish Fillet Knife**

3-6" ▲ Balance Point **Paring Knife**

5" **Boning Knife**

inches. You might want to have a long one for breads and a short one for smaller foods. Avoid slicing knives with sharp, serrated ridges. They tend to tear the food rather than cut it. A proper slicing knife will have smoothly scalloped edges.

Less vital in kitchens today but still handy is the **boning knife**. It is used for what its name implies. Its thin curved blade allows it to cut very close to remove bones from meats and poultry while leaving the meat intact.

The flexible blade of a **fish fillet knife** makes it possible to fillet delicate fish smoothly and cleanly with a minimum of waste. Like the boning knife, it is not a standard item in most kitchens. Still, if you cook and serve a great deal of fish, one of these is a must.

Other important things to consider when selecting knives are as follows:

- *Length:* The length of the knife is measured from its bolster to the tip of the blade. The handle is not included.
- *Metal:* High-carbon stainless steel is the easiest material to care for, and the most practical for most cooks. Carbon steel will hold its edge better, but it interacts chemically with some foods. Also, carbon steel corrodes easily, and that can affect the taste of some foods. Blades made of plain stainless steel are difficult to sharpen, and it is difficult to maintain an edge on the blade. High-chromium "super stainless" or alloy steel blades look pretty, and they do remain sharp in the beginning. But when they become dull (and they will), they are virtually impossible to sharpen.
- *Flat ground or hollow ground:* Blades come with either flat sides (flat ground) or concave sides (hollow ground). Hollow-ground blades will take a sharper edge, but flat-ground blades hold their edge longer.
- *Handle:* Handles made of wood or of wood impregnated with plastic are preferable to plastic ones. Plastic handles are more likely to slip or crack. The most durable handles conform exactly to the full length and shape of the metal part of the blade that they cover (the *tang*).
- *Balance:* How the knife feels—its balance—is extremely important for assuring both comfort and the control needed for avoiding accidents. Test the balance by placing the side of the knife on your finger at the balance point previously described for each type of knife. The knife should feel heavier in the handle so that the blade rises slowly.

□ *The Cutting Board*

Whatever the knife or cutting technique, proper cutting begins with placing the object to be cut on a cutting board. (Never simply hold the object in one hand while trying to cut it with a knife held in the other.) A proper cutting board is made of a firm but not hard material that is non-porous. Nylon, soft plastic, and hard rubber are all good materials. Wooden boards are porous and consequently make natural breeding grounds for bacteria. They are, in a word, unsanitary—so unsanitary, in fact, that many states prohibit their use in public food establishments. They may be pretty, and certainly they are popular, but that does not make them any safer. Boards made of plexiglas, marble, or hard plastic are intended to be used for turning pastry dough. Don't use such a hard surface as a cutting board; it will dull your knives.

Whatever the material from which it is made, the surface of a cutting board should be soft enough to yield slightly to the knife so that the blade's edge is not damaged or dulled as it works against the board. Also, the board should be large enough not to crowd or cramp you or slide around as you work on it. Never use the cutting edge of a knife for moving foods or for sweeping the cutting board. That will dull the blade. Use the back of the blade instead.

Keep your cutting board clean. Wash it frequently with soap or bleach and hot water, especially after meats, chicken, or other fatty foods have been on it. Remember that a food will be only as sanitary as the dirtiest thing it touches, and the cutting board will be only as clean as you keep it.

□ *Cutting Techniques*

The main cutting techniques are slicing, chopping, and dicing or mincing.

Slicing.   This technique is used for cutting foods into pieces of uniform size. The **guiding hand** holds the object securely against the cutting board.

Grip the knife handle securely in the other hand and place the tip on top of the food with the cutting edge at a forty-five degree angle to the board.

Motion: Pressing firmly, push the blade *away* from your body in a smooth, continuous motion so that the cutting edge goes downward through the food in an arc until it is horizontal with the board.

Chopping. This technique is used for cutting smaller foods into pieces of approximately the same size. The **guiding hand** holds the food in place against the cutting board. The fingers should be curved so that the fingertips or the first or second knuckles of one or more fingers are vertical to the food to provide a solid rest and guide for the blade.

Grip the knife handle firmly but comfortably in the other hand. Place the blade so that its side rests lightly against the backs of the fingers of the guiding hand. The cutting edge should be at a forty-five degree angle to the board.

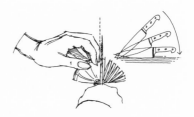

Motion: Using the knife tip as a fulcrum, and the back of the fingers as a guide, roll the blade in one continuous motion downward in an arc through the food to the surface of the board. Notice that the tip of the blade remains in contact with the cutting board.

Dicing or Mincing. This technique is used for cutting foods into smaller pieces of non-uniform size.

Grip the knife handle firmly but comfortably and place the blade tip on the board over the food with the cutting edge at a forty-five degree angle to the board.

The **guiding hand** in this case is used to guide the knife, not the food. With the thumb positioned firmly against the side of the blade, use the fingers to hold the tip against the board and to guide the blade as it is moved to cut the food in different places and at various angles.

Motion: As with the chop position, the tip is used as a fulcrum and the blade is rolled in an arc in one smooth motion down through the food to the board. As each cut is made, roll the knife back up and position it for the next cut. Repeat the motion until the pieces are the size you want. As with chopping, the tip of the blade should not lose contact with the board. Here, though, it is the knife and the guiding hand that move, not the food.

□ *Do's and Don't's of Knife Care*

Good knives aren't cheap, and once you have them you don't want to have to replace them. To save money as well as to have knives that serve you better, follow these simple rules:

· *Do* store knives in a special place—preferably in plain view. A magnetized board mounted on a wall is most visible, most convenient, and most safe.
· *Don't* store knives loosely in a drawer. Not only are loose knives unsafe, but sliding around against the drawer or

other objects will dull and damage their blades.

- *Don't* soak knives in dishwater. It won't hurt them, but a knife hidden in dishwater can be a real safety hazard.
- *Do* wash knives after each use. Wipe them dry and put them in their proper place so that you and they are both safe.
- *Don't* put knives in a dishwasher. The blades might be damaged bouncing against other objects, and the heat might distort the molecular structure of the metal.
- *Don't* try to catch a knife if it is dropped. Get out of its way and let it fall.
- *Don't* use a knife as a screwdriver or bottle opener, or for anything other than the purpose it is intended to serve— cutting.
- *Don't* use kitchen knives for cutting string, paper, or other objects that can dull them.
- *Don't* use metal, marble, glass, porcelain, or other hard surfaces as a cutting board. Hard surfaces of any kind will dull knife blades.
- *Do* keep your knives sharp. When you buy knives, get good, sharp ones, and keep them that way with a sharpening steel. That's the long, round device against which knives are drawn to hone their edges and smooth off the tiny rough spots that come with almost every use. It is a good practice to steel a blade before each use or at least once a day. (See "How to Use a Sharpening Steel," below.)

A steel will help keep a sharp blade sharp, but it won't sharpen a dull one. Although there are any number of gadgets available for sharpening knives, most of them will shorten the life of the blade. For long life as well as sharp blades, it is best to have knives sharpened only by a professional. Almost any hardware store or butcher shop, and many kitchen stores, can sharpen knives at modest cost, or you can purchase whetstones and do it yourself. To do it right, however, requires two to three stones, and they can be rather expensive.

How to Use a Sharpening Steel

1. Hold the knife in your working hand and the steel in the other, keeping your thumb and fingers tucked safely behind the guard of the steel.

2. Hold the blade at a twenty-degree angle to the steel, with the bolster of the knife almost at the tip of the steel.

3. Draw the blade lightly down the length of the steel so that the tip of the blade ends up at the guard of the steel. Be careful not to hit the blade against the guard. Repeat the process on the other side of the blade and of the steel.

4. Use smooth, even, light strokes, always keeping the blade at a twenty-degree angle to the steel. The sound should be a melodic ringing, not a grinding noise. If there is no ring, you are applying too much pressure.

5. Alternate stroking each side of the blade. Stroke each side only five times. Excessive steeling can distort the edge.

6. Clean the steel as needed, using a cloth dampened with vinegar.

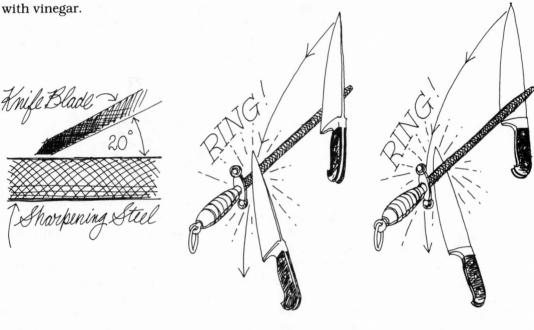

Other Cutting Tools

Even though knives can do almost anything any of the following tools can do, these specialized tools really can do some cutting jobs better and more efficiently.

The double blade of a **vegetable peeler** swivels to follow the contours of vegetables or fruits, removing their peels with a minimum of waste. You can use the sharp tip to pluck out potato eyes, seeds, bruised spots, and so on without putting the peeler down to swap it for a knife. Get a good peeler, one made of stainless steel. If and when it

gets dull, throw it away and get a new one. Peelers are impossible to sharpen.

For grating or making very thin slices of cheese and other hard foods, you need a **grater** of one kind or another. Flat graters are difficult to work with—real knuckle scrapers. Box graters have four sides and are more versatile and kinder to the knuckles than the flat variety. Rotary graters are by far the easiest type to work with, although they won't grate pieces nearly as finely as the other two types. Rotary graters come with one to three blades for grating pieces of different sizes.

For more serious cooks who will get into pureeing, mashing, or grinding, a **food mill** will do the job on almost any food without destroying its texture. Food mills come with different blades for different purposes.

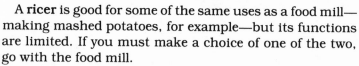

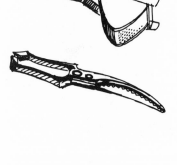

A **ricer** is good for some of the same uses as a food mill—making mashed potatoes, for example—but its functions are limited. If you must make a choice of one of the two, go with the food mill.

Common kitchen tasks such as cutting string, paper, and bones might damage a good knife. **Kitchen shears** do such jobs better without the risk of damage to your precious knives. The best shears are made of carbon steel or stainless steel and have one blade with scalloped edges. Good **poultry shears** can be very useful if you do much fancy cooking with poultry.

Tools for Mixing

Once foods have been cut up, the next task in food preparation usually is to mix them together. Using the correct tool for the task is the best way to save time and effort, as well as to get the results you want.

Mixing bowls generally come in sets (called "nests") of three, in graded sizes. Stainless steel is the most serviceable material. Aluminum can discolor some foods, such as egg whites. Either glass or porcelain might break, and beaten egg whites will slip down their sides. Plastic and other synthetic materials retain fat residue, so that egg whites don't beat up in them very well. If you do a great deal of baking, then you really should have at least one unlined copper bowl for beating egg whites. The chemical reaction that occurs between the copper and egg whites causes them to beat up better.

A lot of fancy cooks and books insist on wooden **spoons** as if wood had some magical quality that makes foods taste better. It doesn't. In fact, wooden spoons can make foods taste bad. About the only good things to be said about wooden spoons are that they are soft and won't damage enamelware or non-stick cooking surfaces and that they do have more charm and warmth than metal or plastic spoons. But wooden spoons, like wooden cutting boards, are unsanitary. Wood is porous and the best possible home for bacteria that can cause sickness and affect the tastes of foods. Also, as with pots made of plain iron, wooden spoons hold flavors, and those flavors can transfer to other foods. Everything that might be done well with wooden spoons can be done just as well with spoons made of plastic or other synthetic materials that offer the additional advantage of being sanitary.

A **loop** is a newer tool usually made of plastic. It is simply a heavy solid loop at the end of a long handle used for mixing almost anything as well as for beating thick, heavy batters.

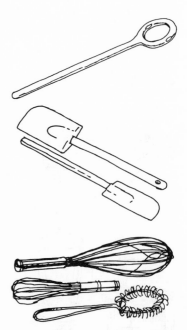

Rubber spatulas or **bowl scrapers** are the thin, long-handled devices with the rubber flap on the end used for mixing thinner batters and liquids as well as for scraping out bowls when you don't have little helpers around to lick them. At least one spatula is a must for every kitchen. If you do much baking, you will want to have two or three of different sizes.

Whisks are indispensable for mixing thinner batters, beating egg whites, and cooking sauces without lumps. They come in various sizes, from one-half inch in diameter to the large "whip" that can be as much as four inches wide. Two or three whisks of different sizes are desirable for most kitchens.

Mixers are the machines that are built to take a lot of the work out of mixing or beating things together. Wonderful things they are, too. They range from the simple, hand-operated rotary mixers through the elaborate pro-

fessional electric mixers and food processors, with all kinds in between. One hand mixer is needed in every kitchen. Do get a good one that will last, one that has a strong handle and blades, and a ball bearing or equally strong metal mechanism. Beyond a hand mixer, whatever electric mixer you should have is a matter of the kind of cooking you intend to do and your bank account. If you do a great deal of bread or pastry making, you should have a heavy-duty mixer on a stand. Otherwise, an electric hand mixer should suit most needs very well.

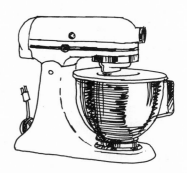

If you intend to do much pastry or bread making, a **pastry blender** is a must. This is an arc of metal blades mounted on a wooden or plastic handle that is used to blend or "cut in" flour with butter or other fat. The thin blades cut through the dough to blend it more evenly than any other mixing tool.

For making everything from frozen daiquiris to cold sauces, with pureed foods for soups or dips in between, a **food blender** is a modern wonder. Blenders range from the inexpensive two-speed type to those with a speed and a button for almost any purpose. Simple or fancy, a blender will find many uses in any kitchen.

The latest, most exotic, and most versatile mixing tool—and one of the most expensive—is the **food processor**. A food processor will slice, chop, grind, mix, blend, puree, and do just about anything but serve the food. This tool is a real luxury, not a must. All of these functions can be

performed by such lesser tools as a good knife and a mul-
tispeed blender, but a food processor does them all, and it
does them very quickly.

Tools for Cooking

The tools described in this section all are used to handle
hot foods. Consequently, they all are subject to two considerations: the working end must be able to withstand
high temperatures, and the handle must be long enough
and made of appropriate material so that the cook isn't
burned. In addition, if you are using a pot or pan with a
non-stick inner coating, the tool must be soft so that it
does not scratch.

Tongs are among the most practical cooking tools you
can have. Like pancake turners, they can be used to turn
or lift foods. Like forks, they can be used to move foods or
hold them steady. Unlike forks, though, tongs don't pierce
the surface of the food and allow its juices to escape.

Pancake turners (also called **offset spatulas**) are used
for turning many things besides pancakes. The wide, flat
blade is usually slotted so that fats or liquids drain off the
food as it is lifted.

Hard spatulas (also called **straight spatulas** or **palette
knives**) are quite different from the soft rubber spatulas
used for mixing. A hard spatula is simply a dull, rounded
blade made of metal or plastic that is used for cutting and
for lifting foods from a baking pan. Hard spatulas come in
various lengths and widths. At least one short one and one
long one are desirable to have.

Long-handled spoons, preferably made of plastic or other
synthetic material, are needed for stirring and basting foods
as they cook. Wooden spoons are unsanitary. It is handy
to have several cooking spoons of various lengths, some
solid and some slotted for draining foods.

Forks used for cooking are distinguished from dining
forks by the number of tines. Cooking forks have only two
or three tines so that they can pierce foods easily. You
should have at least one cooking fork with a long handle
for turning foods, and one with a short handle to hold
foods as they are being cut. (For turning foods, however,
tongs usually do a better job than forks, because they don't
pierce the food's surface and allow its juices to escape.)

Basting brushes are used for applying liquids, sauces, and glazes to foods as they cook. Get at least one good brush about two inches wide with camel-hair bristles. Bristles made of plastic are likely to melt.

Bulb basters are used for reaching under roasting meats or poultry to draw off the pan juices. You could use a spoon, but a basting bulb does the job faster with less chance of burning your hand.

Tools for Draining and Straining

Tools for draining and straining are needed for preparing almost any meal, especially when making sauces, soups, or any foods cooked in liquids.

Slotted spoons are common and handy tools used for lifting solid foods out of hot liquids or fats.

Colanders are large bowls made of wire mesh, metal, or plastic, with holes in the bottom and sides. They are used for draining hot foods and for rinsing and draining fresh foods such as vegetables and fruits.

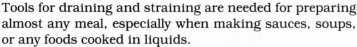

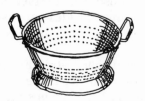

Cheesecloth is especially useful for straining liquids. Get good cheesecloth. Cheap, low quality cheesecloth might shed bits and pieces of itself into the liquid or food being strained. To work with cheesecloth easily, cut the piece to a size that will fit inside a colander or tea strainer. Wet the cheesecloth so that it will stick to the sides and use the colander or strainer to hold it as the liquid is poured through.

Tea strainers of various sizes can be used for straining things other than tea. Used fats, for example, can be strained through them to remove food particles that might burn when the fat is reused. Different strainers have meshes of different densities, and it is worthwhile to have two or three for different needs.

Skimmers are needed for skimming froth and foam off the top of liquids such as soups as they cook. If you don't have a skimmer, a tea strainer can be used instead but won't be quite as satisfactory.

A **China cap** or **"chinois"** is a rather specialized device used for straining broths and other liquids to make purees and sauces. Its uses are limited, and most kitchens won't need one. A tea strainer with a coarse mesh can be used instead.

A **flour sifter** is still a highly desirable item, despite the "no sifting required" message on some flour packages. You should always sift flour in order to measure it most accurately. A small sifter will do unless you do a great deal of baking.

Tools for Measuring

Measuring processes and instruments have changed over the years. The most notable recent change has been the move in the United States to join the rest of the world in using the metric system. As a result, more and more recipes and books include metric measures along with the "English" units (even the English are changing over to the metric system). Cookbooks published in other countries, of course, most often use the metric system. It is easiest when cooking to use measuring instruments that correspond to the units specified in the recipe. If you don't have the proper instrument, refer to the conversion table in the Appendix.

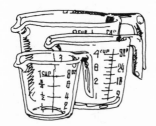

Cups used to measure liquids have extra space at their tops so that they can be handled without spilling. You can use them for measuring dry foods, but the measure is likely to be less than accurate. Wet-measure cups are usually made of heat-proof glass so that they can be used around a hot stove without danger of breaking. To be most serviceable, they should have calibrations for both English and metric units. They range in size from one cup through large measuring bowls with an eight-cup (two-quart) capacity. Since they are inexpensive, it is well worth it to have two or three sizes.

Dry-measure cups are made to exact sizes from one-quarter cup through two cups. Their contents can be leveled off at the top with the back side of a knife blade to ensure accurate measurement. Butter, shortening, and other dense ingredients can form air pockets, and so must be packed down tightly in the cup. Sugar, flour, and other loose ingredients should not be packed for measuring purposes unless a recipe specifies that they should. In either case, packed or not, level off dry ingredients so that they are even with the top of the cup.

Measuring spoons usually come in sets of four in either metric or English units (for example, one-quarter teaspoon to one tablespoon). Spoons with round or oval bowls are easier to work with and scrape out than those with square or rectangular ones. As with measuring cups, the contents of measuring spoons can be leveled off to ensure accurate measurement, unless, of course, you want a "heaping" spoonful. Dense ingredients that might form air pockets should be packed down before being leveled off.

Kitchen scales provide accurate measures of the weights of foods. That can be important for determining cooking times for foods cooked in a microwave oven and for measuring flour and other foods for which differences in weight can affect the product. Sliding-weight scales are best, but they are very expensive. Many accurate scales of the spring type are almost as satisfactory and are likely to cost less.

Another thing to consider when purchasing kitchen scales is the tray. It is a real advantage to have a tray that is large enough to hold the foods without a container whose weight would otherwise have to be accounted for. The tray should also be removable so that foods can easily be poured from it.

A **timer** is a vital tool in any kitchen. Get one that is accurate and that rings loudly. A portable timer is best because you can keep it nearby if you leave the kitchen. It is a good idea to have two or more timers for keeping track of the cooking times for several foods at once. The most accurate timers are the new digital variety, some of which can be set to keep two or more times.

Cooking thermometers are necessary for accurately measuring cooking temperatures, which can determine success or failure as much as any other factor. You'll need several thermometers designed for different purposes.

So that you can know what your oven's cooking temperatures really are, use an **oven thermometer** to check the oven every few months. Test different places in the oven to detect hot spots, and also check different temperature settings. The more you know about your oven, the better you will be able to account for the way it cooks.

Meat thermometers are needed for roasting large cuts of meats as well as whole chickens or turkeys. For oven use, a slow-response thermometer is best. For use with a microwave oven, or for cooking on a rotisserie, you will need one of the rapid-response type that can be inserted into the food to record its internal temperature in about ten seconds.

Fry thermometers, when used at all, are used for deep-fat frying. They usually have handles for hanging them on the side of the cooking vessel. They are not suited for measuring the temperatures of fats in shallow pans except for getting intermittent readings. A good fry thermometer can register temperatures up to 400 degrees Fahrenheit and should be able to be immersed in liquids.

Microwave thermometers are of either the slow-response or rapid-response type. Use a slow-response thermometer made only of plastic, because metal can arc and damage the microwave unit. You can use a metal rapid-response thermometer to measure temperatures of foods outside a microwave oven; just don't use it in the oven.

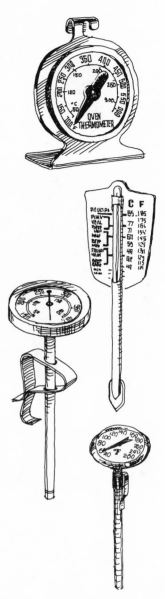

*F*oods and Basic Ingredients
How to Select, Store, Prepare, Cook, Flavor, and Serve Most of Them

PART THREE

This part of the book provides all the essential information most cooks need about foods and basic ingredients in their natural forms. Foods also come in other "unnatural" forms, though, and so Chapter Twelve describes what those are as well as how to work with them. The remaining chapters are about specific groups of fresh foods and include information about how to select, store, and prepare them, determine the cooking methods that suit them best, and select the seasonings and accompaniments that go well with them. Specific instructions for cooking each type of food are given at the end of the chapter in which it is described.

Much of the information in the chapters about foods is presented in "Cook's Guides" designed to convey the most important information about each food in a form that is concise and convenient for quick reference. You can use these guides in two ways: (1) Review the guide for the foods you plan to use before planning your meals and shopping in order to know as much about them as you can. (2) If you buy a food or someone gives you one you've never cooked before, look it up in the appropriate guide. I hope these guides will serve you well and that you will refer to them often.

*U*nnatural Food Forms
Frozen, Canned, and Dried

CHAPTER TWELVE

Frozen Foods
Canned Foods
Dried or Dehydrated Foods

*M*ost good cooks will agree that fresh foods are best to use for virtually every cooking purpose. Fresh foods may not always be available, however, and depending on their seasons they can be more expensive than foods in other forms. Preparing fresh foods also can involve a good deal of time and work, and sometimes a good deal of waste. For these reasons, cooks often use foods in forms that are unnatural: frozen, canned, and dried. Each has its relative advantages in terms of availability, economy, convenience, and flavor.

Frozen Foods

Frozen foods are available at any time of year, require little preparation, and have virtually no waste. The flavor of many of them is about as good as all but the freshest of fresh foods. Depending on the season, frozen foods can be more or less expensive than fresh—more when foods are in season, less when they are not. All in all, frozen foods offer real convenience, but with little sacrifice of quality, nutrition, or economy.

A Cook's Guide to Frozen Foods

☐ *To Select*
Buy frozen foods in packages that are unopened and solid. Make sure there is no sign that the food inside has thawed and been refrozen (look for ice formations or discoloration on one end of the package).

Frozen vegetables and fruits, like canned varieties, may be graded A, B, and C according to their quality. I say "may" because grading is not compulsory. Some packagers use it, others do not. When a grade is shown, it usually conforms to the standards described in the insert on the next page.

You can buy frozen foods in packages containing eight to twelve ounces, which will produce two or three normal portions. Some foods are also available in large bags. These

provide convenience as well as savings since you can use only as much as you need, keeping the remainder frozen for later use.

□ *To Store*

Frozen foods may be stored for a year or even longer, but the fresher they are the better they will taste. They should always be kept in a food freezer or in the freezer compartment of a refrigerator at least below freezing temperature (32 degrees F.) and preferably below zero degrees F. If a frozen food thaws, don't refreeze it unless you cook it first.

A Grading System for Canned and Frozen Foods

Grade A: Reserved for the most tender, succulent, flavorful, and attractive foods. The highest price usually goes with this grade, but not always. Prices vary from brand to brand, and a Grade A from one food packager might be less expensive than a Grade B from another. If appearance is not a consideration (as when the food is to be used in a casserole), either a Grade C or a Grade B can be used just as well and more economically than a Grade A. Most people won't know the difference.

Grade B: Grade B foods don't look as good as Grade A and are a little tougher, but otherwise in many cases it is difficult to tell the difference in taste.

Grade C: There really is a difference between Grade C foods and Grades A and B, both in texture and appearance. Grade C foods are not uniform in color, their flavor is less predictable, and their texture tends to be mushy. Many of the newer generic or "no name" economy brands, by the way, are Grade C whether their labels say so or not.

□ To Cook

Frozen food packages almost always have instructions for cooking printed on them. It is usually best to thaw the food at least partially before cooking so that it will cook evenly. To use a frozen food in a combination dish such as a casserole, thaw it first and then use it as if it were fresh.

Canned Foods

Foods in cans are available in any season, are easily stored for long periods, require no special preparation or equipment for storage, and have virtually no waste. Some people dislike the taste and texture of many canned foods, but taste can vary with the quality of the product as well as with the taste of the individual. The major disadvantage of canned foods is that many of them contain sodium, sugar, or other additives that affect their flavor and are best minimized in a healthy diet. Canned foods may also be less attractive than the same food in its fresh or frozen forms.

A Cook's Guide to Canned Foods

□ To Select

Look for cans that have no dents or other signs of damage that might indicate injury to the contents. If the can bulges out, gas may have formed inside. In that case the contents should not be eaten—not even tasted—for they can be quite dangerous and even deadly.

Cans come in different sizes and should be chosen according to the number of servings planned. Many recipes give the industry terms for the can sizes. The accompanying table shows what those terms mean.

General terms for can sizes and what they mean

Term	Amount	Approximate Measure
#1 or "picnic"	10½–12 ozs.	1½ cups
#300	14–16 ozs.	1¾ cups
#303	16–17 ozs.	2 cups
#2	20 ozs.	2½ cups
#2½	29 ozs.	3½ cups
#3 Special	46 ozs.	5¾ cups

The liquid in canned foods contains many nutrients. Whenever you can, use it to cook the food, save it for use as broth, or both. Be sure to take into account any seasonings in the liquid before adding more (read the label). (See "How to Read a Label," p. 215.) Enough salt or MSG is usually in the liquid so that more is neither necessary nor desirable.

Canned foods are graded to allow the consumer to judge the appearance, texture, and flavor of the food. Almost all food packagers use the U.S.D.A. grading system or one similar to it. (See "A Grading System for Canned and Frozen Foods," p. 277.)

□ To Store
Keep canned foods in a cool, dry place away from direct sunlight. They can be kept safely for as long as several years, but are best if used within one year of purchase.

□ To Prepare
Preparing canned foods is literally as easy as opening the can. However, somewhere between the canner and you the cans have probably been sprayed with insecticides or handled by people whose hands are dirty with just about anything you can imagine. It is a good practice, therefore, to wash the lid with hot soapy water and rinse off the soap before opening the can. That way, if the lid falls in, it won't contaminate the contents.

Always check cans as you open them to be certain no spoilage has occurred. Look for any swelling in the can and watch for any spurting of the liquid when the can is opened. Those are signs of a gas having formed inside by things that might be poisonous. Of course, any off odors, off flavors, or mold are sure signs that the contents are bad and should not be used. "*When in doubt, throw it out.*"

☐ *To Cook*

Canned foods have been cooked at least partially before or after being canned. If you cook them more, do it quickly. If you simply want to heat the contents, use the liquid from the can so that you get full advantage of the nutrients and flavors it contains. When you use canned foods in soups, casseroles, or braises, add them so that they cook only long enough for their flavors to blend with the other ingredients—not so long that they overcook and become soft.

Dried or Dehydrated Foods

(See "About Those Prepackaged 'Convenience' Foods," p. 218.)

Dried or dehydrated foods include everything from dried beans and peas to the more modern prepared and prepackaged processed foods such as cake mixes, dried mashed potatoes, soup mixes, and prepared stuffing mixes. The greatest advantage of dried foods is that they can be stored in very little space at no energy cost for several months. In many cases, however, you pay for that convenience with a much higher price. That is not true of dried beans or peas, but it certainly is true of prepackaged processed foods. Also, and of no little importance, processed foods often contain large amounts of sugar, sodium, and chemicals that many of us would rather not have in our diets. Read labels to be sure of what you are getting.

(See "How to Read a Label," p. 215.)

A Cook's Guide to Dried or Dehydrated Foods

☐ *To Select*

Buy dried foods in packages that have not been opened. (Sometimes the food package is sliced through along with its shipping box. Sometimes the box is opened by children or rude shoppers.) Prepackaged prepared foods are usually sold in boxes containing from two to six servings. Quite often the contents of the entire package must be cooked all together, so don't buy more than you can use. Dried beans and peas, on the other hand, can be cooked in any amounts, so it is safe to buy them in quantities that will be used within a period of up to a year.

☐ *To Store*

Most dried foods keep well unopened for up to one year. If they contain chemical preservatives, many can be stored

much longer. The fresher they are, however, the better they will be. Once a package has been opened, its remaining contents should be transferred to a container that can "seal air out and freshness in." Keep packaged dried foods in a cool place, preferably away from sunlight.

□ *To Prepare*

Any dried or prepackaged food will have instructions for its preparation printed on the package. (Tip: If you open the package and store the contents in a separate container, tear off the instructions and keep them with the food.) Dried beans and peas require overnight soaking before cooking, or you can soften them quickly by parboiling them for two minutes and then soaking them in cold water for one to two hours.

□ *To Cook*

Instructions for cooking most dried foods are printed on the package. Foods such as rice, beans, pasta, and peas will cook up to be much larger than in their dried form, so select a cooking vessel that will be large enough to hold the food after it has cooked.

*B*asic Ingredients

CHAPTER THIRTEEN

*B*asic ingredients are those common things called for in most recipes without which no cook can do much of anything: spices and other seasonings, onions, vinegar, butter, flour, milk and milk products, and the other topics covered here. They are listed alphabetically for easy reference, and some are grouped together with others that are similar and might be used in the same ways. By considering ingredients in groups instead of individually, you will be better prepared to make substitutions when you need to.

A Cook's Guide to Basic Ingredients

Acidic Liquids: Citrus Juices, Vinegars, and Wines

Any liquid that is high in acid content does several things to foods: (1) It affects the food's flavor. If only a small amount is used, it augments the natural flavor of the food. If too much is used, though, it can mask the flavor. (2) It affects the color of the food. Fish, many fruits, and white vegetables such as potatoes, mushrooms, and cauliflower will have their colors heightened. (The acid protects them from the bacteria that cause them to darken when exposed to open air.) Green vegetables, on the other hand, can be turned dark because the acid destroys the chlorophyll in them. (3) It softens the texture of foods, especially proteins, if they remain in the acidic liquid for very long.

(See "Marinades," p. 102.)

For most cooking purposes, any acidic liquid is too strong and must be diluted before it can be used. The "acidulated liquids" called for in many recipes are simply water to which some acidic liquid—usually lemon juice or vinegar—has been added: one tablespoon per cup of water.

☐ Citrus Juices
Lemon juice is the most common of the citrus juices used for cooking. Lime, orange, and grapefruit juices may be used also, but each has a more distinct flavor. Fresh juice always tastes best. (*Tip*: To get the most juice from a fruit,

microwave it for 10 to 20 seconds before squeezing it.) If you use a juice a great deal, you can squeeze a half dozen or so pieces of the fruit at one time and store the liquid in the refrigerator for several days without much loss of flavor. (The juice of one medium-sized lemon or lime equals about three tablespoons.) For added flavor when using any citrus juice, include a little grated rind. The rind contains aromatic oils that add to the juice's flavor. For convenience, you might prefer the frozen juices or the reconstituted lemon or lime juices sold in bottles. Reconstituted juices can have a peculiar flavor, perhaps because of an added preservative. Frozen juices, though, are almost as good as fresh.

☐ *Vinegars*

Vinegars are made from fruits that have fermented. There are different kinds and colors, each with its own special taste.

Apple cider vinegar is probably used more than any other vinegar for most cooking as well as for household cleaning purposes. It is a pale gold-brown color and has an aroma that reminds one of the apples from which it is made.

Wine vinegars have a more subtle taste than vinegar made from apples. They come in red, white, and rosé, just as wines do. Your choice of color should probably be determined by appearance more than taste, for there is not that much difference in their flavors. The taste of wine vinegars is better and more delicate than that of other vinegars, but you pay for it. Wine vinegars may cost three to four times more.

Both apple cider vinegar and wine vinegars contain from 5 to 6% acetic acid, an amount that serves well for most cooking purposes. There are some cooking needs, however, that are served better by a vinegar with a higher acid content. That's where **distilled vinegar** comes in. That's

the **white vinegar** called for in some recipes. It contains up to 12% acetic acid. The higher acid content makes it especially good to use in marinades and for most cleaning purposes.

Flavored vinegar is a convenience if garlic or an herb such as basil or tarragon is used often along with the vinegar. You can buy vinegar already flavored, or make it yourself. Simply place a sprig of fresh herb or a couple of garlic cloves into the vinegar. Remove the flavoring before it deteriorates and clouds the liquid.

☐ *Wines*

Many cooks pride themselves on specialty dishes using wines. In fact, cooking with wine can seem so fancy that some cooks may be intimidated about trying it. Actually, a little experimentation is well worth the effort, because wines do add special flavors to foods.

(See "Beer and Wine," p. 26.)

Wines are used most often for sautés and braises. First the food is browned in fat, and then wine is added to simmer the food and flavor it. For milder flavor, mix water or broth with the wine. Wines may also be used to add flavor to broth and other liquids used for cooking as well as for a part of the acidic liquid in vinaigrette dressings. Don't use too much, though, or the flavor of the original liquid might be overpowered by the wine.

Almost any wine may be used for cooking so long as its flavor and color are compatible with the food. You wouldn't use a hearty burgundy with a delicate fish, for example. It would spoil the white color as well as overpower the flavor of the fish. Never use so much wine that it drowns out the flavor of the food. Delicate dishes require only a little wine, while heartier ones can take more. Add the wine a little at a time, tasting as you go.

As a rule, if the wine is not good enough to drink, it isn't good enough to use for cooking. That is not to say that really good wines should be used for cooking. No, indeed. In fact, their delicate flavors are lost in cooking. However, an inexpensive but flavorful wine is perfectly adequate for any cooking task.

Dry vermouth is a good all-purpose cooking wine that is compatible with most foods. Burgundy is very popular for cooking meats, but other red wines work just as well. There are also wines such as cooking sherry that are made especially for cooking. They contain salt to preserve them and keep them from turning to vinegar. Wines containing salt cannot be used for drinking, and the salt must be accounted for when they are used for cooking.

Baking Powder

See "Leaveners," p. 301.

Baking Soda

See "Leaveners," p. 301.

Bread Crumbs or Breading

Bread crumbs or breading (finely ground bread crumbs) are used as toppings for salads, soups, and casseroles and for adding a crispy crust to fried foods. They are also the primary ingredient in bread stuffing and dressing. You can buy bread crumbs or breading already prepared with seasonings, or you can make them yourself using white or dark bread, corn bread, dried cereal, crackers, or combinations of these. Two to two and one-half slices of bread will make one cup of large crumbs. Six slices will make one cup of fine crumbs. Here is how to do it.

(See "Breading," p. 54.)

How to Make Bread Crumbs

1. **Cut the crust off the bread.**
2. **For large crumbs, use two forks and pull the pieces apart** to keep from compressing the bread too much.

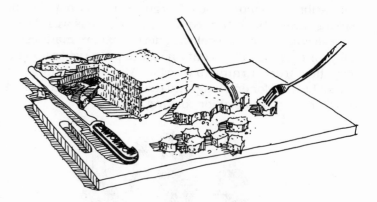

3. **Dry the crumbs** in the open air for one day or longer, or toast them on a cookie sheet in a 300 degree F. oven long enough to dry them without browning.
4. **For finely textured crumbs, chop the dried pieces in a food blender.** Use the pulse button or turn the blender on and off several times. Alternatively, put large dried crumbs into a plastic or paper bag and beat them with the heel of your hand, a rolling pin, or some other broad instrument to crush them.
5. **To butter the crumbs,** use 1 to 2 tablespoons butter or margarine for each cup of crumbs. Melt the butter and pour it over the crumbs, tossing them so that they are covered thoroughly and evenly. For added flavor, use butter in which flavoring vegetables—onions, garlic, and celery—have been sautéed.
6. **To season,** add dried herbs and spices to plain or buttered crumbs.   ■

Bread Stuffing or Dressing

Bread stuffing or dressing is used as a side dish to accompany other foods, especially poultry. It can be cooked by itself or "stuffed" inside a food to cook along with it. Some foods that are often cooked with a bread stuffing are roast birds, fish, pork or veal steaks, and vegetables—especially tomatoes, cucumbers, mushrooms, sweet bell peppers, and eggplant.

There seems to be no end of recipes for bread stuffing. Most of them are good, but rarely do they tell you about a subtle but important consideration: texture. For a light texture, use larger, drier bread crumbs and coat them lightly with a seasoned dip of milk and egg, melted butter or margarine, or a combination of these. For denser, moister texture, use moister or smaller crumbs and more milk/egg dip, butter or margarine, or a combination.

How to Make Bread Stuffing or Dressing

You can think of stuffing as being like a casserole: two parts breading to one part additional ingredients, plus a sauce of milk and eggs.

1. **Prepare bread crumbs.** See "How to Make Bread Crumbs," p. 288.

2. **Cook additional ingredients almost fully.** Some popular ingredients are onions, celery, mushrooms, sausage, giblets, oysters and other shellfish, light flavored nuts such as pine nuts, uncooked apples, raisins and other dried fruits, or combinations of these.

3. **Combine the bread crumbs with the other ingredients.** At least two-thirds of the mixture should be bread crumbs.

4. **Prepare a sauce of equal parts milk and egg.** Egg whites may be used alone to reduce cholesterol. Melted butter or margarine may be added for richer flavor. You can also substitute broth for the milk, or use a combination of milk and broth.

5. **Season the sauce to taste,** accounting for salt and other seasonings that might be in the bread and other ingredients.

6. **Slowly pour the liquid onto the dry ingredients, tossing the dry ingredients to coat them evenly.** The more liquid, the more moist the dressing will be. Do not mix too much or the breading may become pasty.

7. **Stuff the mixture into a food, or pour it into a prepared baking dish.** For lighter texture, do not pack the mixture. It will expand as it cooks. Bake at 325 to 375 degrees F. until the dressing is firm and brown. ■

Butter and Margarine

(See "Fats," p. 194.)

Butter and margarine are the most common fats used as an ingredient or as a topping for foods. Both are high in calories (100 calories per tablespoon), and butter is a major source of cholesterol. If you want to reduce calories in your diet, reduce consumption of both of these fats. If you can't bear to do that, then at least consider cutting back on your cholesterol intake by substituting margarine for butter in your cooking, if not for all uses. If you insist on the flavor of butter but still want to reduce cholesterol, then try a blend of 60% margarine and 40% butter. There are now commercial brands with this combination, and their buttery taste is acceptable to all but the most ardent butter lovers.

Common table butter is lightly salted. This type of butter is either specified or assumed by most recipes published in the United States. Unsalted butter or margarine can almost always be substituted for the salted kind in recipes, and it usually has a richer flavor. When a recipe specifies unsalted butter, it is best to not use the salted kind.

The flavor of butter or margarine is delicate and may become weak if it is stored for too long. For best flavor, refrigerate only as much as will be used in a week and keep it tightly covered. Keep extra butter or margarine tightly wrapped and frozen for up to six months.

☐ Measuring Butter or Margarine

Although you buy butter and margarine packaged as sticks (usually four to a pound) or in tubs containing a certain weight, recipe measures are commonly expressed in terms of cups or tablespoons. A standard stick of butter or margarine weighs four ounces and is equivalent to one-half cup or eight tablespoons. The table on this page gives handy equivalent measures so that you can easily figure the amount of butter or margarine called for in a recipe.

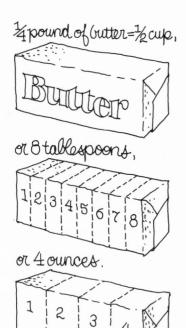

¼ pound of butter = ½ cup,

or 8 tablespoons,

or 4 ounces.

Equivalent measures of butter and margarine

1/4 stick	= 1 ounce	= 1/8 cup	= 2 tablespoons
1/2 stick	= 2 ounces	= 1/4 cup	= 4 tablespoons
1 stick	= 4 ounces	= 1/2 cup	= 8 tablespoons
2 sticks	= 8 ounces	= 1 cup	= 16 tablespoons
4 sticks	= 1 pound	= 2 cups	= 32 tablespoons

☐ *Special Forms of Butter and Margarine*

Whipped butter or margarine is available in tubs and makes a convenient and tasty table spread. In addition, using it is one simple way to cut down on calories. Because a fair amount of air is whipped in, this type of butter or margarine contains fewer calories than solid sticks. For cooking, however, you must make allowances for the air content and use one-third to one-half more to equal the amount called for in a recipe.

Many recipes and cooking techniques call for **melted butter or margarine.** Heat the fat over low heat until it melts and use it while it's hot. Whether used as a topping, for basting, or in a sauce, melted butter or margarine should be stirred just before use to distribute the separated milk particles evenly.

Browned butter is simply melted butter or margarine that is cooked long enough to give it a sweet, nutlike flavor. If it cooks for too long, however, it will taste scorched. Here is one technique that will ensure success: (1) Melt whole butter or margarine over low heat until it foams. (2) Remove it from the heat and stir it once to reduce the foam. (3) Return it to the heat, allow it to come to a foam once again, and then remove it from the heat. Browned butter may be clarified or used as melted butter.

Clarified or "drawn" butter has a clear color and a distinct flavor that is quite different from that of either whole or melted butter. (This cannot be done with margarine, by the way.) Compared with whole butter, clarified butter has fewer calories and can be heated to higher temperatures without burning because the solid milk particles have been removed. Many cooks prefer clarified butter to whole butter for sautéing and for use in sauces. Because it has so many uses, it is easiest to make it up a pint or more at a time and freeze it to use when needed.

How to Clarify Butter

1. **Melt whole butter over low heat,** skimming the foam off as it forms. This can be done on a range burner, in an oven, or in a microwave cooker.

2. **When the butter has melted fully, remove the pot from the heat.** Allow it to sit for 10 to 15 minutes until the solid milk particles have all settled on the bottom.

3. **Separate the clear butterfat on the top** by carefully pouring ("drawing") it off, holding the milk particles back with a spoon. Some cooks even strain the butter through a sieve and/or cheesecloth, but that should not be necessary if you pour slowly and carefully. A much simpler method, if you have the time, is to chill the melted butter. When the butter is solid, the milk particles can simply be scraped off the bottom.

4. **Store** extra clarified butter in ice cube trays, one or two tablespoons per cube.

■

Flavored butter or margarine, including **"savory butter"** or **"herb butter,"** is simply butter or margarine with other ingredients mixed in. Any flavoring can be used. Garlic, onion, herbs, and cheeses are the most popular, but nuts and fruits or fruit juices may be used also.

To make hot flavored butter or margarine, simply add a flavoring ingredient to butter or margarine that has been melted, clarified, or browned. For example, any butter that has been used to sauté onions, garlic, or other vegetables will retain some of their flavors. Flavored hot butter is used as a topping, in sauces, for sautéing, and for basting foods that are being roasted or baked.

To make cold whole butter or margarine (also called "savory butter" or "herb butter"), warm butter or margarine to room temperature and then incorporate chopped herbs, nuts, fruits, or vegetables into it. The fat can then be molded and used as a cold topping for vegetables, fish, or meats, or it can be melted and used hot.

(See "How to Make Cold Butter Sauce," p. 176.)

Buttermilk

See p. 304.

Celery

See "Flavoring Vegetables," p. 296.

Cheeses

There are four to five hundred different names for natural cheeses alone. Add to that the many lowfat "imitation" cheeses and cheese products available to us today, and you

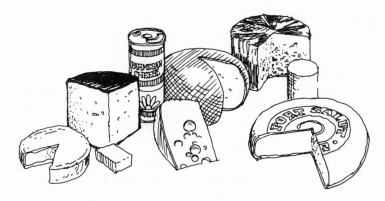

Types of popular cheeses, by texture

Hard		Semihard		Soft	
				Cured	*Fresh*
Parmesan	*Cheddar*	*Fontina*	*Blue*	*Brie*	*Cream*
Parmesan	Cheddar	Fontina	Danish Blue	Fromage de Brie	Cream
Reggiano	American	Bel Paese	Roquefort	Camembert	Neufchatel
Romano	Cheshire	Port Salut	Gorgonzola	Liederkranz	Boursin
Sardo	Tillamook	Reblochon	Stilton	Schloss	Gervais
	Swiss	Teleme Jack		Coulommiers	Cottage
	Gruyère	Monterey Jack		Breakfast	Ricotta
	Edam	Oka			
	Gouda				

From *Cooking for the Professional Chef* by Kenneth C. Wolfe. Albany, New York: Delmar Publishers, Inc. Copyright © 1982. Reprinted with permission.

will appreciate just how complex a task learning about cheeses can be.

The table above groups the most popular cheeses by their common names according to their texture. Hard cheeses are used more than others for cooking, and so it is about them that you should know most.

Classifying cheeses is one thing; knowing how to use them is something else. The "Cheeses Commonly Used for Cooking" table on p. 294 provides a useful summary. In addition, the "Guide to Natural Cheeses" in the Appendix covers both the flavor characteristics and the various uses for all of the most popular cheeses.

□ *Natural, Processed, and Imitation Cheese*
The task of selecting cheeses is complicated even more because there are natural cheeses, processed cheeses, and now even "imitation" cheeses. Any and all are called by

Cheeses commonly used for cooking

Soups	Sauces	Vegetables, eggs, pasta, fish, meat	Salads	Snacks, canape, sandwich, cheese, pastry	Pastry baking
grated	grated	sliced grated	creamed	grated sliced creamed	creamed
Parmesan Romano Sardo Cantal	Cheddar Tillamook Parmesan	Swiss Jack Mozzarella Cheddar Romano Parmesan Provolone	Roquefort Gorgonzola Stilton Blue Brie Camembert	Cheddars Blue Brie Fontina Cream Choice	Cottage Cream Ricotta

How to use them: very hard and dry – grated, semihard – sliced, soft – creamed.

From *Cooking for the Professional Chef* by Kenneth C. Wolfe. Albany, New York: Delmar Publishers, Inc. Copyright © 1982. Reprinted with permission.

common names such as cheddar, Swiss, and Parmesan.

Natural cheeses, of course, are made using products and processes that occur in nature. They all contain butterfat (from 5% to 80%, depending on the cheese), and all have a limited lifespan. For eating, as a spread, or for use as a topping, most people greatly prefer the flavor of fresh natural cheese to that of processed or imitation products. Fresh cheese is always best served at room temperature. Allow thirty minutes to one hour for a soft cheese to warm, one hour or longer for a hard cheese.

Processed cheese is made of fresh or aged natural cheese that is melted, pasteurized, and mixed with an emulsifier and perhaps some other ingredients. The result is a cheese that stops maturing and therefore has a much longer life than natural cheese. The texture of processed cheeses is softer and more uniform than that of their natural cheese counterparts, so that they melt easily and blend well with other foods. Many cooks prefer them for cooking for that reason. Also, they have no rind and consequently no waste. Finally, they are easy to slice. Many come already sliced and ready for use, but at a much higher price and with a much higher sodium content than block cheese.

Both natural and processed cheeses contain butterfat, complete with its calories and cholesterol. They also contain fair amounts of salt. Those of us who care about controlling those substances in our diets can either limit our use of cheeses or use one of the new, low-cholesterol **imitation cheeses**. These are cheeses that do not have enough butterfat to qualify as "real" cheese. By law, these products must go by some name such as "diet" cheese, be identified as an "imitation" product, or have cheese left out of the name altogether. Though the name implies otherwise, the texture, appearance, and even flavor of imitation cheeses may be the same as, or very similar to, those of processed cheeses.

□ *Storing Cheese*

Store cheeses in the refrigerator, with moisture in and air out. Either aluminum foil or plastic wrap will work well for wrapping them. Better yet, take the added step of keeping the wrapped cheese in a sealed jar or plastic bag. To slow the growth of mold as well as to keep the cheese from drying out, soak a small cloth or paper towel with vinegar or lemon juice and wrap the cheese in it before sealing it in a wrap. If mold does grow on the cheese, it won't hurt you. Simply scrape or cut it off.

□ *Cooking with Cheese*

Whether it's fresh, processed, or imitation, when cheese is used as a cooking ingredient or as a topping, one major consideration should guide you: *high heat and prolonged cooking make cheese tough and stringy.* High heat also causes the fat to separate out, making the finished product oily. If cheese is used in a sauce or in a casserole, high heat can make it harden on the bottom of the pot before it can melt evenly and blend with the other ingredients. Here are some other considerations.

To melt cheese, first cut it into small cubes, shred it, or grate it. One-half pound of solid cheese yields 1 to 1 1/2 cups of cubes, 1 1/4 to 1 3/4 cups shredded cheese, or 2 cups grated cheese. Melt the cheese in the top of a double boiler, stirring it frequently until it is a liquid of uniform consistency. To make it thinner, stir in water, milk, cream, wine, broth, or a combination of these.

For casserole dishes or sauces in which cheese is an ingredient, use cheese that has been finely chopped, grated, shredded, or melted so that it can blend evenly into the mixture in very little time. Large pieces won't melt properly. Cook the casserole in a moderate oven (325 to 375 degrees F.) just long enough to melt the cheese thoroughly and/or brown it.

Cheese toppings for casseroles or other foods should be added only after the dish has cooked, and then should be heated only long enough to melt the cheese. Use thin strips or slices, or cheese that has been shredded or grated. If you are using a broiler, place the food so that its top is four to five inches from the heating element and watch it carefully to be certain it does not burn.

For omelets and other egg dishes, use cheese that has been grated or shredded. For omelets, add the cheese just before folding. The heat from the eggs will cook the cheese even after the omelet has been removed from the pan.

Citrus Juices

See "Acidic Liquids," p. 284.

Cooking Oils

See pp. 47–48.

Cream

See p. 304.

Fats

See pp. 46–49 and 194–195.

Flavoring Vegetables: Onions, Garlic, Celery, and Others

As the name implies, flavoring vegetables are used to flavor other foods. Onion, garlic, shallots, and celery are the most common vegetables used for flavoring. Sweet bell peppers, mushrooms, scallions, leeks, carrots, parsnips, turnips, rutabagas, and other root vegetables are in this group also. Detailed descriptions of all these vegetables are given in Chapter Eighteen.

☐ Forms of Flavoring Vegetables

Fresh vegetables are preferable to all other forms for flavoring as much as for eating. No kitchen should ever be without a good stock of fresh onions, a few cloves of fresh garlic, several ribs of fresh celery, and a few fresh sweet bell peppers and carrots. Scallions and shallots are also good things to have on hand when more delicate onion or garlic flavoring is desired. Other vegetables such as turnips are used less frequently and may or may not be available in fresh form, depending on the time of year. Usually fresh flavoring vegetables are sautéed before being mixed with other foods to soften their texture and mellow their flavor, a process called "sweating."

Liquid garlic, onion, and celery juices are now available in bottles. They are convenient, but the flavor is not as good as that of fresh vegetables. Liquid garlic is especially useful because there is no chance of its burning to produce a bitter taste.

Powdered onion, garlic, and celery are always convenient to have on hand to substitute for fresh, especially for making last-minute adjustments. They can be substituted for the fresh vegetable for any cooking, but they don't taste nearly as good.

Dried flakes of onion or garlic have more body than powders and so offer the advantage of adding some texture to foods, especially soups, braises, and casseroles. Flakes are best if they are soaked in liquid for at least ten minutes before use.

Salt forms of onion, garlic, and celery are available, but you don't really need them. Use regular salt plus other forms of the vegetable flavoring instead. You will have more control over the flavor and will use much less salt in your cooking.

☐ *Fresh Garlic and Shallots*

Fresh garlic and shallot bulbs are used almost exclusively for flavoring. The most important thing to know about

these important ingredients is that it is the juice that is desired, not the pulp. Pulp turns bitter when it burns, and it burns easily—especially when it is fried or cooked in dry heat. Here are three ways to extract juice:

1. Rub peeled garlic or shallot over the entire surface of the food.

2. Press peeled garlic or shallot against the bottom of the cooking vessel. Press and rub it around to extract as much juice as you can, and then remove all of the pulp.

3. Preflavor oil or vinegar by putting whole slices into the liquid. Allow the liquid to sit for a week or longer, removing the pieces before they deteriorate. The warmer the liquid, the faster it will become flavored. Add more liquid as needed, and freshen the flavor by adding fresh slices when the flavor becomes weak.

The second most important thing to know about these bulbs is that the longer they cook, the more mellow their flavor becomes. The taste and smell many people find disagreeable about garlic come from either not cooking it long enough or burning the pulp. Apart from these considerations, the "Cook's Guide" on the next page tells you just about everything you need to know about garlic and shallots.

Flour

Flour made from wheat is the most basic ingredient used for making breads, cakes, cookies, and pastries. There are several types, and those that are most common will be covered in detail. First, though, here are some general considerations.

Buy flour in small packages—no more than you are likely to use in a month. The fresher it is, the better the products baked from it are likely to be.

Store flour in a sealable, airtight container to keep the flour fresh and to keep out weevils. Any flour will keep best refrigerated.

To measure flour most accurately, first place a sheet of waxed paper on the kitchen counter or cutting board. Place a dry-measure cup in the center of the paper, and sift the flour directly into it until it is overflowing. Use the back side of a knife to sweep off the excess so that the flour is level with the rim of the cup.

Measuring flour is often inexact because its density and weight vary according to how much it is compacted and

A Cook's Guide to Garlic and Shallots

Plan on having one or more garlic and shallot bulbs on hand at all times. Don't get too many, for if they are too old they become rancid and should be thrown out.

Select bulbs with white, flaky skins. Size has nothing to do with flavor or freshness. By the way, the entire thing is called a "bulb"; individual sections of garlic are called "cloves."

Store in a cool, dry, well ventilated place for several weeks or even months until the cloves become dry.

Prepare by cutting off the tip from each end and peeling off the flaky skin. Individual garlic cloves can be peeled more easily if they are first crushed slightly with the side of a knife blade.

To sauté or fry: To prevent garlic or shallots from burning when fried, use preflavored oil or juice from a bottle. Alternatively, fry whole cloves or large pieces until they brown and remove them before frying other foods in the flavored fat. Small chopped or minced pieces, or pieces pulped in a garlic press, are likely to burn. Cloves that have been sautéed can be chopped, minced, or pressed through a garlic press and used to flavor liquids or for making garlic butter.

To cook in liquids: Use juice or finely minced or pressed pieces. For a more mellow flavor, sauté garlic cloves or large pieces of shallot until they are a golden brown before cutting them up.

To cook in dry heat: Use preflavored cooking oil to coat the surface of the food or rub a garlic clove or a large piece of shallot over the entire surface of the food. You can also soak whole cloves in oil to protect them and then bake or roast them along with the food. Remove the cloves before they burn. (Note: Many instructions for roasting meats or poultry will tell you to pierce the skin and insert slivers of fresh garlic. If you pierce the skin, though, the juices of the food will escape. Besides, you might not pull out all of the pieces, and some unsuspecting diner may get a heavier dose of garlic than he or she wants.)

the amount of moisture it contains. The more compact or moist it is, the more it will weigh compared with the same volume that is loose and dry. You can compensate for compactness by sifting the flour. To account for moisture content, use greater or lesser amounts than those called for in a recipe depending on how moist you think the flour is. During winter months, at high altitudes, or in a dry climate, the amount of moisture will be less than it would be at sea level or in a humid climate. If flour is stored in a self-defrosting refrigerator, it will have less moisture than if it is stored in a conventional refrigerator or at room temperature.

□ *Types of Wheat Flour*

Wheat flours all contain glutenin, or gluten, as it is more commonly called. Gluten is a protein that gives structure and strength to baked goods by forming long elastic strands that hold things together and capture gases in pockets as the dough is heated, causing the dough to rise. It is the gluten content of flours that distinguishes one type from another. Each type is best suited to a special purpose.

All-purpose flour—also called **white, plain,** or **general purpose flour**—is just what its name implies. It can be used in any recipe that does not specify another flour of a particular type. It may be bleached or unbleached. The unbleached variety is more nutritious. It is also slightly heavier, so that you should use less of it when substituting it for bleached white flour. At best, all-purpose flour is a convenient compromise. If you don't want to compromise your baked goods too much, use a flour suited specifically to the baking purpose.

Self-rising flour carries the "all-purpose" idea one step further. It contains a premeasured amount of baking powder, which causes it to rise when heated. When risen dough is desired, self-rising flour can be used directly without the addition of anything else. Pastries made with self-rising flour are usually more spongy and less flaky than those made with regular flour. Also, the baking powder in self-rising flour might lose its potency if the flour is too old, and so results are less predictable than when plain flour with a fresh leavener is used. As a substitute for self-rising flour that gives better results, use all-purpose or other flour plus one tablespoon baking powder per cup of flour. Or instead of baking powder, for each cup of flour use one teaspoon bicarbonate of soda, two teaspoons cream of tartar, and one-half teaspoon salt. (Note: Omit the salt if you are using all-purpose flour.)

Bread flour has the highest gluten content of any flour, which makes it best suited for making risen breads. All-purpose flour may be used instead.

Cake flour is a weak, low-gluten flour especially good for cakes and delicate pastries. As a substitute, use 1 cup minus 2 tablespoons of sifted all-purpose flour for each cup of cake flour specified in a recipe.

Pastry flour is a soft, finely milled flour with a gluten content somewhere between cake flour and bread flour. It is best suited for making cookies, pie pastries, biscuits, muffins, and quick breads.

Whole-grain, whole wheat and graham flours all have more vitamins, minerals, and flavor than the refined flours just described. Any of these may be used as an "all-purpose" flour. Finely ground, one cup equals one cup of all-purpose flour. Coarsely ground, one cup plus two tablespoons equals one cup of all-purpose flour.

"Instant," "quick mix," or "sauce" flour has a granular texture so that it does not need to be sifted. Because it blends readily with liquids without forming lumps, it is especially well suited for thickening liquids and making hot sauces. It cannot be used for most baking, however, so don't think of it as a substitute for any other flour.

Garlic

See "Flavoring Vegetables," p. 296.

Herbs and Spices

See "Seasonings," p. 305.

Leaveners: Baking Soda, Baking Powder, and Yeast

A leavener or leavening agent is any ingredient that is added to flour, ground meal, or other foods to cause them to expand and rise when heated. In the case of beaten egg whites, the action is physical. With all other leaveners, the action is chemical. The most important chemical leaveners are baking soda, baking powder, and yeast.

Baking soda is the chemical bicarbonate of soda. When combined with moisture and some acid—cream of tartar, fruits, fruit juices, buttermilk, sour milk, chocolate, honey, or molasses—the soda releases carbon dioxide gas, which causes the food pieces around it to expand. The most common combination used for baking is two teaspoons cream of tartar, one teaspoon baking soda, and one-half teaspoon salt per cup of flour. If all-purpose flour is used, leave out the salt.

Baking powder is a prepared mix of baking soda plus an acid to react with it along with some starch to prevent absorption of moisture from the air. Baking powder can lose its potency over time. To test it, put one teaspoon into one-third cup of hot water. If it bubbles vigorously, it is okay to use. If it does not, substitute one teaspoon bicarbonate of soda, two teaspoons cream of tartar, and one-half teaspoon salt for each tablespoon of baking powder called for. If all-purpose flour is used, leave out the salt.

There are three types of baking powder. The "tartrate" and "phosphate" types both release most of their gases at room temperature. For this reason, foods using them must be baked in a preheated oven immediately after mixing in order for maximum leavening to occur. "Combination" or "double-acting" baking powders release the major portion of their leavening gases only at oven temperatures. Batters made with these are more stable and can be held for a few minutes before baking without any great loss of leavening. Unless some other form of baking powder is specified in a recipe, it is safe to assume that the "double-acting" type is best.

Yeast is available in two forms: "active dry" and "fresh." Most recipes for home use assume or specify active dry yeast. This type of yeast is granular in form and usually comes in sealed packets. The packet will have a "use by" date after which it should not be used. It will keep fresher longer if stored in a refrigerator. To use active dry yeast, first dissolve it in four times its weight of warm (not hot) water. If the water is too hot, it will kill the yeast.

Active dry yeast is also available in loose form. Substitute 2¾ teaspoons of loose yeast for each envelope of active dry yeast or "cake" of fresh yeast called for in a recipe.

Compressed or "fresh" yeast in cake form is used mostly by professional bakers, although it is available in some stores for home use. If a recipe calls for "one cake" of fresh yeast, use the .6-ounce size. If "two cakes" are specified, use the one-ounce size. Fresh yeast should be kept refrigerated and used within two weeks of purchase.

Mayonnaise

See p. 164.

Milk and Milk Products

As a rule, the greater the amount of butterfat in a milk product, the richer its taste and the more flavorful the foods cooked with it will be. Unfortunately, they will be richer in calories and cholesterol as well.

When cooking any milk product, be careful it does not get too hot; otherwise it might scorch or curdle. Remove milk from heat when bubbles form around the edge of the pan or when it steams. If it does begin to curdle, remove it from the heat and stir rapidly, adding cold milk to cool it.

Whole milk or **"sweet" milk** is used for making soups, custards, cream sauces, gravy, and baked pastries, and for any cooking process in which "milk" is specified. Most of us can get milk only in pasteurized and homogenized forms. Both are safe, hold up well, and are easy to use because the butterfat remains in suspension. Whole milk contains about 3.25% fat. If you prefer to have less fat in your diet, use low-fat milk (0.5% to 2% fat), skim milk (less than 0.5% fat), or non-fat dry milk (fat is 1.5% of its dry weight).

Non-fat dry milk is the least rich form of milk in every way. It is the lowest priced as well as having the fewest calories, lowest amount of fat, and the least cholesterol of any milk product. Because it is powdered, it can be stored for months.

Non-fat dry milk is convenient to have on hand to fill in for whole milk in those emergency situations that no doubt will arise. The thickness and strength of milk made from powder is determined by the amount of liquid added to it. Its flavor may be changed and enriched by making it with broth or the liquid from canned vegetables instead of water. Also, adding a teaspoon of vegetable oil per cup will add to its flavor and give it more body.

Evaporated milk in cans is whole milk from which 60% of the water has been removed. Because it is concentrated, it contains about double the amount of fat as whole milk (a minimum of 7.5%), but much less than cream or even half-and-half. It is also available now in "low-fat" form. When evaporated milk is substituted for an equal amount of whole milk for cooking, the resulting food will be much richer.

Sometimes it will be too rich, which is why many cooks dilute evaporated milk with water or broth.

Half-and-half is half cream and half whole milk. The amount of fat in it is usually between 10% and 14%—more than evaporated milk, but less than either coffee cream or whipping cream. Half-and-half is used most often for coffee, but it can also make a rich substitute for whole milk or a less rich substitute for coffee cream or whipping cream.

Coffee cream (or "light cream") contains about 20% butterfat and is used mostly for what its name implies. It too can be used as a rich substitute for whole milk. Coffee cream can be whipped and used as a substitute for whipping cream if the bowl, the beaters, and the cream are well chilled.

Whipping or "heavy" cream has between 30% and 40% butterfat. Of all the milk products, it is richest in flavor, calories, and cholesterol. It may be diluted with water or milk for general cooking or for use as coffee cream. It is expensive, and so for economic as well as dietary reasons it is best to use it mostly as a whipped topping for desserts. When whipping cream is called for in a recipe, one of the less fatty milk products can usually be substituted. They won't taste quite as good, but they will be better for you.

Buttermilk, whether pure or "cultured" (soured), is used in pancakes, cakes, and many baked goods to give them more body as well as special flavor. Buttermilk contains at least 8.25% milk solids other than fat, and so it is much thicker than other milk products. For those who don't like to drink it, it is now available in powdered form so it can be used for cooking when needed.

Sour milk is called for in some recipes. To make it, simply add lemon juice, vinegar, or baking soda to regular milk. For each cup of milk, add 1 1/2 tablespoons lemon juice, or 1 3/4 tablespoons vinegar, or 1/2 tablespoon baking soda.

Sour cream is a solid milk product that is used as a topping and for enriching sauces, soups, and mayonnaise. Dairy sour cream must contain between 18% and 20% milk fat, but a less rich "half-and-half" form may contain as little as 10%. As with any milk product, when sour cream is cooked it must be heated slowly over low heat or it might scorch or separate. Overstirring also might cause it to thin and curdle. Plain, unflavored, low-fat yogurt (or yogurt mixed with an equal amount of low-fat cottage cheese) makes a suitable low-calorie, low-cholestrol substitute for sour cream. Adding one tablespoon cornstarch per cup will help prevent yogurt from separating.

Onions

See "Flavoring Vegetables," p. 296.

Pepper

See "Seasonings," below.

Pork Fat

Both the fat and the meat of pork products are used to add flavor to foods. Bits of cooked bacon may be used as a garnish on salads, soups, casseroles, and stews. Cooked sausage or bacon add body as well as flavor to soups, casseroles, stews, and bread stuffings. Pork fat added to a cooking liquid will contribute its flavor, and pork fat added to meats and poultry being roasted will moisten and protect them from burning as well as add to their flavor.

(See "Fats," p. 194.)

Pork fat used for cooking comes in many forms: fat back, streak-o-lean, and side meat as well as regular bacon, which is mostly fat. Quite often, pork fat products have been cured in salt. If you don't want them to be too salty, parboil them for five minutes and then wash them thoroughly in cold water before using them for cooking.

Pork fat can be used to moisten steaks and roasts as they cook in two ways, *barding* and *larding.* For barding, simply drape the fat over the top of the meat or bind it in place with kitchen twine. Larding requires a special larding needle used to pierce through thick meat and insert a thin strip of fat (called a "lardon") into it. Lardons should be placed every one or two inches through the meat to moisten and flavor it evenly. (See "How to Bard or Lard Meats," p. 420.)

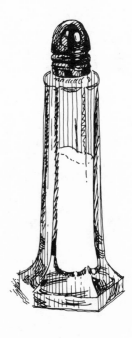

Salt

See "Seasonings," below.

Seasonings: Salt, Pepper, and Herbs and Spices

□ Salt

More than most flavorings, salt used in the right proportions opens the taste buds. It intensifies the natural flavors of foods and brings the tastes of all the individual ingredients together into a harmonious union. In short, salt makes foods taste good.

Salt can also diminish the appearance and texture of foods. Meats, poultry, eggs, and fish may become tough if salt is applied to them too early as they cook. When these foods are cooked in dry heat, salt on their surface will make the surface moist, thereby causing it to brown more slowly. Salt in cooking liquids will draw flavors and nutrients from foods into the liquid.

It is difficult to determine the amount of salt that should be used for cooking even when following a recipe. Most recipes call for more salt than is really needed. Salt is already present in many foods, especially if they are canned, pre-packaged, or frozen. For this reason, it is best to ignore amounts specified in recipes and let "salt to taste" be your guide. This is especially true if the number of servings is different from those covered by a recipe.

(See "Salt and Sugars," pp. 195–197.)

Salt is a major source of sodium, and eating too much sodium can lead to overweight, high blood pressure, and other health problems. Your figure and your health will be much better if you use salt and other high-sodium products sparingly. (MSG, Worcestershire sauce, catsup, and soy sauce are other flavorings that contain large amounts of sodium.) In most cases the amount of salt called for in a recipe can be cut by half if not eliminated altogether without diminishing the taste of the food. Add salt "to taste" after the food has cooked, and don't get into the habit of salting everything before you even taste it. Most foods will taste good without it.

The less salt you use, the healthier you will be. Your figure will likely be more attractive also. "But salt tastes so good," you might protest. Read the opening paragraph once again. It is not the salt that tastes good, but what it does to your taste buds that makes foods taste good. Salt isn't the only thing that can do that. Lemon juice, vinegar, sugar, herbs, and spices will do the same thing. You might also try using a low-sodium salt substitute. These alternatives to salt won't replace it altogether, but the more of them you use, the less salt you will have to use, and the better off you'll be.

□ *Pepper*

Pepper is a spice that is used too often to be abused as much as it is. The flavor of fresh peppercorns begins to

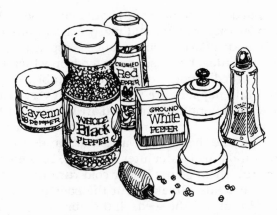

deteriorate the minute they are ground, and the longer ground pepper stands the less flavor it will have. Pepper also changes flavor as it cooks. If it cooks for very long, especially in liquids or frying fats, its flavor becomes harsh and acrid. It is best, therefore, to use pepper that has been freshly ground and to add it to foods toward the end of their cooking period or after they are fully cooked.

Many cooks use ground black pepper that comes in a can. It does come in other forms, though, and the more of them you use the broader the range of pepper flavors you can enjoy.

Black pepper can be bought in whole peppercorns that can be ground just before use. The difference in flavor will amaze you. All you need are the peppercorns and a pepper mill to grind them. To grind a teaspoon or more at one time, use a coffee grinder.

White pepper has a more delicate flavor than black. Because it is white, it is useful in sauces and other things in which the appearance of black specks might be unattractive. White pepper is available in whole peppercorns or ground. Freshly ground peppercorns taste best.

Lemon pepper adds the zest of lemon peel to regular black pepper. You can buy it in cans or just add fresh or dried lemon peel to foods in which freshly ground pepper is used. Either way, you will get a delicate and subtle flavor that can give your foods a special extra touch.

Red pepper flakes are hotter than either black or white pepper. The flakes can be used as they come but are usually better if they are crushed just before use.

Cayenne pepper is a finely ground red pepper with a special flavor all its own. Like any red pepper, it is very hot.

Pepper sauce is red pepper in liquid form. Some brands are stronger than others, and many contain other ingredients for added flavor. Pepper sauce is especially good for spicing up liquids, braises, or any foods in which individual pieces of red pepper might be undesirable.

Fresh chile peppers are very tasty and very hot. They require special handling when you are working with them or they can make your skin and eyes burn. Wear rubber gloves to handle them, and wash your hands thoroughly with soap and warm water after handling. To prepare chile peppers, rub them gently under cold running water and pull out the stems. Break or cut the pods in half lengthwise, and brush out the seeds. If the ribs inside seem soft, cut them out. Soaking chile peppers in salted water for an hour or so before use will mellow their flavor.

☐ *Herbs and Spices*

What is an herb? What is a spice? What's the difference between fresh herbs and spices and those that are dried? How much do you use when you don't have a recipe or if the recipe calls for fresh and you have only dried? What's the best way to store them or blend them into foods? It's a shame that these and other important questions are seldom addressed in cookbooks. About the only information in cookbooks is in the form of a chart such as the one in the Appendix of this book, showing which herbs and spices go with which foods. Those charts can be quite helpful, but they don't address the really important basics. The box on pp. 309–311 presents the fundamentals any cook should know about herbs and spices.

Almost Everything You Will Ever Need to Know about Herbs and Spices

What's the difference? Herbs are leaves. Spices are the seeds and flesh of fruits, unopened flowers, roots, bark, or berries of certain plants. Herbs are available either fresh of dried. Spices are almost always dried.

What herbs and spices are really needed? Special dishes may require special ones, but most cooks will get along quite well with just the following:

- *The Big Ten:* Salt, pepper, dill, paprika, oregano, bay leaves, parsley, sage, rosemary, and thyme
- *The Little Five:* Allspice, nutmeg, dry mustard, sweet basil, and cloves
- *Convenience Combinations:* Chili powder, curry powder, Italian seasoning, and poultry seasoning

What's the best way to buy them? Fresh herbs are far better than dried. The delicate oils in fresh herbs make the difference. It's the difference between a dish that is merely good and one that is great, the difference that makes an expensive meal served in a fine restaurant worth the price. Buy herbs and spices that are as fresh as you can get, and buy small amounts so they don't age too much before use.

What's the best way to store them? Heat and direct light cause herbs and spices to lose their flavors rapidly. Always store herbs and spices in a cool, dry, dark place. Fresh herbs should be refrigerated. Replace dried herbs and spices as they become weak, at least once a year. Fresh herbs freeze well and, once frozen, will keep their aroma and flavor for months. To freeze herbs, simply pick off the unwashed leaves and put them on a sheet of plastic wrap. Cover with another sheet of plastic wrap and roll up tightly. Place the rolled herbs into a labeled jar or sealable plastic bag and freeze.

What about dried herbs? They must be soaked in liquid long enough to replace the water that has been taken out. It is fine to add them right to a cooking liquid, but for other uses they should first be soaked in liquid or cooking oil for at least ten minutes.

How can I tell how an herb or spice will taste or how strong it is? Smell. Crush a little in your hand, allow it to warm a bit, and smell. The stronger the aroma, the stronger the taste. The weaker the smell, the more you will have to use. Even though recipes specify set amounts of herbs and spices, more or less may be required depending on their strength.

continued

How do I use them? Even though recipes specify exact amounts, the flavor and strength of any herb or spice will vary according to its form and freshness. You will do well to make adjustments, using your taste to guide you as much as, if not more than, the amounts specified in a recipe. As a general guide, for each *four* servings use:

- 1/3 teaspoon powder
- 1/2 teaspoon crushed granules
- 1 tablespoon chopped fresh

Crush seeds or other larger pieces just before use to release their flavors. Leaves can be crushed between the heels of your hands. To crush seeds, use a mortar and pestle, or just press them with the back of a spoon against the bottom of a bowl. To flavor a liquid, you can put bay leaves, whole cloves, or other large pieces in a tea ball or a bag made of cheesecloth so they can be removed before the food is served.

How should herbs and spices be added to foods? That depends on how the foods are to be cooked. *For dry heat cooking,* mix the seasonings into cooking oil and spread the oil evenly over the surface of the food during the last thirty minutes of cooking. *For cooking in liquids,* mix the seasonings into the liquid during the last thirty minutes of cooking. If herbs or spices are added to cooking liquids too early, a good deal of their flavor will cook out. You can also use herbs and spices as a garnish on soups and sauces. *For frying,* sprinkle the seasonings evenly over the surface of the food before coating it, or mix them into the dry coating or liquid dip. *Uncooked foods* such as salad dressings benefit from having herbs and spices in them for as long as possible.

How will I know when I have enough? Taste. Use herbs and spices sparingly, adding more gradually to suit your taste. Use only one strong herb or spice per dish and no more than one strongly seasoned dish per meal. Unless you are following a tested recipe (or know what you are doing), do not combine too many herbs and spices in the same dish.

Is there a difference when using them in cold foods as opposed to hot ones? Yes. Cold foods generally require more seasonings than hot ones.

What about foods that are to be frozen? Some seasonings—pepper and garlic, in particular—will have their flavors increased when they are frozen. Others—onion, salt, and chili powder—will lose some flavor. It is best to use a light hand when flavoring foods that are to be frozen, and then make adjustments when they are heated for serving.

continued

What is an "herb bouquet," "bouquet garni," or "sachet"?
These are just fancy terms for a bag or other container that holds herbs, spices, or vegetables used for flavoring foods cooked in liquid so they can be removed easily before the food is served. The term refers to the bag, not to particular flavorings. A typical bouquet garni contains celery, carrot, leek or onion, thyme, bay leaf, and possibly chervil or parsley.

What are "fines herbes"? This term is used in recipes to mean fresh herbs chopped very fine. As with a bouquet garni, there is no one standard for ingredients, although the typical fines herbes would include equal parts of fresh parsley, tarragon, chives, chervil, and perhaps some basil.

Shallots

See "Flavoring Vegetables," p. 296.

Sour Cream

See p. 304.

Spices

See "Seasonings," p. 305.

Tomatoes and Tomato Products

The flavor of **fresh tomatoes** will vary as a function of the time they are picked. The less ripe they are when picked, the less flavor. That's why the vine-ripened tomatoes available from local gardens in the summer taste so much better than those that are picked green in Florida, California, and Mexico, colored artificially, and shipped to market to ripen between the farm and you. (For more information about fresh tomatoes, see Chapter 18.)

The skin and seeds of tomatoes may or may not be desired. Some people like them, others don't. Seeds impart a bitter taste to tomato sauce, for example, and the skin and core are lumpy as well as bitter. To remove the skin, core, and seeds, parboil fresh tomatoes by plunging them into boiling water for thirty seconds and then refresh them in cold water. Peel and slice them and remove the core and seeds with your fingers, or press the tomatoes through a food strainer or food mill.

Canned tomatoes are always cooked to some degree. They come with or without skins, whole or sliced. Grade A is the most tender, flavorful, and attractive. Grade C is less uniform, the flavor is less predictable, and the texture tends to be mushy. Grade B is somewhere in between. Grade A is usually the most expensive, so if you are cooking a sauce or something in which appearance is not a consideration, you can economize by using B or C grades.

The flavor of canned tomato products will vary from brand to brand. Food processors may add sugar, salt, or other preservatives to enhance the appearance and flavor. Read those labels and try different brands to find the ones that suit your own taste, budget, and dietary considerations.

(See "How to Read a Label," p. 215.)

Canned tomato juice, puree, and paste all have had the tomato skins and seeds removed. They differ in thickness, with juice being the thinnest. Puree is concentrated and very thick; it might require thinning with liquid for some uses. Paste is the thickest of all and usually requires thinning for any use. In fact, tomato paste is used as a thickener for thinner tomato products or other liquids. All of these canned products may contain salt, sugar, or other flavorings that you need to account for before adding more. Again, read the label and try different brands to find what suits you.

Canned stewed tomatoes are about the most convenient canned good you can have in your larder. That's because they also contain onion, celery, and sweet bell peppers, all of which go well with cooked tomatoes. For only a little extra cost, you can have most of what you need for cooking most tomato dishes out of the same can, all cooked and ready to go.

Canned or bottled tomato sauce can also be a time and work saver. The more flavorings the sauce contains, the less control you will have and, usually, the greater the cost. For greatest economy as well as control over what goes into what you cook, choose a ready-made sauce that has a minimum of ingredients and add to it what you like.

(See "How to Make Tomato Sauce," p. 151.)

Vinegar

See "Acidic Liquids," p. 284.

Whipping Cream

See p. 304.

Wine

See "Acidic Liquids," p. 284.

Yeast

See "Leaveners," p. 301.

Eggs

CHAPTER FOURTEEN

*T*here isn't a great deal to be said by way of introduction to eggs. Oh, I might say they are "a great way to start your day," and I could repeat the warning that eggs are a major source of cholesterol and caution you to eat no more than two or three a week, including eggs contained in sauces, pies, cakes, pastries, and breads. That having been said, the rest of this chapter gives you the information you need to cook eggs correctly.

A Cook's Guide to Eggs

To Plan

As a main dish, plan one to three eggs per serving, depending on their size and the appetites of the eaters. When working with recipes, you might substitute whites for at least part of the yolks in order to cut down on cholesterol.

To Select

The color of the shell has no bearing on the cooking performance, flavor, or nutritive value of eggs. Size, grade, and freshness are the only real considerations. For most purposes, the fresher eggs are, the better they will taste. If you are going to hard cook them or use the whites for beating, though, use eggs that are at least three days old. Eggs that are to be cooked as main dishes usually should be large, as fresh as possible, and AA or A grade. Most cake and pastry recipes assume eggs of medium to large size, but they need not be of high grade quality. When you buy eggs, open the carton to check that none are cracked or broken (they may contain bacteria that can cause food poisoning). To test eggs for freshness, put them in enough water for them to float. Fresh eggs will lie flat on the bottom. Moderately fresh ones may rise up slightly at one end. If an egg rattles when it is shaken, it is not fresh. An opened egg that has a flat yolk and a runny white is not fresh.

To Store

Eggs do not require washing before storage. They can be kept in the refrigerator for up to five weeks from the date on the carton. Whole eggs should be stored with their small ends pointed down, the way they come in cartons. Egg shells are porous and can absorb odors from strong smelling foods such as onions and some cheeses, so store eggs well away from such foods. Egg whites and yolks that have been separated can be refrigerated for up to six days or frozen for as long as twelve months. (Tip: Freeze whites or yolks in a tightly covered ice cube tray, and then store them in a labeled plastic bag. Two tablespoons equal one whole large egg.) Whites require no special preparation for refrigeration or freezing. Yolks should be beaten together with one-half teaspoon of water and a pinch of sugar or salt for each yolk.

To Prepare

Eggs require no special preparation for cooking, unless they are to be separated or the egg whites are to be beaten. For these topics, see the following "How to's" (pp. 318–321).

To Cook

Eggs can be cooked in their shells in simmering water. Out of the shell, they can be poached, fried, or baked. Specific procedures for cooking them are given in the "How to" sections of this chapter. Eggs also serve as the basic ingredient for mayonnaise and for thickening custard sauces, egg yolk and butter sauces, casseroles, soufflés, and other dishes described in Chapter Three.

To Season

Popular seasonings for eggs include salt, pepper, onion, garlic, dill, basil, paprika, marjoram, tarragon, mustard, nutmeg, mace, mint, chives, chervil, savory, parsley, sage, rosemary, and thyme. Season eggs with salt only after they have cooked; salt on uncooked eggs makes them tough.

To Serve

Eggs may be served plain with just a little salt or other seasoning, or you can top them with flavored butter or margarine, mayonnaise, tomato sauce, catsup, or grated cheese.

Cooking Considerations for Eggs

1. One large egg equals 2 tablespoons or 1/4 cup. Two medium eggs equal 1/3 cup. One tablespoon of egg white or yolk equals the white or yolk of one large egg. Two egg yolks may be substituted for one whole egg in recipes to make them richer. Two egg whites may be substituted for one whole egg to reduce cholesterol.

2. Eggs will taste better when cooked and perform better in recipes if they are at room temperature rather than cold. Allow cold eggs to stand thirty to sixty minutes at room temperature, or place them in warm water for five minutes or longer before use.

3. With the exception of omelets, eggs should be cooked over low to medium-low heat. The lower the temperature, the more tender the cooked egg will be.

4. Eggs will continue to cook after they have been removed from heat. To prevent them from overcooking, remove them from heat before they are cooked to your liking.

5. Salt on uncooked eggs will make them tough. Season eggs with salt only after they have cooked.

6. If a recipe calls for beaten whole eggs and you want the dish to be light in texture, separate the yolks and whites and beat the whites to the foaming or soft foaming stage. Fold the beaten white into the mixture at the last minute, just before cooking. The whites will expand as the dish cooks just as they do in a soufflé.

7. To add eggs to a hot mixture without curdling them, add the hot mixture to the eggs a little at a time, beating the eggs well each time more of the hot mixture is added. When half the mixture has been incorporated, the rest can be added to the eggs safely.

8. If an egg mixture becomes so hot that it begins to curdle, you can save it by removing it from the heat, pouring it into a cold dish, and beating it vigorously. A small amount (1 Tbsp.) of cold liquid or an ice cube added to the mixture will help to rescue it.

9. To clean up spilled raw egg, cover it with salt and let it set until it becomes firm. Use paper towels to pick up the egg.

10. To clean cooked egg off plates and utensils, first soak them in cold water to loosen the cooked protein. Hot water will only cook the egg, making it harder to get off.

How to Separate Eggs

Eggs separate most easily, and with less chance of the yolk and white mixing together, if they are cold. Here's how to separate eggs:

1. **Have two bowls ready,** one for the yolk and one for the white. If the whites are to be beaten, have a third bowl ready, as explained in step 4.

2. **Open the egg.** Crack the egg horizontally along its center by striking it gently against the side of a bowl or

countertop or by rapping it gently with the back side of a knife blade. Be careful not to break the yolk.

3. **Empty the white into one bowl and the yolk into another.** Hold the egg upright over one bowl and pull the top of the shell away so that the white flows out. Use the two halves of the shell to hold the yolk, tipping the egg back and forth between them as the white flows out. When all of the white is out of the shell, pour the yolk into the second bowl.

4. **Optional:** Use a third bowl for separating whites that are to be beaten. Whites to be beaten must not have any yolk in them. To keep the yolk out, separate each white individually in an extra bowl and then add it to the other whites. That way, if some yolk gets into one, you can eliminate it before it spoils the whole lot.

■

How to Beat Egg Whites

Egg whites and yolks are often beaten together—for example, to make scrambled eggs or to use as a thickener in cakes and casseroles. At other times, you will want to separate the whites and yolks and beat them separately. Yolks are easy: simply beat them with a fork or whisk until they are smooth. Beating egg whites, however, requires a special method. Here's how to do it.

1. **Select the eggs:** Eggs that are several days old whip best.

2. **Select the bowl:** The bowl must be large enough to contain the volume of the egg whites after they have been beaten. (Well beaten egg whites will increase in size as much as six times their original volume.) The bowl must be narrow enough so that the whole mass can be in motion at one time or else one part may deflate while the other is being beaten. Any grease present in a bowl will greatly reduce the volume of beaten egg whites. The best material for mixing bowls is stainless steel. Plastic tends to retain grease no matter how well it is cleaned. Aluminum will turn egg whites a grayish color. Copper bowls will give beaten eggs greater volume, but if cream of tartar is present, a chemical reaction with the copper will cause an acid to form that will turn the eggs slightly green. Porcelain or glass bowls should not be used because their sides are so slippery that the whites easily slide down them and lose their volume.

3. **Select a beater:**

· *Fork:* Use when only a little blending is required.

· *Whisk:* A bit of work, but a whisk incorporates air into egg whites more evenly than rotary beaters.

· *Rotary beaters:* Whether you use manual or electric beaters, you must take care not to beat egg whites so much that they become too dry and stiff to be used for some purposes.

· *Food blenders and food processors:* These should not be used to beat egg whites; they invariably make the whites too stiff and dry.

4. **Separate the egg** as described in the preceding "How to." Cold eggs separate most easily. Egg whites will beat up better if allowed to reach room temperature.

5. **Beat the egg white:** Egg whites can be beaten to one of four stages, depending on the purpose for which they will be used.

· *Foaming:* Large bubbles with a transparent mass that flows easily. Used to clarify, to coat, or to thicken, and with breadings.

· *Soft foam:* Smaller bubbles with a white and glossy mass that is moist, will hardly flow, and forms soft peaks. This is the stage at which sugar is added for making meringue. Sugar retards the foaming action of egg whites, so add it a small amount at a time, beating the whites for a few seconds between additions.

· *Stiff foam:* Small bubbles all about the same size. The mass is slightly foamy, glossy, and moist, with soft

Foaming   *Soft Foam*   *Stiff Foam*

rounded peaks that foam when the beater is withdrawn. This is the stage at which the egg whites are folded into other mixtures. (Tip: To stabilize the whites so they will hold more air longer, add 1/4 tsp. cream of tartar and/or a pinch of salt for each 4 egg whites before the whites are beaten or when the whites reach the soft foam stage.)

   • *Dry:* Beyond use. They will probably collapse when heated. The mass is lumpy and gray and will scatter from the beater. You have gone too far. Do not use this mess. Do not pass Go. Do not collect your culinary arts award.

6. **Fold stiff egg whites into other mixtures:** Beat the whites and fold them in just before baking in order to hold in as much of the captured air as possible. Use a whisk to fold the egg into the mixture so that air in the whites is retained. Use long, smooth strokes, plunging the egg down through the middle and folding the mixture up the sides. Blend only enough to incorporate the eggs fully. The more the mixture is worked, the more air will be lost.

■

How to Cook Eggs in Their Shells: "Boiled" or "Coddled" Eggs

Most cooks and books refer to eggs cooked in their shells as "boiled." However, if the water is hot enough to boil, the

whites might overcook before the yolks have time to cook throughout. For the whites and the yolks to cook evenly, eggs should be "coddled"—that is, cooked gently by one of two methods. (1) Follow the instructions given below, turning the eggs occasionally. (2) Use special egg "coddlers"—sealable containers in which an egg is cooked. Shelled eggs are placed into individual containers along with butter and seasonings. The coddler is then sealed, placed in simmering water, and cooked as if the egg were in its shell (follow the directions below).

0. **Before you begin:** Read all steps given below. Review the Cook's Guide and the Cooking Considerations for Eggs if necessary.

1. **Plan** 2 eggs per serving. Allow 10 minutes or longer to warm the eggs, 5 to 15 minutes to bring the water to a boil, plus time to cook and peel the eggs. Cooking times:

   · *Soft:* 2 to 5 minutes
   · *Medium:* 5 to 10 minutes
   · *Hard:* 10 to 20 minutes

2. **Prepare the eggs:** Use eggs of AA or A quality. Eggs that are at least three days old will be easier to peel when cooked. *Optional:* To help prevent the shell from cracking, use a pin or needle to prick a tiny hole in the large end of the egg's shell.

3. **Prepare the vessel:**

   a. Place the eggs in a pot large enough to hold them without crowding. Cover the eggs with cool water so that they are at least 1/4 inch below the surface. *Optional:* Put a few drops of vinegar or lemon juice and/or a little salt into the water. Any of these will prevent egg white from spreading too much if a shell cracks.

   b. Allow the eggs to warm in the water for 10 minutes or longer.

4. **Cook the eggs:**

   a. Cover the pot and heat it slowly until bubbles break on the surface of the water.

   b. Turn the heat off and leave the pot covered. Remove the pot from the burner and let it set covered for the time required to cook the eggs to your liking. Begin timing the moment the pot is removed from the heat. (See Step 1 for cooking times.)

c. As the eggs cook, use a spoon to turn them every minute or so, to cook them more evenly.

5. **Cool the eggs:** Drain off the hot water and immediately cover the eggs in cold water to stop the cooking. This makes them easier to peel and prevents a green film from forming over the yolk.

6. **Peel the eggs:** Tap the shell all over against a hard surface and then roll it gently but firmly on the kitchen counter or between the palms of your hands. Start shelling from the big end; the shell should come off in a few large pieces. Try not to peel any white away with the shell.

7. **Optional:** To slice the cooked egg, dip a knife or egg slicer into iced water before slicing and between each slice to minimize crumbling. For grated yolk pieces to be used as a garnish, use the back of a spoon to press yolks through a fine-mesh tea strainer.

8. **Serve** hot or cold, whole or sliced.

9. **Optional:** Accompany with plain or flavored mayonnaise, butter or margarine, or one of the egg yolk and butter sauces.

10. **For stuffed eggs,** slice the eggs in half lengthwise and carefully remove the yolks. Chop the egg yolks and mix them with mayonnaise and/or mustard plus a little salt and pepper and perhaps a small bit of vinegar. Chopped onion, pickle or relish chips, pimiento, olives, crisp fried bacon bits, and parsley are some popular ingredients that may be mixed in along with the egg yolk. Mound the yolk mixture inside the egg whites and garnish the top with paprika, chopped parsley, or other herbs.

How to Poach Eggs

Poached eggs are cooked in liquid. There are three ways to do it. Commercial devices do a beautiful and virtually fool-proof job. The pan method and the whirlpool method described here can be difficult and require practice.

0. **Before you begin:** Read all steps given below. Review the Cook's Guide to Eggs and the Cooking Consider-ations for Eggs if necessary.

1. **Plan** 2 eggs per serving. Allow 3 to 5 minutes to cook each egg. With the whirlpool method, you can cook only one egg at a time; with the pan method, no more than four. If you plan to serve the poached eggs with a hot sauce, allow time to cook both the sauce and the eggs. You can cook the sauce first and then the eggs, or you can cook all the eggs partially, prepare the sauce, and then reheat the eggs in it just before serving. Pop-ular sauces include tomato sauce, white cheese sauce, and egg yolk and butter sauces such as Hollandaise.

2. **Prepare the eggs:**

   a. Use really fresh eggs of AA or A grade. Cold eggs will hold their shape better than warm ones.

   b. *Optional:* To prevent the whites from spreading, use a pin or needle to prick a tiny hole in the large end of the shell. Dip the eggs into boiling water for about 30 seconds before poaching them.

   c. Break eggs individually into a teacup or saucer. If a yolk breaks, don't try to poach it or you will end up with a poached mess.

3. **Prepare the vessel.** (Tip: For the liquid, use broth, tomato juice, or a thin soup. After the eggs are cooked, add a roux to thicken the liquid to make a serving sauce.)

   · *Pan method:* Use a large frying pan. Coat the bottom and sides lightly with shortening to prevent the eggs from sticking. Add 1 1/2 to 2 inches of liquid.

   · *Whirlpool method:* Use a pot about 8 to 10 inches wide. Fill it with 3 inches of liquid. (Note: This method requires cooking one egg at a time.)

4. **Add a few drops of lemon juice or vinegar to the liq-uid.** This will help to firm up the whites and keep them from spreading. (Note: Salt in the liquid tends to make the whites runny.)

5. **Bring the liquid to a very slow simmer.** Only a few bubbles should be breaking on the surface. Too much agitation will cause the whites to spread.

6. **Add the eggs slowly and carefully:**

   · *Pan method:* Hold the cup or saucer with the egg against the side of the pan at the surface of the liquid. Carefully slide the egg out against the side and into the liquid. Add other eggs one at a time around the edge of the pan but do not crowd them.

   · *Whirlpool method:* Stir the liquid around the side of the vessel until a gentle whirlpool forms in its center. Carefully slide one egg into the center of the whirlpool and continue the circular motion, stirring around it until the white firms.

7. **Smooth the edges of the white with a spoon or knife and trim off "streamers."**

8. **Cover the vessel and cook the eggs 3 to 5 minutes.** The eggs are done when the whites are no longer transparent and the yolks are still runny. If the eggs are to be reheated for serving later on, cook them slightly less, and remove them to a pot of cold water.

9. **Drain the eggs.** Use a slotted spoon to remove the eggs from the liquid. Remove them in the same order they were put in so they are all cooked evenly. Place them on a clean cloth towel. (Paper towels will stick to the eggs.)

10. **Serve hot** with salt and pepper and perhaps topped with plain or flavored butter or margarine. *Optional:* Poached eggs are often served on toast or English muffins accompanied with white sauce, tomato sauce, or one of the egg yolk and butter sauces.

■

How to Bake Eggs ("Shirred" Eggs)

Baked or shirred eggs are prepared in individual containers. Use ramekins, custard cups, or a muffin tin with medium to large cups.

0. **Before you begin:** Read all steps given below. Review the Cook's Guide to Eggs and the Cooking Considerations for Eggs if necessary.

1. **Plan** 2 eggs per serving. Allow 15 to 20 minutes to cook the eggs plus time to bring them to room temperature.

2. **Prepare the eggs.** Use AA or A grade eggs and bring them to room temperature.

3. **Prepare the oven:**

   a. Place a rack on the lowest shelf.
   b. Prepare a "Mary's bath." Use a pan or casserole dish large enough to hold the cups or muffin tin. Place the pan on the oven rack and fill it half full with hot water.
   c. Preheat the oven to 325–350 degrees F.

4. **Prepare the vessel:**

   a. Coat the bottom and sides of each cup with a light coating of butter, margarine, or shortening. *Optional:* Cover the inside bottom of each cup with catsup, partially cooked bread crumbs, grated cheese, or a combination of these. You might also want to line the sides with strips of bacon that have been half cooked.
   b. Break the eggs into the cups, being careful not to break the yolks. Ramekins or large custard cups may hold two eggs.
   c. *Optional:* Top each egg with a light coating of grated cheese, partially cooked bread crumbs, milk or light cream, a small pat of butter or margarine, or a combination of these.

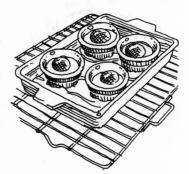

5. **Cook the eggs.** When the oven is preheated:

   a. Place the cups in the Mary's bath.
   b. Close the door and bake the eggs for 10 to 15 minutes.
   c. Remove the eggs when the whites are translucent and the yolks are still soft. (Note: The eggs will continue to cook in their own heat and are, therefore, easily overcooked.)

6. **To serve:** Leave eggs in ramekins or custard cups for individual servings. Remove them from a muffin tin using a large spoon. *Optional:* Accompany with plain or flavored butter or margarine, white sauce, tomato sauce, or one of the egg yolk and butter sauces.

■

How to Fry Eggs

0. **Before you begin:** Read all steps given below. Review the Cook's Guide to Eggs and the Cooking Considerations for Eggs if necessary.

1. **Plan** 2 eggs per serving. Allow time to bring the eggs to room temperature plus 3 to 8 minutes to cook one or two at a time. If necessary, hold them for serving in a warm oven (100 degrees F.). If the oven is too hot, the eggs might overcook.

2. **Prepare the eggs.** Use fresh eggs of AA or A grade and bring them to room temperature.

3. **Prepare the vessel:**

   a. Use a low-sided griddle or pan large enough to hold the eggs apart so each can be turned. Coat the bottom with just enough cooking oil, butter, or margarine to cover it and prevent the eggs from sticking. Too much will cause the eggs to be greasy.

   b. Heat the pan on a burner at a medium-low to medium temperature. Cooking at too high a temperature will toughen the eggs.

4. **Cook the eggs.** Break each egg into the pan and cook as desired:

   · *Sunny side up:* Cook the egg through without turning it. Lift the egg gently with a pancake turner to check for doneness.

   · *Over easy, light or well:* Cook one side a bit less than the way you like it. Turn the egg and cook it the same on the other side.

· *Basted:* Cover the top of the pan so that the top of the egg cooks in the steam as its bottom fries. When the white becomes translucent, baste it with broth, water, butter, or margarine. Re-cover the pan and cook the egg until it is done to your liking.

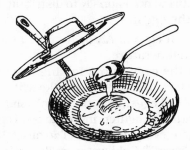

· *Country style:* Cook a meat such as thin beef steak, ham, or corned beef hash. When the bottom has browned, turn the meat over and break one or two eggs on top of it. The heat of the meat will cook the egg "sunny side up" by the time the meat has browned.

5. **Drain the egg.** Use a slotted pancake turner or spoon to remove the egg. Drain off the fat and place the egg on a warm plate.
6. **Serve** hot right away. Top with salt and pepper and (optional) butter or margarine.

■

How to Scramble Eggs

0. **Before you begin:** Read all steps given below. Review the Cook's Guide to Eggs and the Cooking Considerations for Eggs if necessary.

1. **Plan** 2 eggs per serving. Allow time to bring the eggs to room temperature plus 5 to 15 minutes to cook them. Scrambled eggs should be served right away, but they may be held in a double boiler for up to 30 minutes if the water in the double boiler is not boiling and the eggs are stirred occasionally to distribute the heat evenly.

2. **Prepare the eggs:**

   a. Use fresh eggs of AA or A grade and bring them to room temperature.

   b. Break the eggs into a mixing bowl and beat them with a fork or whisk. If you like white streaks in your scrambled eggs, beat them only slightly.

   c. *Optional:* For lighter, more flavorful eggs, add 1 Tbsp. liquid for every two eggs. (Too much liquid will make them "weep.") Cold water, milk, half-and-half, cream, and buttermilk are the most popular liquids.

   d. *Optional:* For special flavor, add crushed herbs such as tarragon or parsley "to taste" and/or 1 Tbsp. per egg of finely chopped cheese, onion, chives, cooked bacon or ham, or combinations of these.

3. **Prepare the vessel:**

   a. Use a griddle or pan with low sides. Coat the bottom with just enough cooking oil, butter, or margarine to cover it and prevent the eggs from sticking. Too much fat will cause the eggs to be greasy.

   b. Heat the vessel on a burner at medium-low to medium temperature. Cooking at too high a temperature will toughen the eggs.

   c. When the fat is hot, remove it from the heat and pour off any excess.

4. **Cook the eggs:** Pour the eggs over the bottom of the heated vessel. When soft curds form, lift them away from the sides and tilt the pan so that the uncooked eggs can flow to the bottom under the cooked eggs. For best appearance, use a pancake turner or a large spoon to avoid breaking up the eggs too much. Frequent stir-

ring will break them into small pieces that can become dry and crumbly. Cook until the eggs are firm but the top is still moist.

5. **Optional:** Undercook the eggs and pour them into a baking dish. Top with grated or thin slices of cheese and bake in a preheated oven at 300 degrees F. until the eggs are firm but still moist and the cheese is melted.

6. **Season** with salt and pepper, chopped parsley, green onions, or other fresh herbs.

7. **Serve** hot right away, or hold for serving in a pan of warm water or in a double boiler. *Optional:* Top with plain or flavored butter or margarine, white sauce, or tomato sauce.

■

How to Make Flat ("French") Omelets

A proper flat omelet should be shiny and delicately browned on the outside, moist and creamy in the center. It can be served plain or with a filling, with or without a sauce topping.

0. **Before you begin:** Read all steps given below. Review the Cook's Guide to Eggs and the Cooking Considerations for Eggs if necessary.

1. **Plan** time to bring the eggs to room temperature plus 2 to 5 minutes to cook each omelet. If necessary, hold omelets in a warm oven (100 degrees F.). If the oven is too hot, the omelet will overcook.

2. **Prepare the eggs:**

   a. Use fresh eggs of AA or A grade and bring them to room temperature. Plan two to three eggs per omelet: two eggs for a 6–7-inch pan, three for an 8–9-inch pan.

   b. Break the eggs into a mixing bowl. *Optional:* For a lighter, more flavorful omelet, add 1 Tbsp. liquid for every two eggs. Cold water, milk, half-and-half, cream, and buttermilk are the most popular.

   c. Beat the eggs with a fork or whisk. If you prefer white streaks in your omelet, beat them lightly. For a lighter, fluffier omelet, beat the eggs in a food blender.

   d. *Optional:* Prepare a filler. Thinly sliced or finely chopped cheese, onion, mushrooms, sweet bell pepper, tomato, cooked bacon or ham, or combinations of these are the most popular fillers. Use 1 Tbsp. per egg.

3. **Prepare the vessel:**

   a. The size of the pan should be such that the eggs will be about 1/4 inch deep. An aluminum pan with a non-stick inner coating gives the best results.

   b. Coat the bottom and sides with just enough cooking oil, butter, or margarine to cover them and prevent the eggs from sticking. Too much will cause the eggs to be greasy.

   c. Heat the pan over medium-high heat.

   d. When the fat begins to bubble, remove the pan from the heat and tilt it to coat the sides. Pour off excess fat and return the pan to the burner.

4. **Cook the omelet:**

   a. Pour the eggs into the center of the pan until the bottom is covered to a depth of 1/8 to 1/4 inch.

   b. Holding the pan flat on the burner, shake it back and forth to stir the eggs and distribute the heat evenly.

   c. Use a hard spatula or pancake turner to pull the congealed eggs away from the sides all around, tilting the pan at the same time to allow the uncooked eggs to flow to the bottom under the cooked eggs.

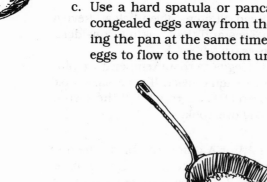

5. **Optional:** When most of the egg is firm but the top is still moist, cover half the egg with a thin layer of the filler.

6. **Fold the omelet.** Tilt the pan and use a hard spatula or pancake turner to lift the top half and quickly fold it over the other. Continue to cook until the bottom is browned.

7. **Flip the omelet over** onto a serving plate with the browned side up.
8. **Season** with salt and pepper, chopped parsley, green onions, or fresh herbs.
9. **Serve** hot right away, or hold in a warm oven (100 degrees F.) for no longer than 10 minutes. *Optional:* Accompany with plain or flavored butter or margarine, white sauce, tomato sauce, or one of the egg yolk and butter sauces.

■

How to Make Puffy ("German") Omelets

The French omelet just described is probably familiar to most readers, but the German omelet is more unusual. Its texture is light—truly "puffy"—somewhat like a soufflé. The puffy omelet is baked in an oven and makes an attractive way to serve simple eggs.

0. **Before you begin:** Read all steps given below. Review the Cook's Guide to Eggs and the Cooking Considerations for Eggs if necessary.

1. **Plan** 2 to 3 eggs per serving. Allow time to bring the eggs to room temperature plus 30 to 45 minutes to prepare and cook the omelet. A puffy omelet, like a soufflé, must be served right away.

2. **Optional:** Prepare a filler. Thinly sliced or finely chopped cheese, onion, mushrooms, sweet bell peppers, tomato, cooked bacon or ham, or combinations of these are popular as fillers (step 4g) or as toppings (step 7).

3. **Preheat the oven to 325 degrees F.**

4. **Prepare the eggs:**

   a. Separate the eggs while they are cold. Use AA or A grade eggs that are at least three days old.

   b. Bring the eggs to room temperature.

   c. Blend the whites with 1 Tbsp. water for each two eggs and beat them until they form stiff peaks. (See pp. 319–321.)

   d. *Optional:* For a firmer omelet, add 1/4 tsp. cream of tartar for each three eggs.

   e. Beat the yolks separately until they are smooth and thick.

   f. Pour the yolks onto the whites and use a whisk to fold them in. Do not blend too much, or the whites may break down.

   g. *Optional:* Blend in herbs and filler. Sauté vegetables and use them as a filler and/or a topping.

5. **Prepare the vessel:**

   a. The size of the pan should be such that the top of the eggs will be about 1/2 to 1 inch below the lip of the pan. The handle should be heatproof to withstand the oven temperature.

   b. Coat the bottom and sides with just enough cooking oil, butter, or margarine to cover them and prevent the eggs from sticking.

   c. Heat the pan on a range burner over medium-high heat until the fat begins to bubble.

   d. Remove the pan from the heat and tilt it to coat the sides. Pour off excess fat and return the pan to the burner.

6. **Cook the eggs:**

   a. Pour the eggs into the center of the hot pan. Use a rubber spatula to spread the eggs evenly, mounding them around the edges of the pan.

   b. Cook the eggs uncovered, without stirring, until they are puffed and firm and golden brown on the bottom.

   c. Remove the pan from the range burner and place it on the center rack of the preheated oven. Bake the omelet 10 to 15 minutes until the surface is golden brown and springs back when pressed lightly.

   d. Test for doneness by sticking a toothpick or knife blade into the center. When it comes out clean, the omelet is ready.

7. **To serve:** Use a hard spatula or pancake turner to loosen the sides and bottom of the omelet all around the pan. You can slice it and serve it like a pie from the pan, or flip the whole thing onto a warm plate and then slice it into individual servings. *Optional:* Cover the top with strips of cheese, sautéed vegetables, cooked ham or bacon, plain or flavored butter or margarine, white sauce, tomato sauce, or one of the egg yolk and butter sauces.

■

P_oultry_

CHAPTER FIFTEEN

Given a choice of any food to cook or serve as a main dish in preference to all others, most people would probably choose one of the birds in the poultry family: chicken, turkey, capon, rock Cornish game hen, duck, goose, or wild fowl. Poultry is tasty, nutritious, and low in fats and calories. Perhaps best of all, it is also inexpensive.

Poultry can be used in an almost endless variety of dishes cooked using one of the basic cooking methods alone, or any and all of the combination methods described in Chapter Three. Even the bones and less desirable pieces can be stewed to yield a flavorful broth for making soups and sauces. Deboned and pounded thin ("scalloped"), chicken or turkey breasts can be substituted for veal in many specialty dishes, but at a fraction of the cost. All in all, poultry is a real winner.

Types of Poultry

Chicken

By far the most popular bird in the poultry family, chicken can be cooked any way and be very good. You can buy chicken whole or cut up, fresh or frozen, and even canned. Fresh whole chicken is usually the most economical form if you are willing to go to a little trouble to cut it up and will use all of the pieces. Otherwise, you can buy it in packages containing all the same or selected pieces already cut up. Those tend to be the most expensive. In between, there are packages containing combinations such as two breasts, two legs, four backs, four necks, and six wings. Such combination packs are popular low-cost price leaders in many food stores.

To save yourself a good bit of money, buy chicken in the combination packages and use the various parts in different ways. Legs and breasts can be broiled or fried to serve as main dishes. Less popular pieces, such as backs and necks, can be stewed along with some breasts and legs and the resulting broth used to make soups and sauces. The meat from the stewed pieces can be removed and used in sandwiches, casseroles, croquettes, soups, and chicken salad. Wings can be served as a main dish, cut up and cooked to make finger foods for parties, or stewed to make broth.

Turkey

Next to chicken, turkey is probably the most popular bird, especially during holidays. That is about the only time the whole bird makes its appearance on the dining table in most American homes, and then it is roasted to serve as the holiday feast. Following the feast, turkey leftovers can be used to make sandwiches, salads, casseroles, hash, and soups.

Other than for serving as a holiday feast, most cooks just can't use as much turkey meat as a whole bird provides. Fortunately, many stores now carry fresh or frozen turkey parts in portions suited for serving four to six persons. Those smaller pieces can be baked whole, or they can be sliced and then fried, baked, or used in many combination dishes.

Capons

For those occasions when a roast bird is desired but a chicken would be too little and a turkey too much, try a capon. Capons are male chickens that have been desexed so that they grow large and fleshy very quickly before their meat gets tough. Their thick layer of fat makes them ideal for roasting.

Rock Cornish Game Hen

These small birds are a delicacy many people have never tried. Their small size (one to two pounds) makes them ideal for roasting when only one to six portions are needed. Cooked and served whole or cut into halves, they can look very fancy, but they are really very economical and easy to prepare and cook. Most food stores carry only frozen game hens, and those are very good. If you can get them fresh, though, you will probably find they have better flavor.

Duck, Duckling, and Goose

Until recently, these birds were available only in a few specialty groceries. Now, though, most of us can buy them frozen any time we want. Frozen birds are really quite good, if not as good as fresh. The high fat level in these birds makes them ideal for roasting whole, but individual pieces can be broiled or fried.

Wild Fowl

Squab, dove, and other wild fowl are rare treats to most people—unless someone in the family is a hunter. These birds won't be covered separately here, but you can prepare and cook wild fowl in the same way as rock Cornish game hens and they will come out just fine.

About Giblets

Giblets are the edible innards of a bird—the heart, liver, and gizzard. Some people like them, some don't. Many who don't like to eat them alone do enjoy gravy or dressing in which chopped giblets are included for flavor. Giblets are very high in cholesterol, so they should be eaten infrequently and in moderation.

To Prepare

Whole birds bought from food stores will already have been cleaned and prepared. The giblets that come with them will be cleaned and prepared also and are usually packaged in a bag inside the bird. Be sure to remove the bag and giblets before cooking the bird. If you have a fresh bird, then the following preparations will be needed.

Heart: Remove the thin membrane as well as any veins and arteries surrounding the heart and discard them. Rinse the heart under cold running water and dry it on paper towels.

Liver: The green sac attached to the liver is the gall bladder. It contains a bitter fluid that will ruin any meat it touches, so it must be removed. Cut into the liver and around the gall bladder where it is attached, being careful not to puncture the gall bladder. Discard the gall bladder. Rinse the liver under cold running water and dry it on paper towels.

Gizzard: Cut away the intestines, membrane, and fat from the gizzard. Remove the hard core of the gizzard by first cutting around it on the concave side of the gizzard. Open the gizzard flat and press the outer side with your thumbs to remove the core. Discard the core and rinse the meat under cold running water. Dry it on paper towels.

Neck: This is not really a giblet, but it is often cooked along with giblets so that its meat can be used to make giblet dressing or gravy. Simmer the neck along with the heart and gizzard, then pick off as much meat as you can.

To Cook

Giblets can be cooked and served whole, or they can be chopped, cooked, and used as an ingredient in giblet gravy or dressing. The liver is tender enough to be broiled or sautéed raw. The gizzard, heart, and neck require simmering before cooking further. Simmer gizzards and neck 60 to 90 minutes and hearts 45 to 60 minutes, depending on their size. For added flavor, cook onions, celery, and garlic along with the giblets. Save the broth to make gravy or dressing.

To cook giblets whole, dip them in a dry coating and fry them. Livers are also good broiled or sautéed until they have lost all but a slight pinkish cast. Livers can be fried raw, but hearts and gizzards should first be simmered, as described above.

To use giblets to flavor gravy or dressing, first boil the gizzard, neck, and heart. Chop them and the raw liver into very fine pieces and then sauté them all until they are browned. Mix the pieces into the gravy or dressing.

A Cook's Guide to Poultry

To Plan

For individual pieces and small whole birds, allow 1/2 to 3/4 pound per serving. For whole birds, use the table on the next page as a guide.

To Select

Choose birds according to how they will be cooked. (See "To Cook," p. 343.) To be safe, use only poultry that has a USDA grade mark. Grade A is the best; grade C is fine for stewing; grade B is acceptable for any cooking method.

Number of servings in whole birds

Weight of Bird	Number of Servings
1–1 1/2 pounds	1
1 1/2–3 pounds	2–3
3–6 pounds	3–6
6–12 pounds	6–12
12–16 pounds	12–24
16–24 pounds	24–36

Note: Birds with a great deal of fat, such as capons or ducks, may yield fewer servings. Lean birds such as big-breasted turkeys may yield more.

The flesh of any bird should be clean-looking, evenly colored, and free of strong odors, blemishes, and other obvious signs of spoilage. Younger birds suited for frying, broiling, or roasting will have a breastbone that is soft with a flexible tip. Older birds with a rigid breastbone are best stewed or braised.

To Store

Store fresh poultry loosely wrapped in the coldest part of the refrigerator. The plastic wrap in which most fresh poultry is packaged is ideal. If the bird comes wrapped in butcher paper, unwrap it, place it on a plate, and cover it with plastic wrap or waxed paper, or in a sealed plastic bag. Take care to keep the juices from leaking out. They are messy and can contaminate other foods with dangerous bacteria. Use fresh poultry within two days of purchase or freeze it.

To Freeze

Wrap pieces tightly in heavy paper, aluminum foil, or heavyweight, sealable plastic storage bags. For convenience, wrap individual pieces separately or in packages suited for one or two servings. Remove the neck and giblets (heart, liver, gizzard) before freezing and store them separately. Store frozen pieces up to six months, frozen giblets no longer than three months.

To Prepare

The following are general instructions for preparing poultry. Additional instructions are given in the "How to" sections for each cooking method later in this chapter.

1. To defrost frozen poultry, keep the bird or pieces wrapped in the refrigerator, or soak them in cold water. Thawing times are given in the accompanying table. If you are using the cold water method, change the water every hour to minimize the growth of potentially harmful bacteria. Thawing at room temperature can result in food poisoning!

Timetable for thawing frozen poultry

Weight of Bird	Thaw in Water	Thaw in Refrigerator
Cut–up pieces	1–2 hours	3–9 hours
Whole, under 4 pounds	1–5 hours	12–16 hours
Whole, 4–12 pounds	4–6 hours	24–48 hours
Whole, 12–20 pounds	6–8 hours	2–3 days
Whole, 20–25 pounds	8–12 hours	3–4 days

2. If the bird has any pin feathers, singe them off over an open flame.

3. Remove any inner parts and cut out the little oil sac above the tail piece if that has not already been done.

4. Cut into halves, quarters, or individual pieces as desired. (See "How to Cut Up a Bird," p. 345.)

5. Cut off excess skin and fat and discard.

6. Rinse under cold running water to minimize bacteria as well as odors that come with aging. Dry thoroughly on paper towels.

To Cook

The choice of cooking method depends in part on the type of bird and its age. **Bake, broil, or grill** halves, quarters, or individual pieces of any birds that are not so old that they should be stewed. **Fry** "fryer/broiler" chicken cut into quarters or individual pieces. Rock Cornish game hens or other small birds should be cut up no smaller than quarters. Turkey, duck, or goose should be cut into small pieces. **Stew or braise** any bird, whole or cut into individual pieces. The older the bird, the longer it must be cooked. **Roast** birds that have a good deal of fat. Cook them whole or cut into halves. Roasters include the following types of birds:

· Chicken: 4 to 7 pounds up to 5 months old
· Turkey: 5 to 25 pounds
· Capon: 6 to 9 pounds
· Rock Cornish game hen: 1 to 2 pounds
· Duck, duckling, or goose: 4 to 10 pounds

To Season

Season with any of the following, or combinations of them: salt, pepper, poultry seasoning, onion, garlic, paprika, bay leaf, tarragon, oregano, basil, cinnamon, allspice, mace, nutmeg, ginger, curry powder, cumin, coriander, dill, marjoram, parsley, sage, rosemary, or thyme.

To Serve

Top with plain or flavored butter or margarine, gravy, or one of the white sauces.

Cooking Considerations for Poultry

1. Salmonellosis is an illness that can be caused by bacteria that thrive in poultry. For safety, keep any poultry at room temperature for as short a period as you can. To avoid contamination of foods from objects that might have come into contact with poultry, use soap and hot water to wash your hands before you touch anything else. Also wash tools, cloths, counter tops, cutting boards, and even the refrigerator door. Anything that has been in contact with poultry, or with hands or other things that have been in contact with it, can be a health hazard as long as it remains unwashed.

2. Undercooked poultry can pose a hazard from food poisoning. For safety, do not cook any poultry partially and then cool it to be completed before serving. If stuffing is to be cooked inside the bird, add it just before the bird is cooked and remove it immediately after cooking.

3. Frozen poultry can be cooked without thawing, but it will cook more evenly throughout if it is thawed first. Cooking times for frozen poultry will be at least half again as long as for thawed and can be as much as twice as long if the bird is very large. If a frozen bird is stuffed, cook it without thawing so that bacteria do not have time to contaminate the stuffing.

4. Cooking times depend on the size and type of bird. "The larger, the longer" is the rule for size. Turkey, duck, and goose require longer cooking times than chicken or rock Cornish game hens.

5. "The lower the heat, the sweeter the meat" is an expression that applies to poultry just as it does to meats.

6. Breasts, wings, and backs require less cooking time than drumsticks and thighs. When cooking individual pieces, start with drumsticks and thighs, and add breasts, wings, and backs about five minutes later. Or cook drumsticks and thighs in one batch and breasts, wings, and backs in another.

7. Do not overcook poultry. If the juices flow clear, it is done. (Note: The meat of very young birds may be red due to coloration from the bone marrow. If the juices flow clear, the poultry is done even though the flesh may still look pink.)

How to Cut Up a Bird

Note: Save any bones and meat scraps for making broth.

Before you begin: Place the bird with the breast and legs down on the cutting board and the back on top. Remove any giblets that may be inside.

To cut into halves: Using a sharp knife or poultry shears, start at the tail and cut through the center of the backbone or through the ribs slightly to the side of the backbone. Cut out the neck if there is one.

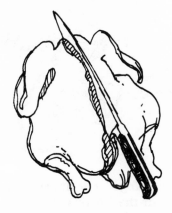

Optional: Cut the backbone away from the ribs on the other side and save it for making soup.

Starting at the neck, slice through the center of the breastbone and down through the tail. Separate the halves. Cut off excess fat and skin, and discard it.

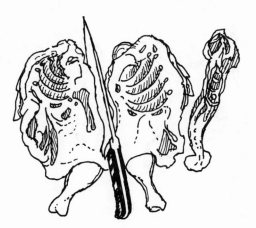

To cut into quarters: Slash the skin between the breast and the thigh.

Press the thigh down and out until the hip joint comes out of its socket.

Cut through the hip joint, releasing the thigh from the breast.

Pull the thigh away to separate the meat from the bone, and then cut through remaining meat and skin. Trim off excess fat and skin, and discard it.

To separate wings: Pull the wing out from the body and cut around the shoulder joint to separate it from the breast. Try not to cut away any white meat from the breast.

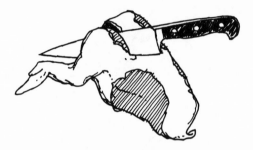

Optional "fancy wings": For finger food for parties, cut off the wingtip. Cut the "drumstick" away from the arm. Cut the little bone in the arm at both ends and then peel the meat back to remove the little bone. This will give two "drumsticks."

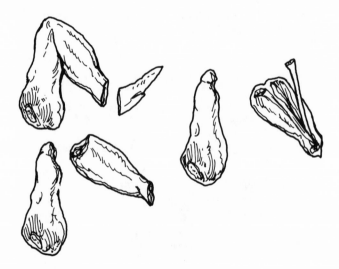

To separate drumstick and thigh: Pull the drumstick back to break the knee joint and slice through it.

To separate breast and back: Pull apart the breast and back to expose the meat-covered shoulder blades that join them. Cut down through the bone and detach the breast.

To debone the breast: Cut and pull the meat away from the bones.

To scallop: Chicken or turkey breasts are used for making specialty dishes such as Chicken Kiev. They are also used as a tasty and low-cost substitute for veal in dishes such as scallopini. To make scallops, use the deboned breast. You can use the pieces whole, but they will be more attractive if you cut them lengthwise into halves or smaller pieces. Pound the pieces with a meat mallet or the back side of a long kitchen knife until they are about ⅛ inch thick.

■

How to Fry Poultry

Sauté, stir-fry, or grill-fry small, cut-up pieces of any poultry with no bones. **Pan-fry, deep-fat-fry, or oven-fry** chicken cut into quarters or individual pieces. Turkey, duck, or goose should be cut into individual pieces.

0. **Before you begin:** Read all the steps below. If necessary, review the Cook's Guide to Poultry, the Cooking Considerations for Poultry, and the principles of frying in Chapter Two.

1. **Plan** 15 to 30 minutes to prepare the food and the coating, and 20 to 45 minutes to fry each batch. If a wet batter is used, allow 1 to 2 hours or longer for the batter to set. *Optional:* Chill food in a dry coating for at least 30 minutes.

2. **Prepare the coating.** (For more detailed information about coatings, see p. 50–54.)
   - *No coating* is needed for sautéing or stir-frying.
   - *Dry coating:* For 4 to 8 servings, use 1/2 cup flour, cornmeal, pancake mix, breading, or combinations of these. Put the coating in a pan or bag, add seasonings, and mix.
   - *Dipped batter:* For 4 to 8 servings, use 1/2 cup seasoned dry coating held in a pan or bag plus a dip of 1/2 cup milk, 1 beaten egg, or a mixture of the two held in a bowl separate from the dry coating.
   - *Wet batter:* For 4 to 8 servings, use 1/2 cup seasoned flour plus 1/2 cup liquid plus 1 whole egg or 2 egg whites. Mix all ingredients and let stand at room temperature for 1 to 2 hours, or refrigerate for 3 to 48 hours. *Optional:* For a lighter crust, add leavening just before dipping the food (see p. 53).

3. **Prepare the bird:**
   a. See the Cook's Guide to Poultry (p. 341) for thawing times and other basic preparations.
   b. Cut small birds into halves. Cut chicken into quarters or individual pieces. Turkey, duck, or goose should be cut into individual pieces.

   (See "How to Cut Up a Bird," p. 345.)

   c. *Optional:* If pieces are very large, parboil them for 3 to 5 minutes and refresh them in cold water.

4. **Coat the pieces:**
   a. Coat evenly with seasoned dry coating or batter. Hold the coated food on a cold plate.
   b. *Optional:* Chill food in a dry coating for 30 minutes before frying.

5. **Prepare the vessel:**
   - *To grill-fry or stir-fry:* Coat the cooking surface with just enough cooking oil to keep the food from sticking.
   - *To sauté or oven-fry:* Use a pan just large enough to

hold the food. Add 1/16 to 1/8 inch of cooking oil.

· *To pan-fry:* Use a pan with sides about 1 inch higher than the food. Add enough cooking oil to cover half the food.

· *To deep-fat-fry:* Use a special appliance or a heavy pan or pot sufficiently deep to hold enough cooking oil for the food to float, with 2 to 3 inches above the food to allow room for foam.

6. **Heat the cooking oil.** Do not allow it to get hot enough to smoke. For garlic flavor, use oil preflavored with garlic, or cook whole cloves of garlic in the oil until they are golden brown, then remove them.

· *On a range burner,* heat the cooking oil at medium-high heat until a small piece of food or batter sizzles when it is dropped in.

· *To oven-fry,* preheat the oven to 450 degrees F. and place the pan on the center shelf. It is ready when the cooking oil sizzles.

7. **Cook.** Slowly add food pieces, skin side down. Do not crowd them. To have everything ready at the same time, start cooking legs 3 to 5 minutes before breasts, wings, and backs; or cook legs in one batch and breasts, wings, and backs in another.

· *To sauté, stir-fry, or grill-fry:* Stir the food around or shake the pan back and forth to brown the food evenly all over.

· *To pan-fry:* Move the food occasionally so that it does not stick and burn. When the bottom has browned, turn the food over and brown the other side.

· *To deep-fat-fry:* Turn the food when the bottom has browned. Cook the other side until brown.

· *To oven-fry:* Using tongs to hold the pieces, coat each one all over in the hot cooking oil. Place them skin side down in the oil. Return the pan to the center shelf of the oven and cook until the top of the food browns. Turn the pieces over and brown the other side.

8. **Remove the food from the cooking oil and drain it on paper towels.**

9. **Before frying more food:** Clean the cooking oil of crumbs, flakes, or stray pieces so that they do not burn. If more cooking oil is needed, allow the hot oil to cool for 2 minutes before adding it.

10. **Optional gravy:** Deglaze the pan and make gravy.   (See "How to Make Gravy," p. 138.)

11. **Serve as quickly as possible,** or hold for up to 30 minutes in a warm oven (150 degrees F.).

12. **Optional:** Accompany with gravy, white sauce, or tomato sauce.

■

How to Braise ("Fricassee") or Stew Poultry

In Chapter Three, *Combination Cookery,* we considered the differences between braises and stews. When cooking poultry, braising is used to cook pieces of more tender birds or small whole birds in only a small amount of liquid, a process many cooks call "fricassee." Stewing, on the other hand, is used for older, tougher birds that are usually cooked fully covered by liquid. The older the bird, the longer it must be cooked.

0. **Before you begin:** Read all the steps below. If necessary, review the Cook's Guide to Poultry, the Cooking Considerations for Poultry, and the principles of braising in Chapter Three.

1. **Plan** 1 to 2 cups per serving. Allow 15 to 30 minutes to prepare the bird and other ingredients. Cooking times will vary all the way from 45 to 60 minutes for smaller pieces of tender fowl to 3 to 4 hours for whole, older birds. Braises and stews taste best if they are cooked partially and allowed to cool for a few hours or overnight before being reheated to completion.

2. **Prepare the bird:**

   a. See the Cook's Guide to Poultry (p. 341) for thawing times and other basic preparations.

   b. Leave the bird whole, or cut it into halves, quarters, or individual pieces.

   c. *Optional:* For added color and flavor, and to thicken the liquid, coat the pieces all over with seasoned white all-purpose flour.

3. **Prepare the cooking vessel(s).** Braising involves two stages: sautéing and stewing. You can use the same vessel for both, or a shallow pan to sauté the meat and a larger pot to stew it. To sauté, heat about 1/16 to 1/8 inch of cooking oil or cooking oil mixed with an equal amount of butter or margarine.

(See "How to Cut Up a Bird," p. 345.)

4. **Brown the meat** by sautéing it until it is golden brown. Remove it from the pan and drain off excess fat.
5. **Prepare flavoring vegetables.** A classic mirepoix of 50% onions, 25% celery, and 25% carrots is most popular. Finely chopped garlic or shallots, sweet bell peppers, mushrooms, and root vegetables such as turnips are also popular. Use 1 to 2 cups, depending on the amount of liquid to be used.

   a. Cut the vegetables into small pieces.
   b. Sauté until the pieces are soft but not browned.
   c. Remove the pieces and drain off excess fat.

6. **Deglaze the vessel:** Remove as much fat as possible from the vessel. Add a small amount of water, broth, or wine and dissolve any browned food particles in it.
7. **Put the foods into the cooking pot.**
8. **Add cooking liquid.** Use water, broth, stewed tomatoes, wine, fruit juices, or combinations of these. Stir in a very small amount of salt. (Salt will not be needed if you are using powdered or canned broth.)

   (See "What Heats and Flavors the Food: Liquids," pp. 23–26.)

   · *To stew:* Cover all the food completely.
   · *To braise:* Cover only half the food.

9. **Cook until the meat is tender:**

   a. On a range burner, slowly bring the liquid to a boil.
   b. When the liquid boils, lower the heat to a slow simmer or "stew." *Optional:* Remove the pot from the range burner to a preheated oven (250–300 degrees F.).
   c. Stir and/or baste the food occasionally as it cooks.
   d. Remove any fat that appears on the surface. (See p. 101.)
   e. *Optional:* Cook the food partially and cool it for several hours or overnight. Remove any fat from the surface before reheating.

10. **Optional:** Remove the poultry and puree the flavoring vegetables. Add the puree to thicken the liquid. For a thicker sauce, add roux, cornstarch, mannie butter, heavy cream, sour cream, or plain yogurt. Return the food to the liquid.

    (See "Thickeners," p. 130.)

11. **Add seasonings** during the last 30 to 45 minutes of cooking. The longer they cook, the more their flavor is diminished.
12. **Optional:** If flavoring vegetables were pureed to thicken the sauce, add fresh vegetables for serving. Potatoes, celery, carrots, onions, mushrooms, sweet bell pep-

pers, and turnips are all popular. Cook them until they are tender but not overcooked. Most vegetables cook in about 30 minutes.

13. **Adjust the thickness of the serving sauce.**

    · *To thin:* Add liquid.

(See "Thickeners," p. 130.)

    · *To thicken:* Add roux, cornstarch, or mannie butter. The sauce will also thicken as it cools.

14. **Serve** in a heated serving bowl or on a heated platter, accompanied by the vegetables and sauce.

      ■

How to Bake, Broil, Grill, or Barbecue Poultry

Any young, tender birds may be cooked by these dry heat methods. **Bake** birds whole, or cut into halves, quarters, or individual pieces. **Broil, grill, or barbecue** quarters or individual pieces.

0. **Before you begin:** Read all the steps below. If necessary, review the Cook's Guide to Poultry, the Cooking Considerations for Poultry, and the principles of dry heat cooking covered in Chapter Two.

1. **Plan** 15 to 30 minutes to prepare the bird. Allow 30 to 45 minutes for cooking smaller pieces, 45 to 60 minutes for larger ones. If you are using charcoal, allow 30 to 60 minutes for the coals to heat.

2. **Prepare the bird:**

    a. See the Cook's Guide (p. 341) for thawing times and other basic preparations.

(See "How to Cut Up a Bird," p. 345.)

    b. Cut small birds into halves. Chicken may be cut into halves, quarters, or individual pieces. Turkey, duck, or goose should be cut into individual pieces.

    c. *Optional:* If pieces are very large, parboil them for 3 to 5 minutes and refresh them in cold water.

(See "How to Make Marinades," p. 105.)

    d. *Optional:* Marinate the pieces in a sauce and skip steps e and f.

    e. Coat all surfaces lightly with cooking oil. (Butter or margarine used alone might burn.)

    f. Sprinkle salt and other seasonings lightly all over the pieces.

g. Refrigerate the food if it must be held for longer than 15 minutes before cooking.

3. **Prepare the heat:**

a. Adjust the height of the grill or rack holder.

   · *If the pieces are small,* set the rack 4 to 5 inches from the heat.
   · *If the pieces are large, set the rack 5 to 6 inches from the heat.*

b. *For oven cooking:* Preheat the oven to 350–400 degrees F. or to "broil."

c. *For charcoal cooking:* Start the fire and allow 30 to 60 minutes for a gray ash to form over all the coals. Tap the coals occasionally before and throughout the cooking to keep the ash from smothering the heat. A fair test of the temperature is how long you can hold your hand over the heat. Place your hand palm down at rack height and count: one thousand one = very hot; one thousand two = hot; one thousand three = medium hot; one thousand four = medium low.

4. **Prepare the vessel:**

   · *For oven cooking:* Use a pan or dish with low sides. Coat the inside lightly with shortening to prevent the food from sticking. Place the pieces of poultry skin side down.
   · *For grill cooking:* Coat the cooking rack or grill with shortening to prevent the meat from sticking. Place the pieces of poultry skin side down.

5. **Cook.** To have everything ready at the same time, start cooking legs 3 to 5 minutes before breasts, wings, and backs; or cook legs in one batch, and breasts, wings, and backs in another.

a. Put the pan into the oven or the grill rack into its holder.

b. Set a timer to the approximate cooking time:

	Bake	*Broil or Grill*
Chicken or game hen	45–60 minutes	30–45 minutes
Turkey, duck, or goose	50–75 minutes	30–60 minutes

c. About two-thirds of the way through the cooking time, turn the pieces to cook on the other side. When cooking on a grill, turn and baste the pieces frequently to prevent burning.

6. **Test for doneness:** Cut into the thickest part of the meat down to a bone. The juices should flow clear with no traces of pink.

7. **Remove from the heat.** Drain off excess fat and place the cooked pieces on a warm serving plate. Serve right away or hold in a warm oven (150 degrees F.) for up to 30 minutes before serving.

(See "How to Make Gravy," p. 138.)

8. **Optional gravy:** If there are any pan drippings, use them to make gravy.

9. **Serve hot right away.** *Optional:* Accompany with barbecue sauce or white sauce.

■

How to Roast Poultry

Birds that have a great deal of fat are good for roasting. Birds are usually roasted whole, but they may be cut into halves. Roast the following types of birds:

- Turkey: 5 to 25 pounds
- Chicken: 4 to 7 pounds, up to 5 months old
- Rock Cornish game hen: 1 to 2 pounds
- Capon: 6 to 9 pounds
- Duck, duckling, or goose: 4 to 10 pounds

0. **Before you begin:** Read all the steps below. If necessary, review the Cook's Guide to Poultry, the Cooking Considerations for Poultry, and the principles of dry heat cooking covered in Chapter Two.

1. **Plan** 15 to 30 minutes to prepare the bird, plus 30 minutes for a stuffing if one is used. Use the table on the next page to estimate the approximate cooking time. Add 15 to 30 minutes to allow the juices to "set" before carving.

(See "Bread Stuffing," p. 289.)

2. **Optional:** Prepare a stuffing.

3. **Prepare the vessel:**

   a. Use a pan with low sides. For easier cleaning, line it with heavy aluminum foil.

   b. Coat the inside of the pan (or foil) and the cooking

Roasting guide for poultry

Kind	Ready-to-Cook Weight (Pounds)	Approximate Total Roasting Time at 325° F. (Hours)	Internal Temperature of Poultry When Done (Degrees F.)
Chickens, whole	1 1/2 to 2 1/2	1 to 2	
	2 1/2 to 4 1/2	2 to 3 1/2	
Capons	5 to 8	2 1/2 to 3 1/2	
Ducks	4 to 6	2 to 3	
Geese	6 to 8	3 to 3 1/2	
	8 to 12	3 1/2 to 4 1/2	
Turkeys			
Whole	6 to 8	3 to 3 1/2	180 to 185 in thigh
	8 to 12	3 1/2 to 4 1/2	180 to 185 in thigh
	12 to 16	4 1/2 to 5 1/2	180 to 185 in thigh
	16 to 20	5 1/2 to 6 1/2	180 to 185 in thigh
	20 to 24	6 1/2 to 7	180 to 185 in thigh
Halves	3 to 8	2 to 3	
	8 to 12	3 to 4	
Boneless turkey roasts	3 to 10	3 to 4	170 to 175 in center

Note that the times given in the table are approximate. They are based on birds that are about 40 degrees and stuffed. Birds that are not stuffed or are warmer will require less time. To be safe, check the temperature every 15 minutes beginning halfway through the times shown. For frozen, commercially stuffed poultry, follow package directions.

Adapted from *Poultry in Family Meals*, United States Department of Agriculture Home and Garden Bulletin no. 110.

rack with shortening to prevent the meat from sticking. Place the rack inside the pan.

4. **Prepare the bird:**
   a. See the Cook's Guide (p. 341) for thawing times and other basic preparations.
   b. Dry the surface thoroughly with paper towels and coat it lightly with cooking oil or shortening. Peanut oil is especially good. Butter or margarine might burn.
   c. *Optional:* For garlic flavor, sauté whole garlic cloves in the oil before using it to coat the bird, or soak cloves in cooking oil and roast them along with the bird.
   d. Sprinkle the inside lightly with white wine or broth.
   e. Sprinkle lightly all over, inside and out, with salt and other seasonings.

f. *Optional:* Stuff whole birds with bread stuffing. Alternatively, place giblets and flavoring vegetables such as garlic cloves, onions, celery, sweet bell pepper, parsley, pieces of lemon or other citrus, or combinations of these, into the cavity to moisten and flavor the meat as it cooks. After the bird has cooked you can chop the cooked vegetables and giblets and use them in the gravy if you like. Secure the legs and wingtips or truss the bird.

(See "How to Stuff a Bird for Roasting," p. 357.)

g. Insert a meat thermometer into the center of the thigh muscle. Be sure the thermometer does not touch a bone. If the bird is still frozen, cook it long enough to thaw before inserting the thermometer.

h. Place the bird on the rack. A whole bird should be placed with the breast and legs on the bottom. (Turn it over one-half to three-quarters of the way through the cooking time to cook the top.) Cook halves with the cavity down.

5. **Prepare the heat:**

a. Place the oven rack so that the bird will be centered in the oven.

b. Preheat the oven to 325 degrees F. for chicken and turkey, and 400 degrees F. for ducks, geese, game hens, and other small birds.

6. **Cook:** Do not start to roast poultry one day and finish it the next. It will become dry and may cause food poisoning.

a. Place the rack and the bird into the preheated oven. Make sure the thermometer does not touch any metal.

b. Use the "Roasting Guide for Poultry" (p. 355) to judge the approximate cooking time, and set a timer accordingly.

c. One-half to three-quarters of the way through the approximate time, turn the bird over so that the breast and legs are on top. Turn the pan so that the end that was facing the rear now faces front. If the legs were bound, release the binding so that the heat can penetrate to the thigh joint.

d. If the surface appears dry, baste it with the pan drippings or cooking oil. Liquids other than these will wash away protective fat and allow the meat to dry. (Note: Duck or goose have enough fat that they probably will not require basting.)

e. Remove excess liquid so that the meat does not steam.

f. Repeat the basting every 15 minutes if needed.

g. If the top becomes too brown, place a piece of aluminum foil lightly over it.

7. **Test for doneness** every fifteen minutes: (Note: If the meat shrinks excessively, or if it splits down the breast or on the legs, it is probably overdone.)

   To test with a thermometer: Use the "Roasting Guide" on p. 355.

   · *Stuffing* should be at least 165 degrees F. If the bird is done but the stuffing is not, remove the stuffing to a pan and finish cooking it as the bird sets.

   · *If the leg is intact,* it should move easily in its socket.

   · *Prick the deepest part of the drumstick.* If it is done, the juices should flow clear without any trace of pink.

8. **Optional:** Remove the stuffing as soon as possible and keep it in a separate container. The longer the stuffing remains in the bird, the greater the risk of salmonella poisoning.

9. **Remove the bird to a warm platter.** Cover it lightly with aluminum foil and leave it to "set" for 20 to 30 minutes to allow the juices to redistribute themselves evenly.

10. **Optional gravy:** Deglaze the pan drippings and make gravy. For giblet gravy, chop cooked giblets very fine and mix them into the gravy. (See "How to Make Gravy," p. 138 and "About Giblets," pp. 340–341.)

11. **Carve the bird.**

12. **Serve** on a hot platter. *Optional:* Accompany with gravy or white sauce. (See "How to Carve Poultry Roasts," p. 360.)

■

How to Stuff a Bird for Roasting

For safety, do not stuff a bird until just before it is to be cooked. Stuffing absorbs fats, and the longer it sits at room temperature, the greater the risk of contamination and possible food poisoning.

1. **Prepare the stuffing,** allowing about 1/2 cup stuffing for each pound of ready-to-cook bird. (See "Bread Stuffing," p. 289.)

2. **Remove the wishbone.** Turn the bird breast up; locate

the wishbone with your fingers and cut around it with
a small knife just enough to free it. This will make the
bird easier to carve as well as to stuff.

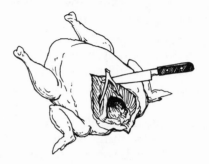

3. **Fill part of the body cavity loosely,** through its tail
   vent, with the stuffing. Do not pack.

4. **Fill the remainder of the body cavity through the neck.**
   Do not pack.

5. **Close the body cavity:** Fold the neck skin over to cover
   the hole. Fasten it with a skewer, or plug it with a thick
   slice of bread. Alternatively, skip this step and truss
   the bird (step 7).

6. **Secure the legs and wingtips.** Cut a small hole in the skin that hangs over the tail and force the leg tips through it. (Note: This has already been done on most commercially produced roasting birds.) To protect wingtips from burning, twist them and fold them back and under the legs.

7. **Optional:** Instead of steps 5 and 6, truss the bird.

   a. Cut a length of kitchen twine 20 to 30 inches long and coat it lightly with shortening to prevent it from burning.

   b. Place the bird with the neck cavity facing away from you and push the legs back close to the body.

   c. Put the center of the string across the end of the legs and bring it around and up between the legs to form a figure 8.

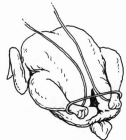

   d. Put the string between the legs and the breast.

   e. Turn the bird over and put the string through the wings.

f. Pull the neck skin over the vent and tie the string in a bow knot over it.

g. Cut off excess string so that it doesn't burn.

h. Place the bird on the roasting rack, with the legs and breast on the bottom.

∎

How to Carve Poultry Roasts

1. Wings: Pull the wings out and away from the body and cut through the joint and the meat until the wing comes free. Serve whole.

2. Legs: Pull the leg out and away from the body and cut through the joint and the meat until it comes free. Twist the thigh and the drumstick back from each other until the joint pulls out, then cut through the joint to separate them.

To slice drumsticks and thighs: Hold them with a carving fork and slice pieces lengthwise parallel to the bone, starting at the outside of one side and working in. Repeat on the other side.

3. Breast:

· *Conventional method:* Use a carving fork to hold the bird steady against a plate or cutting board. Make a horizontal cut into the breast just above the socket for the wing joint, cutting in all the way to the bone. Carve even slices downward, starting from the outside. Start each new slice slightly higher up on the breast. Work inward to the breastbone, keeping the slices thin and even. Repeat this procedure on the other side.

· *Method for large breasts:* Use a carving fork to hold the bird steady against a plate or cutting board. Starting at the neck, cut the breast into halves lengthwise down to the breastbone. Position the fork to hold one half of the breast and carefully follow the contours of the breast-

bone to cut the meat away from it. Remove the breast half to a plate or cutting board. Start at the large end and slice thin, even slices across the grain at a twenty-degree angle. Repeat for the other breast half.

■

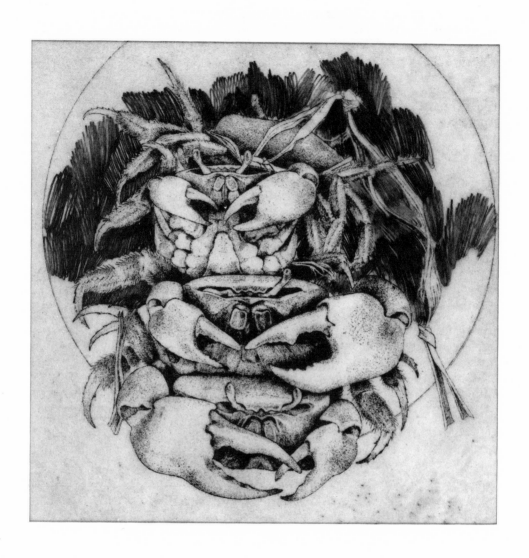

*F*ish and *Shellfish*

CHAPTER SIXTEEN

*T*he variety of fish and shellfish available in most areas of the country is enormous—enough to be confusing if not positively intimidating. However, the Cook's Guides and How to's in this chapter should make the selection, preparation, and cooking of these foods simplicity itself. You can decide what you want and then go to the store and buy it, or you can find what appears to be a good buy in the store and then consult this chapter to determine how to prepare and cook it.

A Cook's Guide to Fish

To Plan

If the fish is **whole,** plan 1 pound per serving. For **dressed** or **drawn** fish (intestines and scales removed), plan 3/4 pound per serving; for **pan-dressed** (intestines, scales, head, tail, and fins removed), plan 1/3 to 1/2 pound per serving; for **steaks or fillets,** plan 1/3 to 1/2 pound per serving.

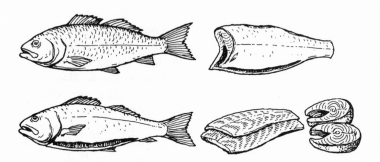

To Select

Fresh fish should have no "fishy" smell or unpleasant odor. If the head is still on, the eyes should be bright, clear, and bulging. The gills should be reddish pink. The body should be shiny, and the scales, if any, should be tight. The flesh should be firm and elastic, springing back to shape when pressed. Fillets or steaks should have a moist, translucent look. If the flesh is milky white, discolored, or dry, it is past its prime.

Fresh fish that has not been frozen is best. Some supermarkets and other vendors sell fish that has been frozen and thawed yet still call it fresh. Excess water in the package indicates that this has been done. Fish that has been frozen and thawed will have less flavor and a softer texture than fish that is really fresh. When you buy fish that has been frozen, keep it frozen until time to cook it.

The chart on pages 366 and 367 is an alphabetical listing of many fish that are popular in the United States. Beside each name, stars appear in the boxes designating the cooking method or methods that best suit that type of fish. Fish are classified according to their fat content: very low, low, low-moderate, moderate, moderate-high, or high. Any fish can usually be substituted for another, provided it has the same fat content. As a general rule, lean fish low in fat is best poached or fried and is often served with a sauce. Fatty fish is best suited to dry heat cooking, although it can be poached. Fatty fish is darker and has a stronger flavor than fish that is low in fat.

To Store

Store live fish in water or sea water. Dressed fish, pan-dressed fish, steaks, and fillets are best stored in crushed ice (no longer than two days). Normal refrigeration causes the surface to dry. When you refrigerate fresh fish, wrap it tightly in nonabsorbent paper, aluminum foil, or a plastic bag, and store it in the coldest part of the refrigerator (again, not longer than two days). Fish that is not well wrapped before refrigeration might come out with a drier, tougher surface.

When freezing fish, use an ice coffin to retain the flavor and texture as much as possible. Prepare the fish in portions to serve one or more persons. Put the portions in plastic containers or bags, or in cardboard containers such as milk cartons that will hold water. Cover the fish completely with water, then freeze. Store fatty fish frozen no longer than two months, lean fish as long as six months.

To Prepare

If the fish is frozen: Frozen steaks or fillets up to eight ounces are best cooked without thawing. Whole fish, fil-

Selection Chart for Fish

Fish	Fat Content	Sauté	Batter-fry	Broil/Bake	Roast	Poach/Steam	Stew
Albacore	moderate	•	•	•	•	•	•
Bass	low-moderate	•	•	•	•	•	•
Bluefish	low	•	•	•			
Bluegill	low	•	•	•			
Bonito	moderate			•		•	•
Bream	low		•	•			
Butterfish	moderate	•	•	•			
Carp	low-moderate				•	•	•
Catfish	low	•	•	•	•	•	•
Cod	very low			•		•	•
Croaker	low	•	•	•		•	
Drum	low			•		•	
Flounder	low	•	•	•		•	
Grouper	low	•	•	•	•	•	•
Haddock	low	•	•	•		•	•
Halibut	very low	•	•	•		•	
Herring	moderate	•	•	•			
Kingfish	moderate	•	•	•	•		
Mackerel	high			•	•		•
Mullet	moderate		•	•	•		
Perch	very low	•	•	•		•	
Pompano	moderate	•	•	•	•		
Porgy	low	•	•	•			
Rockfish	very low	•	•	•		•	
Sablefish	moderate-high			•	•		
Salmon	moderate	•		•	•	•	
Sea bass or trout	very low	•	•	•	•	•	
Shad	high			•	•		
Shark	low	•	•	•	•	•	•

continued

Selection Chart for Fish (continued)

Fish	Fat Content	Sauté	Batter-fry	Broil/Bake	Roast	Poach/Steam	Stew
Smelt	low-moderate	*	*	*			
Snapper	low	*	*	*		*	*
Spot	low	*	*	*		*	*
Swordfish	moderate	*	*	*	*	*	*
Trout	moderate-high	*	*	*	*	*	
Turbot	low	*	*	*		*	
Whiting	low	*	*	*		*	

lets, or steaks over eight ounces should be thawed at least partially so that they can cook evenly throughout. Thawing fish at room temperature or even in the refrigerator breaks down its texture and loses a great deal of flavor. Instead, immerse frozen fish in boiling water only long enough to thaw it and then refresh it in cold water to stop the cooking. Drain the fish well on paper towels, and use it immediately. Do not refreeze fish that has been thawed.

To clean whole fish: Scale and gut the fish, and remove the head, tail, and fins if desired. Catfish, eels, and flatfish must be skinned instead of scaled. If the fish is to be cooked whole, leave the fins or the head and fins on to help hold its shape. Remove the gills by pulling them out with your fingers. Cut the fish into fillets or steaks if desired. Finally, wash the fish in cold water. A little lemon juice in the water will accent the color and flavor of the fish.

(See "How to Clean and Dress Fish," p. 368.)

To Cook

For general pointers, see "Cooking Considerations for Fish and Shellfish" (p. 379).

Saute, pan-fry, oven-fry, or deep-fat-fry small fish, steaks, or fillets that are 1/2 to 3/4 inch thick. Lean fish are best for these methods. Fish with a great deal of fat might taste greasy.

Stir-fry or grill-fry small pieces of lean fish with no bones.

Broil or bake small, pan-dressed fish, steaks, or fillets of more fatty fish less than one inch thick. Lean fish may be baked or broiled if they are well basted with cooking oil.

Roast ("grill") fish, steaks, or fillets that are at least one inch thick. The thicker the fish, the better. Fish with high fat content are best to cook by this method, but lean fish may be used if they are well basted with cooking oil.

Poach or steam dressed or pan-dressed whole fish six inches or longer, and steaks or fillets that are at least one inch thick (the thicker the better). Firm-fleshed fish such as trout are best. Very fat or soft-textured fish tend to fall apart.

Stew or braise chunks and pieces of fish with no bones. For added flavor, cook the heads and trimmings along with the fish, but remove them before serving the fish.

To Season

Season with salt, pepper, onion, garlic, dill, marjoram, savory, bay leaf, paprika, cloves, allspice, nutmeg, mace, ginger, basil, fennel, celery seed, tarragon, mint, parsley, sage, rosemary, or thyme.

To Serve

Top with plain or flavored butter or margarine, lemon juice, white sauce, plain or flavored mayonnaise, tomato sauce, or one of the egg yolk and butter sauces.

How to Clean and Dress Fish

To gut: Hold the fish with one hand and a sharp knife with the other. Starting at the "vent" (anal opening) on the bottom near the tail, cut through the flesh the entire length of the belly to the head. Use your fingers to remove all the viscera, and then run a knife down both sides of the backbone inside the fish to open blood pockets. Rinse the fish in cold running water, and blot dry on paper towels.

To scale (this can be done before or after gutting): Scaling can be done with the dull back of a knife, a vegetable peeler, or a fish scraper. Wash the fish in clean, fresh water.

Place it on a cutting board and hold it firmly by the tail. Holding the tool almost vertical to the fish, start at the tail and scrape toward the head, removing all scales as you go. Be sure to remove all the scales around the fins and head. Repeat on the other side.

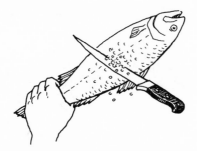

To remove fins: Never try to remove fins with shears or a knife alone, because the root bones at the base of the fins will be left in the fish. Instead, cut along each side of the fin to free it from the flesh. Then pull the fin quickly forward toward the head to remove the fin with the root bones attached. Discard the fins or save them for making broth.

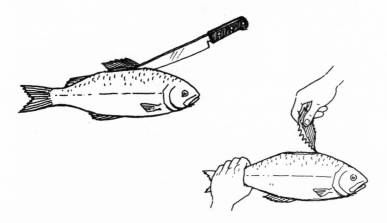

To remove head (optional): Remove the head and pectoral fins by cutting just behind the collarbone. (Note: You can leave the head on if you are making fillets.) If the backbone is large, cut down to it on each side of the fish. Then place the fish on the edge of the cutting board so that the head hangs over, and bend the head down until the backbone breaks. Cut through the bone and any remaining flesh holding the head to the body. Discard the head or save it for making broth.

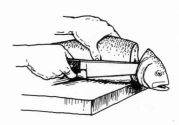

To remove tail (optional): Whole fish is more attractive with the tail left on, and there is no need to remove the tail if you are making fillets. If you want to remove it, though, cut through the flesh at the point where the tail attaches to the body. Discard the tail or save it for making broth.

To skin (optional): Use a sharp knife point to raise a corner of skin from the flesh at the head end of the dressed fish. Use one hand to hold the fish and the other to pull the flap of skin down the length of the fish to the tail. Repeat on the other side. Discard the skin or save it for making broth. (Note: Don't skin the fish if you plan to make steaks.)

To cut into steaks (optional): Steaks are large, cross-cut sections of larger fish such as salmon. Leave the skin on to hold the shape of the steaks. Hold the fish securely with one hand and cut crosswise into steaks of desired thickness, usually 3/4 to 1 inch. If the backbone is large, cut down to it on both sides, then saw through it with a coping saw.

To fillet (optional): Fillets are large, full-length pieces removed in one piece from each side of the backbone of a fish. There is no need to remove the head or tail. Hold the fish steady with one hand, and use a sharp knife to make a vertical cut along the top of the fish down to its backbone from the head to the tail.

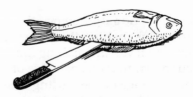

Now turn the knife flat, parallel to the backbone. Starting at the tail, use clean, even strokes to cut the flesh away from one side of the backbone. Be careful not to cut into the flesh. Lift off the whole side of fillet in one piece.

Remove any small bones that might remain on the flesh. Carefully lift the backbone and rib bones off the bottom fillet, or turn the fish over and repeat the cutting process on the other side. (Note: This technique can also be used to debone small cooked fish.)

■

A Cook's Guide to Shellfish

To Plan

For shrimp, one pound in the shell without heads makes about two servings. Figure 1/3 pound more if the heads are on. For **oysters, scallops, or clams,** plan twelve to eighteen per serving, depending on their size. For **crabs, lobster, or crayfish,** plan one per serving unless they are unusually large or small.

To Select

Except for shrimp, fresh shellfish should be cooked alive. (Frozen shellfish is usually prepackaged, with accompanying instructions for preparation and use.) **Shrimp** are usually dead and de-headed, either with or without their shells. They keep best if their shells and heads are left on.

Fresh shrimp should always look fresh and moist and have a rich grayish or green color. Avoid those that are broken, dry, or aged looking.

Mollusks—oysters, clams, mussels, and scallops— should be alive, and their shells should close tightly when touched. Throw out any that are open. They are dead, and there's no telling for how long. If they are already shucked, mollusks should look moist and full. Avoid any that look old or dry.

Crustacea—lobsters, crayfish, and crabs—should be alive and crawling. If they are dead before cooking, the flesh flakes and falls apart when they are cooked.

To Store

Fresh shrimp keep best with their heads and shells left on. Keep them on ice, covered with damp seaweed, sackcloth, or heavy paper. Alternatively, wrap the shrimp tightly in nonporous paper, aluminum foil, or a plastic bag and refrigerate (24 hours at most). Do not store shrimp in water.

Oysters, clams, mussels, and scallops in their shells should be kept alive covered in ice, not water; or they can be wrapped in nonporous paper and refrigerated for two or three days. If you can get them in a bed of their native mud and keep it wet and cool, they will keep for at least a week "just as happy as a clam in mud."

Fresh, live lobsters, crayfish, or crabs should be kept wrapped in cool, wet seaweed and/or sackcloth or heavy paper. Excessive cold may make them appear sleepy and almost dead when they are not. If you can, keep them alive in a tank of sea water until they are cooked.

To Freeze

(See "How to Open Shellfish," p. 374.)

Shell shrimp and shuck mollusks. Boil whole lobsters, crayfish, and crabs, and then pick out the meat before freezing it. Put the meat into a plastic container or milk carton, cover with water, and freeze. The ice coffin will seal in the flavors. Frozen shellfish will keep well up to three months.

To Prepare

Prepare shellfish just before cooking for best flavor. If they are frozen, do not thaw them before cooking.

Shrimp may be boiled or steamed with or without their heads and shells. They are best if the heads and shells are left on. The dark vein along the back should be removed either before or after cooking. It is the shrimp's intestine and may contain dangerous bacteria.

(See "How to Open Shellfish," p. 374.)

Oysters and other mollusks should be scrubbed under cold running water with a stiff brush to remove mud and dirt. If they are soaked in sea water or tap water with 1/3 cup noniodized salt per gallon, they may release any sand and mud in their stomachs. Soak them for one to two hours, changing the water every fifteen minutes. To open, see "How to Open Shellfish," p. 374.

Lobsters, crayfish, and crabs should be cooked live and require no special preparation before cooking.

To Cook

For general pointers, see "Cooking Considerations for Fish and Shellfish" (p. 379).

Boil or steam shrimp, crabs, lobsters, and crayfish in their shells. They are done when their shells turn pink. Cooking for too long can make the meat tough and dry. Oysters, mussels, and clams in their shells should be steamed but not boiled so their juices are not lost. Shelled mollusks may be poached. They are done when their edges turn up.

Roast or bake oysters, mussels, and clams in their shells or on the half shell. They are done when their shells open or when their edges turn up. Overcooking makes them shrunken and dry.

Broil or sauté shelled shrimp or shucked oysters, scallops, mussels, and clams. Shrimp will turn pink when they are done. Oysters, scallops, mussels, and clams are done when their edges turn up.

Pan-fry or deep-fat fry shelled shrimp or shucked oysters, scallops, or clams in a wet batter, dipped batter, or breading.

To Season

Season with salt, pepper, onion, garlic, mustard, dill, paprika, parsley, bay leaf, savory, tarragon, thyme, fennel, anise, or allspice.

To Serve

Top with plain or flavored butter or margarine or mayonnaise, clarified butter, lemon juice, white sauce, or seafood cocktail sauce.

How to Open Shellfish

Shrimp

1. **Remove the head** by twisting and pulling it away from the body. Discard the head.

2. **Remove the vein** that runs along the top of the shrimp. It is the shrimp's intestine and may hold dangerous bacteria. To remove it with the shell still on, insert a skewer or toothpick into one of the joints of the shell nearest the head. Carefully lift the skewer to pull the vein out. Should the vein break, repeat at another point along the back. Discard the vein and wash the shrimp under cold running water.

To take out the vein with the shell removed, run a knife tip, fork tine, or thumbnail down the length of the vein.

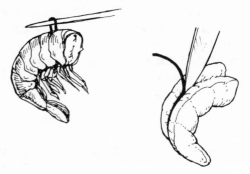

3. **Remove the shell** of cooked or uncooked shrimp by pulling the shell apart along the bottom between the feet. Pull the shell back toward the tail, and either break it off just ahead of the tail or pull the tail off with it. Discard the shell or save it for making broth.

Oysters, Mussels, Scallops, and Clams

1. Before starting, examine the shells to eliminate any that are open or otherwise unfit. Hold the shell in one hand and scrub it with a stiff brush under cold running water to remove as much mud and other dirt as you can.

2. The easiest way to open the shells is to put them in the freezer just long enough to expand the juice and pop the shell. The hard way is to pry them open, using thick, heavy gloves to protect your hands from cuts. Either way, to open the shells fully, hold the shell in one hand and a dull knife in the other. Insert the tip of the knife between the halves of the shell near the hinge. Run the blade the full length of the shell, twisting it to pry the halves apart.

3. Bring the side of the blade across the inside of the upper shell and cut the muscle free from it. Be careful not to cut into the muscle, or it will lose its plumpness.

4. Dislodge and discard the upper shell and then cut the muscle free from the lower shell. If the muscle is served in its shell, remove any pieces of broken shell or other debris that might be present. Keep as much liquor in the shell as you can.

Lobsters and Crayfish

1. Place cooked lobster or crayfish with its back down on the cutting board. With a sharp knife or kitchen shears, cut through the underside of the shell its full length, being careful not to cut into the meat.

Alternatively, place a heavy, sharp knife directly in the center, down the length of the underside, and drive the blade through the shell, cutting the thing into halves by striking its back sharply with a mallet or hammer.

2. Use both hands to pull the shell apart.

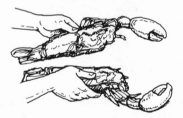

3. Remove the stomach sac and gills just behind the head.

4. Pull out the dark intestinal vein that runs down to the end of the tail. Leave any light-greenish liver and dark roe.

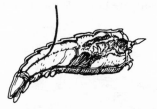

5. Twist the head and tail to separate them. Use a sharp small knife to cut away the thin shell on the underside.

6. Use a hammer, pliers, or nutcracker to break open the shell around the claws and legs.

7. Use a small fork or lobster pick to remove the meat from the shell.

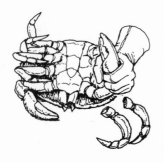

Crab

1. Wear thick gloves to protect your hands from cuts. Grasp the cooked crab firmly and break and twist the claws off where they join the body. Repeat for all claws and legs.

2. To open claws and legs, use pliers or a nutcracker, or hold them with their narrow edge on a cutting board and beat them with a mallet or hammer to crack the shell of each section. Separate the shell pieces with your fingers and pick any shell bits off the meat.

3. To open the body, first use your hands or a dull knife to pull back the "apron" on the underside. Then hold the crab with both hands and insert a thumb under the shell by the apron hinge. Pull the shell away from the body.

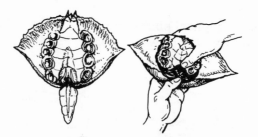

4. Remove and discard gills and spongy parts ("dead man's fingers") in the middle of the body, but save the creamy crab butter.

5. Separate the body into halves by positioning a knife directly in the center between the leg joints on the under-

side. Tap the back of the knife with a mallet or hammer to drive it through the shell, separating it with one clean cut.

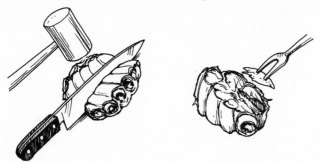

6. Use your fingers, a small fork, or a crab pick to remove the meat.

■

Cooking Considerations for Fish and Shellfish

1. The fresher they are, the better their flavor.

2. The longer a fish keeps its bones and protective skin, the juicer and more flavorful it will be. The intestines, however, should be removed as soon as possible after the fish is caught. They contain bacteria that hastens decomposition.

3. Frozen fish and shellfish are best cooked frozen. If you must thaw them, immerse them briefly in boiling water and then refresh them in cold water to stop the cooking. Do not thaw them at room temperature or in the refrigerator. Slow thawing breaks down the texture.

4. Fish and shellfish require very little cooking. Intense heat and overcooking destroy their flavor, texture, and nutritional value. Since fish continues to cook in its own heat, it is easily overcooked.

5. One kind of fish can usually be substituted for another with the same fat content.

6. Fish with very little fat—such as flounder, bass, red snapper, halibut, and perch—can easily become dry from cooking. For that reason, lean fish is best poached or fried and is often served with a sauce.

7. Fatty fish—salmon, mackerel, trout, tuna, and others—are best suited to dry heat cooking, although poaching suits them also.

8. Cooked fish is ready when the flesh has lost its translucent appearance and turns opaque and milky throughout. Test for doneness by inserting a fork deep into the thickest part and pulling the flesh apart a little. The flesh should just separate into flakes or layers, but not fall apart easily. The flesh of whole fish or steaks should separate cleanly from the backbone.

9. Shrimp, crabs, lobsters, and crayfish are done when their shells turn pink. Oysters, scallops, mussels, and clams in their shell are done when the shell opens. If they are cooked shucked, they are done when their edges curl.

10. Cooked fish must be handled very carefully or it will fall apart.

11. Fish that is cooked in liquid and that is to be served cold will be more moist if it is slightly undercooked and then cooled in the cooking liquid. The heat in the liquid will finish the cooking with little chance of overcooking.

12. Fish that is cooked in liquid is usu-ally accompanied by a sauce. The more delicate the flavor of the fish, the more delicate the sauce should be. Favorite sauces include plain or flavored mayonnaise (especially tartar sauce), plain or flavored butter (whole or clarified), white sauce, or one of the egg yolk and butter sauces.

How to Fry Fish or Shellfish

Sauté or *grill-fry* shelled shrimp or small pieces of deboned lean fish. *Pan-fry, deep-fat-fry,* or *oven-fry* shelled shrimp, shucked oysters, scallops, and clams, or lean fish that is 1/2 to 3/4 inch thick.

0. **Before you begin:** Read all the steps below. If necessary, review the Cook's Guide for fish or shellfish, the Cooking Considerations for Fish and Shellfish, and the principles of frying in Chapter Two.

1. **Plan** 15 to 30 minutes to prepare the food and the coating, and 10 to 15 minutes to cook each batch. If a wet batter is used, allow 1 to 2 hours or longer for the batter to set. *Optional:* Chill food coated with dry coating at least 30 minutes.

2. **Prepare the coating.** (For more detailed information about coatings, see pp. 50–54.)

   · *For sautéing or stir frying,* no coating is needed.
   · *Dry coating:* For 4 to 8 servings, use 1/2 cup flour, cornmeal, pancake mix, breading, or combinations of these. Put the coating in a pan or bag, add seasonings, and mix.
   · *Dipped batter:* For 4 to 8 servings, use 1/2 cup seasoned dry coating held in a pan or bag plus a dip of 1/2 cup milk, 1 beaten egg, or a mixture of the two held in a bowl separate from the dry coating.
   · *Wet batter:* For 4 to 8 servings, use 1/2 cup seasoned flour, plus 1/2 cup liquid, plus 1 whole egg or 2 egg whites. Mix all ingredients and let stand at room temperature for 1 to 2 hours, or refrigerate for 3 to

48 hours. *Optional:* For a lighter crust, add leavening just before dipping the food. (See p. 53.)

3. **Prepare the food.**

   · *Shellfish* must be removed from the shell.

(See "How to Open Shellfish," p. 374.)

   · *Fish* should be no more than 3/4 inch thick, scaled and cleaned. If the fish is small enough to fry whole, leave the fins and tail on. To prevent whole fish from curling as it cooks, score both sides, making diagonal slashes about 1/8 inch deep and an inch or two long, spaced an inch or so apart.

(See "How to Clean and Dress Fish," p. 368.)

   Alternatively, cut fish into fillets or steaks (see p. 370). Wash the fish in cold water with a little salt and/or lemon juice, and dry it on paper towels.

4. **Coat the pieces:**

   a. Coat evenly with seasoned dry coating, batter, or breading. Hold the coated food on a cold plate.

   b. *Optional:* Chill food coated with a dry coating for 30 minutes before frying.

5. **Prepare the vessel:**

   · *To grill-fry or stir-fry:* Coat the cooking surface with just enough cooking oil to keep the food from sticking. Peanut oil is especially good.

   · *To sauté or oven-fry:* Use a pan just large enough to hold the food. Add 1/16 to 1/8 inch of cooking oil such as peanut oil, or equal parts of butter or margarine and cooking oil.

   · *To pan-fry:* Use a pan with sides about 1 inch higher than the food. Add enough cooking oil to cover half the food. Peanut oil is especially good.

   · *To deep-fat-fry:* Use a special appliance or a heavy pan or pot sufficiently deep to hold enough cooking oil for the food to float plus 2 to 3 inches more to allow room for foam.

6. **Heat the cooking oil.** Do not allow it to get hot enough to smoke. For garlic flavor, use oil preflavored with garlic, or cook whole cloves of garlic in the cooking oil until they are golden brown, then remove them.

   · *On a range burner:* Heat the cooking oil at medium-high heat until a small bit of food or batter will sizzle when it is dropped in.

   · *To oven fry:* Preheat the oven to 450 degrees F. and place the pan on the center shelf. It is ready when the cooking oil sizzles.

7. **Cook the food.** Add food pieces slowly. Do not crowd.

   · *To sauté, stir-fry, or grill-fry:* Stir the food around or shake the pan back and forth to brown the food evenly all over.
   · *To pan-fry:* Move the food occasionally so that it does not stick and burn. When the bottom has browned, turn the food over and brown the other side.
   · *To deep fat-fry:* Turn the food when the bottom has browned. Cook the other side until brown.
   · *To oven-fry:* Using tongs to hold the pieces, coat each one all over in the hot cooking oil. Return the pan to the center shelf of the oven and cook until the food browns.

8. **Remove food from oil** and drain on paper towels.

9. **Before frying more food:** Clean the oil of crumbs, flakes, or stray pieces so that they do not burn. If more cooking oil is needed, allow the hot oil to cool for 2 minutes before adding it.

10. **Serve as quickly as possible,** or hold the food for up to 30 minutes in a warm oven (150 degrees F.).

11. **Optional:** Accompany with fresh lemon, plain or flavored butter or margarine, mayonnaise, or white sauce. If you like, serve fish *"à la Meunière"* (mean-yair), a special way of serving fried fish used in fancy restaurants. Put the fried fish on a warm serving plate. Sprinkle it with a little lemon juice and chopped parsley. Brown a little butter (p. 291) and pour it lightly over the fish just before serving.

■

How to Bake, Broil, Roast, Grill, or Barbecue Fish or Shellfish

Broil or *bake* shrimp, oysters, clams, scallops, or fish less than one inch thick. Oysters, mussels, and clams may be roasted or baked either in their shells or "on the half shell." *Grill* or *barbecue* pan-dressed fish, steaks, or fillets that are at least one inch thick. Fish with high fat content are best for these methods, but a lean fish may be used if it is coated with cooking oil.

0. **Before you begin:** Read all the steps below. If necessary, review the Cook's Guide for fish or shellfish, the Cook-

ing Considerations for Fish and Shellfish, and the principles of dry heat cooking covered in Chapter Two.

1. **Plan** 10 to 20 minutes to prepare the food. If you are using charcoal, allow 30 to 60 minutes for the coals to heat. See step 5 for approximate cooking times.

2. **Prepare the heat:**

   · *For baking:* Set the rack on the center shelf of the oven. Preheat the oven to 350 degrees F.

   · *For oven broiling:* Set the rack so that the food will be 3 to 4 inches from the heat. The thicker the food, the farther it should be from the heat. Set the oven temperature on "broil" and preheat the oven.

   · *For charcoal grilling:* Set the rack so that the food will be 3 to 4 inches from the heat. The thicker the food, the farther it should be from the heat. Start the fire and allow at least 30 minutes for a gray ash to form over all the coals. Tap the coals occasionally before and throughout the cooking to keep the ash from smothering the heat. A fair test of the temperature is how long you can hold your hand over the heat. Place your hand palm down at rack height and count: one thousand one = very hot; one thousand two = hot; one thousand three = medium hot; one thousand four = medium low.

3. **Prepare the vessel:**

   · *For oven cooking:* Use a pan or dish with low sides. Coat the inside lightly with shortening to prevent the food from sticking.

   · *For grill cooking:* Coat the grill or rack with shortening to prevent the food from sticking. Fish are best if they are cooked whole in a special rack made expressly for this purpose.

4. **Prepare the food.**

   Fish

   a. Scale and clean the fish.

   (See "How to Clean and Dress Fish," p. 368.)

   b. If the fish is to be cooked whole, remove the fins but leave the head and tail on to help hold its shape. To prevent whole fish from curling as it cooks, score both sides making diagonal slashes about 1/8 inch deep and an inch or so long spaced an inch or so apart on both sides.

   Alternatively, cut the fish into steaks or fillets if desired (see p. 370).

c. Wash the fish in cold water with a little salt and/or lemon juice, and dry it on paper towels.

d. *Optional:* Marinate the fish in a sauce and skip steps e, f, and g. (See "Marinades," p. 102.)

e. *Optional:* Whole fish may be stuffed with a bread stuffing, shrimp or crab meat, or a combination of these. Sew the cavity shut using a trussing needle.

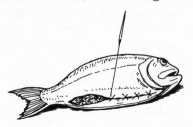

f. Coat the fish lightly all over with butter, margarine, or cooking oil. Peanut oil is especially good.

g. Sprinkle salt and other seasonings lightly all over the fish.

(See "Breading," p. 54.)

h. *Optional:* Coat the fish all over with breading.

i. *Optional:* For added flavor, bard fish by placing strips of blanched raw bacon over it.

Shrimp

(See "How to Open Shellfish," p. 374.)

a. Peel and devein the shrimp.

b. Coat the shrimp liberally with butter, margarine, or cooking oil. Sprinkle lightly with salt and other seasonings.

c. *Optional:* For added flavor, cook the shrimp with pieces of garlic, onion, blanched raw bacon, or combinations of these.

Oysters, Clams, and Mussels

a. Leave in the unopened shell, or open the shell and add lemon or lime juice and other seasonings. (Note: Leave the juices in the shell or add liquid if needed. Mollusks should cook in the liquid, not directly in dry heat.)

b. *Optional:* For added flavor, cook with pieces of garlic, onion, blanched raw bacon, or combinations of these.

5. **Cook the food:**
   a. Place the food in the prepared dish or on the rack or grill.
   b. Place the vessel in the oven or on the grill.
   c. Set a timer for the approximate cooking time. Cooking times will vary depending on the thickness of the food. If fish or shrimp are stuffed, add half again as much time to the times shown here.

   > *Steaks, fillets, small fish, or mollusks:* Bake or roast 10 to 30 minutes; broil 5 to 15 minutes.
   > · *Whole fish (about 3 pounds):* Bake or roast 30 to 35 minutes; broil 15 to 20 minutes.

   d. If the fish is thick, turn it when one surface has browned and brown the other side. Mollusks and thin pieces of fish need not be turned.

6. **Test for doneness:**
   · *Fish* are done when the meat flakes in its thickest part.
   · *Shrimp* are done when they turn pink.
   · *Oysters, clams, and mussels in the shell* are done when their shells open. If they are shelled, they are done when their edges curl.

7. **Remove from the heat** to a warm serving plate, and serve right away. Holding fish or shellfish for any time diminishes their flavor and texture.

8. **Optional:** Garnish with paprika and/or chopped parsley or other fresh herbs.

9. **Optional:** Accompany with fresh lemon, plain or flavored butter or clarified butter, white sauce, or plain or flavored mayonnaise, especially tartar sauce.

∎

How to Boil or Steam Shellfish

Steam shrimp, oysters, scallops, mussels, or clams. *Boil* shrimp, crabs, lobsters, or crayfish.

0. **Before you begin:** Read all the steps below. If necessary, review the Cook's Guide to Shellfish, the Cooking Considerations for Fish and Shellfish, and the principles of cooking with liquids covered in Chapter Two.

1. **Plan** 15 to 30 minutes to prepare the food plus 5 to 30 minutes to cook it.
2. **Prepare the food:**
   a. See the Cook's Guide to Shellfish (p. 371) for basic preparations.
   b. Leave shellfish in the shell.
3. **Prepare the vessel:** Use a pot that is large enough to hold the food. If a steaming rack is used, the pot must be large enough to hold it and the food. Add 1/2 to 1 inch of liquid to the pot. (Use water, beer, fish broth, or combinations of these.) Season the liquid with lemon juice and/or vinegar plus peppercorns, bay leaf, mustard, horseradish, or other seasonings of your choice.
4. **Cook the food:**
   a. Bring the liquid to a boil.
   b. To boil the food, place it in the liquid; to steam it, place it on a steaming rack and then place the rack in the liquid.
   c. Cover the pot and lower the heat to a very slow simmer.
   d. Cook the food until it is done, stirring or shaking it every few minutes so that it all cooks evenly.
      - *Shrimp and mollusks:* 5 to 15 minutes
      - *Crabs:* 20 to 30 minutes
      - *Lobsters or crayfish:* 20 to 25 minutes per pound
5. **Test for doneness:**
   - *Shrimp, crabs, lobsters, and crayfish* are done when their shells turn pink.
   - *Oysters, clams, scallops, and mussels* are done when their shells open or when the edges of the meat begin to curl.
6. **Serve right away** or hold for no longer than 30 minutes in a warm oven (150 degrees F.). *Optional:* Accompany with fresh lemon, plain or flavored butter, white sauce, or plain or flavored mayonnaise, especially tartar sauce.

■

How to Wrap-steam Fish

Use dressed or pan-dressed lean fish that is at least six inches in length, or steaks or fillets at least one inch thick.

Firm-fleshed fish such as salmon, trout, and sole are best. Fat or soft-textured fish tend to fall apart.

0. **Before you begin:** Read all the steps below. If necessary, review the Cook's Guide to Fish, the Cooking Considerations for Fish and Shellfish, and the principles of cooking with liquids covered in Chapter Two.

1. **Plan** 15 to 30 minutes to prepare the fish and to preheat the oven, plus 10 to 30 minutes to cook the fish. For whole fish, measure the fish at its thickest point. Allow 10 minutes cooking time per inch of thickness if the fish is fully thawed. If it is not thawed, allow 12 to 15 minutes per inch.

2. **Prepare the oven:**
   a. Set a rack on the middle shelf.
   b. Preheat the oven to 400 degrees F.

3. **Prepare the food:**
   a. Clean and gut whole fish, removing the gills and fins but leaving the head and tail on to help hold the shape. (See "How to Clean and Dress Fish," p. 368.)
   b. *Optional:* Cut the fish into steaks or fillets 1 inch thick (see p. 370).
   c. Wash the fish in cold water with a little salt and/or lemon juice.
   d. *Optional:* Prepare a chopped mirepoix of 50% onions, 25% celery, and 25% carrots, plus mushrooms, sweet bell peppers, and finely chopped garlic or shallots if desired.
   e. Brush both sides of the fish and the inside of the stomach cavity with butter, margarine, or cooking oil.
   f. *Optional:* Stuff the stomach cavity with bread stuffing, shrimp, crab, lobster, crayfish, or combinations of these.
   g. Sprinkle lightly with lemon juice and/or white wine plus salt and other seasonings to taste.

4. **Prepare the vessel.** Wrap steaming can be done in a covered casserole dish. Alternatively, make a wrap with a piece of aluminum foil or damp, soft cooking parchment that is slightly longer than the fish. Fold the wrap in half lengthwise. Place the fish on it with the bottom of the fish along the folded part of the wrap. Trace the shape of the top of the fish about one inch above it. Cut the wrap along the tracing. The resulting shape should

be roughly that of the fish. Open the wrap and lay it flat on the bottom of a prepared casserole dish.

a. If you are using a wrap, place the fish in the wrap with its bottom along the crease. If you are not using a wrap, place the fish in the prepared casserole dish.
b. *Optional:* Pour the mirepoix of flavoring vegetables over the fish.
c. If you are using a wrap, fold one side of the wrap up and over the top of the fish. Double-fold, crimp, or pinch the two sides of the wrap together to seal the fish inside. Do not cover the dish. If you are not using a wrap, cover the casserole dish.

5. **Cook the fish:**

a. When the oven is preheated, put the baking dish on the center shelf and close the door.
b. Set the timer for the approximate cooking time (see step 1).

6. **Test for doneness:** A minute or so before the approximate cooking time is up, open the wrap and insert a fork into the deepest part of the fish, pulling it apart a little. The flesh should come up in thick flakes or layers and separate cleanly from the backbone.

7. **Serve.** Handle the fish carefully so that it remains intact.

   a. Use a large, wide, hard spatula or pancake turner to lift the fish out of its baking dish and onto a warm serving plate. If a wrap was used, serve with the wrap folded back or slide the fish carefully out of the wrap and onto a warm serving plate.

   b. Pour the warm cooking juices over the fish, or use juices plus milk or a combination of milk and white wine to make a white sauce. Hold the fish in a warm oven (150 degrees F.) while you make the sauce. (See "How to Make White Sauce," p. 144.)

8. **Optional:** Accompany with fresh lemon, plain or flavored butter or clarified butter, white sauce, plain or flavored mayonnaise (especially tartar sauce), or one of the egg yolk and butter sauces.

■

How to Poach Fish

Fish to be cooked by this method should be at least one inch thick—the thicker, the better. Use dressed or pandressed lean fish that is six inches or longer, or steaks or fillets that are at least one inch thick. Firm-fleshed fish such as salmon, trout, and sole are best. Fatty or soft-textured fish tend to fall apart.

0. **Before you begin:** Read all the steps below. If necessary, review the Cook's Guide to Fish, the Cooking Considerations for Fish and Shellfish, and the principles of cooking with liquids covered in Chapter Two.

1. **Plan** 30 to 60 minutes to prepare the fish and cooking liquid, plus 10 to 30 minutes to cook the fish. Measure the fish at its thickest point. Allow 10 minutes cooking time for each inch of thickness if the fish is fully thawed, 12 to 15 minutes per inch of thickness if the fish is still frozen. (Note: Poached fish is usually served with a sauce. Make the sauce in advance, if possible. If you want to make a velouté from the cooking liquid, have the roux and flavorings all prepared so that the fish will have to wait only a short time while the sauce is completed.)

2. **Prepare the fish:**

   a. Clean and gut whole fish, removing the gills and fins

(See "How to Clean and Dress Fish," p. 368.)

but leaving the head and tail on to help hold its shape.

b. *Optional:* Cut the fish into steaks or fillets at least one inch thick (see p. 370).

c. Wash the fish in cold water with a little salt and/or lemon juice.

d. Wrap the fish tightly in cheesecloth that is 6 to 10 inches longer than the fish. The cloth will hold the fish together as it cooks and will be used to lift it from the cooking vessel.

3. **Prepare the vessel:**

   a. Select a pot or pan large enough to accommodate the full length of the fish and deep enough for the fish to be completely covered in the liquid.

   b. Coat the bottom of the vessel lightly with shortening to prevent the fish from sticking.

4. **Prepare the liquid:**

   a. Add just enough liquid to the vessel to cover the fish completely. Use water or a mixture of half milk and half water.

   b. Flavor the liquid. For each cup of liquid, add 1 Tbsp. butter or margarine plus 2 Tbsp. lemon juice, vinegar, white wine, or a combination of these.

   c. Make a "court bouillon" broth. For each two quarts of water, add 1/2 cup chopped onions, 1/4 cup chopped celery, and 1/4 cup chopped carrots plus finely chopped garlic or shallots if desired. Season with salt, pepper, bay leaf, parsley, and thyme to taste.

   d. *Optional:* Add fish trimmings, if any, to the liquid.

5. **Cook the food:**

   a. Simmer the liquid uncovered for 30 minutes before adding the fish.

   b. Put the fish into the water with the ends of the cheesecloth draped over the sides of the vessel.

   c. Cover the vessel only partly to allow steam to escape.

   d. Set a timer to the approximate cooking time. Allow

     10 minutes for each inch of thickness if the fish is fully thawed, 12 to 15 minutes if it is not.

    e. Keep the vessel partly uncovered to prevent boiling. Check every few minutes to be sure the liquid does not boil.

6. **Test for doneness:** A minute or so before the approximate cooking time is up, open the wrap and insert a fork into the deepest part of the fish, pulling it apart a little. The flesh should come up in thick flakes or layers and separate cleanly from the backbone.

7. **Remove from the liquid:** Twist the cheesecloth tightly around the fish and lift it out of the liquid and onto a warm serving platter. Hold the ends apart to support the fish so it does not sag in the middle and break.

8. **Optional sauce:** Strain the broth and use it to make a velouté white sauce. While you make the sauce, hold the fish in a warm oven (150 degrees F.), keeping it covered in its wrap so that it does not dry out. (See "How to Make White Sauce," p. 144.)

9. **Serve as soon as possible on a warm platter.** *Optional:* Accompany with fresh lemon, white sauce, plain or flavored butter or mayonnaise, or one of the egg yolk and butter sauces.

■

How to Make Fish Stew

Stew or braise chunks and pieces of lean fish with no bones. Shellfish can be cooked in their shells. Fish and shellfish can be combined in the stew if you like.

   0. **Before you begin:** Read all the steps below. If necessary, review the Cook's Guides to fish and shellfish,

the Cooking Considerations for Fish and Shellfish, and the principles of braising in Chapter Three.

1. **Plan** 1 to 2 cups per serving. Allow 15 to 30 minutes to prepare the food plus 30 to 60 minutes to cook it.

2. **Prepare the food.** See the Cook's Guides to fish and shellfish for basic preparations. Fish should be cut into small steaks or fillets (see p. 370). You may leave shellfish in their shells, but first scrub them thoroughly with a stiff brush under cold running water.

3. **Prepare the vessel:** Use a pot large enough to hold the food in the liquid with at least a 2-inch space between the top of the liquid and the lid to allow for foam.

4. **Prepare the liquid:**

   a. Add enough liquid to the vessel to cover the food and make the number of servings desired (1 to 2 cups per serving). Use water or a combination of half milk and half water.

   b. For each cup of liquid, add a dash of salt, 1 Tbsp. butter or margarine, and 2 Tbsp. lemon juice, vinegar, white wine, or a combination of these.

   c. Add fish heads and trimmings, if any, to the cold liquid. Bring the liquid to a boil slowly. Reduce the heat and simmer for about 30 minutes.

5. **Prepare flavoring vegetables:** A classic mirepoix is made of 50% onions, 25% carrots, and 25% celery, plus finely chopped garlic or shallots if desired. Allow 1 cup of chopped vegetables for each 2 quarts of cooking liquid. Chop the vegetables and sauté them in butter or margarine until they are tender.

6. **Remove the fish trimmings from the liquid and discard.**

7. **Optional:** Thicken the liquid. Add roux, cornstarch, pureed vegetables, heavy cream, sour cream, or yogurt.

(See "Thickeners," p. 130.)

8. **Season the liquid:** Add pepper, bay leaf, mustard, horseradish, or other special seasonings to taste.

9. **Cook the food:**

   a. Bring the liquid to a boil and add the food to it. If fish and shellfish are being cooked together, cook the longest-cooking shellfish first and then add the other shellfish and finally the fish so that each cooks in only the amount of time needed to make it tender.

   b. When the liquid returns to a boil, cover the pot and lower the heat to a very slow simmer, or "stew."

Optional: Remove the pot to a preheated oven (250–300 degrees F.).

d. Stew the food only long enough to make it tender.

- *Fish, shrimp, or mollusks:* 5 to 15 minutes
- *Crabs:* 20 to 30 minutes
- *Lobsters or crayfish:* 20 to 25 minutes per pound

10. **Test for doneness:**

- *Fish* are done when the meat flakes in its thickest part.
- *Shrimp, crabs, lobsters, or crayfish* are done when their shells turn pink.
- *Oysters, clams, scallops, and mussels* are done when their shells open or the sides of the meat begin to curl.

11. **Serve right away** or hold for no longer than 30 minutes in a warm oven (150 degrees F.).

■

Meats

CHAPTER SEVENTEEN

*T*hat America is a nation of meat eaters is widely acknowledged. What is not widely known, however, is that most American cooks don't really know much about meats. Too many of them cook meats incorrectly or waste money cooking cuts in ways that are inappropriate.

One of the major causes of problems in dealing with meats has been a lack of standardization. In the past, the same meats and cuts were called by different names and cooked in different ways by different cooks. Even butchers working in the same meat market sometimes called the same cut by different names and recommended inappropriate cooking methods for some of them.

It was as recently as 1973 that the National Live Stock and Meat Board finally established a list of 300 or so recommended standard names gleaned from the thousands that had been used all over the country before then. At the same time, standardized methods for cooking each cut were established. Those standardized names and methods are still not used universally, however. Butchers and stores can call any piece of meat whatever they like, and many still do not adhere to the industry standards. Your shopping and your cooking will be a great deal easier if you shop with those who do. Ask your butcher to explain cuts and cooking methods; those who show you a chart issued by the National Live Stock and Meat Board usually adhere to its standards.

To put some order into the confusion surrounding meats, this chapter presents Cook's Guides and Selection Charts for the various types of meats. You can use the guides and charts in two ways. (1) Decide how you want to cook a particular meat (broil, roast, or stew, for example) and then use the appropriate Selection Chart to determine the best cut to buy and the Cook's Guide to determine the best size. (2) Buy what appears to be a good cut of meat and then look it up in the appropriate Chart and Guide to determine the best way to cook it.

The Meat Selection Charts list the cooking methods across the top. For each method, appropriate cuts are listed in order of decreasing tenderness, with the most tender (and usually most expensive) cut at the top and the least tender at the bottom. The names and the cooking methods are those established by the National Live Stock and Meat Board.

Both the Guides and the Charts for beef, veal, and lamb specify different grades. The grades used most often to indicate the quality of meats are those established by the United States Department of Agriculture (U.S.D.A.), as follows.

- *Prime:* This is reserved for meats with the greatest amount of fat. Because it has so much fat, a meat of this grade will be more tender and flavorful than a similar cut of a lower grade, which is why prime grade meat is well-suited for broiling and roasting. Prime grade meats are very expensive; they are usually sold only to restaurants. Beware! Some meat sellers call their meats "prime" even though they do not qualify for this grade under U.S. government standards. To be sure you get your money's worth, ask to see the U.S.D.A. mark on the grading label.
- *Choice:* This is the most abundant and common grade available in most stores. Choice grade meats are tender and flavorful but don't have the excess fat and high price of prime meats. Choice meats are good cooked by any method.
- *Good:* Meats with very little fat are graded good. Their flavor can be very good indeed, especially when cooked slowly in liquid. Cooked in dry heat, however, they are likely to be tough.

A Cook's Guide to Ground Meats

As the National Live Stock and Meat Board has stated, "There is no place in the meat counter with greater chance for consumer misunderstanding and irritation or opportunity for retailer error than the ground beef area." That's because of the enormous variety of methods used for packaging and labeling ground meats. A package labeled "chopped sirloin," for example, could well include trimmings from the shank and chuck, and even pieces of pork or lamb. Moreover, the same meat counter could well have the same ingredients in a package labeled "ground beef" that is priced as much as one-third to one-half less than "chopped sirloin." As a consumer of ground meats, you should be concerned with three things: flavor, fat content, and price.

Beef, pork, veal, and lamb can all be used alone or (more often) mixed together to make ground meat. Ground pork has more and better flavor and less fat than beef, and it can be less expensive. Ground veal also can have much less fat than beef, but its flavor is more delicate, and it is usually much more expensive. Many cooks and books recommend a mixture of equal parts beef and either pork, veal, or a combination of the two, especially for making meat loaf or spaghetti sauce.

Many cooks think of ground beef as the only meat used in making ground meat. They will even pay extra to get a special variety, such as ground chuck, round, or sirloin. However, tests performed by leading food scientists have established that the flavor of a given kind of ground meat is determined mostly by its fat content. The more fat, the greater the flavor.

By law, ground meats can contain no more than 30% fat. The more fat, the greater the flavor and, usually, the lower the price. Much of the fat is cooked away, however, and fat contains calories and cholesterol that aren't good for you. Ground meat with 15% to 20% fat content ("extra lean" or "ground sirloin") is the best for your diet, but probably also the least tasty and the highest priced. Ground meat with 25% to 30% fat ("regular" or "ground chuck") is the cheapest and tastiest, but a fair amount of its volume will be reduced when it is cooked and a good deal of fat will still remain. About the best compromise is to go with ground meat that has between 20% and 25% fat ("lean" or "ground round").

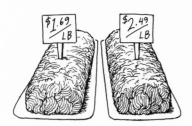

The price charged by meat packagers for ground meats is usually determined more by what they think the customer will pay than by what is in it. "Ground sirloin" certainly sounds more impressive and may cost a good deal more, but it won't taste any better than "ground beef" with the same amount of fat. Since the flavor of ground meat is determined more by the amount of fat it contains than the meat cuts that are used to make it, you will do well to buy the cheapest kind you can get that has the amount of fat you desire.

To Plan

Plan servings of 4 to 8 ounces (1/4 to 1/2 cup) of ground meat, depending on the appetites of the eaters and the amount of fat in the meat. (A good deal of fat will be cooked off.)

To Select

Use the cheapest meat (or meats) you can find with the fat content you want (20% to 25% fat is best). The lighter the color, the fresher the meat or the more fat it contains.

To Store

Wrap ground meats loosely for refrigeration, tightly for freezing. If the outer surface is exposed to air, it will darken and serve as a shield to protect the inner part. Refrigerate one to two days; freeze three to four months.

To Prepare

Note: The more ground meat is handled, or the more compacted it becomes, the less flavor it will have.

1. If you use whole pieces of fresh meat, you can grind them in a meat grinder or in a food processor, or you can use a knife to chop them into small pieces. Many cooks prefer chopped meat to ground meat for use in chili, spaghetti sauce, and stuffing for potatoes and other vegetables.

2. To thaw frozen ground meat, leave it wrapped at room temperature for one to three hours. Frozen meat patties can be cooked without thawing.

3. *Optional:* Bread crumbs may be mixed into ground meat to "extend" it. The combination not only is more economical, but cuts down on calories and cholesterol as well. Use one part bread crumbs to every three or four parts ground meat.

4. *Optional:* Whole egg or egg white mixed into ground meat causes it to brown more, adds flavor, and binds it, making it firmer. Use one whole egg or two egg whites per cup of ground meat.

5. Seasonings and other flavorings can be worked into the meat so that their flavors are distributed evenly. Herbs, onions, garlic, sweet bell pepper, grated cheese, chopped bacon or sausage, or combinations of these add body as well as flavor. Dried onion soup mix (one package per pound of meat) is popular also. Tomato sauce, catsup, chili sauce, barbecue sauce, or one of the meat sauces will add to the moistness and flavor of ground meat (use one tablespoon per cup of meat). Don't mix salt with the raw meat; salt will dry out the meat and make it less tender. Let the mixture of meat and flavoring ingredients stand at room tem-

perature for one hour before cooking so the flavors have time to blend.

To Cook

Broil, pan-broil, or **grill** hamburger steaks. **Pan-broil** pieces for spaghetti sauce, vegetable stuffings, and specialty dishes. **Bake** meat loaf in a preheated oven (325–400 degrees F.). *Tip:* When baking meat loaf, pour off excess fat every ten minutes. If you like, save some of the fat to make gravy to accompany the meat loaf.

To Season

Season with salt, pepper, garlic, onion, paprika, mustard, basil, oregano, curry powder, cumin, coriander, chili powder, cinnamon, allspice, marjoram, poultry seasoning, Italian seasoning, parsley, sage, rosemary, or thyme.

To Serve

Serve plain or topped with gravy or brown sauce, cheese, plain or flavored mayonnaise, tomato sauce, catsup, mustard, or one of the commercial meat sauces.

A Cook's Guide to Beef

To Plan

Plan servings of 4 to 8 ounces of meat with no bone, or 8 to 12 ounces of meat with bone.

To Select

Choose cuts according to the Selection Chart on page 401. The cooking instructions in this Guide describe the best size for each cooking method. As a rule, the darker the color and the more fat marbling, the more flavorful and tender the beef.

To Store

Wrap beef loosely for refrigeration, tightly for freezing. Refrigerate one to four days; freeze six to twelve months.

Beef selection chart

Cut	Broil, Grill, Pan-broil, Pan-fry Prime or Choice Grades	Roast Prime or Choice Grades	Braise or Stew Choice or Good Grades
Loin	Top loin steak T-bone steak Porterhouse steak Sirloin steak Tenderloin steak Tenderloin tips	Tenderloin roast	None
Rib	Rib steak Rib eye steak	Rib roast Rib eye roast	Short ribs Back ribs Rolled cap roast
Round	Top round steak Eye round steak Bottom round steak (pan-fry only) Tip steak Butterfly steak (pan-fry only) Cubed steak (pan-fry only) Cubes for kabobs	Top round roast Eye round roast Bottom round roast Tip roast Rump roast	Top round steak or roast Eye round steak or roast Bottom round steak or roast Tip steak or roast Rump roast Butterfly steak Cubed steak Cubes for kabobs
Chuck	Blade steak Shoulder steak (pan-fry only) Eye steak	Blade roast Under blade pot roast Eye roast	Any and all cuts
Flank	Flank steak Cubed flank steak (pan-fry only) Flank steak rolls (pan-fry only)	Flank steak cubed and rolled	Flank steak Flank steak, cubed or rolled Flank steak rolls
Plate	Skirt steak (pan-fry only) Skirt steak, cubed (pan-fry only) Skirt steak, rolled (pan-fry only)	None	Any and all cuts
Shank	None	None	Any and all cuts
Brisket	None	None	Any and all cuts

To Prepare

The "How to" instructions at the end of this chapter give directions for preparing beef for each cooking method. Otherwise, the following preparations are basic.

1. Beef will taste best if it is brought to room temperature before cooking.

(See "How to Bard or Lard Meats," p. 420.)

2. Trim off excess fat. Use it to bard or lard the meat, or melt it and use it for basting the meat as it cooks.

3. Frozen beef can be cooked without thawing, but add about 50% to the cooking time. To thaw frozen beef, leave it wrapped. Steaks will thaw in two to three hours at room temperature, or in twelve hours refrigerated. Roasts require more time, so to avoid spoilage they should be thawed in the refrigerator: two to four hours per pound for small roasts, four to six hours per pound for large roasts.

4. To make "cubed" or "country" steaks, pound seasoned flour into boneless steaks from one of the tougher cuts until they are tender and won't hold any more flour. Use a meat mallet or the back side of a long knife blade.

(See "How to Fry Meats," p. 425.)

To Cook

Broil or grill steaks that are at least 1 inch to 2 1/2 inches thick. Use well aged, well marbled pieces of prime or choice grades from one of the more tender cuts. Tougher cuts or good grade steaks may be used if they are marinated first.

Pan-broil, sauté, or pan-fry steaks less than 1 inch thick. Use well marbled, well aged pieces of prime or choice grades from one of the more tender cuts. **Pan-fry or braise** cubed steaks.

Roast beef that is at least 2 1/2 inches thick. A roast should weigh at least 3 pounds, although a minimum of 5 pounds is preferable. Use well aged, well marbled pieces of prime or choice grades from one of the more tender cuts. One side should have enough fat to baste the roast as it cooks. Otherwise, purchase extra beef fat or salt pork to bard or lard the roast.

Beef for **braises, pot roasts, and stews** can come from any of the less tender cuts of any grade, or from the good, standard, or commercial grades of the more tender cuts.

1" or Less, Pan-Broil, Sauté, or Pan-fry

1" to 2½" Broil or Grill

2½", 3 lbs. or Larger Roast

To Season

Season with salt, pepper, garlic, onion, bay leaf, cloves, paprika, mustard, basil, oregano, savory, mint, tarragon, poultry seasoning, chili powder, curry powder, cumin, coriander, marjoram, parsley, sage, rosemary, or thyme.

To Serve

Serve plain with seasonings, or top with plain or flavored butter or margarine, gravy, brown sauce, tomato sauce, plain or flavored mayonnaise, one of the egg yolk and butter sauces, or one of the commercial meat sauces.

A Cook's Guide to Veal

To Plan

Plan servings of 4 to 6 ounces of meat with no bone, or 6 to 10 ounces of meat with bone.

To Select

Choose cuts according to the Selection Chart on page 404. The cooking instructions in this Guide describe the best size for each cooking method. Veal should be white to light grayish pink, with little surface fat and no marbling. Bones should be soft and porous and should have a reddish tinge.

To Store

Keep veal tightly wrapped and well refrigerated or frozen. Refrigerate two to four days; freeze six to nine months.

To Prepare

The "How to" instructions at the end of this chapter give directions for preparing veal for each cooking method. Otherwise, the following preparations are basic.

1. Veal will taste best if it is brought to room temperature before cooking.
2. Frozen veal can be cooked without thawing, but add about 50% to the cooking time. To thaw frozen veal, leave it wrapped at room temperature for one to three hours or

thaw it in the refrigerator for two to four hours per pound for steaks and small roasts, four to six hours per pound for large roasts.

3. To make "scallops," pound thin, boneless pieces of veal until they are tender. Use a meat mallet or the back side of a long knife blade. Seasoned flour is usually pounded in. You can buy prepared scallops, but they are very, very expensive. Incidentally, anything that can be done with veal scallops can also be done with scalloped breast of chicken or turkey, but at a fraction of the cost.

Veal selection chart

Cut	Sauté or Pan-fry Prime or Choice Grades	Roast Prime or Choice Grades	Braise or Stew Choice or Good Grades
Loin	Top loin chops Tenderloin chops Kidney chops	Loin roast	Kidney chops
Rib	Rib chops	Rib roast Crown roast	Rib chops
Shoulder	Arm steak Blade steak	Arm roast Blade roast Shoulder roast	Arm steak or roast Blade steak or roast Shoulder roast Stew meat
Leg	Sirloin steak Round steak Cubed steak Cutlets	Sirloin roast Round roast Rump roast	Sirloin steak or roast Round steak or roast Rump roast Heel roast Cubed steak Cubes for kabobs Cutlets
Fore-shank and breast	None	Breast	Breast Riblets Cross cuts

To Cook

Sauté or pan-fry steaks, chops, or cutlets less than 1 inch thick. Use prime or choice grades of one of the more tender cuts. **Sauté, braise, or pan-fry** scallops made from one of the tougher cuts.

Roast roasts, cutlets, or chops that are at least 2 inches thick. Use prime or choice grades of one of the more tender cuts. Since veal has so little fat, bard or lard roasts with fat from beef or pork.

Veal for **braises, pot roasts, and stews** should come from any of the less tender cuts of any grade, or from the good, standard, or commercial grades of the more tender cuts.

Special Cooking Considerations for Veal

1. Veal should always be cooked until it is well done, or it will be tough.

2. Because it is so delicate, veal will pick up the flavors of the fats and liquids in which it is cooked. That is why olive oil and butter are preferred for cooking it.

3. Veal fried in butter or margarine will burn before it is fully cooked. To give it the good taste of butter, first fry it in olive oil or some other vegetable oil and then add butter or margarine a few minutes before the second side is done. Turn once again so the first side cooks in the butter also.

4. Since veal contains so little fat, roasts should be barded or larded and should always be cooked at low temperatures to tenderize the meat and bring out its best flavors.

To Season

Season with salt, pepper, onion, garlic, bay leaf, basil, paprika, poultry seasoning, mustard, oregano, tarragon, cloves, marjoram, savory, parsley, sage, rosemary, or thyme.

To Serve

Serve plain with seasonings, or top with plain or flavored butter or margarine, gravy, white sauce, brown sauce, tomato sauce, plain or flavored mayonnaise, mustard, or one of the commercial meat sauces.

A Cook's Guide to Fresh Pork

To Plan

Plan servings of 4 to 6 ounces of meat with no bone, or 6 to 10 ounces of meat with bone.

To Select

Choose cuts according to the Selection Chart on page 407. The cooking instructions in this Guide describe the best size for each cooking method. Fresh pork meat should be light grayish pink, with fat covering the perimeter. Both the flesh and the fat should yield only slightly to the touch.

To Store

Keep fresh pork tightly wrapped at all times. It should never be left unrefrigerated or uncooked for more than thirty minutes. Refrigerate two to four days; freeze three to six months.

To Prepare

The "How to" instructions at the end of this chapter give directions for preparing fresh pork for each cooking method. Otherwise, the following preparations are basic.

1. Fresh pork should *not* be brought to room temperature before cooking.
2. Frozen pork may be cooked without thawing, but add about 50% to the cooking time. To thaw frozen pork, leave it wrapped in the refrigerator. Chops and steaks will thaw in three to four hours. For roasts, allow two to four hours per pound for small roasts, four to six hours per pound for large roasts.

To Cook

Broil or grill tender cuts at least 3/4 inch to 1 1/2 inches thick with some fat.

Pan-broil, sauté, or pan-fry steaks or chops less than 1 inch thick from one of the more tender cuts.

Roast roasts or crown roasts weighing at least 3 pounds from one of the more tender cuts.

Fresh pork for **braises, pot roasts, and stews** is best if it comes from one of the tougher cuts.

Fresh pork selection chart

Cut	Broil, Grill, Pan-broil, Pan-fry	Roast	Braise or Stew
Loin	Tenderloin Blade chops Rib chops Top loin chops Butterfly chops Sirloin chops or cutlets Assorted chops Spare ribs	Tenderloin Blade roast Center rib roast Top loin roast Center loin roast Sirloin half Rib half Spare ribs Back ribs Country style ribs	Tenderloin Blade chops or roast Rib chops Top loin chops or roast Butterfly chops Sirloin cutlets Assorted chops Spare ribs Back ribs Country style ribs Side pork
Shoulder	Blade steak Cubed steak Cubes for kabobs Arm steak (pan-fry only)	Blade Boston roast Shoulder roast Cubes for kabobs Arm roast Arm picnic	Blade steak or roast Cubed steak Cubes for kabobs Arm steak or roast Pork hock
Leg	Center slice Cubed steak (pan-fry only)	Center roast Roast Shank Rump	Center slice Cubed steak Shank portion

Special Cooking Consideration for Fresh Pork

Pork can contain the parasite *Trichinella spiralis,* which can cause the illness *trichinosis.* To be safe, pork must be cooked thoroughly at a temperature at least high enough to destroy the parasite. The temperature of the meat at its thickest point should be at least 140 degrees F. Many nutritionists recommend at least 185 degrees F.

To Season

Season with salt, pepper, onion, garlic, bay leaf, paprika, basil, cloves, mint, cinnamon, allspice, ginger, poultry seasoning, mustard, marjoram, savory, curry powder, cumin, coriander, parsley, sage, rosemary, or thyme.

To Serve

Serve plain with seasonings, or top with plain or flavored butter or margarine, gravy, brown sauce, white sauce, tomato sauce, mustard, plain or flavored mayonnaise, or one of the commercial meat sauces.

A Cook's Guide to Lamb and Mutton

To Plan

Plan servings of 4 to 8 ounces of meat with no bone, or 8 to 12 ounces of meat with bone. Lamb comes from young sheep; its meat is more delicate and flavorful than that of mutton—older sheep—whose flavor can be rather strong.

To Select

Choose cuts according to the Selection Chart on page 409. The cooking instructions in this Guide describe the best size for each cooking method. Lamb should be light to dark pink; mutton should be dark pink (or light red) to dark red. The flesh of either should be firm to the touch. The fat should be soft and creamy or pinkish in color. The older the animal, the whiter the bones and the greater the amount of fat.

To Store

Store fresh lamb or mutton tightly wrapped and well refrigerated or frozen. Refrigerate two to four days; freeze six to nine months.

To Prepare

The "How to" instructions at the end of this chapter give directions for preparing lamb or mutton for each cooking method. Otherwise, the following preparations are basic.

1. Lamb or mutton will taste best if brought to room temperature before cooking.

2. Frozen lamb or mutton may be cooked without thawing, but add about 50% to the cooking time. To thaw frozen lamb or mutton, leave it wrapped in the refrigerator. Allow three to four hours for chops, three to four hours

Lamb and mutton selection chart

Cut	Broil, Grill, Pan-broil, Pan-fry Prime or Choice Grades	Roast Prime or Choice Grades	Braise or Stew Choice or Good Grades
Loin	Loin chops	Loin roast	None
Rib	Rib chops French chops	Rib roast Rib crown roast	None
Shoulder	Blade chops Arm chops Shoulder com- bination (broil or pan-broil) Cubes for kabobs (broil or pan-broil)	Blade roast Arm roast Shoulder roast Square-cut roast Cushion roast	Blade chops Arm chops Shoulder combination Neck slices Cubes for kabobs Stew meat
Leg	Leg combination Sirloin chops Center slice Cubes for kabobs (broil or pan-broil)	Whole leg Leg roast Short cut, sir- loin off Leg combination Sirloin half Shank half Center roast French-style roast American-style roast	Stew meat Cubes for kabobs
Breast and fore- shank	Spareribs	Spareribs Breast Rolled breast	Breast riblets Breast Rolled breast Shank

per pound for small roasts, four to six hours per pound for legs and large roasts.

3. Remove excess fat. If you like, use it to bard or lard the meat as it cooks.

4. "Fell" is a thin membrane covering some parts of lamb. Some cooks say it imparts a candlewax flavor to the meat. It is usually removed from chops but may be left on legs and roasts to hold in moisture and help hold the shape.

5. For a "butterfly leg," remove the fell and slice through the meat to remove the bone so that the leg lies flat like butterfly wings.

To Cook

Broil or grill steaks or chops at least 1 inch to 2 1/2 inches thick from prime or choice grades of one of the more tender cuts. There should be some fat.

Pan-broil, sauté, or pan-fry steaks or chops less than 1 inch thick from prime or choice grades of one of the more tender cuts.

Roast roasts, crown roasts, or legs weighing at least 3 pounds. The meat should be of prime or choice grades from one of the more tender cuts. One side should have enough fat to baste the roast as it cooks; otherwise, purchase extra fat or salt pork to bard or lard it.

Lamb or mutton for **braises, pot roasts, or stews** can come from any of the less tender cuts of any grade, or from the good, standard, or commercial grades of the more tender cuts.

Special Cooking Considerations for Lamb or Mutton

1. Lamb and mutton pick up odors and flavors from fats and liquids in which they are cooked.
2. Cook lamb and mutton medium-rare to medium-well-done. The juices should be clear, not bloody.

To Season

Season with salt, pepper, garlic, onion, mustard, paprika, bay leaf, mint, dill, oregano, basil, marjoram, poultry seasoning, cloves, curry powder, cumin, coriander, savory, allspice, cinnamon, parsley, sage, rosemary, or thyme.

To Serve

Serve plain with seasonings, or top with plain or flavored butter or margarine, gravy, brown sauce, white sauce, tomato sauce, mint jelly, mustard, plain or flavored mayonnaise, or one of the commercial meat sauces.

A Cook's Guide to Variety Meats

Liver, kidneys, hearts, tongues, sweetbreads, brains, and tripe are known generally as "variety meats." They are also called "offal" and "innards." Many people consider them delicacies; others can't stand them. They are all high in cholesterol and so should be eaten infrequently and in moderation.

Liver

☐ *To Plan*
Plan 1/4 pound per serving.

☐ *To Select*
Whole liver should be moist, with a smooth surface. Sliced liver may appear slightly porous. Most recipes call for slices to be 1/4 inch thick. Slices of 1 inch or more of veal or calves' liver, though, are excellent as broiled steaks.

Veal liver from milk-fed calves is the most tender and flavorful of all livers. Because of high demand and short supply, it may be difficult to obtain and can be costly.

Calves' liver is from calves that are not milk fed. More available and less costly than veal liver, it is still tender and tasty. Calves' liver is the most popular of all livers.

Lamb liver is less flavorful than veal or calves' liver, but it's still popular because it does not have the strong flavors associated with liver from sheep, pork, or beef.

Sheep, pork, and beef livers are the least popular (in that order) because of their strong flavors and their tendency to be tough.

☐ *To Store*
Keep liver tightly wrapped. Refrigerate one to two days; freeze three to four months.

□ *To Prepare*

If frozen, thaw as you would thaw beef (see p. 402).

1. Remove the outer membrane. Use the tip of a knife to loosen the membrane and then pull it off with your fingers.

2. Liver from sheep, mutton, pork, and beef should be soaked in cold milk, water, or a combination of the two in a covered container in the refrigerator for one to two hours to remove some of the strong flavor.

3. Before being cooked, especially if it is to be ground, liver should be parboiled. Pour boiling water over the liver; then rinse it in cold running water and dry it on paper towels. Parboiling "sets" the juices so that they are not lost in the cooking.

□ *To Cook*

Refer to the Timetable for Cooking Variety Meats, p. 419.

Veal or calves' liver: Sauté, pan-fry, broil, or use in a casserole.

Beef, lamb, mutton, or pork liver: Braise, make into a paté, or cook in a casserole.

□ *To Season*

Season with salt, pepper, garlic, onion, paprika, oregano, bay leaf, cloves, mustard, basil, curry powder, cumin, coriander, marjoram, poultry seasoning, parsley, sage, rosemary, or thyme.

□ *To Serve*

Serve plain with seasonings or with plain or flavored butter or margarine, gravy, brown sauce, mustard, or one of the commercial meat sauces.

Kidneys

□ *To Plan*

Plan 1/4 pound per serving.

□ *To Select*

As with liver, the kidneys of veal and calves are the most desirable. Kidneys from lamb, mutton, pork, and beef have a much stronger flavor and require special preparation. Smaller kidneys are more tender than larger ones.

☐ *To Store*
Keep kidneys tightly wrapped. Refrigerate one to two days; freeze three to four months.

☐ *To Prepare*
If frozen, thaw as you would thaw beef (see p. 402).

1. Remove any fat surrounding the kidney.

2. Remove the outer membrane. Use the tip of a knife to loosen a portion of it and then pull it off with your fingers.

3. Slice the kidney lengthwise down the middle and remove the central white core and ducts.

4. Larger kidneys from sheep, mutton, pork, or beef should be soaked in cold milk, water, or a combination of the two in a covered container in the refrigerator for one to two hours to remove some of the strong flavor.
5. Large kidneys should be parboiled before being cooked.

Pour boiling water over them and then refresh them in cold running water.

6. Cut kidneys into thin slices before cooking them.

□ *To Cook*

Refer to the Timetable for Cooking Variety Meats, p. 419.

Veal, calf, and lamb kidneys: Sauté, pan-fry, broil, or use in a casserole.

Sheep or mutton kidneys: Braise, pan-fry, stew, or cook in a casserole.

Pork or beef kidneys: Braise, stew, make into a paté, or cook in a casserole.

□ *To Season*

Season with salt, pepper, garlic, onion, bay leaf, paprika, cloves, mustard, basil, curry powder, cumin, coriander, marjoram, poultry seasoning, parsley, sage, rosemary, or thyme.

□ *To Serve*

Serve plain with seasonings, or top with plain or flavored butter or margarine, gravy, brown sauce, white sauce, mustard, or one of the commercial meat sauces.

Hearts

□ *To Plan*

One beef heart will supply eight to ten portions. One veal heart or pork heart serves two to three. One lamb heart makes one serving.

□ *To Select*

Hearts should be smooth, shiny, and well rounded.

□ *To Store*

Keep hearts tightly wrapped. Refrigerate one to two days; freeze three to four months.

□ *To Prepare*

If frozen, thaw as you would thaw beef (see p. 402).

1. Trim off any blood vessels, gristle, and fat.

2. Soak the heart in salted cold water for one hour to firm it up for cooking.

3. Wash it in cold running water and pat it dry on paper towels.

□ *To Cook*
Roast, boil, braise, or use in casseroles. Refer to the Time-table for Cooking Variety Meats, p. 419.

□ *To Season*
Season with salt, pepper, garlic, onion, bay leaf, paprika, cloves, mustard, poultry seasoning, basil, curry powder, cumin, coriander, marjoram, parsley, sage, rosemary, or thyme.

□ *To Serve*
Serve plain with seasonings, or top with plain or flavored butter or margarine, gravy, brown sauce, mustard, or one of the commercial meat sauces.

Tongues

□ *To Plan*
Plan 1/4 pound per serving.

□ *To Select*
Tongue is available fresh, pickled, or smoked. Smaller tongues (under 3 pounds) are the most flavorful. Because of its texture, beef tongue is the most preferred. Other-wise, there is little difference in flavor in the tongues of different animals.

□ *To Store*
Keep tongues tightly wrapped. Refrigerate one to two days; freeze three to four months.

□ *To Prepare*
If frozen, thaw as you would thaw beef (see p. 402).

1. Tongue that has been pickled or smoked should be soaked in cold water for a minimum of two hours before cooking.

2. Rinse and scrub the tongue thoroughly and simmer it for several hours or as the recipe directs. After it has cooked, plunge it into cold water only long enough to cool it so that it can be handled.

3. Slit the skin on the underside and remove all skin, gristle, and small bones.

4. Rinse in cold water and reheat or cool for serving.

☐ *To Cook*

Boil, braise, or cook tongues in a casserole. Refer to the Timetable for Cooking Variety Meats, p. 419.

☐ *To Season*

Season with salt, pepper, garlic, onion, bay leaf, paprika, cloves, mustard, poultry seasoning, basil, curry powder, cumin, coriander, marjoram, parsley, sage, rosemary, or thyme.

☐ *To Serve*

Serve plain with seasonings, or top with flavored butter or margarine, gravy, brown sauce, white sauce, tomato sauce, mustard, or one of the commercial meat sauces.

Sweetbreads

Sweetbreads are the thymus gland or pancreas of calves or lamb. They are considered a gourmet delicacy.

☐ *To Plan*

Plan 1/4 pound per serving.

☐ *To Select*

Sweetbreads should be very white and tender.

☐ *To Prepare*

Because they are so perishable, sweetbreads should be blanched shortly after purchase.

1. Rinse the sweetbreads thoroughly in hot running water.
2. Simmer the sweetbreads for fifteen minutes in fresh salted water with some lemon juice or vinegar to keep the meat white. Cool them in cold water.
3. Remove the skin and ducts.
4. Slice the sweetbreads or leave them whole for further cooking.

☐ *To Cook*

Sauté, pan-fry, broil, braise, or cook in a casserole. Refer to the Timetable for Cooking Variety Meats, p. 419.

☐ *To Season*

Season with salt, pepper, garlic, onion, bay leaf, paprika,

cloves, mustard, basil, poultry seasoning, curry powder, cumin, coriander, marjoram, parsley, sage, rosemary, or thyme.

□ *To Serve*
Serve plain with seasonings, or top with flavored butter or margarine, white sauce, plain or flavored mayonnaise, or mustard.

Brains

□ *To Plan*
Plan 1/4 pound per serving.

□ *To Select*
Veal and lamb brains are said to be more tender and to have a more delicate flavor than brains from other animals. Any brains should look moist.

□ *To Store*
Store brains tightly wrapped. Refrigerate for one to two days; freeze for three to four months.

□ *To Prepare*
Brains, like sweetbreads, are very perishable and so should be blanched shortly after purchase.

1. Rinse the brains thoroughly in hot running water.
2. Simmer them for ten to fifteen minutes in fresh salted water with some lemon juice or vinegar to keep the meat white. Cool them in cold water.
3. Remove the skin and ducts.
4. Slice the brains or leave them whole for further cooking.

□ *To Cook*
Sauté, braise, or cook in a casserole. Refer to the Timetable for Cooking Variety Meats, p. 419.

□ *To Season*
Season with salt, pepper, garlic, onion, bay leaf, paprika, cloves, mustard, basil, poultry seasoning, curry powder, cumin, coriander, marjoram, parsley, sage, rosemary, or thyme.

□ *To Serve*

Serve plain with seasonings, or top with plain or flavored butter or margarine, white sauce, plain or flavored mayonnaise, mustard, or one of the egg yolk and butter sauces.

Tripe

Tripe comes from the muscular inner lining of the stomach of beef. "Honeycomb" tripe, the most popular as well as the most readily available, comes from the lining of the second stomach. It is said to be more tender and delicate than the so-called smooth tripe from the first stomach.

□ *To Plan*

Plan 1/4 pound per serving.

□ *To Select*

Tripe is available fresh, pickled, or canned. Fresh tripe should be creamy yellow and firm to the touch. If it is slimy or gray, stay away from it.

□ *To Store*

Store tripe tightly wrapped. Refrigerate for one to two days; freeze for three to four months.

□ *To Prepare*

Tripe is sold cleaned and partially precooked. Still, it should be simmered in salted water for at least one hour, especially if it has been pickled.

□ *To Cook*

Sauté, braise, pan-fry, or broil. Refer to the Timetable for Cooking Variety Meats, p. 419.

□ *To Season*

Season with salt, pepper, garlic, onion, bay leaf, paprika, cloves, mustard, basil, poultry seasoning, parsley, sage, rosemary, or thyme.

□ *To Serve*

Serve plain with seasonings, or top with plain or flavored butter or margarine, white sauce, plain or flavored mayonnaise, or one of the egg yolk and butter sauces.

Timetable for cooking variety meats

Kind	Broiled	Braised[a]	Cooked in Liquid
Liver			
Beef			
3- to 4-pound piece		2 to 2 1/2 hours	
sliced		20 to 25 minutes	
Veal (calf), sliced	8 to 10 minutes		
Pork		1 1/2 to 2 hours	
whole (3 to 3 1/2 pounds)		20 to 25 minutes	
sliced			
Lamb, sliced	8 to 10 minutes		
Kidney			
Beef		1 1/2 to 2 hours	1 to 1 1/2 hours
Veal (calf)	10 to 12 minutes	1 to 1 1/2 hours	3/4 to 1 hour
Pork	10 to 12 minutes	1 to 1 1/2 hours	3/4 to 1 hour
Lamb	10 to 12 minutes	3/4 to 1 hour	3/4 to 1 hour
Heart			
Beef			
whole		3 to 4 hours	3 to 4 hours
sliced		1 1/2 to 2 hours	
Veal (calf)			
whole		2 1/2 to 3 hours	2 1/2 to 3 hours
Pork		2 1/2 to 3 hours	2 1/2 to 3 hours
Lamb		2 1/2 to 3 hours	2 1/2 to 3 hours
Tongue			
Beef			3 to 4 hours
Veal (calf)			2 to 3 hours
Pork } usually sold			
Lamb } ready-to-serve			
Tripe	10 to 15 minutes[b]		1 to 1 1/2 hours
Sweetbreads	10 to 15 minutes[b]	20 to 25 minutes	15 to 20 minutes
Brains	10 to 15 minutes[b]	20 to 25 minutes	15 to 20 minutes

[a]On top of range or in a 300–325°F. oven.
[b]Time required after precooking in water.

Source: Lessons on Meat, National Live Stock and Meat Board, Chicago, Illinois. Copyright © 1974. Reprinted with permission.

Cooking Considerations for Meats

1. Meats cooked almost any way will have a better flavor if they are brought to room temperature before cooking. The glaring exception is pork, which should never remain out of refrigeration or away from cooking heat for more than 30 minutes.

2. Frozen meat can be cooked with or without thawing. However, cooking times must be adjusted accordingly. A large fro-

zen roast may require up to 1 1/2 times as long to cook as an unfrozen roast of the same size. Thick frozen steaks must be broiled at a greater distance from the heat to ensure that the center is cooked without burning the surface.

3. You can tenderize less tender meats by rubbing them with lemon or lime juice, vinaigrette dressing, commercial meat tenderizer, or some other marinade. (See "Marinades," p. 102.) Alternatively, you can pound them with a meat mallet, the back side of a long knife, or the edge of a metal pot lid, just as you do when making scallops or cubed steaks.

4. Cooking times will vary according to many things: well-aged meat cooks more quickly; the greater the amount of fat, the slower the meat will cook; small roasts require more time per pound than larger ones; small, chunky roasts cook more quickly than oblong roasts.

5. Despite the many cooks and books that tell you to sear meats, extensive experiments by food scientists have established that there is no need to do so. Meats cooked at a constant low temperature should be juicier, more tender, and more flavorful, with less shrinkage and less cleaning afterwards. This is especially true for roasts.

6. *The larger the meat, the lower the heat. The thinner the meat, the higher the heat.* Both of these are good rules that should produce meats cooked throughout without being tough or dry on the outside or undercooked on the inside.

7. Salt on uncooked meat will draw out moisture so the surface does not brown as well. Steaks will be more attractive if salt is applied after they have cooked. Roasts, on the other hand, will benefit by having salt applied before they cook. The salt will be drawn down into the meat as it warms to flavor it, and the extra moisture on the surface will prevent the roast from browning too quickly. In pot roasts, stews, and braises, a little salt in the liquid is needed to draw the flavor out of the meat so that it blends with the liquid.

8. Any cuts or incisions in a piece of meat will allow its tasty juices to seep out. Consequently, use tongs instead of a fork to hold meats. For the same reason, it is best to cut roasts and large steaks into smaller serving pieces *after* they have cooked.

9. Once cooked, meats will have a better flavor if they are allowed to "set" in a warm oven to cook in their own juices for 10 to 30 minutes, depending on size, before being served. This allows the juices and flavors to redistribute themselves evenly throughout the meat.

10. Meats will be more tender if they are cut across their grain.

How to Bard or Lard Meats

Barding and larding are processes used to add fat to a meat to moisten and flavor it as it cooks. Use fat that has been cut off of the meat, or pork fat or bacon that has been boiled to remove most of the salt.

Barding simply calls for strips of fat to be laid over the meat.

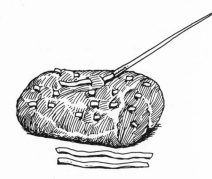

Larding uses a special needle to hold thin strips of fat, called "lardons," and insert them into the meat.

■

How to Broil, Grill, or Barbecue Meats

Cuts cooked by these dry heat methods should be 1 to 1 1/2 inches thick. See the Selection Chart for the meat being cooked to determine the cuts best suited to these cooking methods: beef (p. 401), veal (p. 404), pork (p. 407), lamb (p. 409), variety meats (p. 411–419).

0. **Before you begin:** Read all the steps below. If necessary, review the Cook's Guide for the meat being cooked, the Cooking Considerations for Meats, and the principles of dry heat cooking in Chapter Two.

1. **Plan** 30 to 60 minutes to prepare fully thawed meat and bring it to room temperature. Meats cooked these ways will be done in 10 to 30 minutes, depending on the thickness, but allow an additional 10 minutes after cooking for the juices to "set." If you are using charcoal, allow 30 to 60 minutes for the coals to heat.

2. **Prepare the meat:**

   a. Trim off any excess fat, but leave a narrow strip about 1/4 inch thick around the outer edge for flavor.

   b. To prevent the meat from curling as it cooks, make vertical slashes across the fat every inch or so around the perimeter.

   c. *Optional:* Marinate the meat in a sauce for several hours and skip steps d, e, and f. (See p. 102.)

   d. Coat all surfaces lightly with cooking oil, melted fat, or a combination of the two. (Butter or margarine used alone will probably burn.) For added

flavor, sauté garlic, onions, or both in the oil before basting the meat.

e. Sprinkle on dry seasonings.

f. Bring the meat to room temperature before cooking.

3. **Prepare the heat:**

a. Adjust the height of the grill or rack holder:

· For pieces 1 to 1 1/2 inches thick, set the rack 3 to 4 inches from the heat.

· For pieces 1 1/2 to 2 1/2 inches thick, set the rack 4 to 5 inches from the heat.

b. *For oven cooking:* Preheat the oven to 350 to 400 degrees F. or to "broil."

c. *For charcoal cooking:* Start the fire and allow at least 30 minutes for a gray ash to form over all the coals. Tap the coals occasionally before and throughout the cooking to keep the ash from smothering the heat. A fair test of the temperature is how long you can hold your hand over the heat. Place your hand palm down at rack height and count: one thousand one = very hot; one thousand two = hot; one thousand three = medium hot; one thousand four = medium low.

4. **Prepare the vessel:**

a. Coat the cooking rack or grill with shortening to prevent the meat from sticking.

b. Place the meat on the rack.

c. For oven cooking, put the rack into a pan with low sides. For easier cleaning, first line the pan with aluminum foil.

5. **Cook the meat.** Put the pan into the oven or the grill rack into its holder.

· *If the heat is from above:* When the top surface has browned, turn the meat so that it will cook on the other side.

· *If the heat is from below:* When the juices begin to flow on the top surface and the bottom has browned, turn the meat to cook on the other side.

6. **Optional:** To put grill marks on steaks cooked on a grill:

a. Place the meat on the grill at a 45-degree angle to the line of the grill. Cook for about two minutes.

b. Rotate the meat to the opposite 45-degree angle and continue cooking it on the same side.

c. When the juices begin to flow on the surface of the meat, turn it over, place it at a 45-degree angle to the line of the grill, and cook for one to two minutes.
d. Rotate the meat to the opposite 45-degree angle and cook to completion.

7. **Test for doneness.** Beef may be served rare to well done. Pork, lamb, or mutton should be medium-rare to medium-well done. Veal and variety meats should be well done.

   · *Feel test:* Press down in the center of the meat with your finger or the flat side of a knife. Rare = feels soft and yields to pressure; medium = springs back readily when pressed; well done = feels firm and does not give much to pressure.
   · *Color test:* Make a small incision into the thickest part of the meat and judge it by its color: red = rare; pink = medium; gray = well done.

8. **Remove the meat from the heat.** Place the meat on a warm serving plate and season the second side. Hold the meat in a warm oven (150 degrees F.) for 10 minutes before serving, to allow the juices to become redistributed evenly.

9. **Optional gravy:** If there are any pan drippings, use them to make gravy.

(See "How to Make Gravy," p. 138.)

10. **Serve.** Cut into individual portions, and serve on warm plates.
11. **Optional.** Accompany with plain or flavored butter or margarine, gravy, brown sauce, one of the egg yolk and butter sauces, barbecue or meat sauce.

■

How to Pan-broil Meats

Pan-broil ground or chopped meat or cuts that are less than one inch thick. See the selection chart for the meat being cooked to determine the cuts best suited to this cooking method: beef (p. 401), veal (p. 404), pork (p. 407), lamb (p. 409), variety meats (p. 411–419).

0. **Before you begin:** Read all the steps given below. If necessary, review the Cook's Guide for the meat being cooked, the Cooking Considerations for Meat, and the principles of pan-broiling in Chapter Two.
1. **Plan** 30 to 60 minutes to prepare fully thawed meat and bring it to room temperature. Cooking times will vary from 10 to 30 minutes, depending on the meat, its thickness, and the method.
2. **Prepare the meat:**

   a. Trim off any excess fat but leave a strip about 1/4 inch thick around the outer edge for flavor.
   b. To prevent the meat from curling as it cooks, make vertical slashes across the fat every inch or so around the perimeter (see p. 421).
   c. *Optional:* To tenderize the meat, marinate it in a sauce for several hours or beat it with a meat mallet or the back of a long knife blade.
   d. Sprinkle on seasonings and bring the meat to room temperature.
3. **Prepare the vessel.** Coat the cooking surface with just enough cooking oil or melted fat to keep the food from sticking. (Butter or margarine used alone will probably burn.) For added flavor, use oil or fat in which garlic and/or onions have been sautéed.
4. **Heat the cooking oil.** Do not allow it to get hot enough to smoke.
5. **Cook the meat.** Slowly add the meat pieces to the hot

oil. Do not crowd. Move the meat occasionally so that it does not stick and burn. Turn the meat over when the bottom has browned and brown the other side.

6. **Test for doneness. Beef** may be served rare to well done. **Pork, lamb, or mutton** should be medium-rare to medium-well done. **Veal and variety meats** should be well done.

   · *Feel test:* Press down in the center. The "springier" it is, the rarer it is cooked.
   · *Color test:* Make a small incision into the thickest part of the meat and judge it by its color. Red = rare; pink = medium; gray = well done.

7. **Remove the meat from the heat.** Place it on a warm plate and season. Hold in a warm oven (150 degrees F.) for 10 to 15 minutes before serving to allow the juices to become redistributed evenly.

8. **Optional gravy:** Deglaze the pan and make gravy. (See "How to Make Gravy," p. 138.)

9. **Serve** as quickly as possible or hold for up to 30 minutes in a warm oven (150 degrees F.).

10. **Optional:** Accompany with plain or flavored butter or margarine, gravy, brown sauce, tomato sauce, or one of the commercial meat sauces.

■

How to Fry Meats

Stir-fry, sauté, or oven-fry small chunks or thin pieces of meat with no coating. **Pan-fry** scallops, chops, or steaks with a dry coating. Cuts should be less than 1 inch thick. See the Selection Chart for the meat being cooked to determine the cuts that are best suited to this cooking method: beef (p. 401), veal (p. 404), pork (p. 407), lamb (p. 409), variety meats (p. 411–419).

0. **Before you begin:** Read all the steps below. If necessary, review the Cook's Guide for the meat being cooked, the Cooking Considerations for Meats, and the principles of frying in Chapter Two.

1. **Plan** 30 to 60 minutes to prepare fully thawed meat and bring it to room temperature. If a coating is used, allow 15 minutes to prepare it. Cooking times will vary from 10 to 30 minutes depending on the meat, its thickness, and the frying method.

2. **Prepare the meat:**

   a. Trim off any excess fat. If the meat is to be pan-fried, leave a narrow strip of fat about 1/4 inch thick around the outer edge for flavor.

   b. To prevent the meat from curling as it cooks, make vertical slashes across the fat every inch or so around the perimeter.

   c. Bring the meat to room temperature.

   d. Special preparations:

      · *To stir-fry*, cut the meat into small pieces of about the same size.

      · *To pan-fry*, coat the meat with seasoned white all-purpose flour, cornmeal, breading, or combinations of these. For "country steaks," pound seasoned flour into the meat until it is saturated and won't hold any more.

3. **Prepare the vessel:**

   · *To stir fry:* Coat the cooking surface with just enough cooking oil to keep the food from sticking.

   · *To sauté or oven-fry:* Use a pan just large enough to hold the food. Add 1/16 to 1/8 inch of cooking oil.

   · *To pan-fry:* Use a pan with sides about 1 inch higher than the food. Add enough cooking oil to cover half the food.

   · *To deep-fat-fry:* Use a special appliance or a heavy pan sufficiently deep to hold enough cooking oil for the food to float, with 2 to 3 inches over the food to allow for foam.

4. **Heat the cooking oil.** Do not allow it to get hot enough to smoke. For added flavor, use oil preflavored with garlic, or cook garlic, onions, or both in the oil until they are golden brown, then remove them.

   · *On a range burner:* Heat the cooking oil at medium-high heat until a small amount of food or coating sizzles when it is dropped in.

   · *To oven-fry:* Preheat the oven to 450 degrees F. and place the pan on the center shelf. It is ready when the cooking oil sizzles.

5. **Cook the meat.** Add food pieces slowly. Do not crowd them.

   · *To sauté or stir-fry:* Stir the meat around or shake the pan back and forth to brown the meat evenly all over.

- *To oven-fry:* Using tongs to hold the food pieces, coat each one all over in the hot cooking oil. Return the pan to the center shelf of the oven and cook until the top of the meat browns. Turn the pieces over and brown the other side.
- *To pan-fry:* Move the meat occasionally so that it does not stick and burn. When the bottom has browned, turn the food over and brown the other side.
- *To deep-fat-fry:* Turn the food when the bottom has browned. Cook the other side until brown.

6. **Remove the meat** from the cooking oil and drain on paper towels.
7. **Before frying more:** Clean the cooking oil of crumbs, flakes, or stray pieces so that they do not burn. If more cooking oil is needed, allow the hot oil to cool for two minutes before adding it.
8. **Optional gravy:** Deglaze the pan and make gravy.   (See "How to Make Gravy," p. 138.)
9. **Serve** as quickly as possible, or hold for up to 30 minutes in a warm oven (150 degrees F.).
10. **Optional:** Accompany with plain or flavored butter or margarine, gravy, brown sauce, tomato sauce, or one of the commercial meat sauces.

■

How to Braise or Stew Meats

Use the meat selection chart for the meat being cooked to determine the cuts best suited to these cooking methods. See beef (p. 401), veal (p. 404), pork (p. 407), lamb (p. 409), variety meats (p. 411–419).

0. **Before you begin:** Read all the steps below. If necessary, review the Cook's Guide for the meat being cooked, the Cooking Considerations for Meats, and the principles of braising in Chapter Three.
1. **Plan** 1 to 2 cups per serving. Allow 30 to 60 minutes to prepare the meat and other ingredients. Thin scallops and chops will cook in about 30 minutes; pot roasts and stews require 3 to 4 hours. Braises and stews will taste best if they are cooked partially and allowed to cool for a few hours or overnight before being reheated to completion. (See the Timetable for Braising Meats on the next page.)

Timetable for braising meats

Type	Time (Hours)
Beef	
Small cuts (brisket, chuck, flank, round, rump, sirloin tip, short ribs)	1 1/2 to 2 1/2
Pot roasts	2 1/2 to 3 1/2
Veal	
Small cuts (blade, breast, neck, round, shoulder, flank)	3/4 to 1 1/4
Pot roasts	1 to 1 1/2
Pork	
Shoulder chops, tenderloin, spareribs	1 to 2
Lamb	
Shoulder chops	1/2
Shoulder roast	1 3/4 to 2 3/4
Shank	2
Breast	2
Times are approximate.	

Based on information provided by the National Live Stock and Meat Board.

2. **Prepare the meat:**
   - *Scallops* should be pounded very thin with a meat mallet or the back of a long knife blade.
   - *Stew meat* should be cut into small cubes, about 3/4 to 1 inch.
   - *Pot roasts* may be bound with kitchen twine to give them a better shape.

   - *Optional:* For added color and flavor, and to thicken the liquid, coat the meat all over with seasoned white all-purpose flour. Pound the flour into the meat with the back side of a long knife blade.

3. **Prepare the cooking vessel.** Braising involves two stages: sautéing and stewing. You can use the same vessel for both, or use a shallow pan to sauté the meat and a larger pot to stew it. To sauté, add about 1/16 to 1/8 inch of cooking oil alone or mixed with an equal amount of butter or margarine, and heat it.

4. **Brown the meat.** Sauté the meat until it is light brown. Remove it from the pan to drain off excess fat.

5. **Prepare flavoring vegetables.** A classic mirepoix of 50% onions, 25% celery, and 25% carrots is most popular. Garlic or shallots, sweet bell peppers, mushrooms, and root vegetables such as turnips are also popular. Allow 1 to 2 cups of chopped flavoring vegetables, depending on the amount of liquid to be used.

   a. Cut the vegetables into small pieces.
   b. Sauté the pieces until they are soft but not browned.
   c. Remove the pieces and drain off excess fat.

6. **Deglaze the vessel.** Remove as much fat as possible from the vessel. Add a small amount of water, broth, or wine, and dissolve any browned food particles into it.

7. **Put the foods and deglazed pan juices into the cooking pot.**

8. **Add cooking liquid.** Use water, broth, wine, stewed tomatoes, fruit juices, or a combination of these. Stir in a very small amount of salt. (Salt will not be needed if you are using canned or powdered broth.)

   (See "What Heats and Flavors the Food," pp. 23–27.)

   · *For stew:* Cover all the food completely.
   · *For pot roasts:* Cover about one-third of the meat.
   For scallops and chops: Cover about half of the meat.

9. **Cook until the meat starts to become tender.**

   a. On a range burner, slowly bring the liquid to a boil.
   b. Lower the heat to a slow simmer or "stew." High temperatures will make meats tough. *Optional:* For slower, more even cooking, remove the pot from the range burner to an oven preheated to 300 degrees F.
   c. Stir and baste the food occasionally and add more liquid if necessary.
   d. Remove any fat that appears on the surface.
   e. *Optional:* Cook the foods partially and cool for several hours or overnight. Remove any fat from the surface before reheating.

   (See "How to De-fat Liquids," p. 101.)

10. **Optional:** Remove the meat and puree the flavoring vegetables. Add the puree to thicken the liquid. For a thicker sauce, add roux, cornstarch, mannie butter, heavy cream, sour cream, or plain yogurt. Return the meat to the liquid.

    (See "Thickeners," p. 130.)

11. **Season.** Add seasonings during the last 30 to 45 minutes of cooking. The longer they cook, the more their flavor is diminished.

12. **Optional:** Add fresh vegetables for serving. Potatoes, celery, carrots, onions, mushrooms, sweet bell peppers, and turnips are all popular. Cook them until they are tender but not overcooked. Most vegetables will cook in about 30 minutes.

13. **Adjust the thickness of the serving sauce.**
    · *To thin:* Add liquid.
    · *To thicken:* Add roux, cornstarch, mannie butter, heavy cream, sour cream, or yogurt. Remember that the sauce will also thicken as it cools.

(See "Thickeners," p. 130.)

14. **Serve** in a heated serving bowl or on a heated platter accompanied by the vegetables and sauce.

■

How to Roast Meats

Meats that are roasted should be at least 2 to 2 1/2 inches thick and weigh at least 3 pounds. One side should have enough fat to baste the roast as it cooks; if not, purchase extra beef fat or salt pork to bard or lard it. See the Selection Chart for the meat being cooked to determine the cuts that are best suited to this cooking method: beef (p. 401), veal (p. 404), pork (p. 407), lamb (p. 409), variety meats (p. 411–419).

0. **Before you begin:** Read all the steps given below. If necessary, review the Cook's Guide for the meat being cooked, the Cooking Considerations for Meats, and the principles of dry heat cooking covered in Chapter Two.

1. **Plan** 1 to 2 hours to prepare fully thawed meat and bring it to room temperature. Use the table on page 433 to estimate the approximate cooking time. Add 20 to 30 minutes to allow the juices to "set" before carving.

2. **Prepare the vessel:**
   a. Use a pan with low sides. For easier cleaning, line it with heavy aluminum foil.
   b. Coat the inside of the pan (or the foil) and the cook-

ing rack with shortening to prevent the meat and pan drippings from sticking.

3. **Prepare the meat:**
   a. Cut off any hip bones, back bones, or shoulder bones that might interfere with carving. Any bone that is in the meat should be left so that it can conduct heat to the meat's center.
   b. Trim off excess fat.
   c. For a more attractive appearance, shape the meat and bind it with heavy kitchen twine (see p. 428).
   d. *Optional:* For added flavor, rub the meat all over with a clove of fresh garlic. If the top coating of fat is thick, make small incisions into the fat and insert small slices of garlic. Alternatively, cook garlic, onions, or both in cooking oil or fat and use that to baste the meat.
   e. Coat the meat all over with cooking oil, melted fat, or a combination of the two. (Butter or margarine used alone will burn.)
   f. If the roast has exposed bones (such as a rack of lamb or a crown roast), cover the bone with aluminum foil to prevent it from burning.

   g. Place the meat onto the cooking rack with the fat on the top.
   h. Sprinkle evenly all over with salt and other seasonings.
   i. *Optional:* Bard or lard the meat with fat. (See p. 420.)
   j. Insert a meat thermometer into the thickest part of the meat but away from bone or fat pockets. The tip should reach to the center of the meat.
   k. Bring the meat to room temperature.

4. **Prepare the heat:**
   a. Place the oven rack so that the meat will be centered in the oven.
   b. Preheat the oven to the desired setting. (See the Timetable for Roasting Meats, p. 433.)

5. **Cook the meat.** (*Note:* Many recipes call for vegetables to be cooked along with the meat from the start, but long cooking will destroy the flavor and nutritional value of vegetables. It is best to add vegetables only during the last 30 to 45 minutes of cooking.)

   a. Place the rack and the meat into the preheated oven. Be careful that the thermometer does not touch any metal or bone.

   b. Use the Timetable for Roasting Meats (p. 433) to judge the approximate cooking time and set a timer accordingly.

   c. One-half to three-quarters of the way through the approximate cooking time, turn the pan 180 degrees so that the end that was facing the rear of the oven faces front.

   d. If the meat surface appears too dry, baste it then and every 15 minutes thereafter with pan drippings, cooking oil, or melted fat. (Liquids other than these wash away protective fat and allow the surface of the meat to dry.)

   e. Remove excess liquid from the pan so that the meat does not steam.

   f. Repeat the basting every 15 minutes if needed.

   g. If the top becomes too brown, place a piece of aluminum foil lightly over it.

6. **Optional:** Add serving vegetables such as potatoes, carrots, turnips, mushrooms, or sweet bell peppers to roast along with the meat during the last 30 to 45 minutes of cooking time. Coat the vegetables with cooking oil to prevent them from burning.

7. **Test for doneness** every 15 minutes. Beef may be served rare to well done. Pork, lamb, or mutton should be medium-rare to medium-well done. Veal and variety meats should be well done. (*Note:* A roast will continue to cook in its own heat, so remove it from the heat before it is done to your liking.)

   · *Thermometer test:* Use the Timetable for Roasting Meats (p. 433).

   · *Feel test:* Press down in the center of the meat with your finger or the flat side of a knife. The "springier" it is, the rarer it is cooked.

   · *Color test:* Make a small incision into the thickest part of the meat and judge it by its color. Red = rare; pink = medium; gray = well done.

Timetable for roasting meats

Meat	Cooked at	Will Cook to	In Approximately
Beef or veal	275–325°F.	Rare (125°F.)	15–20 minutes per pound
	275–325°F.	Medium (135°F.)	20–25 minutes per pound
	275–325°F.	Well (150°F.)	25–30 minutes per pound
Pork	300–350°F.	165–175°F.	30–40 minutes per pound
Lamb/mutton	300–325°F.	Rare (140°F.)	20–30 minutes per pound
	300–325°F.	Medium (160° F.)	25–35 minutes per pound
	300–325°F.	Well (170° F.)	30–40 minutes per pound

The times given are approximate. The thicker the cut, the longer it will take for heat to penetrate to its center. Chunky-shaped roasts will cook faster than roasts with an oblong shape. Well-aged meat or meat with a good deal of fat will cook more slowly.

Based on information provided by the National Live Stock and Meat Board.

8. **Remove the meat from the heat before it is fully cooked** (about 5 degrees below the desired temperature for small roasts, 10 to 15 degrees for large ones). The roast will continue to cook in its own heat as it sets.

9. **Allow the meat to set.** Place it on a warm platter and cover it lightly with aluminum foil. Let it set for 20 to 30 minutes to allow the juices to become redistributed evenly throughout the meat. If the roast must be held longer than 30 minutes, place it in a warm oven (150 degrees F.).

10. **Optional gravy:** Deglaze the pan drippings and make gravy. (See "How to Make Gravy," p. 138.)

11. **Carve** as close to serving as possible. Cut across the grain for greatest tenderness. (See "How to Carve Meats," below.)

12. **Serve** on a warm platter or plates.

13. **Optional:** Accompany with defatted pan juices ("au jus"), plain or flavored butter, gravy, brown sauce, white sauce, one of the egg yolk and butter sauces, or commercial meat sauce.

■

How to Carve Meats

Boneless Roasts

1. Hold the meat steady with tongs or a fork and make vertical slices across the grain.

2. If the meat is particularly tough, increase the angle of the cut across the roast by up to 45-degrees.

Loin Roasts, Crown Roasts, and Racks

1. Remove the backbone, leaving as little meat on it as possible.

2. Stand the loin or crown with its thickest part on the bottom. Hold the roast steady with tongs or a fork and cut in the center between the bones.

Standing Rib Roast of Beef

1. Remove the chine bone from the thick end of the meat by cutting between the bone and the meat, leaving as little meat on the bone as possible.

2. Slice a small piece off the large end, if necessary, so that the roast will stand flat.

3. Hold the roast steady with a fork inserted below the top rib. Carve across the "face" of the roast to the rib bone

and free the slice by cutting along the rib bone with the knife tip.

Pot Roasts

1. Cut between the muscles and around the bones to remove one solid section at a time.
2. Cut each section across the grain.

 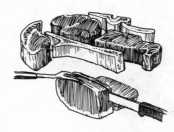

Leg of Lamb or Pork

1. Cut two or three slices lengthwise along the outer (convex) side to form a flat base.
2. Stand the leg on its base. Steady the roast with a fork and make thin vertical slices down to the bone.
3. Release the slices by cutting under them along the bone.

4. When all of the meat is removed from the thick inner side, turn the meat on its side and repeat the process described above on both sides until all of the meat is sliced.

■

*V*egetables
And Other Foods Called Vegetables

CHAPTER EIGHTEEN

*V*egetables and foods that are typically called vegetables (tomatoes, for example, are really a fruit) are vital to a healthy diet and provide added variety in terms of flavor, color, and texture to virtually any meal. There are so many wonderful foods that fall into this category that it would be extremely difficult to cover them all here. Instead, I've included only those vegetables that most cooks are likely to use most often as side dishes or as basic ingredients.

Any fresh foods that are not included in this chapter are likely to be similar to some that are included. By extending the information given for one food, and by generalizing from it a bit, you should be able to determine what you need in order to enable you to work with other foods that are not covered. That will be easier to do if you begin to consider what the foods have in common and ignore their differences. Cabbage, brussels sprouts, and bok choy, for example, may seem quite different from each other. However, when you consider the things they have in common, for cooking purposes they are all about the same. What applies to one applies to all three. Once you begin to consider what similar foods have in common, you'll be amazed at how few important differences there really are among them.

The information in this chapter is of two main types: "Cook's Guides" for individual vegetables or groups of similar ones, and "How to" instructions for cooking all of them. The Cook's Guide entries are considerably more detailed than those for the foods covered in earlier chapters. Cooking times and preparation instructions, especially, are much more explicit. Cooking times, of course, will vary according to the size of the food or food pieces. The smaller they are, the less time they will require. I hope that each entry tells you all you need to know in order to work with the food easily and successfully. The vegetables are listed alphabetically so that you can readily find what you are looking for.

Cook's Guides to Vegetables

Artichokes

Artichokes are globe-shaped and have sharply pointed leaves. Not the most practical vegetables—60 percent or so is waste—globe artichokes are troublesome to prepare, a chore to eat, and a joy to taste.

☐ *To Plan*

Plan one large (4-inch or larger) artichoke or two small (2 1/2-inch) artichokes per serving. The smaller the artichoke, the more tender it will be.

☐ *To Select*

Select plump artichokes with thick green heads and compact, flat-lying leaves. Opened leaves are a sign of a dry, woody texture. Brown leaves or leaves that curl out on the sides are signs of old age. Brown spots on the leaves are only a sign that the leaves were touched by frost; they have no bearing on the texture or flavor of the artichoke. Artichokes are best if they are purchased fresh the day they are to be used. They will keep well, though, for up to five days depending on how fresh they are when purchased.

☐ *To Store*

Store artichokes unwashed and tightly wrapped in paper in a dry part of the refrigerator, not in the vegetable drawer or in a sealed plastic bag.

☐ *To Prepare*

1. Pull off the tough outer row of bottom leaves and any higher leaves that are bruised or discolored.

2. Using scissors, trim the sharp tips (about 1/4 inch) off the top of each leaf. Alternatively, cut off the top fourth of the whole globe with a knife.

3. Cut off the stem to make a flat base upon which the globe can rest.

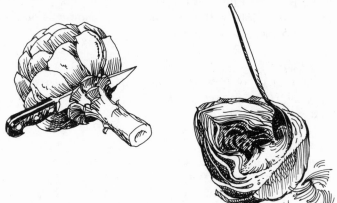

4. Soak the artichoke in a bath of acidulated water (1 to 2 tablespoons lemon juice or vinegar per quart of water). The acid will chase out any little bugs that might be hiding in the leaves and prevent the flesh from discoloring.

5. The fuzzy "choke" in the center is not eaten and must be removed. It is easiest to remove the choke after the whole artichoke has been boiled or parboiled, but it may be removed beforehand. Either way, to remove it, first cut the artichoke into halves or cut off the top and spread the leaves to reveal the hairy center. Use a spoon or melon baller to scrape out the choke, making certain to get all the hairs.

□ *To Cook*

Note: Pots and pans made of aluminum or cast iron will discolor artichokes.

Simmer in acidulated water in an uncovered pot. Cooking times will vary according to size: 15 to 45 minutes if the artichokes are whole, 5 to 25 minutes if the tops and chokes have been removed. Artichokes are done when the base can be pierced easily with a fork. Remove the artichokes from the liquid and refresh them in cold water until they can be handled. Drain them upside down in the sink or on paper towels. If you have not already done so, remove the chokes. Coat the meat with lemon juice to prevent discoloration.

To **fry** artichokes, prepare them and parboil them for 5 to 15 minutes, depending on their size. Refresh them in cold water to stop the cooking. When the globes are cool enough to handle, remove the fuzzy chokes. Set aside the tougher outer leaves and cook them fully by simmering them for another 5 to 10 minutes. **Sauté** the tender inner leaves and the meaty hearts and bottoms without coating or batter until they are slightly browned and tender. **Pan-fry or deep-fat-fry** tender leaves and meaty hearts and bottoms that have been dipped in a dry coating or wet batter. Cook until the crust is golden brown.

Bake artichokes whole or with their tops removed and the cavities stuffed with bread stuffing or other filler. Alternatively, cut each artichoke into halves or quarters and bake the meaty hearts, bottoms, and tender inner leaves. Either way, first parboil the whole artichoke for 5 to 15 minutes, depending on size, and then refresh it in cold water before cooking to completion. Coat the flesh with lemon juice, cooking oil, butter, margarine, or vinaigrette dressing and seasonings before baking. Bake at 350 to 375 degrees F. for 15 to 25 minutes for pieces and quarters, 30 to 60 minutes for whole stuffed globes. Stuffed artichokes may require basting with cooking oil, wine, broth, or seasoned liquid to prevent drying. The artichoke is ready when its bottom can be pierced easily with a fork.

Combination methods: Hearts or bottoms may be used in braises or cooked in casseroles. Chopped or pureed pieces may be used in quiches, puddings, timbales, or soufflés. For any of these special dishes, first parboil the artichoke 5 to 15 minutes and then refresh it in cold water before cooking further.

□ *To Season*

Season with salt, pepper, onion, garlic, oregano, rosemary, tarragon, mustard, sesame seed, dill, or parsley.

□ *To Serve*

You can serve cooked artichokes either with their leaves on the globe or with the leaves pulled off. Serve with a sauce in which diners dip the leaves: hot melted or clarified butter or lemon butter, mayonnaise (plain or flavored), one of the egg yolk and butter sauces, or one of the vinaigrette dressings. The diner removes the meat from the leaf by holding the tip and pulling the leaf across the front teeth. Once the meat is removed, the remaining leaf is discarded. The closer the leaves are to the center of the globe, the more meat they will have. Once the fuzzy choke has been removed, the heart and bottom may be cut up and eaten.

Asparagus

□ To Plan
Plan 1/2 pound (6 to 10 spears) per serving, depending on their size.

□ To Select
Select spears with compact, tightly closed tips and firm, straight, almost brittle stalks of uniform color. To assure uniform cooking, choose stalks of about the same thickness and length. Avoid stalks that are limp. Size makes little difference in flavor, but thinner spears are likely to be more tender.

□ To Store
Store asparagus unwashed in a plastic bag and/or in the vegetable drawer of the refrigerator. Wrap the stems in wet paper towels to keep them moist and tender. It is best to cook asparagus that is as fresh as possible, but it will keep well for four to seven days.

□ To Prepare
1. First cut or break off the tough, woody bottoms at the place where the stalk becomes tender. For more even cooking and more attractive appearance, try to make the spears all about the same length.

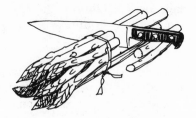

2. Soak the spears in salty water for 10 minutes. Rinse them under cold running water, rubbing each spear gently to remove any dirt, chemicals, or insecticides that may be on them.

3. *Optional:* If a stalk seems tough, peel its lower part with a vegetable peeler. If the stalk is thick, split it up the middle to within an inch of the floret (the flower top) so it will cook evenly throughout without overcooking the floret.

4. To make spears more crisp, soak them in iced water for about 30 minutes before cooking.

5. To cook asparagus in liquid, stand the spears upright with the florets at about the same height, and bind the bunch with kitchen twine.

☐ *To Cook*

Raw asparagus is delicious marinated in a vinaigrette dressing. If the stalks are very thick, steam them for 3 to 5 minutes and refresh them in cold water before marinating.

Simmer spears standing up so that the florets are above the liquid. Cook them in a covered pot for 5 to 10 minutes until the stalks are tender but not limp. (Special devices are made for this, but you can also use a double boiler with the upper pot turned upside down to form a lid.) This method allows the tougher stalks to simmer while the delicate florets steam so that both come out with about the same texture.

Sauté spears without coating or batter until the stalks are tender, about 5 minutes.

Pan-fry or deep-fat-fry asparagus in a wet batter or a dipped batter until the crust is golden brown. Larger spears should first be parboiled for 3 to 5 minutes and refreshed in cold water before being coated with batter.

Bake spears that have been parboiled or steamed for 3 to 5 minutes and refreshed in cold water. Top with butter or margarine or with cheese or cheese sauce and bake in the oven at 400 degrees F. until the fat melts or the cheese browns slightly.

Combination methods: Use asparagus in salads, soufflés, quiches, puddings, soups, and casseroles.

☐ *To Season*

Season with salt, pepper, onion, garlic, dill, basil, paprika, marjoram, nutmeg, allspice, mace, sesame seed, tarragon, mustard, coriander, mint, parsley, sage, rosemary, or thyme.

☐ *To Serve*

Serve cooked asparagus topped with plain or flavored butter or margarine, lemon juice, one of the egg yolk and butter sauces, plain or flavored mayonnaise, white sauce, cheese sauce, or melted cheese.

Avocados

☐ *To Plan*

Plan 1/4 to 1/2 of a large avocado or 1/4 to 1/2 cup of pieces per serving.

☐ *To Select*

Select avocados of uniform firmness that are free of bruises and soft spots. The skin color can vary from shades of green to purplish black and may even have brown spots. Color and spots make no difference. It's the firmness that counts. Avocados are ready for use when they have a slight aroma and the skin yields just slightly to the touch without being soft. If they are really soft, they can still be used for making guacamole.

☐ *To Store*

Store unripened avocados at room temperature until they have ripened enough to yield slightly to the touch. To speed ripening, store them at room temperature wrapped in a newspaper or in a closed paper bag pierced with small holes to allow gases to escape. To slow ripening, store in the refrigerator. The length of time avocados may be stored can be as little as one day or as long as ten days. To store cut avocado, first coat the flesh with lemon juice or lime juice to prevent discoloration. Leaving the seed in will also minimize discoloration.

☐ *To Prepare*

1. Wash the avocados under cold, soapy water to remove the oil, insecticides, and dirt that will get on your hands and contaminate the food. Rinse them thoroughly under cold running water.

2. Slice each avocado lengthwise into halves and scoop out the seed. (Carbon-steel knives will discolor the flesh.)

3. Peel avocados by pulling the flesh away from the shell. Use your fingers, a knife, or a spoon. For fancy serving, use a melon baller to scoop out the flesh.

4. Slice or dice into smaller pieces as desired.

5. Coat all cut surfaces with lemon or lime juice to prevent discoloration.

6. *Optional:* To puree, mash diced pieces with a fork, force them through a sieve, or put them through a food blender or food processor.

☐ *To Cook*

Raw avocado slices or diced pieces are popular as a garnish for green garden salads and for making guacamole dip. You can also mix raw pieces with chicken, crab, lobster, or shrimp together with tomatoes, celery, and mayonnaise to make special salads. For extra-fancy salads, remove the flesh from individual avocado halves, mix it with other ingredients, and serve the salad mixture mounded in the avocado shell.

Sauté slices or diced pieces without coating or batter until they are golden, about 8 minutes.

Combination dishes: Use avocado pieces to make soup or as a filler in casseroles. To preserve the texture of avocados in casseroles, bake them at temperatures below 375 degrees F. for no longer than 30 to 40 minutes.

☐ *To Season*

Season with salt, pepper, dill, garlic, onion, allspice, mace, or nutmeg.

□ *To Serve*
Serve with plain or flavored mayonnaise, vinaigrette dressing, sour cream, or plain yogurt.

Beans and Peas

□ *To Plan*
Plan about 1/4 pound or 1/2 cup per serving, allowing for any shells that will be discarded. One pound of green or wax beans yields about 3 cups cooked. Two pounds of lima beans in pods yields about 2 1/4 to 2 1/2 cups cooked. One pound of peas in their pods yields about 1 cup cooked.

□ *To Select*
Select pods that are crisp, firm, and plump but not bulging. The smaller, the better. The size of all pods should be about the same so that they will cook uniformly. The color should be bright and uniform, free of scars and blemishes. The pods should snap easily with a crisp sound when bent. Avoid any that are limp or wilted.

□ *To Store*
Store beans and peas unshelled and unwashed, loosely wrapped in a paper bag in a dry part of the refrigerator (not in the vegetable drawer). They will keep up to one week but are best if cooked within two days of purchase.

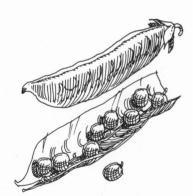

□ *To Prepare*
Wash beans and peas under cold running water, rubbing the pods gently between your fingers to remove dirt, chemicals, and insecticides. Snap off the ends; the string, if any, should come off with them. Leave beans whole, or snap or cut them into pieces of about the same length. Shell peas and lima beans by pulling the inner edge apart to release the peas. Discard any that are dried or discolored.

□ *To Cook*
Simmer green or wax beans 5 to 15 minutes if whole, 4 to 10 minutes if cut up. Whole lima beans will cook in about 10 to 15 minutes. Delicate or young peas require only about 2 to 5 minutes.

   To steam, add about 3 to 5 minutes to the times given for simmering.

   Sauté or stir-fry lima beans or peas out of their pods without coating or batter. Green beans in their pods should be broken or cut into small pieces of uniform size. Before frying beans, first parboil them for 2 to 5 minutes and refresh them in cold water.

Combination methods: Use beans or peas in casseroles, braises, soups, puddings, and quiches.

☐ *To Season*
Season with salt, pepper, onion, garlic, dill, marjoram, turmeric, savory, basil, paprika, oregano, tarragon, allspice, mustard, caraway seed, sesame seed, mace, nutmeg, mint, parsley, sage, rosemary, or thyme.

☐ *To Serve*
Serve beans and peas plain or topped with plain or flavored butter or margarine, vinaigrette dressing, plain or flavored mayonnaise, white sauce, melted cheese or cheese sauce, sour cream, or plain yogurt. Serve alone or mixed with cooked onions, carrots, tomatoes, mushrooms, corn, celery, sweet bell peppers, pimientos, winter squash, water chestnuts, sliced almonds, bacon, or ham.

Beets

☐ *To Plan*
Plan 1/3 to 1/2 pound per serving.

☐ *To Select*
Select small, firm, well-rounded roots no larger than 2 inches in diameter. The skins should be smooth and unblemished with a rich red color. Avoid soft or shriveled beets and beets with rough or bruised skin. The tops, if there are any (and there should be), should be green, fresh looking, and bare of leaves. Because leaves continue to leach out nutrients as long as they are attached, their absence means that the roots are likely to be fresher.

☐ *To Store*
Store beets dry and unwashed in a paper bag in a dry part of the refrigerator, not in the vegetable drawer or in a sealed plastic bag. Moisture causes them to rot. If the tops are still on, remove all but about 2 inches. That 2-inch top will prevent the beets from bleeding their red color when they are cooked. Also, and for the same reason, leave any of the hair-like roots on the bottom. If there are any green leaves on the tops, cut them off and store them as you would other greens. Beets can be stored for up to one week. (See "Greens," p. 464.)

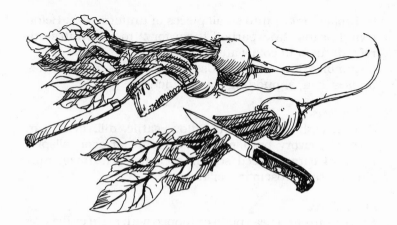

□ *To Prepare*

Scrub beets in cold water with a vegetable brush to remove dirt, chemicals, and insecticides. Don't use soap, and be careful not to break the skin. Do not peel or cut beets until after they have been cooked; that way, they will retain their color and nutrients.

□ *To Cook*

Simmer fresh small beets whole and unpeeled in an uncovered container for 20 to 40 minutes until they are fork tender. Older or larger ones require lengthier cooking, perhaps as long as 3 hours. Refresh the cooked beets under cold running water, rubbing them gently to peel off the skin.

Wrap-steam small, whole beets coated with butter, margarine, or cooking oil and seasonings. Wrap the beets in aluminum foil and bake them in a low-temperature oven (325 degrees F.) until the skins are tender. Baking time will be from 30 minutes to 3 hours, depending on size, freshness, and cooking temperature.

Sauté slices that have been parboiled 5 to 10 minutes, refreshed in cold water, and peeled. Cook them without coating or batter until they are tender.

Combination methods: Braises, casseroles, and soups may be made using beets that have been parboiled 5 to 10 minutes, refreshed in cold water, and then peeled and sliced or diced.

□ *To Season*

Season with salt, pepper, allspice, nutmeg, cinnamon, savory, bayleaf, anise, caraway, clove, dill, ginger, mustard, or thyme.

☐ *To Serve*
Serve plain or topped with plain or flavored butter or margarine, lemon juice, vinegar, vinaigrette dressing, sour cream, or plain yogurt.

Beet Tops

See "Greens," p. 464.

Belgian Endive

See "Lettuce," p. 469.

Bell Peppers

See "Peppers," p. 478.

Bok Choy

See "Cabbage, Brussels Sprouts, and Bok Choy," p. 451.

Broccoli

☐ *To Plan*
Plan 1/3 to 1/2 pound of raw broccoli per serving.

☐ *To Select*
Select bunches with unblemished clusters of dark green or purplish green buds. The stalks should be dark and firm but not hard or woody. The older the broccoli, the tougher it will be. Light-colored stalks and opened yellow flowers are signs of age.

☐ *To Store*
Store in a plastic bag and/or in a vegetable drawer in the refrigerator for as long as five days. It will save time when you cook broccoli if you store it already washed and cut up.

☐ *To Prepare*
   1. Soak broccoli for 10 minutes in salty water to destroy any little bugs that might be hiding out. Rinse it thoroughly under cold running water.
   2. Remove any leaves as well as tough or unattractive lengths of stalk.

3. Cut off the tough lower stalk, leaving about 2 1/2 to 3 inches below the base of the florets (the flower tops). Chop the tougher stalks into small pieces for cooking, or save them for making soup.

4. Cut the florets apart so they are all about the same size. Follow the branching lines for a more attractive appearance.

5. If the stalks still seem thick, split them down the middle to the base of the floret. Alternatively, cut off the florets at the stalk and then cut the stalks into thin strips of even thickness. Either way, the stalk should cook throughout in the same time required to cook the more tender florets. When broccoli is prepared in this way, there is no need to peel the stalk.

6. Before cooking, first parboil the broccoli in an uncovered pot for 3 to 5 minutes and refresh it in cold water for 10 to 15 minutes. This brightens the color and reduces the potential for stomach gas.

□ *To Cook*

Raw or blanched broccoli makes a tasty and attractive addition to crudité trays. Smaller pieces may be used on salads. For an interesting cold side dish or salad, marinate raw broccoli in a vinaigrette dressing either alone or mixed with cauliflower, carrots, pimiento, mushrooms, onions, or combinations of these.

Simmer broccoli uncovered in a seasoned liquid for 5 to 15 minutes for larger whole pieces, 3 to 8 minutes for smaller, cut-up pieces.

Steaming broccoli requires an additional 5 to 10 minutes to the times given for simmering. During the steaming, remove the lid every 2 minutes or so to allow gases to escape. A couple of pieces of stale bread in the cooking liquid will help reduce cooking odors.

Sauté or stir-fry broccoli pieces without coating or batter for about 5 minutes until they are tender.

Pan-fry or deep-fat-fry broccoli pieces in a wet batter until the crust is golden brown.

Combination methods: Use broccoli in braises, soups, casseroles, puddings, soufflés, quiches, or timbales.

☐ *To Season*

Season with salt, pepper, caraway seed, dill, mustard, or tarragon.

☐ *To Serve*

Serve broccoli alone or mixed with cauliflower, onion, pimiento, sweet bell pepper, carrots, celery, tomatoes, bacon or ham, sliced almonds, hard-cooked egg, or combinations of these. Top with plain or flavored butter or margarine, lemon juice, plain or flavored mayonnaise, white sauce, vinegar or vinaigrette dressing, cheese sauce or melted cheese, sour cream or plain yogurt, or one of the egg yolk and butter sauces.

Cabbage, Brussels Sprouts, and Bok Choy

☐ *To Plan*

Plan 1/4 to 1/2 pound per serving.

☐ *To Select*

Select head cabbage or brussels sprouts with heads that are compact and firm. Try to get brussels sprouts all about the same size so they will cook in the same length of time. Leaf cabbage and bok choy should have good color and be clean and free of any signs of age or mishandling.

☐ *To Store*

Store cabbage and brussels sprouts unwashed in a plastic bag and/or in a vegetable drawer in the refrigerator. Brussels sprouts and leaf cabbage will hold up well for four or five days, head cabbage for ten days to two weeks. Bok choy is best stored in a paper bag in a dry part of the refrigerator and will hold up well for two to four days.

□ *To Prepare*

1. Tear off any damaged outer leaves.

2. Soak the vegetable in salty water for 10 minutes to flush out any little bugs that may be hiding out between the leaves. Rinse it thoroughly under cold running water.

3. For **brussels sprouts,** cut off any excess stem and use the point of a paring knife to cut a cross (+) into the stem base deep enough to allow it to cook evenly but not so deep that the leaves will fall off. For **head cabbage,** cut the cabbage from top to bottom through the core into wedges of serving size, or shred it by cutting it crosswise. Cut **leaf cabbage or bok choy** lengthwise into wedges of serving size.

4. Parboil the vegetable for 3 to 5 minutes in an uncovered container and refresh it in cold water for 10 minutes before cooking further. This will brighten the color as well as minimize the stomach gas often associated with these foods.

□ *To Cook*

Simmer cabbage, brussels sprouts, or bok choy in an uncovered container to allow gases to escape. Shredded head cabbage, leaf cabbage, brussels sprouts, or bok choy leaves will cook in 5 to 10 minutes. Quarters of head or leaf cabbage or bok choy ribs will cook in 10 to 15 minutes.

To steam, add 5 to 10 minutes to the times given for simmering. Remove the pot lid frequently to allow gases to escape. To cook a full head of cabbage, steam it for about 30 minutes.

Stir-fry shredded leaves or small pieces of any of these vegetables only long enough to make them tender.

Sauté brussels sprouts without coating or batter for about 10 minutes, individual slices of bok choy or leaf cabbage for 2 to 5 minutes.

Pan-fry or deep-fat-fry brussels sprouts in a wet batter until the crust is golden brown.

□ *To Season*
Season with salt, pepper, onion, dill, oregano, marjoram, mint, allspice, nutmeg, mace, fennel, savory, celery seed, cloves, caraway seed, sesame seed, mustard, sage, thyme, or basil.

□ *To Serve*
Serve plain or topped with plain or flavored butter or margarine, vinegar or vinaigrette dressing, plain or flavored mayonnaise, sour cream or plain yogurt, one of the egg yolk and butter sauces, white sauce, stewed tomatoes, bacon, or ham.

Carrots and Parsnips

□ *To Plan*
Plan 1/4 pound per serving. One pound will make about 2 1/2 cups when cooked.

□ *To Select*
Select roots that are firm and nicely shaped with a rich color. If the tops are still attached, they should be green and fresh looking. Young roots with long rootlets are more tender and have a milder flavor than the more mature, larger ones. Avoid any that are broken or wilted. As with any roots, the tops continue draining nutrients as long as they are attached, so they should be removed.

□ *To Store*

Store carrots and parsnips unwashed in a plastic bag and/or in a vegetable drawer in the refrigerator for as long as two weeks. *Caution:* Do not store these roots with apples. Apples give off a gas that will make carrots and parsnips bitter.

□ *To Prepare*

1. Scrub the root with a vegetable brush under cold running water.

2. Unless the skin is tough, there is no need to peel it. If you do peel the skin, use a vegetable peeler or a sharp knife and remove only a very thin layer.

3. Slice crosswise into rings of equal thickness, or lengthwise into halves, quarters, or "julienne" strips of equal thickness. Thinner strips may be diced if desired. For fancy serving, slice crosswise at a 45-degree angle.

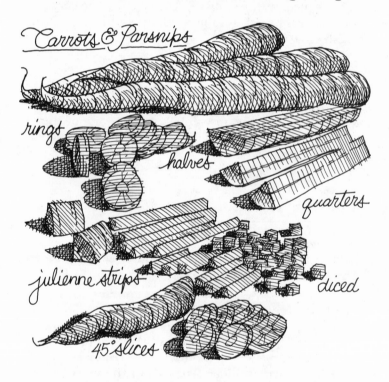

4. If the root is very large or old, its core may be dry, tough, and woody. The woody part should be cut out and discarded.

5. For frying or cooking using one of the combination methods, first parboil the roots for 5 to 10 minutes and then refresh them in cold water for 10 minutes before cooking them further.

□ *To Cook*

Raw or blanched carrots or parsnip slices or strips add color and variety to crudité trays and salads. For a garnish for salads or other dishes, use a vegetable peeler to cut raw pieces into very thin strips. For extra crispness, put raw pieces in iced water for 30 minutes before serving.

Simmer carrots or parsnips in a covered container until tender. Whole roots will cook in 15 to 30 minutes and pieces in 5 to 15 minutes, depending on size.

To steam, add 5 to 10 minutes to the times given for simmering.

Sauté or stir-fry pieces or slices without coating or batter for 10 to 15 minutes until they are tender.

Pan-fry or deep-fat-fry pieces in a wet batter until the crust is golden brown.

Combination methods: Carrots or parsnips are frequently used as ingredients in braises and casseroles. Cook until they are tender, about 30 to 45 minutes.

□ *To Season*

Season with salt, pepper, dill, ginger, onion, parsley, nutmeg, mace, clove, cinnamon, allspice, caraway seed, celery seed, mint, rosemary, anise, marjoram, thyme, tarragon, bay leaf, fennel, mustard, curry powder, cumin, coriander, or brown sugar.

□ *To Serve*

Serve alone or mixed with peas, broccoli, cauliflower, celery, onion, summer squash, potatoes, or combinations of these. Top with plain or flavored butter or margarine.

Cauliflower

□ *To Plan*

Plan 1/4 pound per serving, allowing for tough stems that must be cut off and discarded.

□ *To Select*

Select heads that are almost white, with tight compact

florets and no blemishes. Yellowed or browned florets are a sign of age. Size has no bearing on flavor.

□ *To Store*

Store cauliflower up to two weeks refrigerated in a plastic bag or in a vegetable drawer. Prepare it for storage by soaking it for 5 minutes in acidulated water to chase out bugs and brighten the color.

□ *To Prepare*

1. Cut off the tough lower stalk.

2. Cut the florets apart so they all are about the same size. If the pieces are too big, cut them lengthwise into halves or quarters. Follow the branching lines as you cut for a more attractive appearance.

3. Before cooking cauliflower, first parboil it for 3 to 5 minutes in an uncovered container and then refresh it in cold water for 10 to 15 minutes. This brightens the color and lessens the potential for stomach gas.

□ *To Cook*

Raw or blanched cauliflower makes a tasty addition to crudité trays and salads. For an interesting cold side dish or salad, marinate raw or parboiled cauliflower in a vinaigrette dressing either by itself or mixed with broccoli, pimiento, mushrooms, onions, or combinations of these.

Simmer cauliflower in an uncovered container for 5 to 10 minutes for pieces, or as long as 30 minutes for a full head. A little lemon juice in the cooking liquid will bring out the flavor and heighten the color.

To steam, add 5 minutes to the times given for simmering. Remove the lid frequently to allow gases to escape.

Sauté or stir-fry florets and stems cut to about the same size without coating or batter until they are tender.

Pan-fry or deep-fat-fry florets and pieces dipped in a wet batter until the crust is golden brown.

Combination methods: Use cauliflower in casseroles, puddings, soufflés, timbales, and soups.

□ *To Season*

Season with salt, pepper, onion, garlic, dill, tarragon, nutmeg, mace, paprika, allspice, cinnamon, mustard, oregano, caraway seed, celery seed, curry powder, cumin, coriander, rosemary, or thyme.

□ *To Serve*

Serve cooked cauliflower alone or mixed with broccoli, green peas, mushrooms, tomatoes, carrots, onions, celery, or combinations of these. Top with plain or flavored butter or margarine, vinaigrette dressing, plain or flavored mayonnaise, cheese sauce or melted cheese, one of the egg yolk and butter sauces, tomato sauce, or white sauce.

Celeriac

See "Stalks," p. 492.

Celery

See "Stalks," p. 492.

Chard

See "Greens," p. 464; "Stalks," p. 492.

Chicory

See "Greens," p. 464.

Collards

See "Greens," p. 464.

Corn

□ To Plan

Plan 1 to 2 ears per serving. For kernels already stripped from the cob, plan about 1/4 to 1/2 cup per serving. Two ears will usually yield 1 cup of kernels.

□ To Select

The flavor of corn begins to deteriorate the moment the corn is picked, so select ears that are as fresh as you can get. Ears should be solid and plump, at least 6 inches long. Husks should cover the entire ear and be green and fresh looking. The stem ends should be moist, and the hairlike silk ends should be pale, greenish white, free of decay or worm injury. Peel the husk back a little to check the kernels. They should be full, plump, and firm, with no worm holes. Avoid corn with kernels that are wrinkled or shriveled, or whose husks have been wholly or partially removed.

□ To Store

Store corn in its husks in a plastic bag and/or in a vegetable drawer in the refrigerator. The husk is the best protector for the corn. Cook corn as soon as possible; it will be good for only two to three days.

□ To Prepare

For cooking in liquids, leave corn in the husk or shuck and clean it as described below.

For roasting, corn can be cooked in its husk. The husk adds to the flavor, and it can be shucked more easily after cooking than before. Before roasting the ears, soak them in their husks for 5 to 30 minutes in sugar water (2 tablespoons sugar per quart of water).

For baking, shuck off the husks and clean the corn as described below. Then coat the kernels with butter or margarine. For added flavor, save the clean, tender inner husks and wrap the ears in them for baking. Wrap ears and husks together in aluminum foil or place in a baking dish.

To shuck corn husks:

1. Start at the small end and pull a portion of the husk down to the stalk. Repeat until the husk is removed. *Optional:* Save the clean, tender inner husks to cook with the corn for added flavor.

2. Once the husk is removed, use your fingers or a vegetable brush to pull away as much of the silk as you can while holding the ear under cold running water.

To remove kernels from the cob, use a sharp knife or a special stripping gadget made for the purpose.

□ *To Cook*

Simmer corn in unsalted water. (Salt in the water will make the corn tough.) Sugar, milk, broth, butter or margarine, and/or clean, tender husks may be added to the water to flavor the corn as it cooks. Put the corn in just enough cold liquid to cover it, and bring the liquid to a rolling boil. Cover the pot, turn off the heat, and allow the corn to sit in the water for 15 minutes to cook it fully without overcooking.

Sauté or stir-fry kernels over medium-low heat for 10 to 15 minutes until they are tender and slightly browned around the edges.

Roast or bake ears for 15 to 20 minutes in a preheated oven (325 to 350 degrees F.) or over charcoal. Turn the ears occasionally so that they cook evenly.

Combination methods: Cook corn kernels in casseroles, puddings, timbales, and soufflés.

□ *To Season*

Season with salt and pepper.

□ *To Serve*

Serve topped with plain or flavored butter or margarine. Kernels off the cob can be mixed with onions, tomatoes, lima beans, pimiento, green peas, mushrooms, celery, or combinations of these.

Cucumbers

□ *To Plan*

Plan 1 to 2 inches of cucumber per person for use in salads or crudité trays. To use as a side dish, one medium-size cucumber split lengthwise makes two servings.

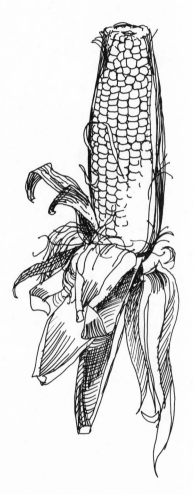

□ *To Select*

Select well-shaped cucumbers that are firm over their entire length and that have a rich green skin. For most uses they should not be too thick. Unless you buy them direct from the farm, it is likely that cucumbers have been coated with wax and/or sprayed with chemicals to keep them fresh and make them more attractive. It's better, therefore, to select them by shape and feel rather than by appearance.

□ *To Store*

Store cucumbers in a plastic bag and/or in a vegetable drawer in the refrigerator for up to seven days. Prepare them for storage by washing them in cool, soapy water, rubbing gently to remove dirt, chemicals, and insecticides that will get on your hands and contaminate other foods. Rinse the cucumbers under cold running water to remove all soap, and dry them thoroughly.

□ *To Prepare*

1. Use a vegetable peeler or sharp paring knife to remove the waxy coating along with a thin layer of skin. (The waxy coating will still have chemicals and insecticides in it no matter how well it has been scrubbed.)

2. Cut crosswise to make slices or lengthwise to make halves, quarters, or strips.

3. To make raw pieces really crisp, soak them in iced water for 10 to 15 minutes before serving.

4. To prepare pieces for baking or frying, coat them with salt and let them sit on paper towels for 30 minutes or so to draw out some moisture. Use clean paper towels to wipe off the moisture and any remaining salt before cooking.

□ *To Cook*

Raw cucumber goes well on crudité trays and in salads, and it makes an attractive garnish for cold soups. For a tasty cold side dish, mix cucumbers with tomatoes and/or onions and marinate the mixture in a vinaigrette dressing, sour cream, or plain yogurt.

Simmer slices or diced pieces 3 to 5 minutes, seeded halves or quarters 5 to 10 minutes.

To steam, add 5 minutes to the times given for simmering.

Sauté or stir-fry pieces without coating or batter for 5 minutes or less, until the edges just begin to brown.

Pan-fry or deep-fat-fry pieces in a dry coating or a wet batter until the crust is a golden brown.

Bake slices or strips coated with cooking oil, butter, or margarine for 5 to 10 minutes in a preheated oven (300–350 degrees F.). Halves with the seeds removed will cook in 10 to 15 minutes. If you stuff the halves, be sure the stuffing requires no more than 15 to 20 minutes of cooking time so that the cucumber doesn't overcook. (Precook the stuffing if necessary.)

Combination methods: Cucumbers can serve as a casserole dish stuffed with a mixture of their own flesh combined with other ingredients such as breading and/or chopped or ground meat or other stuffing. Simply bake the whole cucumber 10 minutes, cut it lengthwise into halves, and scoop out the flesh, leaving a shell about 1/4 to 3/8 inch thick. Mash the flesh and blend it with browned meat, breading, and seasonings to make a stuffing. Mound the stuffing attractively into the shell and bake or broil the stuffed shell until the surface browns.

□ *To Season*

Season with salt, pepper, onion, garlic, dill, basil, mint, or tarragon.

□ *To Serve*

Serve alone or mixed with tomatoes, onions, celery, pimiento, sweet bell peppers, winter squash, or combinations of these. Top with vinegar or vinaigrette dressing, plain or flavored butter or margarine, plain or flavored mayonnaise, sour cream, or plain yogurt.

Dandelion Greens

See "Greens," p. 464.

Eggplant

□ *To Plan*

For use as an ingredient or side dish, one medium-size eggplant will make 4 to 6 servings. One small to medium-size eggplant split lengthwise makes two shells for stuffing.

□ *To Select*

Select eggplant that is heavy for its size with smooth, firm, unblemished skin of uniform color. Avoid eggplant that is soft or shriveled or that has dark spots.

□ *To Store*

Store eggplant in a plastic bag and/or in a vegetable drawer in the refrigerator for up to six weeks. Prepare eggplant for storage by washing it in cool, soapy water, rubbing gently to remove dirt, chemicals, and insecticides that will get on your hands and contaminate other foods. Rinse the eggplant under cold running water to remove all soap, and dry it thoroughly.

□ *To Prepare*

1. Cut crosswise to make slices, lengthwise to make halves, quarters, or strips.

2. Eggplant that is to be fried, baked, or cooked by one of the combination methods should be parboiled whole for 5 minutes and then refreshed in cold water for 10 to 15 minutes before being cooked further.

3. To reduce moisture content, sprinkle salt over all exposed surfaces and let the eggplant stand on paper towels for 30 minutes. Use dry paper towels to wipe off any accumulated moisture and remaining salt before cooking.

□ *To Cook*

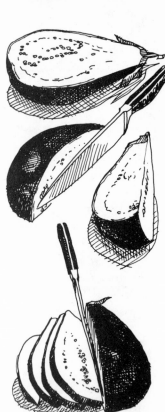

Simmer slices or diced pieces for 5 to 7 minutes.

To steam, add 3 to 5 minutes to the times given for simmering.

Sauté or stir-fry sliced or diced pieces without coating or batter for 5 to 8 minutes.

Pan-fry or deep-fat-fry pieces in a dry coating or a wet batter until the crust is golden brown.

Bake or broil halves or slices that have been coated with cooking oil (preferably olive oil), butter, or margarine. **Bake** in a preheated oven (300–350 degrees F.) for 20 to 30 minutes. **Broil** for 5 to 10 minutes.

Combination methods: Eggplant can serve as its own casserole dish stuffed with a mixture of its flesh together with breading. You can also use browned ground or chopped meat, or cooked fish or shellfish, in addition to or instead of the breading. Simply bake the whole eggplant for 10 minutes, cut it into halves lengthwise, and scoop out the flesh, leaving a shell about 1/4 to 3/8 inch thick. Mash the flesh and blend it with breading, or with breading mixed with browned meat or cooked fish or shellfish, and seasonings. Mound the stuffing attractively into the shell and bake or broil the stuffed shell until the top browns.

☐ *To Season*

Season with salt, pepper, onion, garlic, dill, basil, oregano, paprika, marjoram, parsley, sage, rosemary, or thyme.

☐ *To Serve*

Serve alone or mixed with tomatoes, onion, sweet bell peppers, mushrooms, summer squash, celery, beans, or combinations of these. Top with vinegar or vinaigrette dressing, tomato sauce, melted cheese, or cheese sauce.

Endive

See "Greens," p. 464; "Lettuce," p. 469.

Escarole

See "Greens," p. 464; "Lettuce," p. 469.

Fennel

See "Stalks," p. 492.

Finochio

See "Stalks," p. 492.

Green Onions: Scallions and Spring Onions

☐ *To Plan*

Plan to have several green onions on hand at all times for use in salads, as a garnish, for flavoring, or to serve on a crudité tray. For cooked scallions, plan 2 to 4 stalks per serving.

☐ *To Select*

Select green onions with rich green leaves and small, glossy white bulbs. The larger the bulb, the stronger its flavor.

☐ *To Store*

Store green onions in a plastic bag and/or in a vegetable drawer in the refrigerator for up to ten days.

☐ *To Prepare*

1. Wash the onions under cold running water, rubbing gently to remove dirt, chemicals, and insecticides.

2. Cut off the root hairs as well as any tough ends of the green leaves. Discard any leaves that are soft or slimy.

3. For most purposes, use both the green leaves and the white stem, cutting them crosswise into desired lengths. For crudité trays, you may want to leave the onions whole.

☐ *To Cook*

Raw whole green onions go well on crudité trays. Chop them for use in salads or as a garnish for soups, casserole dishes, meats, poultry, or fish.

Simmer, steam, sauté, or stir-fry green onions over low to moderate heat for 5 to 6 minutes.

Combination methods: Green onions can be used to flavor sauces, soups, braises, casseroles, and other combination dishes.

☐ *To Season*

Green onions, like globe onions, go well with virtually everything, and any seasonings go well with them.

☐ *To Serve*

Serve as a garnish for meats, poultry, or fish, or mix with any and all vegetables.

Greens: Beet Tops, Bok Choy Tops, Chard, Chicory, Collards, Dandelion Greens, Endive, Escarole, Kale, Kohlrabi Tops, Mustard Greens, Sorrel, Spinach, and Turnip Greens

Note: For endive and escarole, see also "Lettuce," p. 469.

☐ *To Plan*

Plan 1 pound with stems to serve 2 to 3 people. Without stems, 1 pound will serve 3 to 4 people.

☐ *To Select*

Select greens with tender, fresh-looking leaves. The leaves should have a good green color and be free of blemishes. Avoid any that are wilted, crushed, or decayed, or that show signs of insect damage. Stems should not be dry or limp.

□ *To Store*

Store greens refrigerated in a plastic bag and/or in a vegetable drawer for three to seven days. Prepare them for storage by first removing any blemished leaves. Separate the leaves and soak them in salty water for 10 minutes to destroy bugs and bacteria. Rinse the leaves in cold running water, rubbing them gently to remove dirt, chemicals, and insecticides.

□ *To Prepare*

Remove any thick stems and blemished leaves. Tear the leaves into smaller pieces if desired. (Cutting with a knife or scissors might discolor the leaves.) Soak the greens for 10 minutes in salted water and rinse them under cold running water.

□ *To Cook*

Note: Plain aluminum or iron cooking vessels may discolor some greens.

Raw endive, escarole, dandelion greens, and spinach make excellent salad greens.

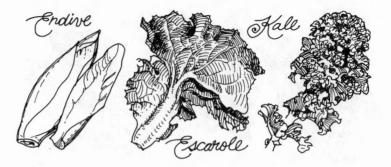

Steam only delicate greens such as spinach, kale, or endive. Steam the greens in just the water that remains on their leaves after they have been washed. Steam only long enough for the leaves to wilt: 3 to 6 minutes.

Stew only strong-flavored greens such as collards, turnip greens, and mustard greens. Stew them for at least 1 hour in just enough liquid to cover them. Flavor the liquid with salt pork, cooking oil, butter, or margarine. Serve the resulting broth (called "pot likker") with the greens or over corn bread.

Sauté or stir-fry spinach, kale, and other delicate greens only long enough to wilt the leaves: about 1 minute.

Combination methods: Use greens in puddings, timbales, quiches, and soufflés.

□ *To Season*

Season with salt, pepper, onion, garlic, basil, dill, mace, nutmeg, allspice, mustard, parsley, sage, rosemary, or thyme.

□ *To Serve*

Serve greens alone or mixed with root vegetables. Top with pot likker, vinegar or vinaigrette dressing, onion, hard boiled egg, stewed tomatoes, blanched almonds, toasted bread crumbs, bacon or ham, or combinations of these.

Kale

See "Greens," p. 464.

Kohlrabi

See "Root Vegetables," p. 487.

Kohlrabi Tops

See "Greens," p. 464.

Leeks

□ *To Plan*

Plan one medium-size rib (about 1/4 pound) for each serving as a side dish.

□ *To Select*

Select ribs that are thick, straight, and well shaped. The green leaves at the top should show no yellowing or other signs of age. Oversized bulbs indicate a fibrous texture. Try to get ribs all about the same size so that they cook evenly in the same length of time.

□ *To Store*

Store leeks in a plastic bag and/or in a vegetable drawer in the refrigerator for up to ten days.

☐ *To Prepare*

1. Soak the leeks for 10 minutes in cold, salty water to destroy any bugs that may be hiding between the leaves.

2. Rinse the leeks under cold running water, rubbing gently to remove dirt, chemicals, and insecticides.

3. Cut off the root ends as well as the tougher ends of the greens. Discard any outer leaves that are soft or slimy.

4. Smaller bulbs are best cooked and served whole. If the bulbs are thick, slice them lengthwise into halves or quarters.

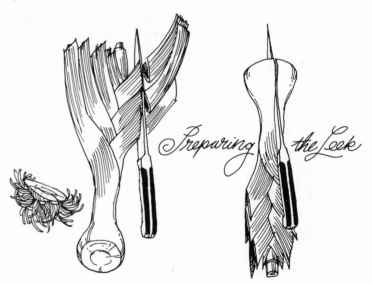

Preparing the Leek

5. For frying or use in a dish cooked by one of the combination methods, first parboil the leeks for 3 to 5 minutes and then refresh them in cold water for at least 5 minutes before cooking them further.

☐ *To Cook*

Simmer medium- to large-size whole leeks for 10 to 15 minutes; quarters, halves, or small whole leeks for about 5 minutes.

To steam, add 5 minutes to the times given for simmering.

Sauté or stir-fry leeks without a coating or batter until they are tender and slightly browned around the edges.

Pan-fry or deep-fat-fry leeks in a wet batter until the crust is golden brown.

Combination methods: Use leeks as a flavoring ingredient in casseroles, soufflés, soups, and braises.

☐ *To Season*

Season with salt, pepper, garlic, tarragon, mustard, dill, marjoram, turmeric, savory, basil, paprika, oregano, mace, nutmeg, allspice, mint, parsley, sage, rosemary, or thyme.

☐ *To Serve*

Serve alone or mixed with onions, tomatoes, pimiento, mushrooms, celery, sweet bell pepper, bacon, ham, or combinations of these. Top with plain or flavored butter, sour cream or plain yogurt, white sauce, vinaigrette dressing, plain or flavored mayonnaise, one of the egg yolk and butter sauces, cheese sauce, or melted cheese.

Lettuce

There are many types of lettuce, any one of which may be used alone or mixed with others to make salads or to garnish dishes for serving other foods.

Crisphead or iceberg lettuce is the most popular form of lettuce used in the United States. Its popularity seems to be due to its crisp texture, not to its flavor, for it is really less flavorful than other lettuce. Crisphead lettuce is solid and round, with medium-green outer leaves that grow paler in color towards the center of the head. For serving, the leaves may be separated individually, or the heads may be cut lengthwise through the center to form attractive wedges.

Romaine and Cos lettuce both have oblong, dark green leaves that grow greenish yellow towards the center. The leaves are crisp, but softer than those of crisphead lettuce. The flavor is mildly pungent.

Romaine Lettuce   *Iceberg Lettuce*

Butterhead Lettuce

Butterhead, Boston, and bibb lettuce all have light green, loosely furled leaves that are soft, not crisp, and that have a delicate, almost sweet flavor. Their special taste and texture make them especially well suited for fancy serving.

Leaf lettuce, including **endive, escarole, notched oakleaf, and red ruby,** has leaves that arrange themselves around the stem. Endive (also called chicory or curly endive) has curly, narrow, ragged leaves. The leaves have a slightly bitter taste. The yellowish inner leaves are milder than the darker green outer ones. Belgian endive is cylindrical in shape, white in color, and succulent to the taste. The core is bitter and is usually not served. Escarole is similar to endive except that the leaves are broader, longer, and less crinkly. In fact, the leaves can be rather tough and so might be cooked as greens. (See "Greens," p. 464) Oakleaf and red-edged ruby lettuces are sweet and rather soft in texture.

Leaf Lettuce

□ *To Plan*

Plan 1 medium-size head for making 4 to 6 salads. Smaller heads of some leaf lettuce may make as few as 2 to 4 salads.

□ *To Select*

Select lettuce that has fresh-looking leaves with good, bright color. The leaves should be free of yellow or brown spots or other signs of deterioration. Avoid lettuce with limp or wilted leaves.

□ *To Prepare*

Remove any wilted or blemished outer leaves. Discard them or clean them and use them for making broth.

1. Cut or tear off the base so that the leaves can be separated. For crisphead lettuce, bang the base on a hard surface and twist out the core.

2. Separate the leaves. Crisphead may be left intact.

3. Soak the leaves in cold salted water. For crisphead, hold the head upside down under the faucet so that the water flows down the core and through the leaves.

4. Rinse the leaves under cold running water, rubbing them gently to remove any dirt, chemicals, and insecticides.

5. Dry the leaves thoroughly in a colander or lettuce spinner. Dry crisphead by placing it upside down in the sink so that the water flows out the core.

□ *To Store*
Store lettuce refrigerated in a plastic bag and/or in a vegetable drawer for up to one week. A little moisture on the leaves will make them more crisp—a good reason for preparing them before storage.

□ *To Cook*
Raw is about the only way most lettuce is ever served. The two exceptions are endive and escarole, which may be cooked as greens (see p. 465).

□ *To Season*
Season with virtually all herbs, onion, or garlic.

□ *To Serve*
Serve alone or mixed with tomatoes, onion, celery, mushrooms, sweet bell pepper, avocado, citrus fruits, cooked shellfish, poultry, or meats. Top with vinaigrette dressing or plain or flavored mayonnaise.

Mushrooms

□ *To Plan*
Buy only cultivated mushrooms. Other varieties found in the woods just might be poisonous. It's a good idea to keep a store of mushrooms on hand at all times to use in salads as well as a filler or garnish for braises, casseroles, and soups. One pound of medium-size sliced caps and stems makes about 4 cups.

□ *To Select*

Select mushrooms with clean white caps. The underside "veil" should cover the "gills" as much as possible. The more gills you see, the stronger the flavor of the mushroom. Size has nothing to do with flavor, so try to get a size that will be attractive for the way the mushrooms will be served: large for stuffing, small for using whole as a side dish or for use in salads or as a garnish.

□ *To Store*

Store mushrooms unwashed in a dry part of the refrigerator. Keep them loosely covered in a brown paper bag so that air can reach them. Mushrooms will keep well for several days and are good for most uses until they become withered and brown. Sprinkling a little lemon juice on them will help to keep them white and moist so that they hold up longer.

□ *To Prepare*

1. Rub the mushrooms gently with a paper towel soaked in lemon water (1 tablespoon lemon juice per cup of water) to remove dirt, chemicals, and insecticides. Place them on fresh paper towels to dry. (*Note:* Soaking or washing will make mushrooms soggy.)

2. Cut off the dried stalk ends. (Save them for soups.)

3. *Optional:* For attractive pieces, slice lengthwise through the stem and the cap.

4. *Optional:* To remove the stem, cut it off evenly with the bottom of the cap. The remaining stem helps to hold the cap's shape.

5. *For stuffing,* carefully twist out the stem.

Tip: Save stems, tips, and scraps. Puree them with a little broth in a food blender. Freeze the liquid in ice cube trays and use the cubes to flavor cooking liquids, sauces, and soups.

□ *To Cook*

Raw mushrooms make a delightful addition to crudité trays or an attractive garnish for salads and soups.

Steam mushrooms whole or in pieces for 5 to 8 minutes until they are tender but not limp. Mushrooms should never be simmered except when being cooked with some other food, and then for only about 5 minutes.

Cut off dried end—slice lengthwise—twist off stem

Sauté or stir fry whole mushrooms or pieces without a coating or batter for 3 to 4 minutes until they are glossy.

Pan-fry or deep-fat-fry whole mushrooms or pieces in a wet batter or dipped batter until the crust is golden brown.

Bake or broil whole mushrooms coated with oil, butter, or margarine, with the bottom side up. Broil or bake them (at 375 degrees F.) plain, or stuff them with sausage, cheese, bread stuffing, crab meat, oysters, or combinations of these. Cook until the mushrooms or stuffings are browned.

Combination methods: Mushrooms and broth make a wonderful soup. Mushrooms are also a popular ingredient or garnish for salads, sauces, braises, casseroles, puddings, quiches, and soufflés.

□ *To Season*
Season with salt, pepper, onion, garlic, mustard, dill, oregano, nutmeg, basil, paprika, parsley, sage, rosemary, or thyme.

□ *To Serve*
Serve alone or mixed with peas, beans, onions, corn, tomatoes, artichokes, blanched almonds, bacon or sausage, or combinations of these. Top with plain or flavored butter or margarine, vinaigrette dressing, or plain or flavored mayonnaise.

Mustard Greens

See "Greens," p. 464.

Okra

☐ *To Plan*
Plan 1/4 pound per serving as a side dish, or 1/8 pound per serving if the okra is to be cooked with tomatoes or some other vegetable.

☐ *To Select*
Select tender pods that are 2 to 4 inches long and bright green in color. The skin should have no breaks, blemishes, or soft spots. The tips should bend to the touch and spring back. Avoid tough or shriveled pods. Try to get pods about the same size so that they will cook evenly in the same length of time.

☐ *To Store*
Store okra refrigerated in a plastic bag and/or in a vegetable drawer for three to five days. It is best used within two days of purchase.

☐ *To Prepare*

1. Wash okra in cold running water, rubbing the pods gently to remove dirt, chemicals, and insecticides.

2. Cut off stems and remove any of the leafy "beard" around the stems.

3. "To cut or not to cut?" That is the question. The sticky sap of okra thickens and flavors the cooking liquid if okra is simmered. Therefore, if the okra is to be served with the liquid, cut it up. If the okra is to be served without the liquid, though, then it's best to leave the okra whole so that its flavor and nutrients are retained. Cut the pods after they have cooked.

4. Okra may be fried whole if the pods are small. Larger pods must be cut up. To prepare cut okra for frying, coat it with salt and let it stand on paper towels for 30 minutes to remove moisture. Use clean paper towels to wipe off accumulated moisture and as much salt as you can before frying.

☐ *To Cook*
Simmer whole pods 8 to 12 minutes, sliced pieces 4 to 7 minutes.

To steam, add 4 to 5 minutes to the times given for simmering.

Sauté whole pods until tender, about 5 minutes. Cut-up okra will be gooey if it is sautéed.

Pan-fry or deep-fat-fry okra whole or in pieces in a dry coating or a wet batter until the crust is golden brown.

Combination methods: Okra is often used as an ingredient in braises, casseroles, and soups.

□ *To Season*

Season with salt, pepper, onion, garlic, oregano, coriander, turmeric, cumin, curry powder, thyme, sage, filé powder, or chili pepper.

□ *To Serve*

Serve alone or mixed with tomatoes, sweet bell peppers, celery, onions, beans, peas, mushrooms, or combinations of these. Top with plain or flavored butter or margarine, vinaigrette dressing, stewed tomatoes, or tomato sauce.

Onions

There are several varieties of onions. Most can be used for almost any purpose, but each has a special role that it alone plays best.

Dry onions (often called **"globe"** or **"maincrop"**) are small and either round or oval. Their strong, pungent flavor makes them popular both for cooking alone and for flavoring other foods. Their color may be white, yellow, brown, or even red and white. The yellow ones tend to have a milder flavor. Yellow dry onions are probably the best general, all-purpose onions.

Dry Onions ~ Creole Type ~ Green Onions

Creole type (Bermuda, Italian, or Spanish) onions are larger and milder in flavor than dry onions. They are excellent raw in sandwiches or salads. Bermuda onions have yellow, white, or brown skins and typically are flat on both ends. Both Italian and Spanish onions are spherical in shape. Italian onions are red; Spanish onions are brown and yellow.

Local onions, those that are grown locally, may look like regular dry or Creole types, but their flavors can be quite different. A "Texas red hot," for example, certainly doesn't have the same mild flavor one would expect from an "Italian" onion, even though the two look very much alike. To really know what you're getting, ask someone who knows.

Green onions (spring onions or scallions) have green leaves and white bulbs. Both the leaves and the bulbs are eaten. The rather delicate flavor of green onions makes them ideal for using raw as a garnish for salads or on crudité trays, or cooked in soups, braises, casseroles, or other combination dishes. For cooking, they can be substituted for regular onions if a milder flavor is desired. (See "Green Onions," p. 463.)

☐ *To Plan*

Plan to have several dry onions on hand at all times for general cooking needs. It is also good to always have some Creole type and green onions ready for any of their many uses. For cooking as a side dish or for use as an ingredient, plan 1 medium-size whole onion (1/4 cup chopped) per serving.

☐ *To Select*

Select dry or Creole type onions that are firm and dry with papery skins. Avoid any that crackle when pressed, have soft spots, or have started to sprout.

☐ *To Store*

Store onions unrefrigerated in a cool, dry, well ventilated place. The better the air circulation, the better they will keep. They should hold up well for several weeks.

☐ *To Prepare*

No matter how you peel or cut onions, they will probably bring tears to your eyes. To minimize or prevent tears:

1. Put the onions in the refrigerator for several hours

Peeling and Cutting an Onion

To peel: Place the onion on a cutting board and slice across it horizontally to remove the top. Leave the root on to hold the onion together. Carefully peel off the skin, starting on the cut end and pulling the skin back to the root. Discard the skin.

For onion rings: Slice the onion horizontally across the grain to make rings of desired width. Discard the root.

For diced onion:

1. Cut the onion in half, lengthwise through the root. Place the halves flat side against the cutting board and make slices lengthwise, along the grain, about 1/8 to 1/4 inch wide. Cut back to—but not into—the root. (The root should remain intact to hold the onion together.)

2. Use your guiding hand to hold the onion together, applying pressure from the top. Working from the top back to the root make horizontal cuts about 1/8 to 1/4 inch wide. Cut across the grain, back to—but not into—the root. (Be careful not to cut your fingers.)

3. Use your guiding hand to hold the onion together from the top and sides. Make slices of desired length, cutting down through the onion across the grain. Start cutting on the end opposite the root, working back to it. The pieces should all be about the same size. Discard the root.

or into a bowl of iced water for 30 minutes before peeling them.

2. Cut each onion in half through the root. Keep one half in the iced water while you peel and cut the other. A little lemon juice in the water reduces tears even more.

3. As you cut, frequently dip the knife blade into the iced water to wash off the juice.

☐ To Cook

Raw slices or diced cubes of onion are often used in salads and sandwiches, or as a garnish for soups and casseroles.

Simmer small onions whole, or large onions cut into halves or quarters. Cook 15 to 30 minutes until they are soft but not squishy.

To steam, add 5 to 10 minutes to the times given for simmering.

Sauté small pieces over low heat for 15 to 20 minutes until they turn translucent and golden but not brown. Cooking slowly over low heat brings out the best flavor.

Deep-fat-fry onion rings in a wet batter until the crust is golden brown. Creole type onions make the best onion rings, but large dry onions may be substituted if they are first parboiled for 1 to 2 minutes and then refreshed in iced water for 30 minutes. The parboiling mellows their flavor, and the iced water makes them firm.

Bake large Creole type onions or dry onions that have been parboiled for 1 to 2 minutes and refreshed in cold water. Cook in a preheated oven at 400 to 450 degrees F. for 30 to 60 minutes.

Combination methods: Onions are used for making onion soup. They can also be stuffed with breading, browned meat, and other things to make a casserole that is eaten "dish" and all. Otherwise, they are an important ingredient for making virtually every casserole or braised dish. They are also frequently used for flavoring sauces, salads, quiches, timbales, puddings, and other combination dishes.

□ *To Season*

It isn't a case of what goes well with onions, but rather that onions go well with almost any food or seasoning. Served alone as a side dish, they can be flavored with salt, pepper, dill, caraway seed, mustard seed, paprika, mace, nutmeg, allspice, parsley, sage, rosemary, or thyme.

□ *To Serve*

Serve with almost any food. There is only one rule to use when adding onions to other foods: You can use too much, but it's difficult.

Parsnips

See "Carrots and Parsnips," p. 453.

Peas

See "Beans and Peas," p. 446.

Peppers: Sweet Bell or Bullnose

□ *To Plan*

Plan 1/4 pepper or less per serving for use on a crudité tray or salad; 1/4 to 1/2 pepper for mixing with other vegetables or for use in a braise or casserole; 1 whole pepper per serving for stuffed peppers to be served as a main dish.

□ *To Select*

Select peppers that are firm, shiny, and well shaped with no soft or pale spots, holes, punctures, or breaks in the skin. Most peppers are green, but occasionally you can get them red or golden yellow. Red bell peppers are sweeter than green, and the golden yellow ones are sweetest of all. Whatever the color, it should be rich and uniform all over. If you plan to stuff the peppers, try to get them all about the same size so that they will cook evenly in the same length of time.

□ *To Store*

Store peppers refrigerated in a plastic bag and/or in a vegetable drawer for up to one week. For convenience, wash them before storage.

□ *To Prepare*

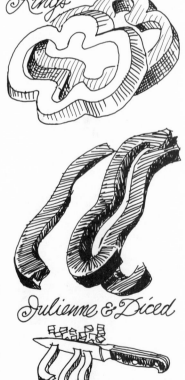

1. Wash peppers in cool, soapy water, rubbing gently to remove dirt, chemicals, and insecticides.
2. Rinse them thoroughly under cold running water.
3. With a small sharp knife, cut out the stem.
4. Cut in half or cut off the top and remove the seeds and inner ribs.
5. Leave peppers whole for stuffing. Cut them crosswise for rings, lengthwise for julienne strips or diced cubes.
6. For stuffing, first parboil the whole pepper 3 to 5 minutes and then refresh it in cold water for 5 minutes.
7. To peel to have softer, sweeter pieces: First bake whole peppers in a preheated oven at 350 degrees F. for 5 to 8 minutes. Place the hot peppers in a paper or plastic bag and seal it. Let the peppers sit for about 15 minutes. Then

remove them from the bag, slice them, remove the seeds, and peel off the skin with your fingers.

□ *To Cook*
Raw slices or diced cubes add color and flavor to crudité trays and salads and make a lovely garnish for casseroles and soups.

Simmer pieces 3 to 7 minutes.

Steam pieces or cored whole peppers 5 to 10 minutes, depending on thickness.

Sauté or stir-fry pieces without coating or batter for 4 to 9 minutes—just long enough to soften them but not long enough to make them limp.

Pan-fry or deep-fat-fry pieces in a wet or a dipped batter until the crust is golden brown.

Bake whole peppers stuffed, until the stuffing is browned. For stuffing, brown ground meat and mix it with breading and/or rice flavored with chopped and browned onion, celery, mushrooms, and perhaps some pieces of semi-hard cheese.

Combination methods: Sweet peppers are frequently used as an ingredient in braises, casseroles, and tomato sauces, or as a stuffed casserole that is eaten "dish" and all.

□ *To Season*
Season with salt, pepper, onion, garlic, basil, coriander, cumin, mustard, turmeric, curry powder, oregano, or parsley.

□ *To Serve*
Serve alone or mixed with tomatoes, onions, celery, lettuce, beans, peas, pimiento, or combinations of these. Top with plain or flavored butter or margarine, vinaigrette dressings, or tomato sauce.

Potatoes: White and Sweet Potatoes

There are any number of names for potatoes of different types. To keep things simple, you can think of the kinds of potatoes as being only three:

1. **Round whites:** "New potatoes" (red or waxy skins), or round "all-purpose whites" are used for simmering or sautéing.

2. **Long whites:** "Russet Burbank," "Idaho," "Irish," or long "all-purpose whites" are used for baking and deep-fat frying, as well as for making mashed potatoes.

3. **Sweet potatoes or "yams"** may be cooked any way.

Round White ~ Long White ~ Sweet & Yam

☐ *To Plan*

Plan 1 large or 2 small potatoes per serving. One pound makes 4 servings of mashed potatoes, 4 to 5 servings of French fries, or about 2 cups of slices or cubes.

☐ *To Select*

Select potatoes according to the way they are to be cooked. (See "To Cook," below.) Potatoes of any kind should be firm and well shaped with reasonably smooth skins that are free of blemishes, cuts, soft spots, or root sprouts. White potatoes with a green tinge may be bitter. Sweet potatoes, as a rule, will be sweeter and more moist the darker their skin.

☐ *To Store*

Store potatoes unwashed and unrefrigerated in a cool, dry, shaded area that is well ventilated. Too much light will give white potatoes a greenish tint and make them bitter. Do not refrigerate potatoes; refrigeration turns their starch to sugar. Sweet potatoes and "new" round whites will keep well up to a month. Long white potatoes may keep well for several months. It is said that onions will spoil potatoes where they touch, so keep them separated.

☐ *To Prepare*

1. Wash potatoes under cold running water, scrubbing with a vegetable brush to remove dirt, chemicals, and insecticides.

2. Cut out any stems and blemished spots.

3. Except when making French fries, it's best to cook potatoes in their skins. They are also easier to peel after

they are cooked. Either way, use a vegetable peeler or a sharp paring knife.

4. When cooking potatoes whole and in their skins, prick the skins in several places with a fork to allow steam to escape.

5. Cut into halves, quarters, or slices for simmering or sautéing, or into slices or julienne strips for frying. Coat cut surfaces with lemon juice or soak the pieces in acidulated water to prevent discoloration.

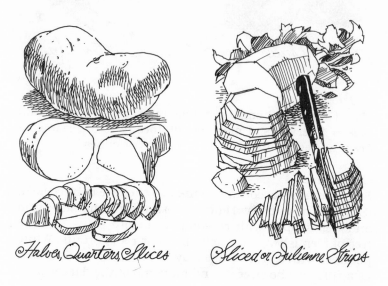

Halves, Quarters, Slices   *Sliced or Julienne Strips*

6. Sweet potatoes that are to be fried should first be parboiled for 5 to 10 minutes and then refreshed in cold water for 10 to 15 minutes before being cooked further.

7. For baked potatoes, coat the skins with vegetable oil, butter, or margarine to prevent them from drying. To speed cooking and to give a more uniform texture throughout, parboil the potatoes for 10 minutes and refresh them for 5 minutes in cold water before cooking them further. This is especially good to do if the potatoes are very large.

□ *To Cook*

Simmer round white potatoes and sweet potatoes. If the potatoes are small, simmer them whole. Start them in cold water rather than hot to allow better heat penetration for more even cooking. Larger potatoes should be cut into halves, quarters, or thick slices. Cook whole potatoes or pieces for 15 to 30 minutes, depending on size, until they can be pierced easily to the center with the blade of a paring knife.

To wrap-steam potatoes, coat them with butter, margarine, or cooking oil and wrap them individually in aluminum foil. Bake or roast the wrapped potatoes at 350 degrees F. for 30 to 90 minutes, depending on size. Turn them occasionally so that they cook evenly. The potatoes are done when they can be pierced easily to the center with the blade of a paring knife.

Fry potato slices or pieces without batter. Sweet potatoes and "home fry" whites should first be parboiled. Potatoes are usually peeled before frying, but you can leave the skins on—they're delicious. To make fried potatoes really crisp, soak cut pieces in acidulated iced water (1 Tbsp. lemon juice or vinegar per pint of water) for about 15 minutes and dry them thoroughly before frying. Fried potatoes can be cooked partially by frying—until they just begin to brown around the edges—drained, held in the refrigerator until needed, and then heated to completion in a preheated oven at 250 degrees F. just before serving. This will make them more crisp than frying them all at once.

Bake or roast whole long white potatoes or sweet potatoes. For a moist skin, coat the skin with butter, margarine, or cooking oil. For a dry, crisp skin, don't coat it with fat. Use the tines of a fork or the blade of a paring knife to pierce through the skin and into the meat in several places to allow steam to escape. Bake the potatoes over hot coals or in a preheated oven (350–400 degrees F.) for 30 to 90 minutes, depending on size, until they are soft enough to be pierced easily to the center with the blade of a paring knife. (Note: Many people now like to "bake" potatoes wrapped in aluminum foil. Really, this is wrap steaming. It gives the potato a moister texture than baking does.)

Combination methods: Use potatoes in casseroles, braises, soups, timbales, puddings, and hash.

Stuffed potatoes make a delicious casserole that can be eaten "dish" and all. To make them:

1. Bake or wrap-steam the potato whole as described above.
2. Cut it in half lengthwise. Scoop the flesh out of the skin, leaving about 1/8 to 1/4 inch to help the skin hold its shape.
3. Mix the flesh with other fully cooked ingredients such as cooked meat and/or vegetables, mixed with breading and/or pieces of cheese.

4. Mound the mixture attractively in the potato skin and top it with cheese, sour cream or plain yogurt, white sauce, melted or grated cheese, and/or cooked bacon bits.

5. Broil or bake enough to brown the top.

To make mashed potatoes:

1. Boil long white potatoes until they are soft.

2. Peel the potatoes.

3. Use a rotary mixer to mash the potatoes, gradually mixing in warmed milk and/or cream until the lumps are gone and the potatoes are light and fluffy.

4. Flavor with butter, salt, and pepper to taste and serve right away.

□ *To Season*

Season white potatoes with salt, pepper, onion, garlic, dill, basil, oregano, mustard seed, caraway seed, celery seed, bay leaf, parsley, sage, rosemary, or thyme. For sweet potatoes, use salt, pepper, sugar, brown sugar, syrup, cinnamon, allspice, cloves, mint, citrus, nutmeg, mace, or cardamom.

□ *To Serve*

White potatoes may be topped with plain or flavored butter or margarine, sour cream or plain yogurt, chives, grated or melted cheese or cheese sauce, stewed tomatoes or tomato sauce, white sauce, or cooked bacon, ham, or mushrooms, or combinations of these. Serve sweet potatoes topped with plain or flavored butter or margarine, and/or marshmallows.

Rice

Here in the United States, we have such an enormous variety of rices to choose from that their selection and preparation can be confusing. Most American cooks today use rice that comes prepackaged, complete with instructions. Even with such convenient instructions, however, by knowing more about rice in general you can vary the way you prepare and cook it to make it more tasty and interesting.

□ *To Plan*

As a rule, one cup of regular, precooked, or wild rice will make three good servings; brown rice will make four. Rice will cook in 5 to 45 minutes, depending on what type it is.

□ *To Select*

There are three main kinds of rice: long grain, medium grain, and short grain. Medium and short grain rice are moist and sticky and so are well suited for making rice pudding and croquettes as well as for fancy serving (for example, baked in a mold). Long grain rice is fluffier, and the grains separate easily. It is best for use in casseroles and as a side dish served with other foods.

Rice in all sizes of grain comes in several forms:

Brown rice has been milled only enough to remove the inedible husk and a small amount of bran. It is light brown and requires more water and a longer time to cook than rice that has had all of the husk removed. Its nutty flavor and chewy texture are quite distinct and provide interesting variety whether brown rice is used alone or mixed with one of the white rices.

Regular or polished rice has been milled to remove the hulls, germ, and most of the bran layers. Unfortunately, most of the nutrients and a good deal of the flavor are removed as well.

Parboiled or converted rice has been steamed before being milled to preserve nutrients and flavors. This forces the thiamine and nicotinic acid from the husk into the white grain so that they remain in the grain when the husk is removed. Converted rice is the tastiest and certainly the most popular form of white rice used in the United States.

Precooked or instant rice carries the converted rice idea a step farther. The rice is cooked entirely and then dehydrated before being packaged. Instant rice is nutritious, flavorful, and very convenient, cooking in about five minutes. However, many good cooks greatly prefer the taste and texture of converted rice.

Wild rice is a long-grained, greenish brown seed of a grass that grows in shallow lakes and marshes. Technically, it isn't rice at all (but who wants to get that technical?). Wild rice can be cooked and served alone, or it can be mixed with white rice, brown rice, or both.

□ *To Store*

Any white rice can be stored for a year or even longer. Brown rice, wild rice, and any seasoned mixes of rice are best used within six months of purchase.

Rice of any kind usually comes in a plastic package or paper box complete with instructions for preparation and cooking. Once a package has been opened, it is a good

practice to empty its contents into a sealable plastic container or glass jar to lock flavors in and keep bugs out. When you store rice in a new container, tear off the instructions from the original package and keep them with the rice. Rice will keep fresher longer if it is stored in a dark, dry place, such as a cupboard.

☐ *To Prepare*
Converted or instant rice and prepackaged fancy rice usually do not require washing. Brown rice and regular milled rice, however, should always be washed before cooking to remove starch, which makes the rice sticky. To wash rice, put it in a colander and rinse it under cold running water, shaking it vigorously for a minute or so until all the white powder is gone. To make any rice crunchier and more flavorful, sauté it in a small amount of butter or margarine before adding it to boiling water to cook.

☐ *To Cook*
Virtually all prepackaged rice will have instructions for cooking on the package. In most cases, use 2 parts liquid to 1 part rice, adding salt and perhaps butter or margarine to taste (1/2 tsp. salt and 1 tsp. butter or margarine per cup of liquid). A little lemon juice in the liquid will make white rice whiter and tastier. For more tender rice, use more liquid and simmer the rice longer.

To simmer: Bring the liquid to a boil, add the rice, reduce the heat to low, and cook covered. Do not stir the rice as it cooks, because that will break up the grains and make them soggy. The longer rice cooks, the drier it will be. Instant rice cooks in 5 minutes or less; converted rice, in about 20 minutes; and brown rice in 30 to 40 minutes. When the rice is fully cooked, fluff it with a fork, place a folded paper towel over it, replace the cover, and let it stand for 5 to 10 minutes. This will produce fluffy separate grains. If rice is left to stand longer than 10 minutes after it has cooked, the grains are more likely to stick together. Fluff the rice once again with a fork just before serving.

To bake: Put the rice and other ingredients in a baking dish and stir in boiling liquid. Cover the dish and bake the rice at 350 degrees F. (see the times given for simmering, above). For fancy serving, bake rice in molds of a size suited to making individual servings. Use medium or short grain rice because those will stick together and hold the shape of the mold better than long grain rice. When the rice is cooked, do not fluff it, but instead invert the mold onto the serving dish. The rice will fall out in one piece, in the shape of the mold.

☐ *To Season*

Most rice is cooked with only a little salt and perhaps butter or margarine. However, there are any number of ingredients you can add to flavor it. For example, notice that the instructions given above specified "liquid," not water. You can use plain water, of course, but to give your rice special flavors you can cook it in broth, very thin soup, tomato juice, or combinations of these. Even fruit juices such as orange juice, pineapple juice, or apple juice make delicious liquids for cooking rice, but they should always be diluted with at least an equal amount of water or broth. When using liquids other than water, be sure to account for salt and other ingredients in them before adding more.

Another way to make plain rice more interesting is to add other ingredients to it. Some of the most popular flavoring ingredients are chopped onion, sweet bell pepper, or a small amount of fresh herb such as parsley. Cook the added ingredients along with the rice.

☐ *To Serve*

Once rice has cooked, you might want to try adding other ingredients such as chopped pimiento, grated cheese, sautéed onions and/or mushrooms, and even slivered nuts such as almonds or pine nuts. The number of possible combinations is enormous, and the adventurous cook can serve rice a different way every day in the week for many weeks.

Cooked rice can be kept warm for a short period in a colander or tea strainer placed in a covered container over hot water, or in a covered container in a warm oven. Reheat cold rice with a little butter or margarine in a double boiler. You can also use leftover rice in casseroles or soups, or cover it with custard sauce to make rice pudding.

Root Vegetables: Kohlrabi, Rutabagas, and Turnips

☐ *To Plan*

Plan 1/4 pound per serving as a side dish, less for use on a crudité tray or salad.

□ *To Select*

Select roots that are firm, shapely, and clean, with a rich color. Avoid any that are soft or that have shriveled skin. The smaller the roots, the more tender and flavorful they will be. Green tops, if there are any, should be green and fresh looking.

□ *To Store*

Store root vegetables unwashed in a paper bag in a dry part of the refrigerator (not in the vegetable drawer) for up to one week. Moisture causes these vegetables to rot. Prepare them for storage by cutting off the tops and root hairs, which will continue to draw nutrients from the root if they are not removed.

□ *To Prepare*

1. Scrub the vegetable with a vegetable brush under cold running water to remove dirt, chemicals, and insecticides. Rutabagas may have a waxy coating that must be peeled off.

2. Unless the skin is tough, it's best to leave it on for the nutrients and flavor it contains. To peel, use a vegetable peeler or sharp paring knife to scrape off a very thin layer of skin.

3. Cut into halves or quarters, or slice or dice.

4. Larger pieces should be parboiled for 5 to 10 minutes and then refreshed in cold water for 10 to 15 minutes before being cooked further.

□ *To Cook*

Raw slices of root vegetables add color, flavor, and crunch to crudité trays or salads.

Simmer small whole roots or slices in a covered container for 20 to 40 minutes until they are tender but not limp. Older or larger roots require longer cooking, perhaps as long as 3 hours. Once cooked, they are often mashed or pureed.

To steam, add 5 to 10 minutes to the times given for simmering.

Sauté or stir-fry pieces without coating or batter for 10 to 15 minutes until they are tender and slightly browned around the edges.

Pan-fry or deep-fat-fry pieces that have been parboiled 5 to 10 minutes and then refreshed in cold water for 10 to

15 minutes. Use a wet batter or a dipped batter and fry the pieces until the crust is golden brown.

Combination methods: Root vegetables are often used in braises and stews and occasionally in casseroles.

☐ *To Season*
Season with salt, pepper, dill, onion, garlic, marjoram, tarragon, savory, mustard, mace, nutmeg, allspice, cinnamon, cloves, ginger, mint, bay leaf, anise, caraway seed, parsley, sage, rosemary, or thyme.

☐ *To Serve*
Serve alone or mixed with greens, beans, peas, broccoli, mushrooms, celery, bacon, ham, or combinations of these. Top with plain or flavored butter or margarine, vinegar, or vinaigrette dressing.

Rutabagas

See "Root Vegetables," p. 487.

Scallions

See "Green Onions," p. 463.

Sorrel

See "Greens," p. 464.

Spinach

See "Greens," p. 464.

Spring Onions

See "Green Onions," p. 463.

Squash

Squash is classified as either winter squash or summer squash. Winter squash, such as Hubbard or butternut squash, has a tough, hard skin that is never eaten. Winter squash tastes a good bit like sweet potatoes and may be substituted for them. Summer squash, such as zucchini

Summer Squash

Winter Squash

or basic yellow squash, has soft skin and lots of seeds, both of which are eaten along with the flesh of the squash.

□ *To Plan*

Plan 1/4 pound per serving of summer squash, 1/2 pound for winter squash (because the skin is not eaten).

□ *To Select*

Select squash that is heavy for its size. Large gourds can be watery and less flavorful. Avoid any with soft spots, bruises, cuts, or other blemishes. Winter squash should have a hard, thick rind. Summer squash should have a skin that is glossy and firm but not tough. Small summer squash are sweeter and more tender than large ones.

□ *To Store*

Store winter squash unrefrigerated in a cool, dry place for up to three months. Summer squash should be refrigerated in a plastic bag and/or in a vegetable drawer and may be stored for up to ten days.

□ *To Prepare*

1. Scrub the squash with a vegetable brush under cold running water to remove dirt, chemicals, and insecticides. Neither variety is peeled before cooking, although winter squash may be peeled after it has been cooked.

2. Leave winter squash whole or cut it into halves, quarters, or slices. For summer squash, cut the tips off both ends and slice lengthwise or crosswise.

3. Winter squash that is to be baked, fried, or cooked by one of the combination methods should first be cut up and then parboiled for 10 minutes, refreshed in cold water for 10 minutes, dried thoroughly, and peeled before being cooked further.

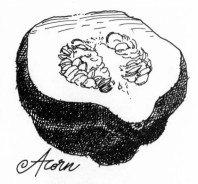

Acorn

□ *To Cook*

Raw summer squash makes a colorful addition to crudité trays and salads.

Simmer squash until the flesh can be pierced easily with the blade of a paring knife. Summer squash whole and unpeeled will cook in 10 to 20 minutes; pieces will cook in 5 to 10 minutes. Winter squash (except for Hubbard or butternut, which are too hard to simmer) must be cut up and will cook in 10 to 15 minutes.

Scalloped

To steam, add 5 to 10 minutes to the times given for simmering.

Sauté or stir-fry cut-up pieces of either type of squash without a batter until the pieces are tender.

Pan-fry or deep-fat-fry either summer or winter squash in a wet batter, dipped batter, or seasoned dry coating until the crust is golden brown. Winter squash should be cut into pieces and parboiled for 10 minutes, refreshed in cold water for 15 minutes, and peeled before being fried.

Crook-neck

Bake squash of any kind for 10 to 45 minutes, depending on the type and the size of the pieces. Halves will cook faster if they are placed flesh side down and baked for about half the time, turned and basted with butter or margarine, and then cooked to completion. Winter squash should be cut into pieces, parboiled for 10 minutes, and refreshed in cold water for 15 minutes before being baked.

Combination methods: Use squash in casseroles, puddings, timbales, and soufflés.

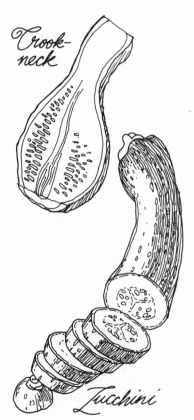

□ *To Season*

Season with salt, pepper, onion, garlic, basil, dill, mustard, oregano, thyme, parsley, marjoram, cardamom, ginger, cinnamon, allspice, nutmeg, mace, cloves, coriander, cumin, curry powder, anise, rosemary, or fennel.

Zucchini

□ *To Serve*

Serve with seasonings alone or top with plain or flavored butter or margarine, or with white sauce. Winter squash is good topped with honey, molasses, or brown sugar.

Stalks: Celery, Celeriac, Chard, Fennel, and Finochio

□ *To Plan*

Plan 2 to 3 ribs per serving as a side dish, less for serving raw or for use in braises or casseroles.

□ *To Select*

Select bunches with ribs that are snappy-crisp, never limp or rubbery. Size makes little difference in flavor or texture, but large celeriac tends to be woody and tough. The color should be definite and glossy, not faded, and leaves should look fresh, not wilted.

Celery   Chard   Fennel

☐ *To Store*

Store refrigerated in a plastic bag and/or in a vegetable drawer for as long as two weeks. To prepare stalks for storage: Leave the bunch whole or cut off the bottom so that the individual ribs separate. Soak the whole bunch or ribs in salted water for 5 to 10 minutes. Rinse the vegetable under cold running water, rubbing gently to remove dirt, chemicals, and insecticides.

☐ *To Prepare*

1. The leaves of most stalks may be left on or removed as desired. Chard leaves should be removed and cooked as greens (see p. 465).
2. It is not necessary to peel the stalks, although some people like to do it to give the stalk a smoother texture. To peel, use a vegetable peeler or sharp paring knife.
3. To make stalks crisper for serving raw, soak them in iced water for 30 minutes before serving.

☐ *To Cook*

Raw stalks go well on crudité trays and add crunch to salads. Raw leaves make a delightful salad ingredient or garnish for salads, soups, or other combination dishes.

Simmer sliced or diced pieces in a covered container for 5 to 10 minutes. Whole bunches cut into quarters or individual ribs require 10 to 20 minutes.

To steam, add 5 to 10 minutes to the times given for simmering.

Sauté or stir-fry smaller pieces without coating or batter until tender.

Combination methods: These stalks are often used as an ingredient in braises, casseroles, and soups.

☐ *To Season*

Season with salt, pepper, onion, garlic, mustard, paprika, parsley, dill, basil, tarragon, or thyme.

☐ *To Serve*

Serve alone or mixed with carrots, peas, onions, tomatoes, sweet bell peppers, mushrooms, potatoes, or combinations of these. Top with plain or flavored butter or margarine, white sauce, stewed tomatoes or tomato sauce, cheese sauce or melted cheese, or one of the egg yolk and butter sauces.

Sweet Potatoes

See "Potatoes," p. 480.

Tomatoes

☐ *To Plan*

Plan to have several tomatoes at various stages of ripeness on hand at all times to use in salads and sandwiches, to use as a garnish, to mix with other vegetables, or to make tomato sauce.

☐ *To Select*

Select tomatoes with a good shape and a smooth, even skin that has no breaks, bruises, or green or yellow patches. They should feel heavy for their size, and they should be red and slightly soft. Firmer tomatoes will ripen given time. Tomatoes that have ripened on the vine will have the best flavor. Small tomatoes are best for making salads and casseroles. Medium and large ones are good for slicing, stuffing, or marinating. Overripe tomatoes of all sizes are best used for making tomato sauce.

☐ *To Store*

Store ripened tomatoes refrigerated in a plastic bag and/or in a vegetable drawer for three to seven days. Long refrigeration will cause them to lose flavor and nutrients. Leave unripened tomatoes at room temperature in a loosely covered paper bag or in a dark drawer until they turn red and slightly soft; then transfer them to the refrigerator. It is said that an apple stored with tomatoes will speed their ripening.

□ *To Prepare*

1. Wash the tomato in cool, soapy water, rubbing gently to remove dirt, chemicals, and insecticides. Rinse it under cold running water.

2. Cut out the stem.

3. *Optional:* To remove the skin, pour boiling water over the tomato or immerse it in boiling water for 1 minute. Refresh the tomato in cold water; then use a sharp paring knife to peel away the skin.

4. Slice vertically through the stem to make wedges or horizontally to make slices. (Note: Wedges drip and leak their liquid less than slices.)

Wedges & Slices

5. *Optional:* To remove seeds, use a pointed spoon such as a grapefruit spoon.

6. *Optional:* To core for stuffing, cut off the top and use a spoon to remove the inner flesh. Leave about 1/4 inch of flesh to help hold the shape.

□ *To Cook*

Raw tomatoes are used in salads and sandwiches, and as a garnish for serving plates or cooked dishes. To make a tasty cold side dish, mix tomatoes with celery, onions, and/ or cucumbers, and marinate the mixture in a vinaigrette dressing, sour cream, or plain yogurt. For a fancy salad, stuff tomatoes with a salad mixture after first removing the core and flesh.

Simmer or **steam** tomatoes for 5 to 10 minutes.

Stew tomatoes with just a little water or broth so that they cook in their own liquid until soft.

Grill-fry or sauté firm slices of green tomatoes, coated with seasoned flour or breading, until they are golden brown.

Deep-fat-fry tomatoes that have been dipped in a wet batter. Firm green tomatoes are best.

Bake or broil whole tomatoes or slices just long enough to make them soft.

Combination methods: Tomatoes may be used alone to make soup. They are often used as an ingredient in casseroles, braises, quiches, timbales, and puddings. Firm whole tomatoes can be stuffed and used as a casserole dish. Simply remove the core and flesh, discard the core, and mix the flesh with the stuffing ingredients. Mound the mixture into the tomato, and bake the stuffed tomato until it is soft.

□ *To Season*

Season with salt, pepper, basil, onion, garlic, dry mustard, oregano, bay leaf, coriander, cumin, curry powder, marjoram, savory, tarragon, dill, celery seed, sesame seed, parsley, sage, rosemary, or thyme.

□ *To Serve*

Serve alone or mixed with onions, okra, corn, lima beans, celery, cucumbers, eggplant, lettuce, avocado, mushrooms, squash, greens, sweet bell peppers, or combinations of these. Top with vinaigrette dressing or plain or flavored mayonnaise.

Turnip Greens

See "Greens," p. 464.

Turnips

See "Root Vegetables," p. 487.

Yams

See "Potatoes," p. 480.

Zucchini

See "Squash," p. 489.

Cooking Considerations for Vegetables

1. The longer vegetables cook, the more they lose flavor, color, texture, and nutrients. To avoid overcooking, prepare and cook them as close to serving time as possible and cook them only long enough for them to become tender. Most are best "al dente," meaning "to the tooth." Firm to the bite, in other words.

2. Whole foods or pieces of foods of this type that are cooked at the same time should all be about the same size in order to cook evenly.

3. Smaller sizes or cuts of any of these foods will cook faster than whole foods or larger pieces.

4. Vegetables that have both tough stalks and tender tips or leaves (such as broccoli or asparagus) require special preparations in order to cook evenly. Split, peel, or chop the stalks so they can cook in the same time required for cooking the tender parts.

5. Any of these foods that have been parboiled ("blanched") require less cooking time.

6. Baking soda and hard water will destroy nutrients and texture and give vegetables a bad taste. Many cooks and books recommend adding baking soda to tomatoes and other vegetables. They are wrong!

7. Green vegetables will lose color, flavor, and texture when cooked in liquids containing vinegar or lemon juice.

8. Red vegetables should be cooked in acidulated water (1 Tbsp. citrus juice or vinegar per pint of water). Acids intensify their colors and flavors.

9. Strong sulphurous vegetables—cabbage, brussels sprouts, broccoli, cauliflower, and turnips—should be cooked in an uncovered container to allow sulphurous gases to escape as well as to lessen the prospects of overcooking. When steaming these foods, remove the lid frequently to allow gases to escape.

10. Sugar, butter, or margarine added to cooking water will make any of these foods taste better. They also add calories, so use them sparingly.

How to Simmer or Steam Vegetables

Any and all of the foods in this category can be cooked in liquids.

0. **Before you begin:** Read all the steps given below. If necessary, see the Cook's Guide for the food being cooked, the Cooking Considerations for Vegetables, and the principles of cooking in liquids in Chapter Two.

1. **Plan** 10 to 15 minutes to prepare the food plus the cooking times listed in the Cook's Guide for the food.
2. **Prepare the food.**
   - *Fresh:* Follow the instructions in the Cook's Guide for the food being cooked.
   - *Frozen:* To use as a substitute for fresh, plunge the frozen food into boiling water and cook it long enough for it to become tender.
   - *Canned:* Drain the liquid and use it for cooking and reheating the food or as a broth.
3. **Prepare the vessel.**
   - *To simmer:*
     a. Use a pot or pan large enough to hold the food and the liquid with an extra 2 inches at the top to account for any foam.
     b. Add enough liquid to cover the food. If the food was canned or parboiled, use that liquid.
     c. Season the liquid if desired. It is best to use only a pinch of sugar plus other seasonings, but no salt or pepper. Add salt and pepper after the food has cooked.
     d. Add 1 tablespoon of butter, margarine, or cooking oil per quart of liquid. The oil will hold some of the flavors and nutrients to the vegetable when the liquid is poured off.
     e. Bring the liquid to a boil. The thicker the liquid, the more slowly it should be heated and the more frequently it should be stirred.
   - *To steam:* Use 1/2 inch liquid and place the food in a steaming rack. (For delicate greens, use only the liquid that remains on the greens after they are washed.)
   - *To butter-steam:* Melt enough butter or margarine to coat the bottom of a pot or pan to a depth of 1/8 inch. For more delicate flavor, use butter or margarine mixed with an equal part of water or broth.
   - *To wrap-steam:* Follow the instructions for wrap-steaming fish (p. 386).
4. **Cook the food:**
   a. When the liquid boils, lower the food or the steaming rack slowly into it.
   b. When the liquid returns to a boil, lower the heat so that the liquid simmers. Bubbles should just barely break on the surface.

   c. Cover the pot unless the Cook's Guide or other instructions advise otherwise.

   d. Stir the food occasionally to keep it from sticking on the bottom and to distribute the heat for even cooking.

   e. Cook only long enough to make the food tender.

   f. Adjust seasonings and flavorings before serving.

5. **Drain the food.** Either lift it out of the liquid with a slotted spoon or pour the food and the liquid into a colander, catching the food in the colander and the liquid in a pot or bowl. Save the liquid for reheating the food or making broth.

6. **Serve** the food hot in a previously warmed serving plate or bowl as quickly as possible. To hold for serving, cover the food and hold it in a warm oven (100 degrees F.).

7. **Optional:** Accompany with plain or flavored butter or margarine, white sauce, plain or flavored mayonnaise, one of the egg yolk and butter sauces, cheese sauce, or melted cheese.

■

How to Bake, Broil, or Roast Vegetables

Foods in this category that are cooked by these dry heat cooking methods include whole or stuffed artichokes, asparagus, corn on the cob, sliced or stuffed cucumbers, sliced or stuffed eggplant, whole or stuffed mushrooms, sliced or stuffed onions, sliced or stuffed sweet bell peppers, whole or stuffed potatoes, sliced or stuffed squash, and whole or stuffed tomatoes.

0. **Before you begin:** Read all the steps given below. If necessary, see the Cook's Guide for the food being cooked, the Cooking Considerations for Vegetables, and the principles of dry heat cooking in Chapter Two.

1. **Plan** 10 to 15 minutes to prepare the food plus the cooking times listed in the Cook's Guide for the food.

2. **Prepare the food.** Foods cooked in dry heat should be coated with butter, margarine, shortening, or cooking oil to keep them moist.

   • *Fresh:* Follow the instructions in the Cook's Guide for the food being cooked.

- *Frozen:* To use as a substitute for fresh, plunge the frozen food into boiling water and cook only long enough to defrost. Refresh in cold water to stop the cooking.
- *Canned:* Drain the liquid and save it to use as broth.

3. **Prepare the heat.**

   - *To bake or roast:* Place the oven rack on the center shelf and preheat the oven to the desired temperature. Usually the cooking temperature should be 325 to 375 degrees F.
   - *To broil:* Place the rack so the food will be 3 to 4 inches from the heat. The thicker the food, the farther it should be from the heat. Preheat the oven or grill.

4. **Prepare the vessel.** For baking, use a pan or dish with low sides. For individual servings, use small dishes or ramekins. Coat the inner surface lightly with shortening to prevent the food from sticking. Distribute the food evenly inside.

5. **Cook the food:**

   a. Place the food or the dish on the cooking rack.
   b. Set a timer for the approximate cooking time. (See the appropriate Cook's Guide.)
   c. Halfway through the cooking time, turn the dish 180 degrees so that the end that was at the rear of the oven faces front.

6. **Test for doneness:** When the food is tender and browned to your liking, remove it even if the cooking time is not up.

7. **Serve right away,** or cover and hold in a warm oven (100 degrees F.).

8. **Optional:** Accompany with plain or flavored butter or margarine, white sauce, tomato sauce, plain or flavored mayonnaise, one of the egg yolk and butter sauces, cheese sauce, or melted cheese.

■

How to Fry Vegetables

Any of the foods in this category are good cooked by the sauté or stir-fry methods. Foods that are good cooked by the pan-fry, oven-fry, or deep-fat-fry methods include artichoke bottoms and hearts, asparagus, broccoli, brussels sprouts, carrots and parsnips, cauliflower, cucumbers, eggplant, kohlrabi, leeks, mushrooms, okra, sweet bell peppers, potatoes, rutabagas, summer squash, tomatoes, and turnips.

0. **Before you begin:** Read all the steps below. If necessary, see the Cook's Guide for the food being cooked, the Cooking Considerations for Vegetables, and the principles of frying in Chapter Two.
1. **Plan** 10 to 15 minutes to prepare the food and the batter, plus 10 to 15 minutes to fry each batch. If a wet batter is used, allow 1 to 2 hours or longer for it to set. *Optional:* Chill food with a dry coating for at least 30 minutes.
2. **Prepare the coating.** (For more detailed information about coatings, see pp. 50–54.)
   - *No coating* is needed for vegetables that are sautéed or stir-fried, or for fried white potatoes.
   - *Dry coating:* For 4 to 8 servings, use 1/2 cup flour, cornmeal, pancake mix, breading, or combinations of these. Put the coating in a pan or bag, add seasonings, and dredge or shake the vegetables in the bag to coat them.
   - *Dipped batter:* For 4 to 8 servings, use 1/2 cup seasoned dry coating held in a pan or bag plus a dip of 1/2 cup milk, 1 beaten egg, or a mixture of the two held in a bowl separate from the dry coating.
   - *Wet batter:* For 4 to 8 servings, use 1/2 cup flour plus 1/2 cup liquid plus 1 whole egg or 2 egg whites. Mix all ingredients and let stand at room temperature for 1 to 2 hours, or refrigerated for 3 to 48 hours. *Optional:* For a lighter crust, add leavening just before dipping the food. (See p. 53.)
3. **Prepare the food:**
   - *Fresh:* Follow the instructions given in the Cook's Guide for the food being cooked.
   - *Frozen:* To use as a substitute for fresh, plunge the frozen food into boiling water and cook only long enough to defrost. Refresh the food in cold water to stop the cooking.
   - *Canned:* Vegetables from a can do not fry well.
4. **Coat the food:**
   a. Coat evenly all over with seasoned dry coating or batter. Hold coated food on a cold plate.

b. *Optional:* Chill food with a dry coating for 30 minutes before frying.

5. **Prepare the vessel.**
   - *To grill-fry or stir-fry:* Coat the cooking surface with just enough cooking oil to keep the food from sticking.
   - *To sauté or oven-fry:* Use a pan just large enough to hold the food and add 1/16 to 1/8 inch of cooking oil, or cooking oil mixed with up to an equal amount of butter or margarine.
   - *To pan-fry:* Use a pan with sides about 1 inch higher than the food. Add enough cooking oil to cover half the food.
   - *To deep-fat-fry:* Use a special appliance or a heavy pan or pot sufficiently deep to hold enough cooking oil for the food to float with 2 to 3 inches over to allow room for foam.

6. **Heat the cooking oil.** Do not allow it to get hot enough to smoke. For garlic flavor, use oil preflavored with garlic, or cook whole cloves of garlic in the oil until they become golden brown, then remove them.
   - *On a range burner:* Use medium-high heat and heat the cooking oil until a small bit of food or batter sizzles and cooks when it is dropped in.
   - *To oven-fry:* Preheat the oven to 450 degrees F. and place the pan on the center shelf. It is ready when the cooking oil sizzles.

7. **Cook.** Add food pieces slowly. Do not crowd them.
   - *To sauté, stir-fry, or grill-fry:* Stir the food around or shake the pan back and forth until the food browns evenly all over.
   - *To pan-fry:* Move the food occasionally so that it does not stick and burn. When the bottom has browned, turn the food and brown the other side.
   - *To deep-fat-fry:* Turn the food when the bottom has browned and brown the other side.
   - *To oven-fry:* Using tongs to hold the pieces, coat each piece all over in the hot cooking oil. Return the pan to the center shelf of the oven and cook until the food browns. Turn the pieces and brown the other side.

8. **Remove the food from the cooking oil** and drain it on paper towels.

9. **Before frying more food, first clean the cooking oil** of crumbs, flakes, or stray pieces so that they do not burn.

If more cooking oil is needed, allow the hot oil to cool for 2 minutes before adding it.

10. **Serve as quickly as possible,** or hold the food for up to 30 minutes in a warm oven (100 degrees F.).

11. **Optional:** Accompany with plain or flavored butter or margarine, white sauce, tomato sauce, plain or flavored mayonnaise, cheese sauce, or melted cheese.

■

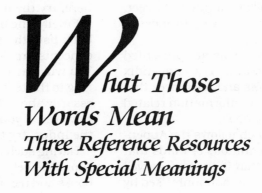

What Those Words Mean
Three Reference Resources With Special Meanings

PART FOUR

Any field that requires much skill or technical expertise has its own special vocabulary or jargon. So it is with cooking. In fact, knowing what the words mean is a large part of what cooking is all about.

The language of cookery is complicated, because so many of its words come from different countries, and because many cooks and books use words in different ways. The lack of a consistent vocabulary has made it necessary for recipes and cooking instructions to spell out each and every step in such great detail. If only the language of cookery had well-established meanings, used consistently, many of the explicit instructions used in recipes could be minimized or eliminated entirely. The entire cooking process would be much simpler as a result. For example, a typical set of instructions in a recipe can read as follows. "In an 8-inch pan, heat 2 Tbsp. of butter until it foams. Slice mushrooms lengthwise through the stem and cook in the hot fat until they are shiny." The phrase "sauté sliced mushrooms" says the same thing, but only to those who know the language.

It is the goal of this part of the book to provide a reference work for the language of cookery. Many of the technical words and concepts used in this and other books about cooking are listed, with at least one meaning for each. That is not to say that it is the only meaning, or that everyone will agree with these definitions. However, the definitions are arguably correct, so they should serve you well in most of your cooking needs.

The words and concepts are presented in one of three ways. The Appendix includes several tables and references that provide more detailed information related to some topic in the book.

The Glossary, which follows the Appendix, gives concise definitions of words that are explained more fully in the text, as well as some words that are commonly used by cooks and other books but are not used in this text. If you don't find a word defined here, try the Index.

Finally, the Index in the very back of the book lists the text pages where words or concepts are defined or covered in detail. You will learn a great deal more by referring to the text than you can from the necessarily short definitions in the Glossary. However, if you don't find a word listed in the Index, try the Glossary.

Having such extensive resources as these should be helpful as you use this and other books and recipes. I hope you will find them useful and refer to them often.

Appendix

A Cook's Guide to Herbs and Spices

Herb or Spice	How It Is Available	How It Tastes	How It Is Used
Allspice	Whole or ground	Like a blending of cinnamon, nutmeg, and cloves	Spices meat, fish, seafood dishes, soups, juices, fruits, spicy sauces, spinach, turnips, peas, red and yellow vegetables
Anise	Whole or ground	Aromatic, sweet licorice flavor	Sweet rolls, breads, fruit pies and fillings, sparingly in fruit stews, shellfish dishes, carrots, beets, cottage cheese
Basil, sweet	Fresh, whole, or ground	Aromatic, mild mint-licorice flavor	Meat, fish, seafood dishes, eggs, soups, stews, sauces, salads, tomato dishes, most vegetables, fruit compotes
Bay	Dried whole leaves, ground	Aromatic, woodsy, pleasantly bitter	Meat, game, poultry, stews, fish, shellfish, chowders, soups, pickled meats and vegetables, gravies, marinades
Burnet	Fresh, dried leaves	Delicate cucumber flavor	Soups, salads, dressings, most vegetables, beverages, as a garnish
Caraway	Whole or ground seed	Leaves and root delicately flavored, seeds sharp and pungent	Beans, beets, cabbage soup, breads, cookies, dips, variety meats, casseroles, dressings, cottage cheese, cheese spreads, sauerbraten
Cardamom	Whole or ground, seed	Mild, pleasant ginger flavor	Pastries, pies, cookies, jellies, fruit dishes, sweet potatoes, pumpkin
Cayenne	Ground	Blend of hottest chili peppers	Sparingly in sauces, meat or seafood dishes, casseroles, soups, curries, stews, Mexican recipes, vegetables, cottage and cream cheeses
Chervil	Fresh, whole	Delicate parsley flavor	Soups, salads, stews, meats, fish, garnishes, eggs, sauces, dressings, vegetables, cottage cheese
Chili powder	Powder	Blend of chilies and spices	Sparingly in Mexican dishes, meats, stews, soups, cocktail sauces, eggs, seafoods, relishes, dressings
Chives	Fresh, frozen, dried	Delicate onion flavor	As an ingredient or garnish for any dish complemented by this flavor

Herb or Spice	How It Is Available	How It Tastes	How It Is Used
Cinnamon	Whole sticks or ground	Warm, spicy flavor	Pastries, desserts, puddings, fruits, spiced beverages, pork, chicken, stews, sweet potatoes, carrots, squash
Cloves	Whole or ground	Hot, spicy, penetrating	Sparingly with pork, in soups, desserts, fruits, sauces, baked beans, candied sweet potatoes, carrots, squash
Coriander	Whole or ground, seed	Pleasant lemon-orange flavor	Pastries, cookies, cream or pea soups, Spanish dishes, dressings, spiced dishes, salads, cheeses, meats
Cumin	Ground, seed	Warm, distinctive, salty-sweet, reminiscent of caraway	Meat loaf, chili, fish, soft cheeses, deviled eggs, stews, beans, cabbage, fruit pies, Oriental meat cookery
Curry	Powder	Combination of many spices, warm, fragrant, exotic, combinations vary	Meats, sauces, stews, soups, fruits, eggs, fish, shellfish, poultry, creamed and scalloped vegetables, dressings, cream or cottage cheeses
Dill	Fresh, whole or ground, seed	Aromatic, somewhat like caraway, but milder and sweeter	Seafood, meat, poultry, spreads, dips, dressings, cream or cottage cheeses, potato salads, many vegetables, soups, chowders
Fennel	Whole or ground, seed	Pleasant licorice flavor somewhat like anise	Breads, rolls, sweet pastries, cookies, apples, stews, pork, squash, eggs, fish, beets, cabbage
Ginger	Fresh, whole root, ground, crystallized	Aromatic, sweet, spicy, penetrating	Cakes, pies, cookies, chutneys, curries, beverages, fruits, meats, poultry, stews, yellow vegetables, beets, soups, dressings, cheese dishes
Mace	Whole or ground	This dried pulp of nutmeg kernel has a strong nutmeg flavor.	Chicken, creamed fish, fish sauces, cakes, cookies, spiced doughs, jellies, beverages, yellow vegetables, cheese dishes, desserts, toppings
Marjoram	Fresh, whole or ground	Faintly like sage, slight mint aftertaste, delicate	Pork, lamb, beef, game fish, fish sauces, poultry, chowders, soups, stews, sauces, cottage or cream cheeses, omelets, soufflés, green salads, many vegetables
Mint	Fresh, dried	Fruity, aromatic, distinctive flavor	Lamb, veal, fish, soups, fruit, desserts, cottage or cream cheeses, sauces, salads, cabbage, carrots, beans, potatoes
Mustard	Fresh, whole or ground	Sharp, hot, very pungent	Salads, dressings, eggs, sauces, fish, spreads, soups, many vegetables

Herb or Spice	How It Is Available	How It Tastes	How It Is Used
Nutmeg	Whole or ground	Spicy, sweet, pleasant	Desserts of all kinds, stews, sauces, cream dishes, soups, fruits, beverages, ground meats, many vegetables
Oregano (wild marjoram)	Fresh, whole or ground	More pungent than marjoram, but similar, reminiscent of thyme	Italian cooking, Mexican cooking, spaghetti, tomato sauces, soups, meats, fish, poultry, eggs, omelets, spreads, dips, many vegetables, green salads, mushroom dishes
Parsley	Fresh, dried flakes	Sweet, mildly spicy, refreshing	As a garnish, ingredient in soups, spreads, dips, stews, butters, all meats, poultry, fish, most vegetables, omelets, eggs, herb breads, salads
Poppy seed	Tiny whole dried seed	Nut flavor	Breads, rolls, cakes, soups, cookies, dressings, cottage or cream cheeses, noodles, many vegetables, fruits, deviled eggs, stuffings
Rosemary	Fresh, whole	Refreshing, piny, resinous, pungent	Sparingly in meats, game, poultry, soups, fruits, stuffings, eggs, omelets, herb breads, sauces, green salads, marinades, vegetables
Saffron	Whole or ground	Exotic, delicate, pleasantly bittersweet	Expensive but a little goes far; use for color and flavor in rice dishes, potatoes, rolls, breads, fish, stews, veal, chicken, bouillabaisse, curries, scrambled eggs, cream cheese, cream soups, sauces
Sage	Fresh, whole or rubbed	Pungent, warm, astringent	Sparingly in pork dishes, fish, veal, lamb, stuffings, cheese dips, fish chowders, consommé, cream soups, gravies, green salads, tomatoes, carrots, lima beans, peas, onions, brussels sprouts, eggplant
Savory	Fresh, whole or ground	Warm, aromatic, resinous, delicate sage flavor—winter savory stronger than summer savory	Egg dishes, salads, soups, seafoods, pork, lamb, veal, poultry, tomatoes, beans, beets, cabbage, peas, lentils, summer squash, artichokes, rice, barbecue dishes, stuffings
Sesame	Whole seed	Toasted, it has a nutlike flavor	Breads, rolls, cookies, fish, lamb, eggs, fruit or vegetable salads, chicken, thick soups, vegetables, casseroles, toppings, noodles, candies

Herb or Spice	How It Is Available	How It Tastes	How It Is Used
Tarragon	Fresh, whole or ground	Licorice-anise flavor, pleasant, slightly bitter	Sparingly in egg dishes, fish, shellfish, veal, poultry, chowders, chicken, soups, butters, vinegar, sauces, marinades, beans, beets, cabbage, cauliflower, broccoli, vegetable juices, fresh sprigs in salads
Thyme	Fresh, whole or ground	Strong, pleasant, pungent clove flavor	Sparingly in fish, gumbo, shellfish, soups, meats, poultry, tomato juice or sauces, cheeses, eggs, sauces, fricassees, tomatoes, artichokes, beets, beans, mushrooms, potatoes, onions, carrots
Turmeric	Whole or ground	Aromatic, warm, mild	Substitutes for saffron in salads, salad dressings, butters, creamed eggs, fish, curries, rice dishes with saffron, vegetables, used partially for orange color
Watercress	Fresh	Pleasing, peppery	Garnish or ingredient in salads, fruit or vegetable cocktails, soups, cottage cheese, spreads, egg dishes, or sprinkled on vegetables or sauces

Approximately 1/3 teaspoon ground herbs or 1 teaspoon dried herbs is equal in strength to 1 tablespoon fresh herbs.

From Joyce Daly Margie, M.S., and James C. Hunt, M.D., *Living with High Blood Pressure: The Hypertension Diet Cookbook.* Copyright © 1978 by HLS Press. Reprinted with permission.

A Cook's Guide to Natural Cheeses

Cheese	Characteristics	Uses
Bel paese (*bel pah-ay-say*)	Mild, sweet flavor; light, creamy-yellow interior; slate-gray surface; soft to medium-firm, creamy texture	Appetizers, sandwiches, desserts, and snacks
Blue	Tangy, piquant flavor; semisoft, pasty, sometimes crumbly texture; white interior marbled or streaked with blue veins of mold; resembles Roquefort	Appetizers, salads and salad dressings, desserts, and snacks
Brick	Mild to moderately sharp flavor; semisoft to medium-firm, elastic texture; creamy white-to-yellow interior; brownish exterior	Appetizers, sandwiches, desserts, and snacks

Cheese	Characteristics	Uses
Brie (*bree*)	Mild to pungent flavor; soft, smooth texture; creamy-yellow interior; edible thin brown and white crust	Appetizers, sandwiches, desserts, and snacks
Caciocavallo (*ca-cheo-ca-val-lo*)	Piquant, somewhat salty flavor—similar to Provolone, but not smoked; smooth, very firm texture; light or white interior; clay-colored or tan surface	Snacks and desserts; suitable for grating and cooking when fully cured
Camembert (*kam-em-bear*)	Distinctive mild to tangy flavor; soft, smooth texture—almost fluid when fully ripened; creamy-yellow interior; edible thin white or gray-white crust	Appetizers, desserts, and snacks
Cheddar (often called American)	Mild to very sharp flavor; smooth texture, firm to crumbly; light cream to orange	Appetizers, main dishes, sauces, soups, sandwiches, salads, desserts, and snacks
Colby	Mild to mellow flavor, similar to Cheddar; softer body and more open texture than Cheddar; light cream to orange	Sandwiches and snacks
Cottage	Mild, slightly acid flavor; soft, open texture with tender curds of varying size; white to creamy white	Appetizers, salads, used in some cheesecakes
Cream	Delicate, slightly acid flavor; soft, smooth texture; white	Appetizers, salads, sandwiches, desserts, and snacks
Edam	Mellow, nutlike, sometimes salty flavor; rather firm, rubbery texture; creamy-yellow or medium yellow-orange interior; surface coated with red wax; usually shaped like a flattened ball	Appetizers, salads, sandwiches, sauces, desserts, and snacks
Gjetost (*yet-ost*)	Sweetish, caramel flavor; firm, buttery consistency; golden brown	Desserts and snacks
Gorgonzola (*gor-gon-zo-la*)	Tangy, rich, spicy flavor; semisoft, pasty, sometimes crumbly texture; creamy-white interior, mottled or streaked with blue-green veins of mold; clay-colored surface	Appetizers, salads, desserts, and snacks
Gouda (*goo-da*)	Mellow, nutlike, often slightly acid flavor; semisoft to firm, smooth texture, often containing small holes; creamy-yellow or medium yellow-orange interior; usually has red wax coating; usually shaped like a flattened ball	Appetizers, salads, sandwiches, sauces, desserts, and snacks

Cheese	Characteristics	Uses
Gruyere (*grew-yare*)	Nutlike, salty flavor, similar to Swiss, but sharper; firm, smooth texture with small holes or eyes; light yellow	Appetizers, desserts, and snacks
Liederkranz (*lee-der-krontz*)	Robust flavor, similar to very mild Limburger; soft, smooth texture; creamy-yellow interior; russet surface	Appetizers, desserts, and snacks
Limburger	Highly pungent, very strong flavor and aroma; soft, smooth texture that usually contains small irregular openings; creamy-white interior; reddish-yellow surface	Appetizers, desserts, and snacks
Monterey (Jack)	Semisoft; smooth, open texture, mild flavor; Cheddar-like; hard when aged	Appetizers, sandwiches; aged cheese can be grated
Mozzarella (also called Scamorza) (*mottza-rel-la*)	Delicate, mild flavor; slightly firm, plastic texture; creamy white	Main dishes such as pizza or lasagna, sandwiches, and snacks
Muenster (*mun-stir*)	Mild to mellow flavor; semisoft texture with numerous small openings; creamy-white interior; yellowish-tan surface	Appetizers, sandwiches, desserts, and snacks
Mysost (*mews-ost*)	Sweetish, caramel flavor; firm, buttery consistency; light brown	Desserts and snacks
Neufchatel (*new-sha-tel*)	Mild, acid flavor; soft, smooth texture similar to cream cheese but lower in fat; white	Salads, sandwiches, desserts, and snacks
Parmesan	Sharp, distinctive flavor; very hard, granular texture; yellowish white	Grated for seasoning
Port du Salut (*pore du sa-loo*)	Mellow to robust flavor similar to Gouda; semisoft, smooth elastic texture; creamy white or yellow	Appetizers, desserts, and snacks
Provolone (*pro-vo-lo-na*)	Mellow to sharp flavor, smoky and salty; firm, smooth texture; cuts without crumbling; light creamy yellow; light-brown or golden-yellow surface	Appetizers, main dishes, sandwiches, desserts, and snacks
Ricotta (*ri-cot-ah*)	Mild, sweet, nutlike flavor; soft, moist texture with loose curds (fresh Ricotta) or dry and suitable for grating; white	Salads, main dishes such as lasagna and ravioli, and desserts
Romano	Very sharp, piquant flavor; very hard, granular texture; yellowish-white interior; greenish-black surface	Seasoning and general table use; when cured a year, it is suitable for grating

Cheese	Characteristics	Uses
Roquefort	Sharp, peppery, piquant flavor; semi-soft, pasty, sometimes crumbly texture; white interior streaked with blue-green veins of mold	Appetizers, salads and salad dressings, desserts, and snacks
Sap sago	Sharp, pungent, cloverlike flavor; very hard texture suitable for grating; light green or sage green	Grated for seasoning
Stilton	Piquant flavor, milder than Gorgonzola or Roquefort; open, flaky texture; creamy-white interior streaked with blue-green veins of mold; wrinkled, melon-like rind	Appetizers, salads, desserts, and snacks
Swiss (also called Emmentaler)	Mild, sweet, nutlike flavor; firm, smooth, elastic body with large round eyes; light yellow	Sandwiches, salads, and snacks

Adapted from "Cheese in Family Meals," *U.S.D.A. Home and Garden Bulletin* #112.

A Cook's Guide to Metric Conversion: Weight

Weight: U.S. to metric		Weight: metric to U.S.	
1 oz = 0.06 lb = 28.35 g	1 lb = 0.454 kg	1 g = 0.035 oz	1 kg = 2.205 lb
2 oz = 0.12 lb = 56.70 g	2 lb = 0.91 kg	2 g = 0.07 oz	2 kg = 4.41 lb
3 oz = 0.19 lb = 85.05 g	3 lb = 1.36 kg	3 g = 0.11 oz	3 kg = 6.61 lb
4 oz = 0.25 lb = 113.40 g	4 lb = 1.81 kg	4 g = 0.14 oz	4 kg = 8.82 lb
5 oz = 0.31 lb = 141.75 g	5 lb = 2.27 kg	5 g = 0.18 oz	5 kg = 11.02 lb
6 oz = 0.38 lb = 170.10 g	6 lb = 2.72 kg	6 g = 0.21 oz	6 kg = 13.23 lb
7 oz = 0.44 lb = 198.45 g	7 lb = 3.18 kg	7 g = 0.25 oz	7 kg = 15.43 lb
8 oz = 0.50 lb = 226.80 g	8 lb = 3.63 kg	8 g = 0.28 oz	8 kg = 17.64 lb
9 oz = 0.56 lb = 255.15 g	9 lb = 4.08 kg	9 g = 0.32 oz	9 kg = 19.84 lb
10 oz = 0.62 lb = 283.50 g	10 lb = 4.54 kg	10 g = 0.35 oz	10 kg = 22.05 lb
11 oz = 0.69 lb = 311.85 g	11 lb = 4.99 kg	11 g = 0.39 oz	11 kg = 24.26 lb
12 oz = 0.75 lb = 340.20 g	12 lb = 5.44 kg	12 g = 0.42 oz	12 kg = 26.46 lb
13 oz = 0.81 lb = 368.55 g	13 lb = 5.90 kg	13 g = 0.46 oz	13 kg = 28.67 lb
14 oz = 0.88 lb = 396.90 g	14 lb = 6.35 kg	14 g = 0.49 oz	14 kg = 30.87 lb
15 oz = 0.94 lb = 425.25 g	15 lb = 6.81 kg	15 g = 0.53 oz	15 kg = 33.08 lb
16 oz = 1.00 lb = 453.59 g	16 lb = 7.26 kg	16 g = 0.56 oz	16 kg = 35.28 lb

A Cook's Guide to Metric Conversion: Liquid Measure

Liquid measure: U.S. to metric			*Liquid measure: metric to U.S.*		
1 fl oz = 29.573 ml	1 qt = 0.946 l	1 gal = 3.785 l	1 ml = 0.034 fl oz	1 l = 1.057 qt	1 l = 0.264 gal
2 fl oz = 59.15 ml	2 qt = 1.89 l	2 gal = 7.57 l	2 ml = 0.07 fl oz	2 l = 2.11 qt	2 l = 0.53 gal
3 fl oz = 88.72 ml	3 qt = 2.84 l	3 gal = 11.36 l	3 ml = 0.10 fl oz	3 l = 3.17 qt	3 l = 0.79 gal
4 fl oz = 118.30 ml	4 qt = 3.79 l	4 gal = 15.14 l	4 ml = 0.14 fl oz	4 l = 4.23 qt	4 l = 1.06 gal
5 fl oz = 147.87 ml	5 qt = 4.73 l	5 gal = 18.93 l	5 ml = 0.17 fl oz	5 l = 5.28 qt	5 l = 1.32 gal
6 fl oz = 177.44 ml	6 qt = 5.68 l	6 gal = 22.71 l	6 ml = 0.20 fl oz	6 l = 6.34 qt	6 l = 1.59 gal
7 fl oz = 207.02 ml	7 qt = 6.62 l	7 gal = 26.50 l	7 ml = 0.24 fl oz	7 l = 7.40 qt	7 l = 1.85 gal
8 fl oz = 236.59 ml	8 qt = 7.57 l	8 gal = 30.28 l	8 ml = 0.27 fl oz	8 l = 8.45 qt	8 l = 2.11 gal
9 fl oz = 266.16 ml	9 qt = 8.52 l	9 gal = 34.07 l	9 ml = 0.30 fl oz	9 l = 9.51 qt	9 l = 2.38 gal
10 fl oz = 295.73 ml	10 qt = 9.46 l	10 gal = 37.85 l	10 ml = 0.34 fl oz	10 l = 10.57 qt	10 l = 2.64 gal

Adapted from *Handbook of Food Preparation*, American Home Economics Association, 1975.

A Cook's Guide to Temperature Conversion

The numbers in the body of the table on the next page give in degrees F. the temperature indicated in degrees C. at the top and side.

To convert 178° C. to Fahrenheit scale, find 17 in the column headed degrees C. Proceed in a horizontal line to the column headed 8, which shows 352° F. as corresponding to 178° C.

To convert 352° F. to Celsius (Centigrade) scale, find 352 in the Fahrenheit readings, then in the column headed degrees C., find the number that is on the same horizontal line: 17. Next, fill in the last number from the heading of the column in which 352 was found (8), resulting in 178 °C., which is equivalent to 352° F.

Otherwise (for the mathematically inclined), the following formulas may be used to convert:

$$T° C. = 5/9 (T° F. - 32)$$
$$T° F. = 9/5 (T° C.) + 32$$

Degrees

C.	0	1	2	3	4	5	6	7	8	9
−2	−4° F.	−6° F.	−8° F.	−9° F.	−11° F.	−13° F.	−15° F.	−17° F.	−18° F.	−20° F.
−1	14° F.	12° F.	10° F.	9° F.	7° F.	5° F.	3° F.	1° F.	0° F.	−2° F.
−0	32° F.	30° F.	28° F.	27° F.	25° F.	23° F.	21° F.	19° F.	18° F.	16° F.
0	32° F.	34° F.	36° F.	37° F.	39° F.	41° F.	43° F.	45° F.	46° F.	48° F.
1	50° F.	52° F.	54° F.	55° F.	57° F.	59° F.	61° F.	63° F.	64° F.	66° F.
2	68° F.	70° F.	72° F.	73° F.	75° F.	77° F.	79° F.	81° F.	82° F.	84° F.
3	86° F.	88° F.	90° F.	91° F.	93° F.	95° F.	97° F.	99° F.	100° F.	102° F.
4	104° F.	106° F.	108° F.	109° F.	111° F.	113° F.	115° F.	117° F.	118° F.	120° F.
5	122° F.	124° F.	126° F.	127° F.	129° F.	131° F.	133° F.	135° F.	136° F.	138° F.
6	140° F.	142° F.	144° F.	145° F.	147° F.	149° F.	151° F.	153° F.	154° F.	156° F.
7	158° F.	160° F.	162° F.	163° F.	165° F.	167° F.	169° F.	171° F.	172° F.	174° F.
8	176° F.	178° F.	180° F.	181° F.	183° F.	185° F.	187° F.	189° F.	190° F.	192° F.
9	194° F.	196° F.	198° F.	199° F.	201° F.	203° F.	205° F.	207° F.	208° F.	210° F.
10	212° F.	214° F.	216° F.	217° F.	219° F.	221° F.	223° F.	225° F.	226° F.	228° F.
11	230° F.	232° F.	234° F.	235° F.	237° F.	239° F.	241° F.	243° F.	244° F.	246° F.
12	248° F.	250° F.	252° F.	253° F.	255° F.	257° F.	259° F.	261° F.	262° F.	264° F.
13	266° F.	268° F.	270° F.	271° F.	273° F.	275° F.	277° F.	279° F.	280° F.	282° F.
14	284° F.	286° F.	288° F.	289° F.	291° F.	293° F.	295° F.	297° F.	298° F.	300° F.
15	302° F.	304° F.	306° F.	307° F.	309° F.	311° F.	313° F.	315° F.	316° F.	318° F.
16	320° F.	322° F.	324° F.	325° F.	327° F.	329° F.	331° F.	333° F.	334° F.	336° F.
17	338° F.	340° F.	342° F.	343° F.	345° F.	347° F.	349° F.	351° F.	352° F.	354° F.
18	356° F.	358° F.	360° F.	361° F.	363° F.	365° F.	367° F.	369° F.	370° F.	372° F.
19	374° F.	376° F.	378° F.	379° F.	381° F.	383° F.	385° F.	387° F.	388° F.	390° F.
20	392° F.	394° F.	396° F.	397° F.	399° F.	401° F.	403° F.	405° F.	406° F.	408° F.
21	410° F.	412° F.	414° F.	415° F.	417° F.	419° F.	421° F.	423° F.	424° F.	426° F.
22	428° F.	430° F.	432° F.	433° F.	435° F.	437° F.	439° F.	441° F.	442° F.	444° F.
23	446° F.	448° F.	450° F.	451° F.	453° F.	455° F.	457° F.	459° F.	460° F.	462° F.
24	464° F.	466° F.	468° F.	469° F.	471° F.	473° F.	475° F.	477° F.	478° F.	480° F.
25	482° F.	484° F.	486° F.	487° F.	489° F.	491° F.	493° F.	495° F.	496° F.	498° F.
26	500° F.	502° F.	504° F.	505° F.	507° F.	509° F.	511° F.	513° F.	514° F.	516° F.
27	518° F.	520° F.	522° F.	523° F.	525° F.	527° F.	529° F.	531° F.	532° F.	534° F.
28	536° F.	538° F.	540° F.	541° F.	543° F.	545° F.	547° F.	549° F.	550° F.	552° F.
29	554° F.	556° F.	558° F.	559° F.	561° F.	563° F.	565° F.	567° F.	568° F.	570° F.
30	572° F.	574° F.	576° F.	577° F.	579° F.	581° F.	583° F.	585° F.	586° F.	588° F.

Glossary

acidulated water Water to which vinegar or lemon juice has been added (1 Tbsp. per cup liquid) to prevent discoloration and darkening of certain foods, such as avocados or mushrooms.

al dente *(ahl dain-tay)* An Italian term meaning "to the tooth"—that is, not too soft; offering a slight resistance to the teeth. Used to describe the way pasta should be cooked, but applies equally to most vegetables.

à la *(ah lah)* A French term used as a prefix, meaning "such as" or "according to the style of." *See* the entries below.

à l'Anglaise *(ah lawn-glaze)* In the English style. Usually, cooked by boiling or steaming.

à la broche *(ah lah brosh)* In the style of a brochette—on a skewer.

à la carte "Menu" style, in which individual items are priced separately.

à la Florentine *(ah lah floor-en-teen)* Served in the manner of Florence, Italy; e.g., on a bed of spinach, usually covered lightly with a cheese sauce.

à la hongroise *(ah lah ohng-wahz)* Served Hungarian style, which usually means with onions, sour cream, paprika, and perhaps sweet bell pepper, cabbage, or leeks.

à la king Served in a rich cream sauce that usually contains mushrooms, green peppers, and pimiento and perhaps is flavored with sherry. Often, the food and the sauce are served on toast.

à la marengo *(ah lah mah-rehn-go)* Served with mushrooms, tomatoes, olives, and olive oil.

à la mode Usually refers to ice cream on top of pie, but may refer to other toppings, such as whipped potatoes, for other dishes.

à la Provençale *(ah lah pro-vohn-sahl)* Dishes cooked in the style of Provence, France—with lots of garlic and olive oil.

à la Russe *(ah lah roose)* Dishes served in the Russian style, e.g., with sour cream.

allumette *(ah-loo-met)* Cut like large matchsticks. Shoestring potatoes, for example.

amandine *(ah-mahn-deen)* A garnish of almonds (usually toasted or sautéed), such as would be served on fish or vegetables.

antipasto In Italian, this means "before the pasta." The first, or appetizer, course, usually consisting of relishes, olives, tomatoes, smoked or pickled meat or fish, cold cuts, and the like, coated with oil and vinegar. Usually served cold.

apertif *(ah-pear-teef)* A small glass of wine or a cocktail served before a meal, as an appetizer.

appetizer Small amounts of foods, such as hors d'oeuvre, canapés, antipasto, soup, or salad. Served before the main course, to whet the appetite.

arrowroot A dry starch used to thicken liquids.

aspic A jelly made from broth thickened with gelatin. For soups, add one envelope unflavored gelatin to 3 cups of broth. For molded dishes, use 1 envelope of gelatin to 2 cups of broth.

au gratin *(oh grattin)* A topping for casseroles, consisting of breading and/or cheese browned in an oven.

au jus *(oh zhoos)* Meat served with its own natural juices or gravy.

au lait *(oh lay)* Served with milk or cream such as café au lait (coffee with cream).

au naturel *(oh nah-too-rell)* Cooked in a natural state, plain and simple.

bain-marie *(bahn mah-ree)* *See* Mary's bath.

bake To cook in an oven using dry heat.

baking powder A leavening agent used for baking.

baking soda (bicarbonate of soda) A leavening agent used for baking.

barbecue   1. A method of cooking using dry heat. 2. Foods (usually meats or poultry) cooked in a spicy sauce by dry heat.

bard   To drape pieces of fat over meat or poultry, so as to baste them as they cook in dry heat.

baste   To moisten foods as they cook, so as to avoid burning and to give them more flavor. For example, meats and poultry cooked in dry heat are usually basted, using either pan drippings or cooking oil applied with a brush or bulb baster.

batter   A semi-liquid mixture, containing flour or other starch. Used to make breads, cakes, and fritters and as a coating for fried foods.

beat   To stir or mix rapidly to make a mixture smoother or lighter by incorporating air into it.

beurre *(burr)*   French word for butter.

beurre manié *(burr mahn-yay)   See* mannie butter.

bicarbonate of soda   *See* baking soda.

bind   To add an ingredient such as white sauce, eggs, or eggs mixed with melted fat to pieces of food in order to hold them together, as in making croquettes or hash. Also, to thicken a soup or a sauce using flour or other thickener.

blanch   To cook partially in a boiling liquid; to parboil.

blend   To mix two or more ingredients thoroughly.

boeuf *(buff)*   French word for beef.

boil   Method of cooking in liquids, in which the liquid bubbles profusely.

bone   To remove bones from meat, poultry, or fish.

bouquet garni *(boo-kay gahr-nee)   See* herb bouquet.

bouillon *(bull-yon)   See* broth.

braise   A method of combination cookery in which a food is browned in fat and then completed in liquid.

brazier *(brah-zee-yay)*   A large, heavy, shallow-walled pot with loop handles. Used for searing, braising, and stewing.

breading   A coating of bread or cracker crumbs, added to foods to provide a crusty coating.

brine   A liquid of salt and vinegar, used for pickling.

broche *(brosh)*   A wooden or metal skewer used to suspend and turn meat or poultry as it roasts.

brochette *(brosh-et)*   Any food cooked and served on a broche (skewer).

broil   A method of cooking in dry heat, in which the food is exposed directly to very high radiant heat.

broth, stock, or **bouillon**   The flavorful liquid in which a food has been cooked.

brown   To cook a food until its surface browns slightly. Usually done by sautéing.

buffet *(buff-ay)*   A method of serving in which all foods are presented together for guests to serve themselves.

butter steam   A method of cooking in liquids, in which foods are cooked in butter or margarine in a closed container. Also called sweating.

calorie   The unit of measure used to express the energy-producing value of food. The heat required (3.968 B.T.U.) to raise 1 gram of water 1 degree Celsius.

canapé *(can-a-pay)*   An appetizer made of crackers or small pieces of fried or toasted bread, topped with such foods as cheese, caviar, and anchovies.

candy   To cook a food such as carrots or sweet potatoes in sugar and butter, or in syrup, so as to give it a sweet, glossy coating.

capers   Pickled green buds of the hyssop plant. Used for flavoring sauces or as a garnish for salads and other foods.

capon   A male chicken that has been desexed so that it grows fat but remains tender. Ideal for roasting.

caramel   Sugar, jelly, or syrup, heated until it becomes slightly brown. Used for many purposes, including as a glaze for meats such as ham, or for vegetables such as carrots or sweet potatoes, or as a sauce topping for ice cream and other desserts.

carbonade *(car-bohn-ahd)*   Meat that has been browned until it has a crust and then cooked in liquid (braised).

carcinogenic   Causing cancer.

casserole   One or more foods combined with a sauce and cooked in a dish or vegetable skin.

champignons *(shahm-pee-nyohn)*   French word for mushrooms.

chiffonade *(shiff-on-ahd)*   Shredded vegetables or meats used as a garnish in soups or salads.

chill   To refrigerate until thoroughly cold but not frozen.

China cap   A cone-shaped strainer or sieve with a long handle and a hook for hanging it on the side of a pot. Also called a Chinois, this tool got its name because it resembles a cap worn by Chinese laborers.

cholesterol   A chemical substance that builds up in blood vessels, causing them to narrow and perhaps become clogged.

chop   1. Noun: a thin cut of pork or lamb with some bone. 2. Verb: to cut into coarse or fine pieces.

chutney   A spicy, somewhat sweet relish, made from several fruits and vegetables, sugar, vinegar, and spices. Served as a condiment for meats, especially in East Indian cookery. Also makes an excellent salad dressing when mixed with mayonnaise or a vinaigrette dressing.

clabber Milk that has soured to the point where it is thick and curdy but not separated.

clarify To make a liquid clear by removing solids from it.

clarified or **drawn butter** Butter that has been heated so that the solid milk particles separate from the butterfat, which is then poured ("drawn") off.

cleaver An extra-wide, square-shaped knife with a heavy blade. Used to chop through bones or heavy cartilage of meats.

coat To cover with a thin film of an ingredient such as flour or melted fat, usually as a prelude to browning.

coddle To cook gently in a liquid just below the boiling point.

colander A perforated bowl used for draining vegetables, fruits, pasta, and the like.

collop To tenderize a piece of meat by beating it with a mallet or the back side of a knife blade or by slicing it very thin.

combine To mix two or more ingredients until they are thoroughly blended.

compound butter or **herb butter** Raw, cold butter that has been flavored with herbs or other ingredients.

concasser *(cohn-cah-say)* To chop coarsely.

condiment An appetizing addition to a dish. Used to flavor foods at the table. Mustard, chutney, catsup, and meat sauces, for example.

consommé *(cohn-so-may)* Clear broth, usually served as a soup, but also used for cooking.

coquille *(co-key)* A shell or small dish made in the shape of a shell. Used for baking and serving foods such as fish in white sauce.

core To remove the center of a fruit or vegetable.

court bouillon Broth in which fish is poached.

cracklings The crisp, browned bits of pork that remain after the fat has been melted away.

cream or **cream together** To stir and mix liquid or semi-liquid foods together until they are smooth and creamy.

crème fraîche *(crem fresh)* A tangy-sweet, thick cultured cream. Used as a flavoring ingredient or topping.

Creole A style of cooking associated with the Creole people of Louisiana. Usually highly seasoned, combining vegetables (especially tomatoes, okra, and peppers) with meat, chicken, or fish.

crisp To make firm and crisp. Raw vegetables are made crisp by placing them in iced water. Bread crumbs, potato chips, crackers, and other foods are made crisp by drying them in a moderate oven.

crustaceans Sea animals, such as lobsters and shrimp, that have segmented shells and jointed legs.

croutons Small cubes of bread that have been sautéed or toasted in seasoned butter or oil. Used as topping for salads and soups and for making bread stuffing.

crown roast A special roast of lamb or pork, made by folding the ribs into a circle to form a crown shape. Often filled with a stuffing.

crudité *(croo-dee-tay)* Crisp, raw vegetables served with a seasoned salt or dip as an appetizer or hors d'oeuvre. Sliced cucumbers, carrots, celery, summer squash, sweet bell peppers, and mushrooms are most popular.

cruet A small jar with a lid, used for making and storing vinaigrette dressing, vinegar, or other liquids.

cube 1. To cut into cube shapes of equal size, usually 1/4 to 1/2 inch. 2. To tenderize a meat by pounding it with a mallet or the back of a knife blade. Seasoned flour is usually pounded in until the meat won't hold any more, as in making cubed round steak.

curdle What happens to eggs, milk, and milk products (except heavy cream) when heated too much: They separate and form solid particles.

cut To separate into pieces using a knife or scissors.

cut in To mix fat with flour or other dry ingredient until pieces of uniform size are formed. This may be done with a fork, two knives, or a pastry blender.

cutlet A small, thin, boneless piece of meat cut from the leg or ribs of pork or lamb. Usually broiled or fried.

dash A very small amount, less than 1/8 teaspoon.

de-fat To remove accumulated fat from the surface of a liquid.

deglaze To remove the "glaze" of caramelized food particles (the fond) from the bottom of a cooking pan.

de-grease *See* de-fat.

demiglaze *(dem-ee-glahz)* A very thick brown sauce, used to baste meats to give them a flavorful, glossy coating.

deviled A food prepared with hot seasonings such as pepper and mustard. Deviled eggs or deviled crab, for example.

dice To cut into very small cubes, about 1/8 to 1/4 inch.

disjoint To cut into pieces at the joint. Usually done to prepare poultry, using a knife or poultry shears.

dissolve To mix a dry substance such as flour with a liquid to form a solution.

dot To scatter small bits of food (such as butter or breading) over a larger food (such as a casserole) so as to moisten it or to give it added flavor.

dough   A thick, pliable mixture of flour and liquid that is firm enough to be shaped or kneaded.

drawn butter   *See* clarified butter.

dredge   To sprinkle or coat a food lightly with a fine, dry ingredient such as sugar or flour.

dress   To prepare poultry or fish for cooking.

dressing   1. A blend of breading with seasonings, milk, and eggs. 2. A cold sauce used mostly on salads.

drippings   Fat and juices that drip from a meat while it's being cooked. Often deglazed and used to make gravy.

drizzle   To coat the surface of a food with a liquid such as melted fat or sugar syrup. Usually, the liquid is poured in a fine stream, making a zigzag pattern.

dust   To sprinkle or coat lightly with an ingredient such as flour, sugar, or breading.

Dutch oven   A deep, heavy cooking pot with a cover, used mostly for cooking braises and stews.

duxelles *(duke-sell)*   A combination of sautéed mushrooms and shallots or garlic. Used as a garnish or added to enrich the flavor of another sauce. Sometimes mixed with breading to make a stuffing.

émincé *(ay-mahn-say)*   Chopped into small pieces; minced.

emulsion   A suspension of small fat globules in a liquid, such as oil in a vinaigrette dressing.

en brochette *(ahn brosh-et)*   Cooked on a skewer, usually by broiling.

en papillote *(ahn pah-pee-yawt)*   Cooked in a wrapping of aluminum foil or parchment so that the food cooks in steam.

enricher   An ingredient such as cream, sour cream, or a liaison. Added to a sauce to give it more flavor.

entrée *(ahn-tray)*   In the United States, this is the main course of a meal. In France, the entrée is the course that is served just before the main course.

epicure or **epicurean**   One who loves and knows a great deal about foods and wines. *See also* gourmand and gourmet.

escallope *(ess-cah-lopp)*   1. A thin slice of meat, poultry, or fish. 2. A casserole coated with buttered bread crumbs and/or cheese so that the top browns.

eviserate   To remove the entrails of an animal, bird, or fish.

fatback   Pure fat from the back of a pig. Used to flavor a cooking liquid for cooking vegetables "Southern style," as well as for larding meats.

F.D.A.   Abbreviation for the United States Food and Drug Administration.

fell   The thin membrane that covers some cuts of lamb.

filé *(fee-lay)*   Spice used in Cajun cooking to thicken and flavor stews.

filet or **fillet** *(fill-lay)*   1. Noun: a strip of lean, boneless meat (usually a choice cut) or of fish with no bones. 2. Verb: to cut into thin slices, as in cutting the sides of fish away from the bones.

fines herbes *(feenz ehrb)*   A combination of herbs such as parsley, tarragon, chives, and chervil, all finely chopped.

finish   To add a pat of butter or margarine to the surface of a sauce or liquid, so as to prevent a film from forming.

flake   To break lightly into small, flat pieces. Usually done with a fork, as in flaking the flesh of a cooked fish.

flambé *(flam-bay)*   Served flaming.

floret *(floor-ay)*   A small flower or one of a cluster of flowers, such as those of broccoli and cauliflower.

flour   1. Noun: a powdery starch used as a dry coating and as a basic ingredient. 2. Verb: to coat a food lightly with flour or other dry coating.

flute   To make decorative indentations around the edges of pastry, vegetables, or fruits.

fold or **fold in**   To combine ingredients gently, using a spoon, whisk, or fork. Often done when combining egg whites with other foods, so that little air is lost.

fond   See pan drippings.

frizzle   To fry a food (usually meat) in a small amount of fat until the edges curl.

frost   To cover a pastry or cake with frosting.

fry   To cook in fat.

fumet *(foo-may)*   A concentrated broth made from fish or game.

garnish   To decorate a dish with small pieces of food, so as to make it more attractive.

gel   To make a liquid become firm by adding gelatin to it.

gelatin   An unflavored thickening agent used to gel liquids. One envelope will gel 2 cups of liquid.

giblets   The heart, liver, and gizzard of poultry birds.

glaze   The glossy, semi-transparent coating achieved by cooking foods (such as meat or poultry) coated with a sugary substance such as jelly, sugar, or brown sugar mixed with melted butter. Cold foods can be glazed with aspic.

gluten or **glutenin**   The protein part of wheat or other cereal. Gives flour dough the ability to hold together when it expands.

gourmand *(goor-mand)* A person who enjoys eating—even to the point of eating ravenously—and is considered a knowledgeable judge of good food and cooking.

gourmet *(goor-may)* An expert or connoisseur of food and drink.

gram The basic unit of weight in the metric system; approximately one-thirtieth of an ounce.

grate To reduce a solid food into grains or small particles by rubbing it against the rough surface of a grater. Can also be done in a food processor or by chopping very finely with a knife.

grater Any device with holes surrounded by raised, rough edges, used to break foods into bits and small pieces.

gratin or **gratinée** *(grah-tin-ay)* A casserole made with a topping of bread crumbs and/or cheese.

gravy A sauce made from the fat in which meat or poultry is cooked.

grease 1. Noun: the liquid obtained from heating fat. 2. Verb: to rub fat or oil on a cooking surface so as to prevent food from sticking to it.

griddle A flat, solid metal surface used for grill-frying and pan-broiling.

grill 1. Noun: an open grate on which foods are roasted in the open air. 2. Verb: to cook on a grill.

grind To reduce a food such as meat or poultry into very small particles by cutting and crushing it in a food grinder or food processor.

heavy cream Whipping cream.

herb bouquet, bouquet garni *(boo-kay gar-nee)*, or **sachet** *(sah-shay)* A combination of fresh herbs and spices, tied in a loose cloth bag such as cheesecloth or held in a tea ball. Used to flavor a cooking liquid so that the herbs can be retrieved.

herb butter *See* compound butter.

hors d'oeuvre *(or derve)* Bite-sized appetizers. Served as finger food before the first course of a meal or at a cocktail party.

hydrogenated fat Solid fats made by treating liquid oils (such as corn oil) with hydrogen.

infuse To add flavoring or seasoning to a food by soaking it in a flavored liquid or oil.

jardinière *(zhahr-deen-yare)* A garnish of diced fresh vegetables such as carrots, green beans, broccoli, and cauliflower.

julienne *(zhoo-lee-ehn)* Food cut into thin, match-like strips. Often used as a garnish.

jus *(zhoos)* French word for juice. Usually the deglazed pan drippings of cooked meat, served without any thickener.

kebobs Meat and/or vegetables cooked on skewers.

knead To work and press dough with the palms of the hands so as to make it smooth and elastic.

kneaded butter *See* mannie butter.

kosher Cooked according to Jewish dietary restrictions.

lard 1. Noun: rendered animal fat used for cooking. 2. Verb: to insert thin strips of fat into a meat roast in order to baste it as it cooks.

larder A room, cupboard, or cabinet in which foods are kept.

lardon A thin strip of fat or salt pork used to lard or bard meat or poultry.

leavener A substance, such as baking powder or yeast, that is added to a food to cause it to expand when heated.

liaison *(lee-ay-zohn)* A mixture of cream and eggs, used as a thickening agent.

light cream A milk product, such as coffee cream or half-and-half, that is heavier than milk but lighter than whipping cream. Can be made by mixing equal parts of milk and whipping cream.

liter The basic unit of volume in the metric system; slightly more than a quart.

macerate To infuse a food (usually fruit) with flavor by letting it stand in a flavored liquid such as wine or brandy.

mannie butter, beurre manié *(burr mahn-yay)*, or **kneaded butter** Equal parts of flour and butter or margarine, kneaded together to make a smooth paste. Used as a thickener for sauces, soups, and stews.

marinade *(mare-a-naid)* A liquid in which foods are soaked to give them special flavor.

marinate To soak a food in flavored liquid so that it takes on the flavors of the liquid.

Mary's bath or **bain-marie** A pan of hot water in which another vessel containing food is held, to prevent it from cooking too quickly or to keep it warm for serving.

mash To crush or reduce a food to a soft, smooth, even texture. For example, mashed potatoes.

melt To change a solid substance such as butter to a liquid by heating it.

mince To cut or chop a food into very small pieces, usually with a knife.

mirepoix *(mee-rep-wah)* A mixture of chopped vegetables such as onions, carrots, and celery. Used to flavor broth, soups, sauces, braises, and stews.

mise en place *(meez ahn plahss)* French term meaning approximately "a place for everything, and everything in its place."

mix To combine two or more ingredients, usually by stirring.

mother sauce A basic sauce, such as white sauce, brown sauce, or mayonnaise.

oeuf *(uff)* French word for egg.

offal Another name for variety meats.

oignon *(oyn-yohn)* French word for onion.

oven An enclosed space used for baking and roasting.

ovenizing The process of frying foods in an oven.

pan-broil To cook a fatty food such as bacon in a shallow pan or griddle, with no added fat.

pan drippings or **fond** The crust of burned fat and food particles that accumulates on the bottom of a pan in which meat or poultry is cooked. May be deglazed and made into a sauce.

pan-fry To fry in enough oil to cover one-half the depth of the food.

papillote *(pah-pee-yawt)* 1. A frilled paper cover used to decorate the bone end of a cooked chop or cutlet. 2. The parchment paper in which foods are steamed.

parboil To cook partially in simmering or boiling liquid.

parch To brown in dry heat.

pare To remove the outer covering from fruits or vegetables using a paring knife or vegetable peeler.

paring knife or **vegetable peeler** A special cutting device with a swiveled blade, used to pare fruits and vegetables.

pasta A dried paste used in many Italian dishes.

paste A smooth mixture of a starch (such as flour) and a liquid.

pasteurize To sterilize a food or liquid partially, by heating it to at least 140 degrees F. for 30 minutes to destroy potentially harmful microorganisms.

peel To remove skin or rind by stripping or cutting. Usually done with a thin knife or vegetable peeler.

piquant *(peek-ahnt)* Highly seasoned so as to have a pungent aroma.

poach To cook in water that is hot enough to bubble only slightly.

poisson *(pwa-sohn)* French word for fish.

pound To beat a food with a heavy object in order to break down its texture and make it tender.

preheat To turn on heat so that it reaches the desired cooking temperature before food is introduced to it.

prepared pan A pan thinly coated with fat and perhaps dusted with flour, so that foods baked in it won't stick to the insides.

prick To make small holes in something, using a sharp object such as a thin knife blade or the tines of a fork.

purée *(pure-ay)* 1. Noun: a food that has been reduced to a mushy, thick pulp or paste of uniform texture. 2. Verb: to turn a solid food into a puree, using a blender, food mill, ricer, or food processor.

ragout *(rah-goo)* French word for stew.

ramekin A shallow dish used for cooking individual servings, especially casseroles.

range An appliance with surface burners on which foods are cooked.

reduce To make a liquid more concentrated and thicker by boiling or simmering it to lessen its water content.

refresh To plunge hot food into cold water to stop it from cooking.

render To heat a piece of meat so that the fat becomes liquid and separates.

ricer A cone-shaped sieve with a solid bottom and a plunger. Used to press cooked vegetables such as potatoes into long strings.

roux *(roo)* A mixture of flour cooked in fat. Used to thicken liquids.

sachet *(sah-shay)* *See* herb bouquet.

salamander A small broiler oven with an open front. Used in restaurants to brown or glaze the tops of foods.

salmonella A food-borne disease, spread by improper sanitation and food handling.

sauté *(saw-tay)* To fry foods quickly in only a small amount of fat (usually butter, margarine, or olive oil).

scald To heat a liquid such as milk to a temperature just below the boiling point—the point at which tiny bubbles begin appearing around the outer edge of the pan.

scallop 1. A shellfish. 2. To make an ornamental border of rounded indentations around the outer edge of a dish or food. *See also* escallope.

score To cut shallow grooves or slits into the outer surface of a food to prevent it from curling as it cooks.

scramble To mix a food or foods until well blended.

sear To brown the surface of a food quickly. Usually applied to meats. Some cooks and books say this will seal in the juices and make the meat more flavorful. However, many food studies indicate that meats will shrink less, retain more juices, and therefore taste better if they are cooked at lower temperatures, without searing.

shortening A white, almost tasteless, solid fat. Made by hydrogenating vegetable oils to make them solid. Some shortenings contain cholesterol; others do not.

shuck To remove an outer coating from a food—for example, shells from oysters or husks from corn.

sieve 1. Noun: a round metal frame with a mesh bottom. Used to sift foods. 2. Verb: to pass a food through a sieve.

sift To pass one or more dry ingredients through a sieve or sifter in order to remove lumps and achieve a lighter texture.

simmer To cook in liquid just below the boiling point.

skewer 1. Noun: a long stick made of wood or metal, on which a food is placed and held while it cooks. 2. Verb: to stick a food onto a skewer.

skillet A heavy metal pan (usually made of iron) with a handle. Used for pan-frying and pan-broiling.

skim To remove accumulated scum, grease, and other floating substances from the surface of a liquid. May be done with a slotted spoon, a skimmer, or a bulb baster.

slice To cut a food into thin pieces.

sliver To cut or shred into long pieces or slivers.

small sauce Any sauce made by adding ingredients to a basic mother sauce.

spit A pointed rod used to hold meat or poultry and turn it as it roasts.

sprinkle To distribute an ingredient evenly over the surface of a food.

steam 1. Noun: the gaseous form of a liquid, heated to its boiling point. 2. Verb: to cook a food in a closed container so that it cooks in steam without touching the liquid.

steel 1. Noun: the long, round tool used to hone the edges of kitchen knives. 2. Verb: to hone the edges of a knife using a steel.

steep To poach a food in liquid to extract color, flavor, or other qualities from it.

sterilize To destroy bacteria and other microorganisms by boiling, steaming, or exposing them to very hot, dry heat (above 140 degrees F.).

stir To mix ingredients using a circular motion.

stir-fry To fry small pieces of food using very little fat, stirring almost constantly so that everything cooks quickly and evenly.

stock *See* broth.

strain To drain liquids from solid foods. This may be done either by lifting the food from the liquid (using a slotted spoon) or by pouring the food and its liquid into a colander.

stud To stick seasonings such as cloves into the surface of a food in order to garnish it and add flavor.

stuff To fill a cavity in a food with a mixture. For example, putting bread stuffing inside a turkey.

sweat To cook in a small amount of fat over low heat (sometimes covered), so as to soften a food slightly and mellow its flavor. Onions, celery, mushrooms, and sweet bell peppers are often sweated before adding them to cook with other foods.

thicken To add a thickening agent to a liquid.

toast To cook a food in dry heat until its surface browns.

tongs A scissors-like utensil used to hold and turn foods.

toss To mix ingredients lightly without mashing them.

truss To tie, lace, or sew together an opening in meat, fish, or poultry.

try out To cook solid fat or fatty meat cut into small pieces, in order to render fat from it.

U.S.D.A. Abbreviation for United States Department of Agriculture.

variety meats The edible innards of four-legged animals: liver, kidneys, heart, tongue, sweetbreads, brain, and tripe.

vessel Any container in which a food or liquid is stored or cooked.

wash 1. A solution of thickening agent (such as flour) in a cool liquid. 2. Egg, milk, or mixture of the two, in which foods are dipped to give them a crust when fried.

whip To beat rapidly so as to incorporate air, in order to lighten the food and increase its volume.

whisk 1. Noun: a tool used for mixing foods to incorporate air. 2. Verb: to beat with a whisk until blended and smooth.

wok A vessel used to stir-fry foods.

wrap cooking A method of cooking foods in steam.

zest The oily, colored part of the peel of citrus fruits. Grated zest adds more of the fruit's flavor to foods in which its juices are used.

Index

Accidents, how to avoid, 60, 246–247, 262
Acidic liquids, 165, 173, 284–287 (*see also* Fruit juices; Vinegar; Wine)
Aioli mayonnaise, 166
Altitude, effect of on boiling, 37
Aluminum foil, 28, 31, 32, 33, 40, 42, 44, 64, 89, 90, 342, 365
  drugstore wrap, 31, 32
  pyramid wrap, 31, 33
  soufflé collar, 89–90
American style serving, 230
Arrowroot, 59, 130
Artichokes, 439–442
Asparagus, 442–444
Au gratin, 71, 77–78
  defined, 71
  how to make, 77–78
  pastry crust for, 79–82
Au jus, 129
Avocados, 444–446

Bacteria, 37, 102, 106, 153, 240–244, 316
  temperature chart, 241
Bain-marie, 40, 85, 90, 93
Baked custard, 159–161
  how to make, 160–161
  ingredients, 159–160
Baking, 38, 41–42, 62–63
  cooking considerations for, 41–42
  eggs, 326–327
  fish and shellfish, 382–385
  meats, 400
  poultry, 352–354
  vegetables, 499–500
Baking powder, 301
Baking soda, 301
Barbecuing, 45
  fish and shellfish, 382–385
  meat, 421–424
  poultry, 352–354
Barding, 44, 305, 420–421
Bargain shopping, 211
Basic food groups, 189
Basic ingredients, guide to, 283–313 (*see also* name of ingredient)
Basting, 44, 268

Batter
  dipped, 51–52, 348, 380, 501
  fritter, 52–54
  for fritters, 123
  wet, 52–54, 348, 380, 501
Beans, 446–447
Béarnaise sauce, 153–159
Béchamel, 28, 140
Beef, 400–403
  barbecued, 421–424
  braised, 402, 427–430
  broiled, 402, 421–424
  fried, 402, 425–427
  grilled, 402, 421–424
  pan-broiled, 424–425
  pot roast, 402, 427–430
  roast, 402, 430–433
  selection chart, 401
  stew, 427–430
Beer
  batter, 52, 123
  cooking in, 26
  marinating in, 102, 103
Beets, 447–449
Beet tops, 464–467
Belgian endive, 470
Bell peppers, 478–479
Bercy sauce, 143
Beurre manié, 133 (*see also* Mannie butter)
Birgarde sauce, 147
Bisques, 109
Blanching, 34–35, 104
Blenders, 155–157, 167–170, 266
Blood pressure, 194, 219
Blue cheese dressing, 167, 173
Boiling, 32–34
Bok choy, 451–453
Bordeaux sauce, 153–159
Botulism, 243
Bouillon
  cooking in, 24
  how to make, 111–113
  in soups, 106–108
Bouquet garni, 311
Bourguignonne sauce, 147
Bowl scrapers, 265
Brains (meat), 417–418

Braising, 12, 17, 35, 37, 95–102
  defined, 95
  fish, 368, 391–393
  how to do it, 98–100
  ingredients, 96–97
  meat, 427–430
  poultry, 350–352
  timetable for meats, 428
  vessels for, 97–98
Bread, 16, 40, 41, 62–63, 189
Bread crumbs, 287–289
Breading
  as a basic ingredient, 287–289
  as a coating for fried foods, 54
  for croquettes, 119
  how to make, 288
Bread stuffing, 288–289
Breakfast, 200–201
Broccoli, 449–451
Broiling, 38, 39, 43
  cooking considerations for, 43
  fish and shellfish, 382–385
  meat, 421–424
  poultry, 352–354
  vegetables, 499–500
Broth, 24, 37, 338
  cooking in, 24
  how to make, 111–113
  kinds of, 107
  in sauce, 146
  in soups, 106–108
Browning liquid, 63
Browning tray, 63
Brown sauce, 145–149
  gravy, 136–140
  how to make, 148–149
  ingredients, 146–147
  small sauces, 147
Brussels sprouts, 451–453
Buffet style serving, 230
Bulb basters, 168, 268
Bullnose peppers, 478–480
Burns, how to avoid, 247
Butter
  as a basic ingredient, 290–292
  browned, 291
  clarified or drawn, 47, 291–292
  in cold sauce, 175–177

525